AF478100

A DICTIONARY OF
BRITISH
SPORTING PAINTERS

A Dictionary of

BRITISH SPORTING PAINTERS

by

SYDNEY H. PAVIÈRE

F.S.A., F.M.A., F.R.S.A., A.R.D.S.

Author of 'The Devis Family of Painters'
'A Dictionary of Flower, Fruit and Still-Life Painters'
Floral Art–'Great Masters of Flower Painting'

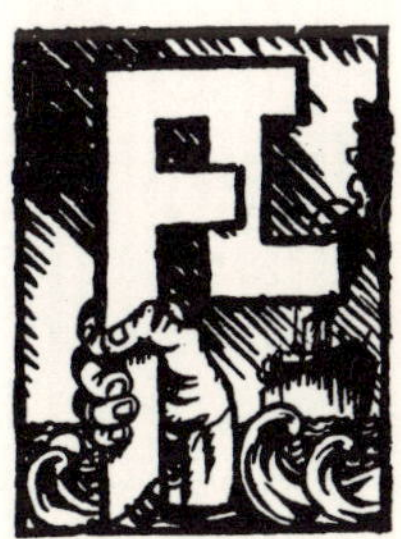

F. LEWIS, PUBLISHERS, LTD.

PUBLISHERS BY APPOINTMENT TO THE LATE QUEEN MARY

The Tithe House, Leigh-on-Sea, England

PRINTED AND MADE IN ENGLAND

F. LEWIS, PUBLISHERS, LIMITED
THE TITHE HOUSE, LEIGH-ON-SEA, ENGLAND

First published 1965
Reprinted with corrections 1980

ISBN 0 85317 940 9

PRINTED IN GREAT BRITAIN BY
CLARKE, DOBLE & BRENDON LTD., PLYMOUTH AND LONDON

FOREWORD

More than thirty years have elapsed since Walter Shaw Sparrow wrote his last book on sporting painters[1] and forty years since his work on angling in art.[2]

During this time many more pictures have been discovered, fresh facts have been unearthed, and a new generation of painters has appeared. This being so, it is appropriate that an attempt should be made to revise what was then known, to add new names to the list of artists, and to give details that have come to light in recent times.

As with flower painters so with sport, there is hardly a known artist who has not produced the odd picture with a sporting interest, and many an artist is known only by the one example and usually an example of considerable merit. This raises the question as to what, if anything, has happened to his other work.

It should be clearly understood that in the case of well-known artists who can hardly be termed 'sporting painters' only such pictures as come under this heading are listed. Similarly, only brief biographical details are given of the well-documented artists.

It is surprising that so many of the pictures by well-known sporting artists which were exhibited at the Royal Academy annually have now disappeared. Here it might be added that only in a few cases are exhibits at the Society of Artists, the Free Society, and the British Institution, listed. The question of space has forced this limitation upon author and publisher.

Details of living artists have been much more difficult to obtain than was so with the older generations. Even now it is doubtful if this dictionary contains all the names it should do, and one is very conscious of the fact that there are bound to be omissions both of artists and paintings.

Thanks are due to many who have given considerable help in the compilation of the dictionary, notably Messrs. Arthur Ackermann & Son Ltd. and Messrs. Frost & Reed Ltd., of Bristol. Others include the Kent County Archivist and the Directors of National and Provincial Galleries, particularly Bath, Doncaster, Hull, Leicester, Newcastle upon Tyne, Norwich, Nottingham and Preston.

Finally, thanks are due to my publisher, Frank Lewis, for help and encouragement in a difficult task.

SYDNEY H. PAVIÈRE

[1] *A Book of Sporting Painters.* John Lane. 1931
[2] *Angling in British Art.* John Lane. 1923

ABBREVIATIONS USED IN THIS VOLUME

A.G.	Art Gallery
auct.	Auction
b.	Born
B.I.	British Institution (1806–1867)
Benezit	'Dictionnaire des Peintres, etc.' (1948–1955)
Bryan	Bryan's 'Dictionary of Painters and Engravers' (1905)
Christie's	Christie, Manson & Woods, Auctioneers, London
coll.	Collection of
d.	Died
exhib.	Exhibited
F.S.	Free Society of Artists (1761–1783)
G.G.	Grosvenor Gallery (1878–1890)
Grant	'A Dictionary of British Landscape Painters, 16th to 20th Centuries' (1952) 'A Chronological History of the Old English Landscape Painters (in oils)' (1957–1961). Revised ed., 8 vols.
Graves	'Dictionary of Artists who exhibited in London 1760–1880'
lit.	Literature
N.E.A.C.	New English Art Club
N.G.	New Gallery, London (1888–1893)
N.W.C.S.	New Water Colour Society, London (1832–)
Norwich 1927	Exhibition of Norwich School Pictures, Castle Museum and Art Galleries, Norwich, October 1927
Norwich 1950	Loan Exhibition of Sporting Pictures and Prints from Norfolk and Suffolk Houses, July-October 1950
O.W.C.S.	Old Water Colour Society
op.	Operating
P.O.U.	Present owner or whereabouts unknown
Preston 1943	Exhibition of British Sporting Painters (1943)
R.A.	Royal Academy of Arts, London (1796–)
R.B.A.	Royal Society of British Artists (1826–)
R.H.A.	Royal Hibernian Academy (1823–)
R.I.	Royal Institute of Painters in Water-colours
R.O.I.	Royal Institute of Oil Painters
R.S.A.	Royal Scottish Academy
R.W.S.	Royal Society of Painters in Water Colours (1805–)
repr.	Reproduced
S.A.	Society of Artists, London (1760–1791)
S&D	Signed and dated
S.S.	Suffolk Street Galleries
Sotheby's	Sotheby & Co., Auctioneers, London
V. and A.	Victoria and Albert Museum, London
V.E.	Various exhibitions

ABBOTT, LEMUEL FRANCIS (c. 1760–1803). A portrait painter famous for his pictures of Nelson, of which many replicas exist. *coll.* London, National Maritime Museum; National Portrait Gallery; Tate Gallery. *exhib.* R.A., 1788–1800 (portraits). *repr.* 'Mr. Innes, Member of Blackheath Society of Golfers', engraved in mezzotint by Valentine Green, 1790; 'Henry Callender, Member of Blackheath Society of Golfers', engraved by William Ward.

ABBOTT, RICHARD (Shaw Sparrow), **RICHMOND** (Graves) (op. 1860–1866). Liverpool address. Animal painter. *exhib.* B.I. (3); S.S. (4).

ABSOLON, JOHN, R.I., R.O.I. (b. Lambeth 1815, d. 1895). Pupil of Ferrigi. Employed by Grieve as a scene painter at Drury Lane and Covent Garden. Spent some time in Paris, 1835. Returned to London 1839. Member and Treasurer of the New Water Colour Society. *exhib.* R.A. (16); B.I. (7); S.S. (22); N.W.C.S. (660); V.E. (3), Graves says 'Domestic'. *repr.* 'The Compleat Angler', 1844 edition. 'Angling in British Art', Shaw Sparrow.

ADAM, JOSEPH (op. 1858–1880). London address. A Glasgow landscape painter. Father of Joseph Denovan Adam, R.S.A., R.S.W. *coll.* Glasgow Art Gallery (1). *exhib.* R.A. (17); B.I. (10); S.S. (13); V.E. (15). Graves says 'Landscape'.

ADAMS, DOUGLAS (op. 1880–1905). London address, residing at 7 James Street, Haymarket. Landscape and wild fowl painter, occasionally sport. *exhib.* R.A. (18); S.S. (6); G.G. (2); N.G. (5); V.E. (3). Graves says 'Landscape'. *repr.* Prints after paintings of 'Otter Hunting', 'Sea Trout Fishing', 'Trout Fishing', 'Landing the Salmon', 'The Tight Line', 'Trout Fishing in the Highlands'.

ADAM, EMIL (b. 1834 in Germany, d.). Settled in England, receiving commissions from the Prince of Wales, Duke of Westminster, Duke of Portland and others. Became the finest racehorse painter of his day. The Jockey Club owns a number of his works.

AGASSE, JACQUES LAURENT (b. Geneva 1767, 24th March, Benezit; 1780, Basil Taylor. d. London 1849, 27th December. d. 1846, Bryan's; 1767–1849, Shaw Sparrow). Pupil of David and Horace Vernet in Paris. Visited England about 1790 in company of his patron, the Hon. George Pitt (later Lord Rivers). Also studied at the Veterinary College in Paris. Returned to London 1800, residing with the Chalon family, remaining until his death. *coll.* Bucharest. Geneva (Musee d'Art). H.M. The Queen; Mr. and Mrs. Paul Mellon, U.S.A.; Major Guy Paget (the late). *exhib.* R.A., 1801–1810.

AINSLIE, Miss (op. 1823–1835). Hon. Exhibitor at Royal Academy. No address given. Painted game and sporting. *exhib.* R.A. (11).

AINSLEY, SAMUEL JAMES (b. 1820, d. 1874). Leyton and London addresses. Painter, engraver and lithographer. Visited Rome. *exhib.* R.A. (2); B.I. (4); S.S. (1).

AITKEN, JAMES ALFRED, A.R.H.A., R.S.W. (b. Edinburgh 1846, d. Glasgow 1897, 21st December). Resided for some time in Dublin. Returned to Edinburgh for art instruction. Visited Europe and America. Painted animals and landscapes. *coll.* Glasgow Art Gallery, landscape. *exhib.* R.A. (1); G.G. (3), Graves says 'Figures'.

ALDIN, CECIL CHARLES WINDSOR (b. Slough 1870, 28th April, d. 1935, 6th January). Educated at Eastbourne College. Studied at South Kensington and under Frank W. Calderon. First drawing published in 'Graphic' 1891. Published 'Romance of the Road' 1908; 'Rat catcher to scarlet' 1926; 'Dogs of Character' 1927; 'Scarlet to M.F.H.' 1913. Lived in Mallorca. M.F.H. South Berks Foxhounds. *coll.* National War Museum.

ALDRIDGE, DENIS (Living). Exhibiting at The Tryon Gallery, London. Sporting subjects.

ALEXANDER, D. This artist's name appears as the painter on prints of shooting subjects.

ALEXANDER, ROBERT, R.S.A., R.S.W. (b. Dolgaren, Ayrshire, 1840, d. Edinburgh 1923). Apprenticed to a Kilmarnock house painter who also painted landscape. Held a position in the workshop of the Royal Scottish Museum, Edinburgh. In 1868 devoted himself to painting domestic animals--horses and dogs. Visited Paris in 1906. *coll.* Edinburgh N.G. (1); Glasgow A.G. (2); W. H. Cook (1); J. H. Pillman (1); Sir Robert Usher, Bt. (1). *exhib.* R.A., 1878 (1).

ALFRED, HENRY JERVIS (op. 1855–1882). *exhib.* S.S. (2), 'Fish'. *auct.* Christie's, 20th November 1964 (106). Three pictures, 'Not caught yet' and two 'Fish on the Hook'.

THE ALKEN'S. Originally came to England from Denmark, the family name was originally 'Seffrien' or 'Sefferin'; this they changed to Alken, after a village in North Jutland. First settling in Suffolk and later moving to London.

ALKEN, GEORGE (d. before July 1837). Son of Samuel Alken, architect and engraver. Painted sporting subjects in watercolour, miniatures, and engraved. *repr.* 'A Book of Sporting Painters', Shaw Sparrow, 1931; Four racing coloured aquatints published by S. W. Fores 1827; St. Leger winners drawn and engraved in aquatint in 1827; four lithographs of shooting.

***ALKEN, HENRY THOMAS,** called Old Henry Alken. (b. London 1785, 12th October, baptized 4th November 1785; d. 1851, 7th April, Shaw Sparrow; b. 1774, d. 1850, Benezit). Son of Samuel Alken, architect and engraver and the most famous of the family of sporting artists. Pupil of John Thomas Barber (Lincoln catalogue says John Thomas Booker). Miniature painter to the Duke of Kent. About 1802–1809 in Ipswich, marrying Maria Gordon in 1809. Suggestion that he went to Persia with James I. Morier not confirmed. Visited Waterloo and prints of the 1815 battle and portraits of Wellington, Blucher, and the Marquess of Anglesey were published by S. & J. Fuller in 1815. Visited Leicestershire and rode with the Meltonians. Used the pseudonym 'Ben Tally Ho', but Meltonians were unaware of this until later, he having gone to Melton to study his favourite sport. *exhib.* Henry Alken Exhibition, Lincoln, 1948, showing 16 oils and 32 water-colours loaned by the Hon. Mrs. Mountjoy Fane, of Holywell Hall, near Stamford. The oils mainly stage-coach scenes, several snow scenes of which Henry was fond, the others hunting scenes and studies of horses and dogs, with one or two pugilistic and of like interst. *coll.* Dunedin A.G. (5); Leicester A.G. (3); London, V. and A. Museum (3); Manchester, Whitworth A.G. (1); Preston A.G. (4); Major the Hon. H. R. Broughton (4); Lord Exeter (4); Hon. Mrs. Mountjoy Fane (48); Lord Hastings (6); C. G. Hoare (4); Major Sir Reginald Macdonald-Buchanan (12); Mr. and Mrs. Paul Mellon (4); Chas. H. Thieriot, New York (2). *repr.* 'The Beauties and Defects of the Horse', 1816; 'National Sports of Gt. Britain', 1821; Jorrock's Jaunts and Jollities', 1869; 'A Book of Sporting Painters', 1931; 'Angling in British Art', by Shaw Sparrow; 'Animal Painting in England', by Basil Taylor, 1955. *lit.* 'New Sporting Magazine', 1844, by Wildrake; 'Henry Alken', by Shaw Sparrow, 1927; 'Story of British Sporting Prints', by Siltzer.

ALKEN, HENRY, Junior (*see* SAMUEL HENRY ALKEN)

ALKEN, SAMUEL (b. 1756, 22nd October; d. London 1815; buried St. James's, Piccadilly, 4th November) Son of Sefferin Alken, wood and stone carver. Architect and engraver. Not certain if he painted in oils. Published 'A New Book of Ornaments', designed andetched by himself, 1779. *coll.* Charles H. Thieriot, New York (1, since sold). *exhib.* R.A. 1780, 'Architecture' (1). *lit.* 'A Book of Sporting Painters', Shaw Sparrow, 1931.

ALKEN, SAMUEL, Junior (b. London 1784, 10th April; d. c. 1825). Son of Samuel Alken, architect and engraver. Painted sporting subjects, some signed 'S. Alken, Jnr.' Many works are given to a mythical Samuel Alken, 1750–1825. *coll.* Liverpool, Walker A.G. (2); Manchester, Whitworth A.G. (1); Major Jack Lloyd (1). *auct.* Four angling subjects were included in the A. N. Gilbey Sale at Christie's 25/26th April 1940. *repr.* 'Angling in British Art', Shaw Sparrow; 'A Book of Sporting Painters', Shaw Sparrow; 'Sporting Pictures of England', Guy Paget (1945); 'Drawing Cover', watercolour, G. P. Fores.

***ALKEN, SAMUEL HENRY,** miscalled HENRY ALKEN, JUNIOR (b. Ipswich 1810, 1st August; d. 1894, 5th July, in Poplar Workhouse). Also known as Henry 'Gordon' Alken. Son of Henry Thomas Alken. Married Martha Dormer. Copied his father's style and used his father's signature, 'H. Alken'. Died at the age of 84. Had worked as 'biscuit-baker's journeyman' at Poplar Workhouse. *coll.* Manchester, Whitworth A.G. (1). *repr.* 'Renewal of Acquaintance with Hounds', oil; 'A Book of Sporting Painters', Shaw Sparrow, p. 127.

ALKEN, SEFFERIN JOHN (b. London 1796, 14th May; d. London 1857). Brother of Samuel Junior, Henry Thomas and George Alken, Son of Samuel Alken, architect and engraver. Married Sarah Ann Cawood. Known as 'Seffrien'. *coll.* G. P. Fores (1). *repr.* 'Shooters outside a Cottage with Dogs', G. P. Fores; 'A Book of Sporting Painters', Shaw Sparrow.

ALKEN, SEFFERIN, Junior (b. 1821, d. 1873, 19th January, at Newington, Surrey). Married Mary Ann Johnson in 1840 when 19 years old. Had two sons and three daughters. Signed sporting pictures 'S. Alken', so can be confused with Samuel Alken. *coll.* George Kendall (1). *repr.* 'The New Race Stand at Brighton'; 'A Book of Sporting Painters', Shaw Sparrow, 1931.

ALLAN, DAVID (b. Alloa 1744, d. Edinburgh 1796). Studied Academy of Art established by Foulis's, the printers, in Glasgow. Went to Rome 1764, where he won a gold medal and became a member of the Academy of St. Luke. Returned to London in 1777 and settled in Edinburgh in 1780, being made Master of the Academy of the Board of Manufacturers. Was a friend of Robert Burns and illustrated his poems, also Allan Ramsay's 'Gentle Shepherd', 1788. Made five humorous drawings of the 'Sports of the Carnival of Rome', which were engraved by Paul Sandby. *coll.* Edinburgh, N.G. of Scotland, 'Portraits and Figures'. *exhib.* R.A. (12); S.A. (3); F.S. (4). *repr.* 'Conversation Pictures' by S. Sitwell (cricket painting).

ALLEN, W. (op. 1789). W. Allen, who exhibited a single picture at the R.S.B.A., is possibly the same. *coll.* Birmingham A.G., 'A Birmingham Prize Fight between Tom Johnson, Champion of England, and Isaac Perrins of Birmingham' (canvas S&D 1789).

ALLEN, W. H. (op. 1865–1874). London, Ebury Street address. *exhib.* R.A. 1868, 'A Bite'.

ALLINSON, ADRIAN PAUL, R.B.A. (b. London 1890, 9th January; d. 1959). Painter, sculptor, designer. Art master at Westminster Technical Institute; sometime stage designer to Beecham Opera Company. Studied Slade School. *coll.* Lord's (1). *exhib.* at R.A., N.E.A.C., etc.

ALMA-TADEMA, Sir LAURENCE, O.M., R.A. (b. Dronrijp, Friesland, 1836; d. Wiesbaden 1912). Studied under Wappers, Louis de Taeye, and Baron Leys at Antwerp. Came to England in 1870; naturalised 1873. Painted classical subjects. *repr.* 'Angling in British Art', Shaw Sparrow; 'A Roman Lady Watching her Rod and Line', oil.

ALPENNY, J. S. (op. 1825–1853). Kew address. Painted portraits. His R.A. exhibit of 1825 was 'Ancient Irish Hunting the Moose Deer'. *exhib.* R.A., 1826–1853, portraits.

AMBROSE, C. (op. 1824–1848). London address. *coll.* Lord's (1). *exhib.* R.A. (30); B.I. (2); S.S. (49), 'portraits'.

ANDERSON, JOHN CORBET (op. 1852). Illustrated 'Sketches at Lord's', lithographed by Hulmandel. *coll.* Lord's (12 sketches). *repr.* 'The Picture of Cricket', John Arlott, 1955; 'Surrey Players Sherman, Caesar, Caffyn and Lockyer'. *lit.* Arlott.

ANDREW, F. W., the Elder (op. 1826–1827). London address. *exhib.* S.S. (3), game.

ANDREWS, H. (b. 1804, d. 1868, 30th November). A painter of genré and follower of Watteau. *coll.* Glasgow A.G., 'The Pet Dove'; Mr. and Mrs. R. Richards, 'Mary Queen of Scots returning from Hawking'. *exhib.* R.A. (8); B.I. (17); S.S. (14). Graves says 'Historical'. *auct.* The Gilbey Sale (Christie's, 25/26th April 1940) included an angling canvas. Christie's, 22nd January 1965 (154), 'The Hawking Party'.

***ANSDELL, RICHARD, R.A.** (b. Liverpool 1815, d. Farnborough 1885, 20th April). Educated at the Blue Coat School, Liverpool, 1824–28. Pupil of W. C. Smith, portrait painter at Chatham. Returned to Liverpool. Attended Liverpool Academy, eventually becoming President. Removed to Kensington in 1847. Spent some time in lodge beside Loch Laggan. Ansdell and his family occupied 'Starr Hills', a house the artist built at Lytham in 1861. First a road, then a railway station, and finally a whole district near 'Starr Hills' became known as 'Ansdell'. Today the railway station still bears the name 'Ansdell and Fairhaven'. About 1864 the artist sold the house at Lytham. It would appear to have been used only as a summer residence. Ansdell etched a few plates of animals. *coll.* Cheltenham A.G. (1); Liverpool, Walker A.G. (2); London, R.A. (1); Tate Gallery (1); Lytham St. Annes, Town Hall (23); Preston, H.M. & A.G. (3); J. M. Cheetham (1); Major Sir Reginald Macdonald-Buchanan (1). *exhib.* R.A., 1840–1885 (17). *repr.* 'Angling in British Art', Shaw Sparrow; 'A Book of Sporting Painters', Shaw Sparrow.

ANSELL, CHARLES (op. 1780–1781). A watercolour artist who exhibited four views at the Royal Academy. Grant questions identity of sport with this artist. The following engravings are known after paintings by Charles Ansell: 'Life of a Racehorse' (6), engraved by Jukes, 1784; 'Hunting Scenes' (10), engraved by Sutherland; 'Shooting', engraved by Sutherland.

ANSTED, WILLIAM ALEXANDER (op. 1888–1893). Exhibited four works at the Royal Academy, including 'Woodcock Shooting' in 1892. Graves says 'Etching'.

APPART, A. A painting entitled 'Group of Sportsmen watching Cocks Fighting in a Barn', canvas 19½ by 23½in., signed, was sold at Christie's 12th October 1962 (158).

APPELBEE, LEONARD, A.R.C.A. (b. London 1914, 13th November; living). London address. *exhib.* R.A. 1956–1964 (4), all angling pictures.

***APPLEYARD, JOSEPH** (b. 1908, 3rd January), living. Sporting painter in oil and watercolours. Residing in Leeds. *coll.* Doncaster A.G. (8); Huddersfield A.G. (2); Newcastle A.G.; Wakefield A.G.; Sir Eric Ohlson, Bart.

ARCHER, ARCHIBALD (op. 1810–1845). London address. *exhib.* R.A. (16); B.I. (6); S.S. (1). Graves says 'Scriptural', but only one such subject in R.A. The 1836 exhibit was 'A Young Archer'. A coloured lithograph by Pollard, a portrait of Thomas Yudgeon, Gamekeeper to Lord Gaze, is said to have been painted by Archer.

ARCHER, J. S. (op. 1850). Address unknown. *exhib.* R.A. (1), 'Zuleika, Mare belonging to J. L. Gaskin, Esq.'.

ARGENT (op. 1782–1783). London address. Animal painter exhibited three works at the Free Society. A 'W. Argent', op. 1837, with a London address, is recorded.

ARMFIELD, GEORGE, the name of George Armfield Smith (op. 1836–1867). Painter of animals and sporting subjects. London, 1840–1847; Clapham, 1848–1850; Camberwell, 1851–1853; Larkhall Rise, 1855–1856; Wandsworth, 1858–1862. Not infrequently his small works passed off as by Sir E. Landseer. *coll.* Glasgow A.G. (1); Liverpool, Walker A.G. (1); H. K. Fores, Esq. (1); Lieut. John S. Clarke, U.S.A. (1). *exhib.* R.A. 1840–1858 (12); B.I. 1841–1867 (6); under the name 'Smith' R.A. 1836–1839 (5); B.I. (2); S.S. (1). *repr.* 'Spaniels putting up a Bird', Walker A.G., Liverpool. Colour plate Bibby's Calendar 1963.

ARMSTEAD, —. A canvas entitled 'Taking a Fence—Steeplechasing' was exhibited at Ackermann's, London. This is possibly ARMSTEAD, HUGH WELLS, M.D., F.R.C.S. (b. London, 8th November 1865), son of H. H. Armstead, R.A. Lecturer on artistic anatomy of animals at Calderon's School of Animal Painting, and artistic comparative anatomy at City and Guild's School of Art, 1932. His recreation was painting.

ARMOUR, G. DENHOLM (b. 1864, 30th January; d. 1903, 11th July). Edinburgh; London 1893; Welwyn 1894; Devizes 1903. *coll.* Bath, Victoria A.G., 'Member of the Beaufort Hunt with Hounds'; 'Hound Feeding'. *exhib.* R.A. (7); N.G. (4). *repr.* Painting of 'Three Greynounds' was engraved by W. Brooke.

ARNALD, GEORGE, A.R.A. ('Bryan', says Arnold). (b. in Berkshire 1763, d. Pentonville 1841, 21st November). Pupil of W. Pether, painter of landscapes, although his R.A. exhibit of 1801 was 'Three Spaniels belonging to Mr. Nowel', while the Gilbey Sale at Christie's 25/26th April 1940 included 'Two Young Anglers'. *exhib.* R.A. (176); B.I. (63); N.W.C.S. (2).

ARNOLD, Mrs., *née* HARRIOT GOULDSMITH (Graves gives 'Harriett' and 'Harriot') (b. 1787, d. 1863). Married Captain Arnold, R.N., in 1839. Painted in oils and watercolour; also etched and produced lithographs. *exhib.* As Gouldsmith: R.A. 1807–1838 (27); B.I. (81); S.S. (28); O.W.C.S. (34); N.W.C.S. (4). As Arnold: R.A. (15); B.I. (15).

ARNULL, G. (c. 1825). Arthur Ackermann & Son had a pair of racing subjects, 'Going Out' and 'The Finish', attractive and of good quality. Both signed but not dated.

ASHFORD, WILLIAM, P.R.H.A., F.S.A. (b. Birmingham 1746, d. Dublin 1824, 17th April). Went to Ireland in 1764 and settled in Dublin. President of the Irish Society of Artists 1813. President of the Royal Hibernian Academy 1823. Painted flowers, fruit, dead game, and landscapes. Some of interest to anglers. *exhib.* R.A. (25); S.A. (23) landscapes; 1775 from a Dublin address; 1789–1811 from a London address.

ASHTON, G. R. (op. 1874–1877). London address. Painted animals and some sporting. *coll.* Sydney A.G., Australia (1), 'Coursing in Victoria' *exhib.* S.S. (4); V.E. (5).

ATKINSON, E. (op. 1793–1797). London, Long Acre address. *exhib.* R.A. (3); 1793, Snipe; 1794, Woodcocks; 1797, Fish.

ATKINSON, J. (op. 1796). No address given. *exhib.* R.A. (1), 1796, 'Portraits of a Horse and Dog'.

ATKINSON, JOHN AUGUSTUS (b. London 1775, living in 1833). Painter in oils and watercolour and engraver. Subjects were battles, military, figures, and some sporting. Member of Old Water Colour Society. *exhib.* R.A. (60); B.I. (45); S.S. (24); O.W.C.S. (68).

ATTWOOD, THOMAS (op. 1857). Messrs. Arthur Ackermann had a painting, 'The Southdown Steeplechase at Ringmer', S&D 1857.

AUMONIER, JAMES (b. London 1832, d. 1911). Principally a landscape painter. Commenced career as a designer of calicoes.Took up painting after 1873. Residing at Hornsey 1870; Petersfield 1884; Steyning 1887; and London 1888. *exhib.* R.A. 1888, a painting, 'Football'.

AUSTEN, Miss WINIFRED M. L., R.I., R.E., F.Z.S. (b. Ramsgate, d. 1964). Painter in oil and watercolour of birds and animal life. Now residing at Orford in Suffolk. Married Oliver O'Donnell Frick. Some of her bird and animals subjects might be regarded a sporting. *exhib.* R.A. (from 1899).

BACKSHELL, W. (BACKSHEEL, Benezit). op. 1848. Exhibited two pictures at S.S. in 1848. Graves says 'Domestic'. Shaw Sparrow refers to Sporting Magazine V.145.

BACON, D'ARCY (op. 1855–1874). Painted animals. *exhib.* R.A. (1); B.I. (3), 'The Twelfth of August', 'The Haunt of the Heron' and 'Haunt of the Red Deer'; S.S. (10); V.E. (6).

BACON, H. D. (op. 1861). London address. Exhibited a sporting picture in London.

BAKER, ARTHUR (op. 1864–1911). London and Tunbridge Wells addresses. Painted sporting and mainly cattle subjects in oils and water-colours. *exhib.* R.A. (2), Cattle; B.I. (3); S.S. (2); V.E. (4). Graves says 'Sporting'.

BAKER, THOMAS (b. 1809, 8th October; d. 1869, 10th August). Painted mainly landscapes. Well-known figure in Midland art, friend of J. V. Barber, David Cox, and others of the local coterie. Exhibited mainly in Birmingham. An 'Angling at Ambleside' was in the A. N. Gilbey sale at Christie's 25/26th April 1940. Graves gives a Thomas Baker exhibiting landscapes from a Leamington address between 1831 and 1860. *coll.* Birmingham A.G. (1); Glasgow A.G. (1); V. and A. Museum (5 drawings); Wolverhampton A.G. (1). *exhib.* R.A. (4); B.I. (19).

BAKER, W. CARMICHAEL. *coll.* Lord Exeter, 'Troilus', oil. Signed.

BALDERY, J. K. (op. 1793–1794). Holborn address. Exhibited a portrait at the R.A. 1793 and a Portrait of a Gamekeeper in 1794.

BALDOCK, CHARLES E. (op. 1900). Nottingham address. Exhibited at R.A. 1900, picture 'Hard Pressed—S. Notts. Hounds'.

***BALDOCK, JAMES WALSHAM** (op. 1867–1887). Worksop address. Painted cattle and horses in oils and water-colours. A canvas S&D 1879, 'Two Bay Horses and a Dappled Grey in a field', was in the Hutchinson Gallery of Sport (now dispersed). *exhib.* S.S. (16); N.W.C.S. (6).

BALDOCK, T. (op. 1854). A painting known of 'Honeydew', a favourite greyhound. Canvas 14¼ by 23¾ in. S&D 1854. This may be by James Baldock.

BALFOUR-BROWNE, VINCENT, R., J.P. (b. London 1880, 30th May). Painter in water-colour, mainly stalking subjects. *Exhib.* Tryon Gallery, London. *repr.* 'A Day's Stalking', 'Story of a Stag', 'The Corrie Dubh Royal', etc.

BALMER, GEORGE (b. North Shield 1805, d. Ravensworth 1846, 10th April). Worked much in Newcastle and Edinburgh, chiefly scenes of the North-east coast, mostly in water-colours, some oils are known. Shaw Sparrow says 'angling ideas in his water-colours'. Visited Holland and Switzerland. Assisted J. W. Carmichael. *exhib.* B.I. (5); S.S. (42). *coll.* Gateshead A.G. (1); Leeds A.G. (1); Newcastle A.G. (1).

BARBER, CHARLES BURTON (b. Great Yarmouth 1845, d. London 1894, 27th November). Studied at the R.A. Schools. Painted sporting and animal subjects. *exhib.* R.A. (32); S.S. (2); G.G. (1).

***BARENGER, JAMES, Junior** (b. 1780, 25th December; d. 1831, 1st October). Son of a painter and glazier of Kentish Town, a breeder of pointers and a painter of insects, who was related to Woollett and Pouncy, the engravers. He himself was devoted to sporting and animal painting. His 'Lord Derby's Stag-hounds' (Mellon Collection) probably his best pure hunting scene. This artist should not be confused with one named BERRINGER (op. 1774–1775), a painter of still-life, who exhibited five pictures at the Society of Artists. *coll.* Mr. and Mrs. Paul Mellon, U.S.A. (1); Charles H. Thieriot, New York (1). *exhib.* R.A. (48); B.I. (8); S.S. (3). *repr.* Engraved by Charles Turner, Sutherland, C. Hunt and R. Woodman. *lit.* New Sporting Magazine, Vol. II, 1831, pp. 145–146.

BARKER, A. (op. 1834). Exhibited a sporting painting at Suffolk Street.

BARKER, BENJAMIN, Senior (b. Newark, d. Bristol 1793, 12th June). Founder of the painter family, the 'Barkers of Bath' and father of Thomas Barker (1769–1847). Was at Pontypool employed in the decoration of the elaborate Japan ware. Said to have owned stables and then turned his attention to painting his horses. Only one of these pictures said to be extant.

BARKER, BENJAMIN, Junior 'of Bath'. (b. 1776, d. Totnes 1838, 2nd March). Second son of the preceding, brother of Thomas and Joseph, and father of Marianne. Exhibited over two hundred and forty works, all landscapes, at R.A., B.I., S.S., O.W.C.S., N.W.C.S. and V.E. *coll.* Bath, Holburne Museum (8).

BARKER, THOMAS, 'of Bath' (b. near Pontypool 1769, d. Bath 1847). Son of Benjamin Barker, Senior, and best known of the 'Barkers of Bath'. Painted landscapes, country life, and a few sporting pictures, including his 'Lansdown Fair with men Playing at Ninepins', a 44 by 55 inch canvas shown at the B.I. in 1813. *coll.* Bath, Holburne Museum (15); Victoria A.G. (several, including a self portrait); Dublin N.G. (1); London, N.G. (2); V. and A. (2 oils and 5 drawings); Glasgow A.G. (2); Nottingham A.G. (4); Wolverhampton A.G. (2). *exhib.* R.A. (18); B.I. (97); S.S. (3).

BARKER, THOMAS JONES (b. Bath 1815, d. Haverstock Hill, London, 1882, 29th March). Painted military, battle and sporting pictures. His 'The Horse Race at Rome' was shown at the R.A. in 1860. *exhib.* R.A. (29); B.I. (34); S.S. (15). Graves says 'Historical'.

BARKER, WRIGHT (op. 1891–1893). Painted hunting subjects and domestic. *auct.* 'Full Cry', sold Christie's 16th October 1964. *exhib.* R.A. (2); S.S. (1), 'Domestic'.

BARLOW, FRANCIS (b. Lincolnshire 1626, d. 1704, 11th August), buried St. Margaret's Churchyard, Westminster. (d. 1702, Benezit). Painter and etcher of birds, animals, and sporting subjects in the manner of Hondius and Hondecoeter. *coll.* Bedford, Cecil Higgins Museum (1); London, British Museum (52); Painter's Company (1); V. and A. Museum (1); Witt Library (1); Plymouth M. and A.G. (1); Preston H.M. and A.G. (1); Captain T. Tyrwhitt Drake (several); Mr. and Mrs. Paul Mellon, U.S.A. (1); Lord Onslow (1). *repr.* 'British Sporting Painters', Shaw Sparrow; 'A Book of Sporting Painters' Shaw Sparrow; 'Angling in British Art', Shaw Sparrow. *lit.* See above-mentioned three books. Shaw Sparrow also mentions a painting, 'Southern Hounds'.

BARNARD, EDWARD (b. 1785, d. 1861, aged 76). *repr.* 'Angling in British Art', Shaw Sparrow.

BARNARD, GEORGE (d. 1890). London address. Pupil of J. D. Harding, Painted sporting subjects and landscapes. *exhib.* 1832–1884, R.A. (19); B.I. (7); S.S. (52); N.W.C.S. (8); V.E. (9).

BARRABLE, H. (op. 1873–1887) and **STAPLES, R. P.** (1875–1893). A painting by these two artists is to be seen in the M.C.C. Gallery at Lord's Cricket Ground, London. H. Barrable is probably George Hamilton Barrable (op. 1873–1887). *exhib.* R.A. (13); S.S. (16); G.G. (1); V.E. (9), 'Domestic'.

BARRATT, THOMAS (op. 1852–1893). Stockbridge address. Painted deer, horses, dogs and landscapes. *exhib.* R.A. (17); B.I. (6); S.S. (11); V.E. (4).

BARRAUD, FRANCIS P. (op. 1877–1891). London address. *coll.* Lord's (1). *exhib.* R.A. (1); S.S. (11) N.W.C.S. (4), 'Churches'.

BARRAUD, HENRY (b. 1811, d. London, Marylebone, 1874, 17th June, aged 63). Painted sport, landscapes, portraits and figures. *exhib.* R.A. (33); B.I. (48); S.S. (19); V.E. (86).

***BARRAUD, HENRY** (1811–1874) and **WILLIAM** (1810–1850). Brothers, grandsons of Barraud the chronometer maker. Painted many sporting pictures together. *coll.* Major Sir Reginald Macdonald-Buchanan (3). *exhib.* R.A. 1842–1849 (4); B.I. 1840–1849 (4).

***BARRAUD, WILLIAM** (b. 1810, d. Kensington, London, 1850, 1st October). Pupil of Abraham Cooper, R.A. Painter of sporting pictures, some in conjunction with his brother Henry. *exhib.* R.A. 1830–1849 (18); B.I. 1835–1849 (4). *repr.* 'Angling in British Art', Shaw Sparrow.

BARRINGTON-BROWNE, W. E. (living). Paints stalking, shooting and fishing subjects. *exhib.* Tryon Gallery, London. (Two one-man shows, the second June-July 1962).

BARROW, THOMAS (b. Great Eccleston in the Fylde 1737, 15th January; d. there 1822). No work by this artist has yet been traced. Nodal says he painted animals, landscapes, portraits, and history. *exhib.* 1769–1819, S.A. (11); F.S. (1); R.A. (13). All portraits from a London address. *lit.* 'Art and Artists in Lancashire and Cheshire', J. H. Nodal.

BARRY, JAMES (op. 1813). London address. *exhib.* O.W.C.S. (1), Sporting.

BARTLETT, WILLIAM H., R.O.I., R.B.A.(op. 1874–1904). Chelsea address. Painted fishing, poaching and games, also views on the Continent, in the East, and America. *coll.* Leeds. *exhib.* R.A. (19); S.S. (40); G.G. (15); N.G. (8); V.E. (19). A 'William Henry Bartlett', b. Kentish Town 1809, d. 1854, travelled on the Continent, in the East, and America (see Grant's Dictionary).

BARWICK, J. (op. 1844–1849). Painted portraits of huntsmen and horses, often in nicely executed landscapes. *exhib.* R.A. (2), 'Horses property of Lord Willoughby D'Eresby' was the 1849 R.A. exhibit. *repr.* Print by C. Chalot.

BASBE, C. J. (op. 1849). Painted a number of cricket portraits. The Gallery at Lord's has a number of sketches by this artist. *repr.* 'The Picture of Cricket', by John Arlott, 1955.

BATCHELOR, ARTHUR. *repr.* 'Angling in British Art', Shaw Sparrow. 'After Wiltshire Grayling', oil.

BATEMAN, HENRY MAYO (b. Sutton Forest, Australia, 1887, 15th February; living in Devon 1964). Studied at Westminster and New Cross Art Schools. Humorous artist and illustrator. His drawings included many sporting subjects.

BATEMAN, JAMES (b. 1815, d. Holloway, London, 1849, 24th March; b. 1814, Benezit). Painted fishing, shooting and hunting subjects. *exhib.* R.A. (19); B.I. (29); S.S. (34). *repr.* 'An Angler fishing in Mountain Stream', S&D 1840, engraved in the 'Sporting Magazine'. 'Angling in British Art', Shaw Sparrow.

BATEMAN, JAMES, R.A. (b. Kendal 1893, 22nd March; d. 1959, 2nd August). Painter, wood-engraver and art master. Studied Slade, R.C.A. *coll.* Cheltenham A.G. (2); Leeds A.G. (Mare and foal). *exhib.* R.A., N.E.A.C.

BATMAN, J. E. (op. 1871). A pen and ink drawing of a Spaniel, 3 inches in diameter, exhibited in 'British Sporting Paintings', H. M. and A. G. Preston, 1943. Property of Miss E. M. Woods.

BAXTER, GEORGE (b. Lewes 1804, 31st July; d. Sydenham 1867, 11th January. Painter in water-colour and lithographer. *coll.* Lord's (1). *exhib.* R.A. (1), 'Historical'.

BAXTER, THOMAS (op. 1802–1821). A 'Portrait of Honest Baxter' of Surrey Cricket Club as a Young Cricketer holding his Bat on Richmond Green was sold at Sotheby's 29th July 1964. *exhib.* R.A. (16); V.E. (1), 'Enamels'.

BAYES, ALFRED WALTER (op. 1858–1903). Painted portraits, landscapes and fishing subjects. *exhib.* R.A. (49); B.I. (9); S.S. (91); N.W.C.S. (21); V.E. (83). Graves says 'Domestic'.

BAYLEY, CHAPMAN (op. 1818–1832). Painted landscapes, views and shooting subjects in oil and water-colour. His R.A. exhibit 1825 was 'Pheasant Shooting, Didlington, Norfolk'. *exhib.* R.A. (15); B.I. (15); S.S. (7).

BAYNES, THOMAS MANN (1794–1854). London address. Like his brother James (1766–1837), a water-colourist of the topographical kind. He is also described as an architect. A few oils are known. *coll.* Lord's (1). *exhib.* R.A. (41); S.S. (5); N.W.C.S. (5), 'Landscape'.

BEATTIE, L. (c. 1835). A painting of the racehorse 'Elis' with jockey up, on a racecourse, signed but not dated, was exhibited by Arthur Ackermann & Son in their London Gallery.

BEAUFORT, C. (op. 1831). Three sporting subjects in possession of Major R. E. H. Finch, The Old School House, Merstham, Surrey. A pair depicting a 'Groom taking out a spare Horse' and its return after a day's hunting. The third a sporting subject. All three of merit by a good painter. But these are possibly colour prints.

BEAUMONT, Sir GEORGE HOWLAND, Bart. (b. Dunmow 1753, 6th November; d. Coleorton 1827, 7th February). Painted landscapes. *coll.* London, Tate Gallery (Landscape with Jaques and the Wounded Stag). *exhib.* R.A. 1779–1825, all landscapes.

BECKWITH, H. (op. 1832–1854). Painter and engraver. 'Woodland Angling', drawn and engraved by this artist 1854, mentioned by Shaw Sparrow. 'Nature and Art—River Scene with Anglers', a water-colour mentioned by Grant.

BEDDINGTON, ROY (b. 1910, 16th June; living). Landscapes and angling subjects in water-colours and oils. Studied art at The Slade and Florence. *exhib.* R.A.; N.E.A.C.; Ackermann's. *repr.* Illustrations to many books on angling.

BEDFORD, JOHN READE. An example by this painter is at Lord's.

BEER, JOHN. *repr.* 'Pretty Polly' in 'Sportsmen's Pictures', by Guy Paget; Studio", Vol. CXXX, No. 629, August 1945. *auct.* Lady Nelson's 'Ally Sloper'; Views of Becher's Brook; 'The Fifth Fence'; 'The Water Jump'; 'The last Fence at Grand National 1915' (all signed), sold at Christie's 16th October 1964.

BEERBOHM, Sir MAX (b. London, 1872, 24th August, d. 1956, 20th May). Caricaturist. Nine one-man exhibitions of his drawings in London; there are also nine volumes published on his drawings. *coll.* Lord's.

BELANGER, LOUIS DE (BELLANGÉ, BOULANGÉ), also known as Belanger le Romain (b. Paris 1736, d. Stockholm 1816). London address. Painter to the Duke of Orleans. *coll.* H.M. The Queen, 'A Cricket Match'; Lord's. *exhib.* R.A. (3), landscapes.

BELL, J. C. (op. 1850–1868). Newcastle and Scarborough addresses. Not John Clement Bell (b. 1860) of London. *exhib.* Preston A.G. 1943, a 'Sheldrake', S&D 1857, property of the late Dr. H. J. Taylor. *repr.* 'British Sporting Painters'.

BELL, EDWARD (op. 1811–1847). Worcester address. In 1816 London, 1847 Shefford, Beds. Painted still-life, game, fish and fishing, and some sporting. May have mezzotinted four pictures of Fox-hunting after Morland 1800. *coll.* London, British Museum. *exhib.* R.A. (22); B.I. (24); S.S. (22).

BELLEW, W. H. du (op. 1866). Executed a drawing of Cricket for 'Jerks in from a Short Leg', by R. A. Fitzgerald, 1866. *repr.* 'The Picture of Cricket', John Arlott, 1955. Pen drawing.

BELLINGER, —. (op. 1803). Kentish Town address. *exhib.* R.A. (3), 1803 'Bear Hunting'; 'A Mare and Spaniel'.

BENHAM, THOMAS C. S. (op. 1878–1904). London and Southwold addresses. Painted portraits and landscapes. Exhibited a 'Poachers' at R.A. 1883. *exhib.* R.A. (23); N.W.C.S. (2); G.G. (2); V.E. (17).

BENNET, THOMAS (op. 1796–1799). Woodstock address. Painted sporting subjects. Charles Turner mezzotinted nine of his pictures, all hunting. Graves gives a second entry, 'Thomas Bennett—Woodstock'. Exhibiting O.W.C.S. (6), 1816–1819, Animals'. *exhib.* R.A. (7).

BENNETT, F. M. (op. 1930–1937). A painting, 'The Snail Race', S&D, 1930 was sold by Sotheby's 10th February 1960, and 'The Hunt Breakfast', S&D 1936, while Christie's (5th February 1965) auctioned 'Sportsmen's return at Close of Day', S&D 1937. A Frank M. Bennett exhibited at the R.A. 1898–1928, mostly portraits and figures; the following might be termed sporting: R.A. 1900, 'The Greek Runner Ladas falling dead as he goes to receive his Crown at Olympia'; 1913, 'The Falconer'.

BENSON, J. (op. 1805–1811). Landscape and sporting. His R.A. exhibits include 'Coursing' 1807; 'A Pointer' 1809; 'Warrior, a favourite Hunter' 1811.

BENSTEAD, J. (Shaw Sparrow); **BENSTED** (Grant, Graves and Benezit) (op. 1828–1847). Chiefly a sporting painter of animals, game birds, etc., his subjects set in landscape. *exhib.* R.A. (7), including 'Dead Game', 'Snipes and Heron', 'Shot Mallard'; S.S. (4). *repr.* Two paintings lithographed, 'Tally-Ho!' by J. W. Giles and the 'Maidstone Grand Steeplechase 1839'.

BENTLEY, CHARLES (b. London 1806, d. there 1854). Articled to Theodore and Thales Fielding. First worked as an engraver. Member of the Old Water Colour Society. Painted coast and river scenes. *exhib.* R.A.; B.I. (11); S.S. (3); O.W.C.S. (209); N.W.C.S. (10). *repr.* 'Angling in British Art', Shaw Sparrow.

BERKELEY, STANLEY, R.E. (op. 1878–1902, d. 1909, 24th April). Epsom, Esher and London addresses. Painter of animals and sporting. His R.A. exhibits included a 'Coursing', 'Gone Away' and 'Full Cry'. His wife, Mrs. Stanley B. (Edith) exhibited figure subjects from 1883–1893 at R.A., S.S.; N.W.C.S.; and G.G. *exhib.* R.A. (16); S.S. (14); N.W.C.S. (9); G.G. (1); V.E. 18.

BERRIE, JOHN ARCHIBALD ALEXANDER, R.C.A., A.R.C.A., F.R.S.A. (b. Fallowfield, Manchester, 1887, 28th December). Studied Liverpool School of Art and Paris. Living in Johannesburg 1964. Portrait painter. *exhib.* Paris Salon 1935 (Portrait of Gordon Richards in jockey's silks).

BERTHOUD, HENRY (b. London 1790, d. Paris 1864). *exhib.* S.S. (2), Game. *repr.* Two poaching pictures engraved by R. G. Reeve.

BEST, JOHN (op. 1750–1792). A once well-known painter of game-cocks, sporting animals and prize cattle. *exhib.* R.A. (3); S.A. (7).

BEST, T. (18th century). Author of 'A Concise Treatise on the Art of Angling', 1798 (see 'A Book of Sporting Artists', by Shaw Sparrow). He was Keeper of History, Drawing Room in Tower of London (see 'Angling in British Art', by Shaw Sparrow. Here name given as Thomas Best). Shaw Sparrow says he had seen two paintings by this artist, one an oil of a 'Horse, boy and Groom'.

BESTOESMITH, W. (op. 1836–1837). A painter of fish in a later version of Elmer's manner. Sudbury address. *exhib.* R.A. (2).

BEVAN, ROBERT POLHILL (b. Hove 1865, d. London 1925). Studied Westminster School of Art and Julian's in Paris. Visited North Africa and the Continent. Settled in Hampstead. Founder member of the Camden Town Group 1911. Member London Group. Visited Poland 1921. *coll.* Leicester Art Gallery (1); London, Tate Gallery (2). *exhib.* Lefevre Gallery, London, 'Bevan Paintings', 1944.

BEWICK, THOMAS (b. Cherryburn, Ovingham, Northumberland, 1753; d. Gateshead 1828). Famous wood engraver. Also painted birds in water-colour. *coll.* London, British Museum (230); V. and A. Museum; Witt Library. *lit.* 'Thomas Bewick', Selwyn Image; Print Collectors Club No. 11, 1932. Illustrations: Pl. IX(A), X(A), XI(B), XVII (A & B), all sporting.

BIDDULPH, S. 'A Hawk attacking a Duck', signed, was sold at Sotheby's 2nd March 1960.

BIEDERMANN, J. C. (op. 1799–1831). Said to have painted some sporting subjects. *exhib.* R.A. (16), all landscapes with figures; B.I. (19).

BIEGEL, PETER (b. Croxley Green 1913, 22nd April). Father a naturalized Dutchman, mother Irish. Educated Downside. Went into City for five years. Then studied at Lucy Kemp Welch Studio at Bushey. War service with 4th Batt. Wiltshire Regiment. Invalided out 1945. Met Lionel Edwards when travelling by train from Salisbury to London. Meeting led to a year at the Bournemouth School of Art and a year with Lionel Edwards. Lives at Gillingham, Dorset. *coll.* Messrs Silcock & Sons Ltd., 'March Morning —Huntsmen and Hounds'. Picture reproduced in Silcock Calendar 1963. *exhib.* Tryon Gallery, London, 'One Man', 1960 and 1963 (80 racing and hunting scenes).

BIGG, WILLIAM REDMORE, R.A. (b. 1755, January; d. London 1828, 6th February). Painted mostly domestic subjects and some sporting. *coll.* R. W. Ketton-Cremer ('A Shooting Party', S&D 1803); Lord's ('John Charles Reade with Bat and ball'). *exhib.* R.A. (129); B.I. (30); F.S. (1).

BINKS, REUBEN WARD (b. Bolton, living 1934, New York). Painter of sporting scenes and especially of sporting dogs. Illustrated 'Gun Dogs', by Patrick Chalmers; 'About our Dogs', by A. Croxton Smith. *exhib.* Preston, H.M. & A.G. 1943, 'British Sporting Paintings', four water-colours.

BIRCH, S. J. LAMORNA, R.A. (b. Egremont, Cheshire, 1869, d. 1955, 5th June). Painter of landscapes in oils and water-colours, many with angling interest. *repr.* 'Angling in British Art', Shaw Sparrow.

BIRCH, WILLIAM. A groom in a tandem gig, gentlemen meeting for a hunt to the right, signed and inscribed '13 Cooper's Row, Tower Hill', was sold at Sotheby's 6th November 1963. A William Birch exhibited enamels and miniatures 1775–1794 from a London address. A view in America, whither he emigrated in 1794, is known, and a view of Warwick and some others. *exhib.* R.A. (41); S.A. (2).

BIRD, EDWARD, R.A. (b. Wolverhampton 1772, 12th April; d. London 1819, 2nd November). Painted landscapes, history, and a few sporting. *coll.* London, R.A. Diploma Gallery; Guildhall A.G.; Aberdeen; Bristol and Nottingham. *exhib.* R.A., 1810, 1812, 1813, 'sporting'.

BIRD, HARRINGTON (op. 1870–1899). Painted sporting subjects and animals. 'An Arabian Horse led by a Groom', S&D 1899, was sold at Sotheby's 16th March 1960. *exhib.* R.A. (5), not sporting; S.S. (3); V.E.3.

BIRLEY, Capt. Sir OSWALD HORNBY JOSEPH (b. Auckland, New Zealand, 1880, 31st March; d. 1952, 6th May). Educated Harrow and Trinity College, Cambridge. Studied Dresden, Florence and Paris. Travelled in America, Mexico, Siam and India. Enlisted 10th Batt. Royal Fusiliers 1914. Vice-President Royal Portrait Society. Known work, 'Portrait of a Falconer—Mr. G. Blackhall-Simmonds', 1927.

BISHOP, WALTER FOLLEN, R.B.A. (b. Liverpool 1856, 16th June; d. 1936, 20th July). London and St. Helier, Jersey, addresses. Painted principally landscapes, but his R.A. exhibit for 1899 was 'A Hunting Morning'.

BLACK, ARTHUR JOHN, R.O.I., R.B.C. (b. Nottingham 1855, d. 1936, February). Painter of figures and landscapes, some with angling interest. Nottingham, Wimborne and London addresses. *exhib.* R.A. 1882–1902.

BLACK, T. (op. 1839). Shaw Sparrow suggests 'T. Black' may be a misspelling for T. Blake. Engraving known of J. Raines with celebrated Greyhounds by T. Black, Edinburgh 1839.

BLACKBURNE, E. R. IRELAND (op. 1891–1901). Newlyn address. Painted landscapes and shooting subjects. *exhib.* R.A. 1897, 'Rough Shooting, A right and left'.

BLAKE, C. (op. 1826). Engravings, eight illustrations of a 'Poacher's Progress', by Charles Turner after this artist.

BLAKE, T. (op. 1821). Engraving known of 'Interior of Five's Court, With Randall and Turner Sparring', by C. Turner, 1821.

BLAND, BEATRICE (b. 1870, d. 1951). Painter of flowers, figures, etc., in oil and water-colour. *coll.* London, Tate Gallery (Yachts at Lymington).

***BLINKS, THOMAS** (b. 1860, d. 1912). Painter of sporting subjects. *coll.* Leicester M. and A.G. (2). *exhib.* R.A. 1886–1904, all sporting; S.S. (4); V.E. (8). *repr.* 'A Book of Sporting Painters', Shaw Sparrow.

BLYTH, ROBERT HENDERSON (b. Glasgow 1919, 21st May). Studied at Glasgow and Arbroath. Painter in oil; water-colours, etc. *coll.* Aberdeen A.G. (1); Perth A.G. (1), not sporting. *exhib.* R.A. 1964, 'The Goal-mouth' (football).

BODGER, J. (op. 1770–1821). Stilton address. Said to have been a land surveyor at Stilton. Was represented in the Hutchinson Gallery of Sport (now sold). *exhib.* R.A. 1821, 'A view of Newmarket, Racehorses in exercise', engraved.

BONE, ROBERT TREWICK (b. London 1790, d. 1840, 5th May). Son of H. Bone, R.A. Painted portraits, figures, genré and historical. *exhib.* R.A. (50); B.I. (74); S.S. (25); N.W.C.S. (3).

BOTTOMLEY, JOHN WILLIAM (b. Hamburg 1816, 31st July; d. 1900, 13th April). Painted sporting subjects. Said to have painted the cattle in pictures by T. Creswick, R.A. Studied Dusseldorf and Munich. Visited Italy. *exhib.* R.A. (37); B.I. (16); S.S. (3); V.E. (61).

BOUGH, SAMUEL, R.S.A. (b. Carlisle 1822, d. Edinburgh 1878, 19th November). Scene painter, Theatre Royal, Manchester, 1845, and in Glasgow and Edinburgh. Settled in Glasgow 1848. Edinburgh 1855. Awarded Heywood Gold Medal at Royal Institution. Shaw Sparrow, 'Angling in British Art', mentions two paintings, 'A Trout Stream in Cumberland 1861' and 'Salmon Weir on the Eden 1864', as not having been traced; but a 'Full Cry' water-colour S&D 1865 was sold at Christie's 30th October 1964 (48). *coll.* Glasgow A.G. (2), 'Cadzow Forest with three Sportsmen and a dog', S&D 1869; 'The Mail Coach', S&D 1855. Carlisle M. and A.G. (1), 'The Cricket Match' (c. 1845). *exhib.* R.A. 1856–1876, landscapes.

BOUGHTON, GEORGE HENRY, R.A. (b. Norwich 1833, d. London 1905). Painted landscapes, portraits and some sporting. Visited Paris. Member of the National Academy of New York. *exhib.* R.A. 1863–1904.

BOULDING, G. Angling illustrator.

***BOULT, A. S.** (op. 1815–1853). London address. Began life in the 'Stag' brewery. Painted sporting subjects with considerable accomplishment in water-colour and oils. *exhib.* R.A. (10); B.I. (4); S.S. (3).

BOULT, FRANCIS CECIL (op. 1885). *exhib.* S.S. (1), sporting.

***BOULTBEE, JOHN** (b. c. 1745, d. c. 1812). Sporting painter, chiefly of horses, but also some pure landscapes. London and Loughborough address. Lived in 1776 with his brother Thomas at 338 Oxford Street, London. Worked at Loughborough for T. W. Coke and painted the portrait of the stallion 'Pensorosa' there. *coll.* Lytham Hall, Lancs. (1 S&D 1811); Major Guy Paget (1); Lt.-Colonel E. C. Packe (1); Mr. V. R. Pochin (1); Major Sir Reginald Macdonald-Buchanan (1). *exhib.* R.A. (6); S.A. (3); F.S. (3). *repr.* 'A Book of Sporting Painters', Shaw Sparrow.

BOULTBEE, JOHN, Junior. Shaw Sparrow says he had seen one picture signed 'John Boultbee Junior'.

BOULTBEE, THOMAS (op. 1775–1783). Brother of John Boultbee. Living together in 1776 at 338 Oxford Street, London. Like his brother, to whose art he so closely approximates, he too exhibited twelve paintings. *exhib.* R.A. 1783, 'A Hunter and Shooting Horse', property of T. W. Coke; 'An Old Charger'; 'Old Hunter'.

BOURGEOIS, Sir PETER FRANCIS, R.A. (b. 1756, d. 1811). Principally a landscape painter. Had as pupil R. B. Davis. The R.A. exhibits included 'Hunting the wild Boar' and 'Hunting the Royal Tiger' in 1787; 'Horses watering' in 1793, and 'Bathing Horses' in 1796. *coll.* Dulwich College; Soane Museum. *exhib.* R.A. (103); B.I. (5). Preston H.M. and A.G., 1943, 'Horse', S&D 1781.

BOWDEN, —. (op. 1852). Apart from 'A Cricket Match in 1852', by Bowden, at Lord's, London, nothing is known of this elusive painter. A Bowden working around Gosport, specialising in engraving, is known, but apart from one picture exhibited in 1764 he appears lost, and is presumably another artist. A 'J. Bowden' exhibited a landscape at S.S. in 1862.

BOWMAN, JEAN. Living American artist. Has painted racehorses in England.

BOWYER, WILLIAM. Living artist. Chiswick address. *exhib.* R.A. 1964 (77), 'The Marksman' (target shooting).

BOYS, THOMAS SHOTTER (b. Pentonville, London, 1803; d. Marylebone 1874). Articled to G. Cooke the engraver. Worked with W. Callow in Paris. Member of the New Water Colour Society. Painted landscape and views of towns and produced lithographs. *exhib.* R.A. (2); S.S. (14); N.W.C.S. (158). Agnew's London, 91st Annual Exhibition of Water Colour Drawings 1964, 'Fishing'.

BRACKETT, W. *exhib.* At the Great Fisheries Exhibition the following: 'The Rise', 'The Leap', 'The Struggle', 'Landed'.

***BRADLEY, BASIL, R.W.S.** (b. Hampstead 1842, d. 1904, 30th October). Painted principally landscapes in water-colours from a Milford address. A painting, 'Taking a Rest', was in the Hutchinson collection of sporting pictures (now dispersed). *exhib.* from 1866–1893 at R.A. (7); S.S. (1); O.W.C.S. (141); V.E. (7).

BRADLEY, CUTHBERT (d. 1943). *coll.* Major Guy Paget, 'Lord Lonsdale and The Hon. Lancelot Lowther Arriving at Borrough Hill Races in Carriage and Postillion, Greeted by "Lobengula" the Quorn runner', 1895. *exhib.* Lincoln 1947.

BRADLEY, WILLIAM (b. Manchester 1801, 16th January; d. there 1857, 4th July). Portrait painter. Painted a picture of 'Old Billy', a horse 63 years old, which was engraved by Sutherland. *exhib.* R.A. (21); B.I. (13); S.S. (8), portraits.

BRANSCOMB, J. (op. 1805) A 'Coursing' two greyhounds and a terrier standing over a dead hare, S&D 1805 sold at Sotheby's 17th February 1965 (179).

BRANWHITE, CHARLES (b. Bristol 1817, 17th June; d. 1880, 15th February). Pupil of William Muller. Member O.W.C.S. *coll.* V. and A. Mus. (2); Bristol A.G. (6). *exhib.* R.A. (9); B.I. (25); S.S. (2); O.W.C.S. (265), 'Landscape'. *auct.* Christie's, 20th November 1964 (100), 'Eel Butts on the Thames near Streatley'.

BREACH, E. R. (op. 1868–1886). *exhib.* R.A. 1875, 'A Brace; steady at the Point'; S.S. (30); V.E. (1).

BRETLAND, THOMAS W. (b. Nottingham 1802; 21st April; d. there 1874). Painter of animals. Born in a house in Carlton Street, Nottingham. Patrons included Dukes of Buccleugh and Montrose. Travelled to country houses, his works passing directly into private collections. Apparently did not exhibit in his lifetime. *coll.* Nottingham A.G.; York, City A.G. (S&D 1843); Mrs. Leader ('Rockingham with Sam Darling up', S&D 1833).

BRIGGS, ERNEST E., R.I. (b. Broughty Ferry, near Dundee, 1866, d. 1913). Studied first at London University and Leeds University for a mining engineer. Owing to health reasons took up art and studied at the Slade School and Heatherleys. Visited Italy. At Ambleside 1891–1893. *exhib.* R.A. 1891, 'A Mixed Bag'; 1892, 'Wild Duck Shooting in Mull'; 1903, 'Trout Fishing in Galloway'. *repr.* 'Angling and Art in Scotland', E. Briggs, 1908; 'Angling in British Art', Shaw Sparrow.

***BRISTOW, EDMUND** (b. Windsor 1787, 1st April; d. 1876). Spent whole of his life at Windsor. Painted a number of portraits, chiefly of a sporting character, several of which, and some of his sporting scenes, were engraved. Painted landscapes, portraits, figures and animals. *coll.* Hull, Ferens A.G. (1); Leicester A.G. (1). *exhib.* R.A. (12); B.I. (11); S.S. (8). *repr.* 'Angling in British Art', Shaw Sparrow; 'Animal Painters', Sir Walter Gilbey (1905).

BROADHEAD, W. SMITHSON (op. 1937). London address. *exhib.* R.A. 1937, 'A Hunter'.

BROCAS, WILLIAM. (c. 1794–1868). Of Dublin. Third son of Henry Brocas. Member Royal Hibernian Academy. Mainly landscape but included equestrian portraits. His 'Freney' with her trainer, jockey and groom, was sold at Sotheby's 9th December 1964 (86).

BROMLEY, CLOUGH W. (op. 1872–1904). Painted flowers, landscapes, etc. His 'Pigeon Fanciers' was shown at the R.A. 1882. *exhib.* R.A. (15); S.S. (40); N.W.C.S. (2); V.E. (43).

BROMLEY, WILLIAM, A.R.A. (b. Carisbrooke, Isle of Wight, 1769; d. 1842). Pupil of W. Wooding, an engraver. Worked for Trustees of the British Museum, engraving the Elgin Marbles from drawings by Henry Corbould. One of the family of well-known engravers. *coll.* Mr. and Mrs. R. Richards, Gawsworth Hall, Macclesfield, 'Waiting for Master—a stable-boy holding a chestnut Hunter in a landscape'. Lord's have a portrait of Alfred Mynn (1807–1861). *exhib.* R.A. (51); S.A. (3); S.S. (2); N.W.C.S. (1). Graves says 'Engraving'.

BROOKE, EDWARD (op. 1846). London address. Showed four landscapes at the R.A. An exhibit of 1878 under this name is probably by a different artist. *exhib.* R.A. 1846, 'A Boy Fishing'.

BROOKS, W. (op. 1792). A Full Cry hunting painting in the style of J. Seymour, S&D 1792, was at one time in the possession of Arthur Ackermann & Son. Could be William Brooks (op. 1780–1801), who exhibited seventeen of his works at the R.A.?

BROWN, E. (op. 1840–1857). Shaw Sparrow gives this artist as painting sporting subjects, but mostly animal painter and some military subjects. Worked mainly in Warwickshire.

BROWN, Miss ELLA G. (op. 1887–1888). Lytham address. *exhib.* R.A. 1887, Partridges; 1888, Grouse.

BROWN, Sir JOHN A. ARNESBY, R.A. (b. 1866, d. 1955). Painted landscapes in oils and water-colours. *repr.* 'Angling in British Art', Shaw Sparrow; 'The River with Children fishing', exhibited at R.A 1909.

BROWN, Mrs. (op. 1822). *exhib.* R.A. 1822, 'A Foxhound'.

***BROWN, NATHANIEL** (op. 1753–1779). Painted portraits, fruit, sea-pieces, etc. A 'Hunter and Sportsman with his dogs in a landscape', S&D 1753, was exhibited in the Gallery of Frank T. Sabin, London. *exhib.* F.S. (54).

BROWN, W., Junior (op. 1798–1808). A 'Portrait of Charles Loraine Smith on a Horse', lent by Captain R. H. Bevan, and exhibited Leicester 1951 (Leicestershire Hunting Pictures), was probably by this artist. *exhib.* R.A. (2), the painting shown in 1808 was 'Sportsman with Setters'.

BROWNE, HABLOT KNIGHT 'PHIZ' (b. Lambeth 1815, d. Hove 1882, 8th July). Comic illustrator and water-colour painter. *coll.* Preston A.G., 'He's Out of it' (hunting scene). *exhib.* R.A. (3); B.I. (14); S.S. (10); N.W.C.S. (4); Preston A.G., 'British Sporting Paintings', 1943 (2).

BROWNE, PHILIP (op. 1824–1861). Shrewsbury address. Painted landscapes, flowers, fruit and sporting. R.A. exhibit 1855, 'A Stray Shot'. *exhib.* R.A. (70); S.S. (13).

BROWNING, ROBERT BARRETT (b. 1846, d. 1912). Painter and sculptor. Son of Robert and Elizabeth Browning. Studied at Antwerp. Bronze medal Paris Exhibition 1889. *exhib.* R.A. 1880, 'Watching the Skittle Players'.

BRYAN, J. Painting of 'Birmingham', a bay racehorse with jockey up, and owner at Newmarket, S&D 1832, sold at Sotheby's 13th June 1966.

BRYANT, J. (op. 1850). A set of four hunting paintings were shown by Arthur Ackermann & Son, London. Grant's Dictionary gives two other artists as this, op. 1798–1809 and op. 1764 respectively, but apparently each are different men.

BUCKLEY, C. F. (op. 1841–1869). Landscape painter, mostly in water-colour. Messrs. Frank T. Sabin, in their Autumn Exhibition 1959, showed a 'River scene with Anglers'. *coll.* V. and A. Museum (2 landscapes). *exhib.* B.I. (2); S.S. (31).

BUCKMAN, EDWIN, A.R.W.S. (b. 1841, d.). *exhib.* R.A. 1874, 'North Country Wrestling'; 'Skittles'; 1876, 'Tug of War'.

BULLEY, ASHBURNHAM H. (op. 1841–1851). London address. His three exhibits at the R.A. 1846, 1848 and 1850 were portraits of a Vixen, of Two Scotch Terriers, and of a Spaniel respectively. *exhib.* R.A. (3); B.I. (13); S.S. (7). Graves says 'still-life'.

BUNBURY, HENRY WILLIAM (b. 1750, d. 1811). Amateur painter and caricaturist, some landscapes included among his twenty R.A. exhibits from a Mildenhall address. *coll.* V. and A. Museum (11 drawings); Mr. and Mrs. Paul Mellon (Angling water-colour). *exhib.* R.A. (20), the 1774 exhibit a Billiard Table. *repr.* 'Angling in British Art', Shaw Sparrow. Colour plate of 'Anglers of 1611'. 'Black George', engraved by I. Chapman 1800. Four caricatures of Riding engraved by J. Bretherton 1799.

BURBANK, J. M. (op. 1825–1872). London, Camberwell, address. Painted animals. The R.A. exhibit 1825, 'Dog's Head'; 1841, 'The Dying Heron'; and 1845 was a 'Giraffe attacked by a Lion'. *exhib.* R.A. (12); B.I. (6); S.S. (19); N.W.C.S. (21).

BURGESS, F. L. (op. 1778). London address. *exhib.* R.A. 1778, 'Return from Shooting'.

BURKE, L. (op. 1864). *auct.* Sotheby's, 25th March 1964, 'Prince' and 'Flora'; King Charles Spaniels seen in a landscape, a pair, S&D Oct. 1864.

BURNET, JOHN, F.R.S. (b. Musselburgh 1784, d. Stoke Newington, London, 1868, April). Elder brother of James M. Burnet, a cattle painter. Studied under Robert Scott, an engraver in Edinburgh and Trustees' Academy. In London 1806. Visited Paris 1813. *coll.* Dublin, N.G.; Glasgow A.G.; London, Guildhall A.G.; V. and A. Museum; Wolverhampton A.G. *exhib.* R.A. (5); B.I. (30); S.S. (6); R.A. 1808, 'Draught Player'.

BURR, ALEXANDER HOHENLOHE (b. 1835, d. 1899). Studied Trustees' Academy, Edinburgh. Removed to London in 1861. *coll.* Glasgow A.G., 'Shuttlecock'. *exhib.* R.A. and R.S.A.

BURRAS, T. (op. 1880). Oil of 'Two Spaniels putting up a snipe', S&D 1880, shown in Oscar and Peter Johnson's 'Sport and the Horse' exhibition June 1969.

BURT, REVELL (op. 1890). A pair 'Hunt in Full Cry' and 'Pheasant Shooting', S&D 1890 sold at Sotheby's 12th March 1965, (132).

BUSH, Mrs. H. (*see* NOEL L. NISBET)

BUTLER, THOMAS (op. 1750–1759). A bookseller and stationer in Pall Mall, London, till middle of 18th century. Shaw Sparrow suggests that pictures bearing this name may not be all painted by Butler himself. He employed assistants who would, according to the advertisements, travel the country to paint hunts, dogs and horses, and living game. A fine portrait of a Horse was in the Hutchinson Sporting Gallery. *exhib.* 'Paintings of English Life', Rutland Gallery, June-July 1963; 'Brisk—a Hunter'; 'A Hunter', a pair, S&D 1759.

BUTTERSWORTH, THOMAS (op. 1798–1827). Grant gives the name as Butterworth. Painter of sea-pieces of the Napoleonic period. His 'Trafalgar' (B.I. 1827) considered his finest. *exhib.* R.A. (1); B.I. (1); S.S. (1). *auct.* Christie's, 3rd April 1964. A pair of yachting pictures.

BYLES, WILLIAM HOUNSOM (op. 1872–1899). London address. *exhib.* R.A. *auct.* Sotheby's, 11th November 1964 (129), 'Milenko winning the 1921 Cambridgeshire Stakes', signed, 15¼ by 23½ inches.

***BYNG, ?** (op. 1706). A Robert Byng or R. Byne said to have been an assistant to Kneller, painting drapery and backgrounds. Colonel Grant suggested they could not be the same artists. Benezit gives Robert and Edward Byng or Bing—brothers—date of death as late as 1850. A S&D 1706 canvas, 57 by 93 inches 'Master with Hounds and Attendants' is known and was sold at Christie's 20th November 1964; catalogued as by Robert Byng. *lit.* Grant, 'Old English Landscape Painters', Vol. 2, pp. 94–5, pl. 43 (new ed.).

CAFFIERI, HECTOR, R.I., R.B.A. (b. Cheltenham 1847, d. 1932). Pupil of Bonnat and J. Lefebvre in Paris. Working in London. Member of the New Water Colour Society. Painted flowers, landscapes and some sporting subjects. *exhib.* R.A. (31); S.S. (84); N.W.C.S. (45); G.G. (2); V.E. (41).

CAFFYN, WALTER WALLOR (op. 1874–1897, d. 1898). Dorking address. Painted landscapes for angling pictures by H. L. Rolfe. *exhib.* R.A. (10); S.S. (26); V.E. (6).

CALDECOTT, RANDOLPH, R.I., R.O.I. (b. Chester 1846, d. St. Augustine, Florida, 1886). Son of an accountant. Educated King's School, Chester. Became a bank clerk. Drew for 'Punch', 'Graphic', etc., from 1868. Settled in London 1872. *coll.* London, Tate Gallery (1); V. and A. Museum (7); Manchester, City A.G. (13); Newport (Mon.) A.G. (1). *exhib.* R.A. (4); N.W.C.S. (10); G.G. (7); V.E. (14);. The R.A. exhibit 1878 was titled 'So They Hunted and they Holla'd'.

CALDERON, PHILIP HERMOGENES, R.A. (b. Poiters 1833, d. London 1898). Studied Leigh's School, London, and Paris. *exhib.* R.A. (100); B.I. (6); S.S. (9); G.G. (6); N.G. (1); V.E. (12); The Fine Art Society, 1907, 'The Captain of the Eleven'.

CALDERON, W. FRANK, R.O.I. (b. London 1865; d. 1943, 21st April). Painted portraits, landscapes, and some sporting subjects. *exhib.* R.A. (19); S.S. (3); G.G. (1); V.E. (7).

CALDWELL, EDMUND (b. Canterbury 1852, d. after 1915). Working in London and Guildford. Painted animals and landscapes. Produced many illustrations for 'The Gun at Home and Abroad' (4 vols., 1912–15). *exhib.* R.A. (6); S.S. (4); N.W.C.S. (11); V.E. (10). R.A. 1884, 'Run to Ground'.

CALKIN, LANCE, R.O.I. (b. London 1859, 22nd June; d. 1936, 10th October). Painted portraits mainly. Trained Slade and R.A. Schools. His 1892 R,A. exhibit was 'Salmon Poachers'. *exhib.* R.A. (18); S.S. (14); G.G. (4); N.G. (4); V.E. (14).

CALLCOTT, Sir AUGUSTUS WALL, R.A. (b. Kensington 1779, d. there 1844). Chorister at Westminster Abbey. Studied music before taking up painting at R.A. Schools 1797. Pupil of Hoppner. Painted portraits first, then landscapes in oils and water-colours. *coll.* Greenwich, Maritime Museum (Fishing scene); London, N. G.; Tate ('Fishing in the Mere'); V. and A. *exhib.* R.A. (129); B.I. (13).

***CALVERT, HENRY** (op. 1813–1861). An important sporting artist of whom little is known, reputed to have been born in Manchester. Working mainly in Wales. His work was of very fine quality. 'A mounted Huntsman', S&D 1813, was sold at Sotheby's 3rd June 1959. 'Jack, a Favourite Hunter', and 'Vic', a favourite Terrier, aged 16, belonging to John T. Ord, Esq., S&D 1834, was sold at Sotheby's 11th November 1964. *exhib.* R.A. (4). *repr.* His 'Vine Hunting Meeting', engraved by H. W. Simmons 1844; 'The Wynnstay Hunt' shown at the R.A. 1852 was engraved by W. T. Davey in 1855.

CAMDEN, P. (op. 1805–1809). Known only by two paintings, one 'A Fishing Party' (a scene at the New Lock, Medmenham), illustrated in the 'Farington Diary', Vol. I, p. 50. The figures possibly painted by Zoffany. *lit.* Grant, 'The Old English Landscape Painters', Vol. 7, p. 518, illus.

CAMERON, ANGUS (op. 1870). 'Out for a Day's Shooting', S&D 1870, *exhib.* Frost & Reed Ltd.

CAMERON, Sir DAVID YOUNG, R.A., R.S.A., R.W.S. (b. Glasgow 1865; d. 1945, 16th September). Studied at Glasgow and Edinburgh Academies. Painted landscapes, architecture in oils and water-colours and etched. Some landscapes have an angling interest.

CAMPION, GEORGE B. (b. 1796, d. Munich 1870). Water-colour painter. Went to live in Germany and devoted some time to sporting subjects. Said to have executed Four Coaching Snow Scenes after Pollard. Published 'Adventures of a Chamois Hunter'. Member of the New Water Colour Society. *coll.* Dublin, National Gallery of Ireland. *exhib.* S.S. (10); N.W.C.S. (463).

CAMPIONE, S. (op. 1831–1833). Painted animals, birds, and still-life. *exhib.* R.A. (2); B.I. (6).

CANE, HERBERT COLLINS (op. 1883–1891). Painted animals, some sporting. *exhib.* R.A. (3); N.W.C.S. (5).

CARLAW, JOHN, R.S.W. (b. Glasgow 1850, d. Helensburgh 1934). Water-colour painter of landscapes and sporting subjects. Commenced career as designer in a local foundry. *coll.* Glasgow A.G. *exhib.* R.A. (8); N.W.C.S. (1).

CARLINE, NANCY M. (Mrs.) (op. 1964). Living Pont Street, London. *exhib.* R.A. 1964 (551), 'Fishing at Richmond'.

CARR, THOMAS, R.W.S. (op. 1964). *exhib.* R.W.S. 1964, 'Lagan Landscape' (fishing).

CARSTAIRS, JOHN PADDY (op. 1963). Kingston Hill. *exhib.* R.A. 1963, 'The School Match—Rugger'.

CARTER, SAMUEL JOHN, R.O.I. (b. Swaffham, Norfolk, 1835, d. 1892). Included animals, sport, equestrian portraiture among his paintings. *coll.* London, Tate; Preston A.G.; Lytham St. Annes, Town Hall. *exhib.* R.A. (49); B.I. (3); S.S. (10); G.G. (1); V.E. (15).

CASSIE, JAMES, R.S.A. (b. 1819, d. 1879). A painting of 'Gentlemen with three greyhounds', S&D 1853 was sold by Arthur Ackermann & Son.

CASTAN, LOUIS (b. Berlin 1828, d. 1909). London address 1865–1867. A sculptor. His R.A. exhibit for 1865 'Horse with dog'. *exhib.* R.A. (2).

CATTERMOLE, CHARLES, R.I., R.B.A. (b. 1832, d. 1900, 21st August). Nephew of George Cattermole. Painted figures in oil and water-colours. Some sporting. *coll.* Birmingham A.G. ('A Hawking Party'). *exhib.* R.A. (1); B.I. (5); S.S. (85); N.W.C.S. (188); V.E. (2).

CATTERMOLE, GEORGE (b. Dickleburgh, near Diss, 1800, d. Clapham Common 1868, 24th July). Pupil of John Britton. Member of the Old Water Colour Society; Amsterdam Academy and Belgian Water Colour Society. Medal Paris 1855. *coll.* Birmingham A.G. 'The Castle: Rook Shooting'. *exhib.* R.A. (6); B.I. (2); O.W.C.S. (97), Figures.

CATTON, CHARLES, R.A. (b. Norwich 1728, d. London 1798). Commenced as a painter of heraldry on coaches and hatchments, then turned to history, classics, animals and landscapes. Foundation member of the Royal Academy. *coll.* London, Painters' Hall; V. and A. Museum; Mrs. Ketton-Cremer (Happisburgh Beach, Norfolk, with Huntsmen, 1766). *exhib.* R.A. (43); S.A. (16).

CATTON, CHARLES, Junior (b. 1750, d. in America 1819). Son of Charles Catton, R.A. Emigrated to America in 1804. Painted animals. His R.A. exhibit of 1786, 'A Horse Race', was engraved. *coll.* V. and A. Museum (5 drawings). *exhib.* R.A. (37).

CERVENG, JOHN (op. 1771–1773). Painted portraits and animals. *exhib.* S.A. (5); R.A. (2).

CHALMERS, Sir GEORGE, Bart. (d. 1791). Pupil of Allan Ramsay. Portrait painter working in Edinburgh. *coll.* Armand Blackley, Esq., 'Portrait of a Huntsman'. *exhib.* R.A. (24).

CHALON, ALFRED EDWARD, R.A. (b. Geneva 1780, d. Kensington, London, 1860, 3rd October). Brother of John James Chalon. Portrait painter in oils and water-colours. Executed some miniatures, drama, genre and landscapes. *coll.* Lytham Hall, Lancs., 'J. Talbot Clifton with Cricket Bat', S&D 1834. *exhib.* R.A. (396); B.I. (21); V.E. (15), portraits.

CHALON, FRANCIS (b. 1776, d. 1836). A sporting painter of repute.

***CHALON, HENRY BARNARD** (b. London 1770, d. there 1849). Of Dutch parentage. Became student at the R.A., exhibiting first in 1792 and continually to 1846. Animal and sporting painter. Animal painter to William IV, the Prince Regent, and the Duchess of York. Published 'Passions of the Horse' 1837. *coll.* London, R.A. (Dip. Gall.); V. and A. Museum; H.M. The Queen, Windsor Castle; Commander Robert T. Bower, R.N. (11); Mr. and Mrs. Paul Mellon, U.S.A. (1); H. Parkin Smith, of Bath (1). *exhib.* R.A. (198); B.I. (28); S.S. (21); O.W.C.S. (1); V.E. (2). *repr.* 'Sporting Pictures of England', Guy Paget, 1945; 'Sir Mark Sykes's Hounds Breaking Cover', p. 19; 'Sporting Prints—The Makers', Guy Paget, 'Apollo', May 1945; 'British Sporting Artists (1770–1850)', H. A. Bryden, 'A Book of Sporting Painters', Shaw Sparrow. *lit.* 'Passions of the Horse', 1837.

CHALON, JOHN JAMES, R.A. (b. Geneva 1778, d. London 1854). Elder brother of A. E. Chalon. Friend of J. Agasse, who painted his portrait. *coll.* Birmingham A. G., 'The Angler's Pool', S&D 1809. *exhib.* R.A. (86); B.I. (49); O.W.C.S. (55).

CHAPMAN, W. J. (op. 1853–1864). *auct.* Christie's, 18th December 1964, 'Minette' a bay hunter in a loose-box, S&D 1853. A S&D 1864 painting advertised in 'Country Life' (13th June 1968) by Chichester Antiques.

CHARLTON, JOHN, R.B.A., R.O.I. (b. Bamborough, Northumberland, d. 1917, 5th November). Studied Newcastle School of Art and South Kensington. Painted battles, portraits and sporting. *coll.* Earl Spencer (4). *repr.* 'Book of Sporting Painters', Shaw Sparrow. *exhib.* R.A. (37); S.S. (21); N.W.C.S. (1); G.G. (2); N.G. (4); V.E. (34).

***CHINNERY, GEORGE** (b. London 1774, 5th January; d. Macao 1852, 30th May). Travelled and resided much in the East. Painted landscapes in India and China and portraits in oils and water-colours. A few sporting. *coll.* John Galvin (4 sporting). *exhib.* R.A. (39), miniatures. *lit.* George Chinnery, 'Artist of the China Coast', by Henry and Sidney Berry-Hill. (Leigh-on-Sea 1963.)

CHRISTIE, JAMES ELDER (b. Guardbridge, Fifeshire, 1847; d. London 1914). Removed to Paisley. Studied at the local school. Studied South Kensington from 1874 and R.A. Schools. Gold Medal at latter for historical painting in 1877. Paris 1882–1885. Returned to London. Associated with the New English Art Club. Went to Glasgow. Returned to London, where he died. Hon. Mention Paris Salon 1905. *coll.* Paisley A.G., 'The Red Fisherman'. *exhib.* R.A. (19, included pictures of poachers and fishermen); S.S. (7); G.G. (10); N.G. (6); V.E. (8), 'Domestic'.

CHRISTMAS, THOMAS C. (op. 1819–1825). London address. R.A. exhibits were portrait of a horse and study of dogs. *exhib.* R.A. (2); B.I. (11); S.S. (6); O.W.C.S. (5).

CLARK, JOHN COSMO, A.R.A., C.B.E. (b. London 1897, 24th January; living). Son of James Clark. Studied Goldsmith's College School of Art, R.A. Schools, and Julian's, Paris. Work includes all kinds of sport: rowing, skating, boxing, hurdling, fishing, sailing. *coll.* Huddersfield A.G. (1). *exhib.* R.A. 1931–1964.

CLARKE, FREDERICK (op. 1834–1870). London and Leicester addresses. Painted game birds. *exhib.* R.A. (10).

CLARKE, JAMES. *exhib.* Rutland Gallery, London, June-July 1963, 'Fred Chandler Driving Kate'. *auct.* Sotheby's 10th February 1960 (65), 'Pretty Jane' and 'Fair Maid of Perth'. Two prizewinning hackneys in a stable yard. Christie's, 1st August 1961 (221), 'The Old Hunter', signed.

CLARKE, WILLIAM HANNA (b. Glasgow 1882, d. 1924). Resided in Kirkcudbright. Painted landscapes. Met a premature and tragic end by an accident. *coll.* Glasgow A.G., 'Flying the Kite'.

CLENNELL, LUKE (b. Ulgham, near Morpeth, 1781; d. Newcastle 1840, Shaw Sparrow and H. M. Cundall; d. London, Benezit). Apprenticed to Bewick 1797. Went to London 1804 and painted in oils and water-colours. Worked at one time with Ben Marshall. His 'The Jovial Foxhunters' was engraved by Lupton. *coll.* London, V. and A. Museum (7); Nottingham A.G. (6). *exhib.* R.A. (6); B.I. (15); O.W.C.S. (18); V.E. (31). Newcastle, Laing A.G., 1951 (Tyneside's Contribution to Art), first exhibition of collected works.

CLEMINSON, ROBERT (op. 1865–1868). Painted sporting, mainly Highland deer, dead game, dogs, etc. *exhib.* B.I. (10); S.S. (5).

CLEVELEY, ROBERT (b. London 1747, d. Dover 1809). Twin brother of John Cleveley, also an artist. Marine draughtsman to the Prince of Wales and H.R.H. the Duke of Clarence. Painted shipping, naval battles, etc. Apparently in the Navy. *coll.* London, V. and A. Museum, 'The Rowing Match at Richmond', S&D 1793. Exhibited R.A. 1793. *exhib.* R.A. (57); B.I. (1); F.S. (15).

CLIFTON, F. (op. 179–). *auct.* Christie's, 18th December 1964, 'York Minster', a bay horse standing in a loose-box. Canvas S&D 179–.

CLOWES, DANIEL (c. 1790–1849). Sporting painter. Apparently did not exhibit any works. Given same dates as J. Clowes. *coll.* Lytham Hall, Lancs., Racehorse with jockey up in Clifton colours; racecourse in middle distance with town beyond (Nottingham?), signed 'D. Clowes, pinxt' and dated 1826. *auct.* Sotheby's, 15th January 1964, 'Coursing – the Famous Match at Bristol Meeting, Feb. 14, 18[illegible]3', signed and inscribed.

CLOWES, J. (op. 1790–1849). Sporting painter. Given same dates as Daniel Clowes. Apparently did not exhibit any work. This artist not mentioned by Shaw Sparrow, Guy Paget or Basil Taylor; and only Shaw Sparrow mentions Daniel Clowes. *coll.* 'Dodger Vernon with Jockey Up' (Chester Racecourse?), signed 'J. Clowes, pinxt 1824', is in private ownership.

COBBETT, EDWARD JOHN, R.B.A. (b. London 1815, d. 1899). Painted genre, landscapes, etc. Two of his R.A. exhibits were of dead game and angling. *exhib.* R.A. (50); B.I. (49); S.S. (343); V.E. (36).

COCKEN, EDMUND. *coll.* Lt.-Col. Sir Edward Preston, Bt., 'Robert Hewitt, Lord Nelson's Waterman, with catch of Fish and Barton Broad in background'.

***COLE, GEORGE** (b. Portsmouth 1810, d. 1883, 7th September). Father of George Vicat Cole, R.A. Painted landscapes, etc. Working in London. Two Chestnut Hunters in Landscape Overlooking a River, S&D 1855, were recently in possession of Messrs. Frost & Reed. *exhib.* R.A. (16); B.I. (35); S.S. (209).

COLEMAN, EDWARD (op. 1813–1848). Painted game and shooting subjects. *coll.* Birmingham A.G., 'Dead Game'. *exhib.* R.A. (16). Ackermann's recently had a signed 'shooting' painting.

COLLET, JOHN (COLLETT, Grant; **COLET,** Arlott) (b. London 1725, d. 1780). Pupil of G. Lambert. Painted landscapes in oils and water-colours. Walpole 'anecdotes' gives the painter's death in 1771, and E. Edwards 'Anecdotes' 1808 suggests there were two artists of a similar name, one the Landscape painter, the other the painter of humorous subjects. *repr.* 'Miss Wicket and Miss Trigger, 1778'; Lady with cricket bat and lady with gun, dead birds, and dogs in landscape is a colour plate in 'The Picture of Cricket', John Arlott, 1955, from the coloured engraving. *exhib.* F.S. (47), 'Domestic'.

COLLINS, ISAAC. *auct.* Sotheby's, 15th July 1959 (153), 'The Derby'. Sold with an oleograph of the picture.

COLLINS, WILLIAM, R.A. (b. London 1788, d. there 1847). Pupil of Morland and R.A. Schools. Landscape and figure painter. Two angling pictures engraved: 'Two boys in a boat by reed-fringed bank with trees overhead', and 'The River Brent'. *coll.* Bury A.G. (Minnow Catchers).

***COLMORE, NINA** (*née* Murray) (b. 1889, living at Upton, Hants). Painter of equestrian portraits, race-horses, hounds, etc., also landscape. Studied at Heatherley's and Julien's in Paris. *coll.* Cairo, Fuad I Museum (2); Sir Hugh Arbuthnot, M.F.H. (4); Herbert Blagrave (4); the late Major Hilton Green, M.F.H. (2); Nicholas Hall (4); Hon. David Hely Hutchinson (3); H.H. the Maharajah of Jaipur (2); H.H. the late Prince Ali Khan (2); Major Sir Reginald and Lady Macdonald-Buchanan (8); Major Dermot McCalmont (6); Sir Harold Nutting, M.F.H. (3); Lord Rosebery; the late Lord Stalbridge, M.F.H. (3); Sir Harold Werner; The Duchess of Westminster (3); W. Holden White (7); H.R.H. the Duke of Windsor (2); Young's Brewery. *exhib.* Paris Salon (diploma); N.E.A.C., etc. *lit.* The British Racehorse, Vol. 13, No. 5.

CONSTABLE, JOHN, R.A. (b. East Bergholt, Suffolk, 1776; d. London 1837). Son of a miller and for some years in his father's business. Went to London to study art in 1795 and entered R.A. schools in 1799. Painted landscapes. *coll.* C. Clifton Brown, 'The Young Waltonians'; Mr and Mrs Paul Mellon (portrait of his father's horse). *auct.* Christie's, 25th/26th April 1940 (31), 'The Young Waltonians'. A group of children angling from the bank of a river beside a watermill. A framed mezzotint by David Lucas sold with the drawing.

COOK, D. *auct.* Sotheby's, 10th February 1960 (114), 'Two Greyhounds in a landscape setting, signed.

COOK, JOSHUA (op. 1838–1848). London address. Painted birds, game, fruit, and sporting. A 'Return from Hawking' was shown at the R.A. 1838. *exhib.* R.A. (8); B.I. (14); S.S. (5).

COOPER. A Claude Cooper exhibited a picture of Fish in 1870. *auct.* Christie's, 25/26th April 1940, 'Anglers with a Trout beside a Stream'. *coll.* A. N. Gilbey.

***COOPER, ABRAHAM, R.A.** (b. London 1787, d. Greenwich 1868). *coll.* London, Tate G. (1); Major The Hon. Henry R. Broughton (1); Mr. and Mrs. Paul Mellon, U.S.A. (1); Miss Margaret Powney and John Powney (1); Major The Lord Shuttleworth, M.C. (1). *exhib.* R.A. (332); B.I. (74); S.S. (1); O.W.C.S. (13). *repr.* 'The Old Sporting Magazine'; 'The New Sporting Magazine'; 'Angling in British Art', Shaw Sparrow.

COOPER, ALEXANDER DAVIS (op. 1837–1880). Son of Abraham Cooper, R.A. Painted portraits, including one of his father, landscape and sporting. His R.A. exhibits included 'Spaniel and Game'; 'The Hon. G. W. C. Byng's Horses'; 'A Good Day's Sport'; 'Blackcock' and 'Mountain Hare'. *exhib.* R.A. (65); B.I. (27); S.S. (16).

COOPER, ALFRED EGERTON, R.B.A. (b. Tettenhall 1883, 5th July). Working in London. Painted portraits, figures, landscape and a few sporting subjects. *exhib.* R.A. 1924–1945, including 'Derby Day, seventy-seven years after Frith'; 'Paddock at the Pony Races'.

***COOPER, EDWIN** (b. Beccles, op. 1803–1831). Painter of horses and sporting scenes, his early paintings were virtually all coaching subjects, a number of which have been shown at the Ackermann Gallery, London. Grant's Dictionary gives Edwin and Edward with same dates. Shaw Sparrow gives Edwin and Graves merely E. The Norwich 1950 catalogue gives Edwin. A signed 'En COOPER PINXT 1825' 'Two Hounds in a Landscape', recently in the possession of Messrs. Frost & Reed, against several signed E. COOPER is perhaps responsible for the assumption of E for Edward. 'A Black Hunter in a Landscape with Spaniel', S&D 1806 as E. F. Cooper, exhibited at the Rutland Gallery, April 1960, is doubtless the same. 'A Cock-Fight' was in the now dispersed Hutchinston Gallery of Sport. *exhib.* R.A. (2). *coll.* E. Cooper Bland; Lt.-Colonel Michael St. John Burne; Lord Hastings (5); Colonel Vivian Lockett; Major E. H. Evans Lombe; Charles H. Thieriot, New York (2); V. and A. Museum (a drawing).

CORBOULD, ALFRED (op. 1831–1875). London address. Studied horses at Tattersall's Sale Ring, then resident in Grosvenor Place. A painting by A. Corbould was in possession of M. Bernard, of London, 'The Duke of Bedford with Groom and Pony out Shooting', 28 × 36 in. S&D 1849. His R.A. exhibits include a 'Retriever and Wounded Pheasant'; 'Pheasant-Shooting'; 'Retriever and Dead Game'; 'Termination of the Day's Sport'. *exhib.* R.A. (22); B.I. (21); S.S. (16); V.E. (14).

CORBOULD, ALFRED HITCHENS (op. 1844–1863). Painted portraits and sporting subjects. His exhibit at R.A. 1844 was 'Fitz-James and His Dying Horse—Woe was the Chase'. *exhib.* R.A. (20); B.I. (18).

CORBOULD, ASTER R. C. (op. 1842–1877). Brother of Alfred Hitchens Corbould. Painted sporting subjects. *exhib.* R.A. (35); B.I. (32); S.S. (48).

CORDREY, JOHN (op. 1765–1825). A painter principally of coaching subjects and occasionally hunting. 'The Peace Coach, 1814', in the Charles H. Theriot collection, is interesting, depicting one of the Edinburgh and London Royal Mail Coaches, the flag bearing the words 'Peace, June 4th, 1814', carrying the news of the peace concluded between Great Britain and France. *coll.* The Hon. David Astor (1); Charles H. Thieriot, New York (1). *repr.* 'British Sporting Artists, 1770–1850', H. A. Bryden, 1931.

CORNISH, J. Was only known by one painting, which appeared to be a copy of 'Racing at Newmarket', after Tillemans, Shaw Sparrow.

COTES, FRANCIS, R.A. (b. London 1725, d. there 1770, 20th July). Pupil of Knapton. Founder member of the R.A. *coll.* M.C.C. Gallery, Lords. (Copy of portrait, property of Lord Brocket.)

COTMAN, JOHN SELL (b. Norwich 1782, d. 1842). Worked in London for a time. Returned to Norwich. Visited Normandy in 1817–18 and 1820. In London again in 1834. Painted landscapes in oils and water-colours. *coll.* Norwich A.G., 'Evening; Boys Fishing'. *lit.* 'John Sell Cotman', by V. Rienaecker.

COTTRELL, H. S. (op. 1840–1860). Messrs. Arthur Ackermann & Son have had several Racehorse and Jockey paintings of this period through their hands.

COX, DAVID (b. Birmingham 1783, d. 1859). Studied under Varley. Visited Holland and Belgium in 1826 and France in 1829 and 1832. Principally a painter in water-colours. Took up oil-painting under Muller in 1840. *coll.* P.O.U., 'Fly Fishing on the Wye at Haddon Hall'. Reproduced as colour-plate, 'Angling in British Art', Shaw Sparrow, p. 128.

COZENS, WILLIAM (op. 1820–1828). Aveley, Essex, address. R.A. exhibit 1820, 'Hon. John Jocelyn with Favourite Pony and Harriers'; 1828 'Horses'. *exhib.* R.A. (6); B.I. (1).

CRADOCK, MARMADUKE (b. Somerton, near Ilchester, 1660; d. London 1717). Painted birds, dead game, and animals. Close follower of Francis Barlow. *auct.* Christie's, 20th November 1964 (77), 'A Peacock, a Cock Pheasant, a Hen and her chicks and other birds in a landscape'.

CRAIG, JAMES STEPHENSON (op. 1854–1870). Two of his three R.A. exhibits were, 1854 'Young Anglers'; 1861 'Ghillie Callum'. *exhib.* R.A. (3); B.I. (7); S.S. (12), 'Domestic'.

CRANMER, C. (op. 1801–1839). There were two of this name, father and son, and they exhibited works from identical addresses and so overlap that, in the absence of any sure knowledge as to the life-dates of either painter, it is not easy to distinguish their respective performances. Cranmer *senior*, first heard of in 1793, ceased to exhibit in 1815. Cranmer *junior* exhibited 82 pictures in London from London address. A pair of G. Morland-style peasant scenes, S&D 1801, known. *exhib.* R.A. (31); B.I. (51). *repr.* Works by them were engraved by W. Barnard. *lit.* Grant, 'Old English Landscape Painters', Vol. 6, pp. 469/470.

CRANE, R. (op. 1832, d. c. 1834, very young). Newmarket address. A lithograph from his picture, 'Royal Bowmen at Eaton Hall', is dated Oct. 18. 1832.

CRANE, THOMAS (b. Chester 1808, d. Bayswater 1859, July). Studied at R.A. Schools at 16 years of age. Returned to Chester 1825. Worked in Liverpool, member of the Liverpool Academy. Shaw Sparrow says some of his work had a sporting interest. *exhib.* R.A. (9); B.I. (3); S.S. (3), 'Historical'.

CRAWFORD, ROBERT CREE (b. Glasgow 1842, d. there 1924). Lived some time on the Continent and three years in Canada. Took up art as a profession. Painted landscapes and then portraits. His R.A. exhibit in 1881 was 'Wild Fowl Shooting'. *exhib.* R.A.; R.S.A.; Royal Glasgow Institute of Fine Arts; Glasgow International Exhibition 1901; Paris Salon.

CRAWFORD, SUSAN (b. 1941, living). Lives at Haddington, East Lothian, where her father is a trainer. Studied under Signorina Simi in Florence. First exhibited at the Tryon Gallery, London in 1969, again in 1972 at the Tryon Gallery, 'Horse Artists of the World' exhibition. Her equestrian portraits include 'Sir Ivor'; 'Nijinsky'; 'Park Top'; 'Arkle'. Visited U.S.A. to paint 'Stage Door Johny' for Mr. Jock Whitney and 'Art and Letters' for Mr. Paul Mellon. Also paints portraits. Exhibits at R.S.A. and Nat. Portrait Gallery.

CRAWHALL, JOSEPH (b. Morpeth, Northumberland, 1861; d. London 1913). Trained by his father and studied under Aime Morot in Paris. Being dissatisfied, he destroyed many of his drawings. Painted animals, especially horses, dogs, and fowl. Gold Medal, Munich; Silver Medal, Paris. *exhib.* Newcastle, Laing A.G., 1951 (Tyneside's Contribution to Art). *coll.* Berwick-on-Tweed, Museum and A.G. (1); Birmingham A.G. (1); Edinburgh National Gallery of Scotland (2); Glasgow Museum and A.G. (6); Burrell Coll. (132); Daniel B. Fearing (1). *repr.* Crawhall Exhibition Catalogue, Glasgow, 1935. *lit.* 'Joseph Crawhall', Adrian Bury.

CRIBB, PRESTON (b. Portsmouth 1876, d. Birmingham 1937). Studied art at Portsmouth and London. Specialised in marine subjects and was a constant visitor at Cowes for the yacht racing. Painted Jubilee Review from H.M.S. *Ramilies*. Etcher and illustrator. Exhibitor at R.A., R.O.I., R.B.A. and most other societies. *coll.* Birmingham A.G., 'Making for the Mark Buoy'.

CROME, JOHN (b. Norwich 1769, d. there 1821). Usually known as 'Old Crome'. Painted landscapes in oils and water-colours. Founder member of the Norwich Society of Artists. *coll.* Bury A.G., 'Peasant fishing from rustic Bridge'. *exhib.* 'The Beaters' in 'International Art Treasures', V. and A. Museum, 1962.

CROME, JOHN BERNEY (Norwich A.G. catalogue 1927 and Grant); **BERNAY** (P. and L. Murray and others) (b. Norwich 1794 (Norwich Catalogue and Grant), 1793 (National Gallery of Scotland and others); d. 1842). Eldest son of John Crome. President, Norwich Society, 1819. Landscape painter to H.R.H. the Duke of Sussex. Painted in oils and water-colour. *coll.* John Lane, 'Fishing from a Rustic Bridge'. *repr.* 'Angling in British Art', p. 111.

CROOME, J. D. (op. 1839–1852). London address. Painted still-life, etc. His R.A. exhibit in 1846 was 'Two Arabian Horses', presented to Her Majesty by Sir Jamsetjee Jejeebhoy of Bombay. *exhib.* R.A. (7); B.I. (2); S.S. (3), 'Figures'.

CROWQUILL, ALFRED (ALFRED HENRY FORRESTER) (b. London 1804, d. there 1872, May). The R.A. 1845 painting was titled 'The Huntsman's Rest'. *exhib.* R.A. (4), 'Domestic'.

CRUIKSHANK, GEORGE (b. 1792, d. 1878). Caricaturist, etc. Occasionally produced sporting subjects. Etching known of 'Portrait of a Huntsman—Stag Hunt in the Distance' and 'Angling a la Mode'. *repr.* 'Angling in British Art', Shaw Sparrow, p. 126. *exhib.* R.A. (8); B.I. (15) 'Humorous'

CRUIKSHANK, ROBERT ISAAC (b. 1789, d. 1856). Brother of George Cruikshank. 'Archers Target Shooting at Warings Archery, Bayswater', was exhibited at the R.A. 1817. Some sporting prints after his own designs are known: 'Going to the Derby'; 'John Anderson, Falconer'; 'Going to a Fight'; 'Berkeley Hunt' 'Sportsmen Resting'. *exhib.* R.A. (8), 'Portraits'.

CUITT, GEORGE (b. Moulton, Yorkshire, 1743; d. Richmond, Yorkshire, 1818). Painted 'The Ketton Ox', 1801, engraved in aquatint by Robert Pollard. *exhib.* R.A. (14), 'Landscape'.

CUNDALL, CHARLES ERNEST, R.A., R.W.S. (b. Stretford, Manchester, 1890, 6th September; living 1964). Studied at the Slade School and Royal College of Art, London. *coll.* Birmingham A.G., 'Boat-Race Day, Hammersmith, 1925'. *exhib.* R.A. 1934, 'The Derby 1933'; 1938 'The Derby'; 1939 'The St. Leger'; 1959 'Henley Regatta'.

CUNLIFFE, DAVID (op. 1826–1855). Painted military and sporting subjects and landscape. Painted two portraits of Phillip Booth of the Oakley Hounds, Bedfordshire. *exhib.* R.A. (11); B.I. (3); S.S. (7), 'Landscape'. *repr.* 'A Book of Sporting Painters', Shaw Sparrow; 'Breaking Cover', Vicars Bros., London.

CUST (op. 1784–1785). Probably the Hon. C. Cust, of the family of Lord Brownlow, known as an enthusiast in art and not an unskilful etcher. *exhib.* R.A. (2), views in Wales and in Westmorland. *coll.* M.C.C. Gallery, Lord's, have a 'Cust', presumably the above.

DADD, FRANK, R.I., R.O.I. (b. London 1851; d. 1929, 7th March). Studied S. Kensington and R.A. Schools. Painted figures and sporting in oils and water-colours. Produced some woodcuts, one of 'Salmon Spearing'. *exhib.* R.A. (7); S.S. (9); N.W.C.S. (19); V.E. (42). *repr.* Badminton Library, volume on Polo.

DAGLEY, RICHARD (op. 1785, d. 1841). Poet and etcher. Published 'Death's Doings', 30 plates designed and etched by himself. Contains 'The Angler' and 'Death and the Angler'. *exhib.* R.A. (65); B.I. (3); S.S. (3); V.E. (1).

***DALBY, DAVID** (op. 1780–1849). Residing in York, later moving to Leeds. Painted Gentlemen's Seats and Sporting, including a series of hunting subjects in 1824 called 'Lord Harewood's Hunt'. Sometimes known as 'Dalby of York'. *coll.* Liverpool, Walker A.G.; Major Sir Reginald and Lady Macdonald-Buchanan (2); N. C. Selway (2); Charles H. Thieriot, New York; Hutchinson Gallery of Sport (3 now sold).

DALBY, JOHN (op. 1826–1853). Apparently residing in York. Possibly related to David Dalby. Known for his numerous fine quality hunting scenes. *coll.* Liverpool, Walker A.G. (2), 'Finish of a Race at Hoylake' and 'A Steeplechase'. *exhib.* Rutland Gallery, London, April 1960, a racehorse, 'Colonel', S&D 1828. *auct.* Sotheby's, 3rd June 1959, 'A Chestnut Hunter', S&D York 1826.

DANBY, FRANCIS, A.R.A. (b. Wexford 1793, 16th November; d. Exmouth 1861, 10th February). Went to Bristol with his tutor, J. A. O'Connor, in 1813 (Grant), 1821 (Cundall). Later in London, where owing to quarrel with R.A. in 1892 did not become a full member and retired to the Continent till 1847 (Grant). Cundall says he lived in Switzerland from 1830 to 1841. Painted landscapes, scriptural and angling subjects in oils and water-colours. *coll.* London, V. and A. Museum, 'Fisherman's Home at Sunset'. *exhib.* R.A. (48); B.I. (17); S.S. (2).

DANCE, NATHANIEL (SIR NATHANIEL DANCE-HOLLAND, BART., M.P., R.A.) (b. 1734; d. 1811, 15th October). Portrait groups with sporting interest. Messrs. Arthur Ackermann and Son report having had a very fine one of a Gentleman with his three sons shooting in a Landscape, S&D 1776. *lit.* Grant, 'Old English Landscape Painters', Vol. 3, pp. 206/7.

DANIEL, T. LLEWELYN (b. Aberdovey 1891, 26th April, living at Ilford, Essex). Water-colour artist painting landscape, marines, and in particular animals and sporting scenes. *exhib.* R.I. 1963, 'Straying Horses, New Forest'; 'Round Up, Brecon'; 'The Meet, Exmoor'.

DANIELL, SAMUEL (b. Chertsey 1775, d. Ceylon 1812). Brother of William Daniell, R.A. Pupil of Thomas Medland. Visited South Africa 1799. Under Secretary to the Governor for a short time. Secretary and Draughtsman to a mission to Bechuanaland. Returned to England 1803. In 1805 left for Ceylon. Works reproduced in 'African Scenery and Animals', 2 vols., 1804–5, 'A Picturesuqe Illustration of the Scenery, Animals and Native Inhabitants of the Island of Ceylon', 1808. 'Sketches of South Africa' (animals, tribes and scenery), 1820. 'Account of Travels into Interior of South Africa in years 1797 and 1798', by Sir John Barrow. Sporting scenes or subjects may appear in many of the illustrations. *lit.* 'The Daniells', by Thomas Sutton, F.S.A., 1954.

DANIELL, THOMAS, R.A., F.R.S., F.S.A. (b. Kingston-on-Thames 1749, d. London 1840). Son of John Shepard Daniell, innkeeper of 'The Swan', Chertsey. Apprenticed to a coachbuilder. Later with Charles Catton, R.A. Entered R.A. Schools in 1773. Took up aquatint engraving with his nephew William. Went to India with William in 1785. Returned to England 1794. *exhib.* R.A. (125); B.I. (10). Walker Gallery, London, 1933. *repr.* 'Oriental Scenery', 24 plates drawn and engraved by Thomas Daniell, 1795, 1797, 1801 and 1816 (150 pls.). *lit.* 'The Daniells', by Thomas Sutton, F.S.A., 1954; 'Thomas and William Daniell', by Martin Hardie and Muriel Clayton, 1932 (Walker's Quarterly). Many of the illustrations may have sporting interest, such as the following: R.A. 1798, 'Tiger Hunting in the East Indies'; 1799, 'Forest Scene in Northern Part of Hindoostan with a Rhinoceros'.

DANIELL, WILLIAM, R.A. (b. 1769, d. London 1837, 16th August). Son of William and Sarah Daniell and nephew of Thomas Daniell. Pupil of his uncle. Travelled with him to India in 1785. Returned to England in 1794. Married Mary Westall, eldest sister of Richard Westall, A.R.A. Travelled through England and Scotland. Later visited Devonshire and Wales in 1807; Ireland in 1828. *coll.* London, V. and A. Museum, 'A Hippopotomus Hunt'. *exhib.* R.A. (168); B.I. (64). *repr.* 'Oriental Scenery', 1797 and 1816. 'A Picturesque Voyage to India by Way of China', 1810. *lit.* 'The Daniells', by Thomas Sutton, F.S.A., 1954; 'Thomas and William Daniell', by Martin Hardie and Muriel Clayton, 1932 (Walker's Quarterly).

DANIELS, ALFRED (op. 1952). London address. *exhib.* R.A. 1952, 'Cricket at Kew'.

DANIELS, WILLIAM (b. Liverpool 1813, 9th May; d. there 1880, 13th October). Buried in St. James' Cemetery. Son of a brickmaker and publican. Apprenticed to Alexander Mosses (1793–1837). Painted portraits. *coll.* Liverpool, Walker A.G., 'Chess Players'; 'The Card Players'.

DARWIN, Sir ROBIN (b. 1910), living. Head of the Royal College of Art. *coll.* Hove Museum of Art, 'Ice Hockey at the Empress Hall', S&D '49.

DAVID, S. (op. 1841) Said to be a French artist working in this country. *auct.* Christie's, 25/26th April 1940, A. N. Gilbey Collection, 'Dibbing for Chub', S&D 1841.

DAVIDSON, THOMAS (op. 1871). Graves gives a Thomas Davidson, Junior, London, op. 1863–1893, and exhibiting R.A. (26); B.I. (5); S.S. (65); V.E. (45), 'Figures'. *exhib.* R.A. 1871, 'Hawking'.

DAVIES, ARTHUR A. (op. 1887). 'Huntsman and Hounds in a Wooded Landscape', S&D 1887. *exhib.* London, Trafalgar Galleries, September 1966.

DAVIES, W. (op. 1818–1819). London and Shrewsbury addresses. A William H. Davies, London address, exhibited R.A. (8), Still-life, between 1818 and 1838. *exhib.* R.A., 1818, Flowers; 1819, Game and Poultry.

DAVINCI, L. (op. 1839). London address. Exhibited a sporting painting at the B.I. in 1839.

DAVIS, HENRY WILLIAM BANKS, R.A. (b. Finchley 1833, 26th August; d. 1914). Son of a barrister. Studied R.A. Schools. Painted landscapes, animals, and angling subjects. Had a house at Boulogne, living there occasionally. Painter and sculptor. *coll.* London, Tate, 'Mother and Son' (Horses). Exhibited R.A. 1881. *exhib.* R.A. (100); B.I. (5); S.S. (17); N.G. (5); V.E. (14). *auct.* Christie's, 23rd/30th May 1913, McCulloch Collection, 'A Gleamy Day, Picardy'. Two horses on a green pasture, beyond are cattle, a mare and foal Exhibited R.A. 1891.

***DAVIS, RICHARD BARRETT, R.B.A.** (b. Watford 1782, d. Kensington 1854, 13th March). His father was Huntsman to the Royal Harriers. King George III placed the artist under Sir Francis Bourgeois, R.A. Also studied R.A. Schools and under Sir William Beechey, R.A. Appointed animal painter to four Sovereigns. *coll.* Hull, Ferens A.G.; H.M. The Queen; Lord Fairhaven; Mr. and Mrs. Paul Mellon. *exhib.* R.A. (70); B.I. (57); S.S. (141); O.W.C.S. (3); N.W.C.S. (2). *lit.* Grant, 'Old English Landscape Painters', Vol. 7, pp. 535–536.

DAVIS, TYDDESLEY R. T. (op. 1831–1857). Worked at Brighton, Oxford and Ruabon. *exhib.* B.I. (7), Sporting.

DAVIS, T. exhibited one work at R.A. 1852, 'Hounds running into a Fox'; possibly same as above.

DAVIS, WILLIAM HENRY (op. 1803–1849). London address. Appointed Animal Painter to the King in 1837. Visited Rome. *coll.* Lord Exeter (2); Charles H. Thieriot, New York (1), since sold at Sotheby's 15th July 1959, No. 97, a S&D 1836 canvas. *exhib.* R.A. (30); B.I. (7); S.S. (8).

DAWSON, HENRY (b. 1811, d. 1878). Painted views of the River Thames with angling interest.

DAY, G. F. (op. 1849–1850). One painting, portrait of Mr. John Purser, of the Cardington Club, with his greyhounds, 'Pansey and Pilot', S&D 1849, is known. Engraved for the 'Sporting Magazine', Vol. 1, p. 116, 1850.

DAYES, EDWARD (b. 1763, d. London 1804, May). Pupil of W. Pether. Water-colour landscape painter. *exhib.* S.A. (5); R.A. (64). *auct.* Christie's, 25/26th April 1940, A. N. Gilbey Collection. 'Two Men Fishing from opposite banks of a stream'.

DE DREUX, ALFRED (b. 1810, d. 1860). Although French, worked in England and his sporting paintings are very good. Apart from animals he painted historical and portraits. *coll.* Mr. and Mrs. Paul Mellon, U.S.A.

DEIGHTON, JOSHUA (op. 1899). *exhib.* Rutland Gallery, London, 'English Sporting Life', April 1960. 'Manifesto, The Racehorse, with Jockey Up', winner of Grand National Steeplechase 1899.

DE LATRE (op. 1834–1838). Painter of animals, sometimes in collaboration with P. Reinagle. A Jean Marie Delatre (b. Abbeville 1746, d. Fulham 1840), a pupil of Bartolozzi, may possibly be the same. *exhib.* B.I. (1).

DE LOUTHERBOURG, PHILIP JAMES, R.A. (b. Basle 1740, d. 1812). Mainly landscape and fully dealt with elsewhere, but his painting of coaching subjects brings him into this volume. One extremely fine one, entitled 'The Evening Coach', showing a coach climbing Greenwich Hill, with a view of London in the distance, is an example. *coll.* London, N. G.; V. and A. Museum; Bethnal Green; Dulwich; Greenwich Hospital; Nottingham A.G.; Glasgow A.G.; Derby; Dublin. *lit.* Grant, 'Old English Landscape Painters', Vol. 3, pp. 230/235.

DEMAISTRE, ROY L. (b. Australia 1894). Won Society of Artists travelling scholarship 1923 and went to Paris. Worked in London since 1938. *exhib.* Paris Salon; Australian Section of Biennale, 1926; Leeds; Birmingham; New York; R.A. 1964 (358), 'The Match' (Rugby).

DENOW, R. *coll.* Lord Exeter, 'Stockwell', oil, signed.

DE PRADES A. F., or PRAEDES (see under P).

DESVIGNES, HERBERT CLAYTON (op. 1833–1863). London address. Painted coaching and hunting scenes. *coll.* Charles H. Thieriot, New York (1). *exhib.* R.A. (20); B.I. (27); S.S. (36), 'Cattle'. *auct.* 'Coaching Scenes' sold London 1927 and 1929, and 'Hunting Scenes' sold 1922, 1929 and 1938. A Miss Emily E. Desvignes (op. 1855–1876) exhibited cattle and sheep R.A. (6); B.I. (6); S.S. (28).

DETTI, CESARE AUGUSTE (b. Spolete 1847, 28th December; d. Paris 1914, 19th May). London address 1889, Duke St., St. James's. *exhib.* R.A. (1), 'Departure of the Hawking Party'.

DEVIS, ARTHUR (b. Preston, Lancs., 1711, 19th February; d. Brighton 1787, 25th July). Pupil of Tillemans. London 1742, Preston 1745. Painter of conversation pieces. *coll.* Earl of Bathurst; J. Heseltine Carstairs; Lady Josephine Chance; Mrs. Lytle Hull, U.S.A.; Major Sir Reginald Macdonald-Buchanan; J. C. Meyer, U.S.A.; Colonel John Parker; Uppark, Sussex (National Trust); Hon. F. Wallop; Viscount Wimborne; Preston, H.M. and A.G. *lit.* 'The Devis Family of Painters', by S. H. Paviere, 1950.

DEVIS, ARTHUR WILLIAM (b. London 1762, 10th August; d. 1822, 11th February, at Caroline Street, Bedford Square). Buried churchyard of St. Giles-in-the-Fields. Nineteenth child of Arthur Devis and pupil of his father, also R.A. Schools. Visited Canton and India. Returned to England 1795. *coll.* Preston, Harris Museum and Art Gallery, 'John Addison, Tiger shooting in India'; 'Portrait of Dog "Dido" '. *lit.* 'The Devis Family of Painters', by S. H. Paviere, 1950.

DE WINT, PETER, R.W.S. (b. Stone, Staffs., 1784; d. London 1849). Studied under John Raphael Smith and at R.A. Schools. Painted landscapes in oils and water-colours, a number with angling interest. *coll.* Glasgow A.G. (Landscape with Pond and sluice, man fishing by the side); Earl of Inchcape ('Partridge Shooting', a pair); M.C.C. Gallery, Lord's (1). *repr.* 'Memoir of Peter de Wint', by Walter Armstrong, 1880.

DIGBY, GEORGE (op. 1888–1889). *exhib.* R.A. (6); S.S. (2); V.E. (1), 'Sea pieces'. R.A. 1888, 'Salmon from the Stake Nets'.

DIGHTON, ROBERT (b. 1752, d. London 1814). Painted portraits and drew caricatures. Shaw Sparrow, 'Angling in British Art', mentions a drawing entitled 'August'—over-dressed lady angler leaning against some timber rails. *exhib.* F.S. (14); R.A. (6). *auct.* Christie's, 9th July 1961, Portrait of a sportsman in green coat, standing in landscape (one of a pair), S&D 1791; also Sotheby's, 11th November 1962 (No. 48), same pair.

DIXON, CHARLES (b. Goring 1872, 8th December; d. 1934). Painted marines and history and some sporting apparently, as a 'The Leeds London Stage held up by a Hunt in full cry', S&D 1912, sold at Christie's 16th October 1964, testifies. *exhib.* R.A. (8); N.W.C.S. (1); V.E. (1).

DOBSON, WILLIAM (b. London 1610, d. there 1646, October). *coll.* London, Tate 'Endymion Porter, c. 1642, with gun, dog and dead game'. *repr.* 'English Painting', by Mark Roskell, 1959, in colour.

DOCHARTY, JAMES, A.R.S.A. (b. Bonhill, Dumbartonshire, 1829; d. Egypt 1878; d. Glasgow, Benezit). Son of a calico block cutter. Pattern designer. Studied Glasgow School of Art. Died whilst travelling and sketching in Egypt. *coll.* Glasgow A.G., 'A Salmon Stream—the Lochy Water'—with an angler, S&D 1878. *exhib.* R.A. (13), 1875, 'Gaffing a Salmon', 1877; 'A Good Fishing Day, Loch Lomond'. *repr.* 'Angling in British Art'.

DODDS, W. (op. 1879–1885), represented in the M.C.C. Gallery at Lord's Cricket Ground, London, with an example. *exhib.* S.S. (1); V.E. (8), 'landscape'.

DOLLMAN, JOHN CHARLES, R.I., R.O.I., R.W.S., F.E.S. (b. Hove 1851, 6th May; d. 1934). *coll.* Newport, Mon., Museum and Art Gallery, 'Going to the Meet'; Preston, Harris Museum and Art Gallery, 'During the Time of the Sermonses' (Golf).

DONALD, JOHN MILNE (b. Nairn 1817, d. Glasgow 1866; b. 1819, d. 1858, Benezit). Apprenticed to house painter in Glasgow. Worked for some time in London in the shop of a picture restorer. Returned to Glasgow, where he died. *coll.* Glasgow A.G., 'Loch Eck with Angler', S&D 1863. *exhib.* R.A. (2); B.I. (1).

DONNE, J. P. Three examples by this artist are in the M.C.C. Gallery, undated.

DORRELL, EDMUND (b. Warwick 1778, d. London 1857, 28th February). Working in Chelsea, painting principally in water-colours. *exhib.* R.A. (15); S.S. (14), 'Landscapes'. Picture, 'Cricket near Richmond', engraved by F. C. Lewis.

D'ORSAY, COUNT ALFRED (b. 1798, d. 1852). Produced original lithographs of steeplechases. *exhib.* R.A. (17); S.S. (3), 'Scriptural'.

DOUGLAS, EDWARD ALGERNON STUART (op. 1880–1892). Barnes address. *exhib.* R.A. (10); V.E. (1). The Academy exhibits included, 1880, 'Foxhounds in Covert'; 1883, 'After a Long Run'; 1884, 'The Huntsman's Favourites'; 1887, 'Listen how the Hounds and Horses, etc.'; 1890, 'Lord Portman's Hounds'; 1891, 'A Hunting Morning'; 1892, 'The First Flight'.

DOUGLAS, EDWIN (b. Edinburgh 1848). Studied R.A. Schools. *exhib.* R.A. (41); V.E. (17). The R.A. exhibits included: 1874, 'Mountain Shooting'; 1876, 'The Bagged Fox'; 1882, 'Ferreting'; 1883, 'A Licensed Poacher'. *auct.* Sotheby's, 11th March 1959, 'Persimmon', the Triple Crown Winner 1896 in a stable interior, S&D 1896.

DOWNMAN, Lieutenant J. T. (op. 1810–1840) of the 83rd Regiment: two series of prints published between 1810 and 1840. *lit.* Captain Frank Siltzer, 'The Story of British Sporting Prints'.

DOYLE, JOHN – 'H.B.' (b. Dublin 1797, d. London 1868, 2nd January). Caricaturist and portrait painter. *repr.* 'Angling in British Art', Shaw Sparrow. 'Lord John Russell Angling in Conservative Waters, aided by Palmerston and Watched by Peel and Wellington'. 'Sir Robert Peel and Wellington Angling for Morgan O'Connell'. *exhib.* R.A. (6). The 1825 exhibit, 'Turning out the Stag'.

DOYLE, RICHARD (b. 1824, d. 1883). Represented in the M.C.C. Gallery, Lord's, London, with one example. *exhib.* R.A. (2); G.G. (61), 'Landscape'.

DRAKE, NATHAN, F.S.A. (b. Lincoln 1727, d. York 1778, 19th February). Buried at St. Michael-le-Belfrey, York. Son of the Rev. Samuel Drake, Minor Canon of Lincoln, Vicar of St.Mary, Lincoln, and Rector of St. Mary, Nottingham. Mother was Elizabeth, daughter of Zachary Sugar, Vicar of Felix Kirk, Yorkshire. Nathan was the second son; his elder brother, Samuel, born in 1724, educated Merton and Trinity, Oxford, became Vicar of Gunby in Lincolnshire. Nathan went to York in 1752, advertising as a limner and landscape painter and teacher of drawing and painting in water-colours. Terms were one guinea entrance and two guineas a quarter. Married Martha Carr (b. 1742), daughter of Thomas Carr, keeper of a coffee shop in Minster Yard, York, on 31st May 1763. Had two daughters, Anne and Mary, and two sons, Nathan and Richard. Around 1766 had a new patron, William Joliffe Tufnell, of New Munckton Priory, near York. Three pictures he painted are still in the family. Painted topographical views in Lincolnshire, portraits, country houses, landscapes, and owners' horses and dogs of sporting activities. Often confused with Nathaniel Drake, a London colourman and artist, possibly a relative. *coll.* Mr. John Joliffe Tufnell (3). *exhib.* S.A. (5); F.S. (1).

DRING, WILLIAM, R.A. (b. 1904, 26th January; living). Studied Slade School. *exhib.* R.A. 1964 (102), 'Dr. Marsden Roberts with Gun'.

DUBOIS, SIMON (baptized Antwerp 26th July 1632; buried London 26th May 1708). Pupil of C. P. Bercham at Haarlem and P. Wouverman. In Venice 1657. Came to England in 1685. Painted cattle, horses and portraits. *auct.* London 1928, 'Partie de Chasse'.

DUBOST, ANTOINE (b. Lyon 1769, 16th July; d. Paris 1825, 6th September). Pupil of Vincent and C. Vernet in Paris. Visited Italy and Switzerland. Came to England in 1813. Produced lithographs of Newmarket Races, etc., 1809–1818. *exhib.* R.A. 1806, 'Preparations for a Horse Race'. *lit.* 'Art in England', Whitley.

DUKE, A. A painting, 'The Kill', sold at Christie's 22nd January 196 (225).

DUMAURIER (or DU MAURIER), GEORGE LOUIS PALMELLA BUSSON, A.R.W.S. (b. 1831, d. 1896). *coll.* M.C.C. Gallery, Lords (3). *exhib.* R.A. (39); O.W.C.S. (38); N.G. (6); V.E. (61), 'Illustrations'. *repr.* 'Angling in British Art', Shaw Sparrow.

DUNCAN, EDWARD, R.W.S. (b. London 1803; d. London 1882). Articled to Robert Havell, the engraver. Painted landscapes, marines, etc. Member O.W.C.S. and N.W.C.S. *exhib.* R.A. (7); B.I. (13); S.S. (18); N.W.C.S. (188); O.W.C.S. (332). *repr.* 'Angling in British Art', Shaw Sparrow; a set of 'Shooting' prints published.

DUNCAN, THOMAS, R.S.A., A.R.A. (b. Kinclaven, Perthshire, 1807; d. Edinburgh 1845). Entered lawyer's office in Perth before studying art at Academy of the Board of Manufacturers, Edinburgh. *coll.* Edinburgh, National Gallery of Scotland, 'Bran, a Celebrated Scottish Deerhound'. *exhib.* R.A. (8); S.S. (1), 'Historical'; R.A. 1842 exhibit, 'Deer Stalking'.

***DUNN, Miss EDITH** (*see* MRS. THOMAS O. HUME)

DUNSTAN, BERNARD ANDREW HAROLD, A.R.A. (b. 1920, 19th January). Living artist. Pupil of Ernest Jackson. Slade and Byam Shaw Schools. *exhib.* R.A. 1953, 'Cricket on Kew Green'.

DUNTHORNE, JOHN, Junior

***DUPONT, RICHARD, J. M.** (b. 1920, 20th July; living). Resident in Dedham, Essex. Painter of horses and sporting subjects. *coll.* H.M. The Queen (2); Hon. J. J. Astor; Earl and Countess of Derby (2); Harry F. Guggenheim, U.S.A. (2); Jockey Club, Newmarket; Baron Guy de Rothschild, Paris; Sir Humphrey de Trafford (2). *exhib.* Ackermann Gallery, London.

***DUVAL** or **DUVALL, JOHN** (op. 1834–1881). Ipswich and London addresses. *coll.* Howell, U.S.A. (formerly Messrs. Frost & Reed Ltd.), Huntsman on dappled grey horse, other huntsmen with pack of hounds in near distance. *exhib.* R.A. (18); B.I. (10); S.S. (49), 'Domestic'.

DYCE, WILLIAM, R.A. (b. Aberdeen 1806, d. Streatham 1864, 15th February). Visited Rome. *exhib.* R.A. (41); B.I. (4), 'Mythological'. Painted a picture, 'George Herbert at Bemerton', now in the Guildhall Art Gallery, London. Herbert was accompanied by Izaac Walton seated and fishing. Told as a joke that Herbert and Walton were not contemporaries. Walton was painted out but not his fishing-basket. Walton and Herbert both born same year, 1593.

EARL, GEORGE (op. 1856–1883). London and Banstead addresses. Painted animals and sporting. *exhib.* R.A. (19); B.I. (9); S.S. (18).

EARL, MAUD (op. 1884–1901). London address. Painted animals. *exhib.* R.A. (3); S.S. (1). R.A. 1884, 'Red Deer'.

EARL, THOMAS (op. 1836–1885). London address. Painted animals and sport. *exhib.* R.A. (47); B.I. (62); S.S. (108); V.E. (21).

EARL, T. P. (op. 1903). *auct.* 'The Mighty Sceptre', A bay racehorse with groom in a landscape, sold Sotheby's 14th October 1964.

EARLE, F. (op. 1839). London address. *exhib.* R.A. (2), 'Dogs'.

EARP, HENRY (op. 1871–1884). Brighton address. Painted animals and cattle. *exhib.* S.S. (4); N.W.C.S. (2).

EAST, Sir ALFRED, R.A., R.I., R.B.A., R.P.E. (b. Kettering 1849, d. London 1913). Studied Glasgow School of Art and in Paris. Landscape painter. *exhib.* R.A. (22); S.S. (30); N.W.C.S. (25); G.G. (11); N.G. (11); V.E. (17), 'Landscape'. R.A. 1910, 'Morning Sunshine' (has two fishermen).

ECKSTEIN, JOHN (op. 1770–1802). London address. *exhib.* S.A. (1); F.S. (1); R.A. (19). Graves says 'Sculpture'. R.A. 1799, 'A Boy Fishing'; 1801, 'Newfoundland Dog Saving a Child'; 1802, 'Gelert and Llewellyn'.

EDOUART, A. (op. 1815–1816). London address. Painter of animals. *exhib.* R.A. (5); 1815, 'Portrait of a Horse'; 'Portraits of Dogs'; 1816, 'Portraits of Dogs'; 'Portrait of a Dog'.

EDWARDS, EDWARD, A.R.A. (b. 1738, d. 1806). Painted portraits, landscapes, etc., also etched. Well known for his 'Anecdotes of Painters', 1808. *exhib.* R.A. (104); S.A. (6); F.S. (1); B.I. (1). R.A. exhibit 1796, 'Portrait of a Spaniel'; 1804, 'Two Pomeranian Dogs'; 1805, 'Portrait of a Spaniel'.

EDWARDS, EDWIN (b. Framlingham 1823, d. London 1879). Sunbury address. Painted fishing subjects. *exhib.* R.A. (54); B.I. (3); S.S. (1); V.E. (101), 'Sea-pieces and etching'.

EDWARDS, LIONEL, R.I., R.C.A. (b. 1878, living). Contemporary artist painting sporting subjects in oils and water-colours and illustrator of books on sport. *coll.* Bath A.G. (4); Mr. and Mrs. George Earle; Captain Jack Gilbey; Major Sir Reginald Macdonald-Buchanan (4). *repr.* 'Country Life Annual', 1959; 'Country Life', 23rd November 1961; 'Shires and Provinces', by Sabretache. *lit.* 'A Leicester Sketch Book'.

EDWARDS, SYDENHAM (b. Usk, Monmouth, 1768; d. Chelsea, London, 1819). Painted portraits, etc. *exhib.* R.A. (12), 'Portraits'. R.A. 1798, 'A Cocking Spaniel'; 1810, 'Portrait of Staghounds in Kennel'; 1813, 'Red Grouse'; 1814, 'Unkennelling Hounds with portrait of a Hunter'.

EDWARDS, S. R. W. (op. 1818–1822). *exhib.* R.A. (3).

***EGERTON, DANIEL THOMAS, R.B.A.** (op. 1824–1840, d. 1842). Painted landscapes and some sporting. Visited America and Mexico. Murdered in Mexico 1842. *exhib.* B.I. (1); S.S. (65).

EGERTON, M. (op. 1825). Painted coaching scenes. A 'The London Royal Mail' is in the Charles H. Thieriot collection, New York. It was engraved in aquatint by George Hunt in 1825.

EGLINGTON, SAMUEL (op. 1833–1855). Liverpool artist, President of the Liverpool Academy 1842–1844. *coll.* Liverpool, Walker A.G., 'Trout Fishing in North Wales'. *exhib.* R.A. (2); B.I. (13); S.S. (4); N.W.C.S. (5).

ELEN, PHILIP WEST (op. 1839–1872). Painted landscapes, principally in water-colours and some oils. Streams and pools in Wales, Devon, and other parts of England. *exhib.* R.A. (64); B.I. (57); S.S. (46); V.E. (75). R.A. 1846, 'A Trout Stream in Yorkshire'; 1847, 'A Trout Stream, Yorkshire'; 1850, 'A Trout Stream'.

ELMER, STEPHEN, A.R.A. (op. 1764, d. Farnham 1796). Well known painter of fish, game-birds, placing them in pretty landscapes, for the most part scenes around Farnham. Although he painted a large number, they are scarce from the destruction of many in a fire in 1801. Graves gives 1811 as last date of exhibiting; however, he had died in 1796, so there is an error. *exhib.* F.S. (113); R.A. (117); B.I. (4), 'still-life (four at the B.I. under this name, in 1810, 1811, are either posthumous or by another hand—a son?)

ELMER, WILLIAM (op. 1778–1799). Son or nephew of Stephen Elmer, A.R.A. Resided with Stephen at Farnham. Visited Dublin. Grant says a picture, 'Fox with a Dead Cock Disturbed by Hounds', is extant. *exhib.* S.A. (19); R.A. (6); R.A. 1797, 'Spaniels pursuing a Wounded Pheasant'.

ELSLEY, ARTHUR JOHN (op. 1878–1893). *exhib.* R.A. (19); S.S. (4); V.E. (14). R.A. 1878, 'Portrait of an Old Pony'.

ELSLEY, J. (op. 1845). *exhib.* B.I., A Group of Horses.

ELVERY, JAMES (op. 1762). A painting of a Gentleman mounted on a hunter with dog, S&D 1762, was in the possession of Messrs. Arthur Ackermann & Son.

EMERY, JAMES (op. 1777–1822). Actor and artist. Painted sea-pieces and horses. Exhibiting as from 'Covent Garden Theatre'. Shaw Sparrow mentions Messrs. Ellis & Smith, London, as having sketches by Emery and 'A Racehorse Galloping'. Benezit gives 'John Emery', b. Sunderland 1777 (22nd December), d. London 1822 (25th July). Obviously the same as above. *exhib.* R.A. (19). 1807, 'Portrait of a Horse'; 1808, 'Portrait of an Irish Mare'. *See also* ELVERY, JAMES.

EMMS, JOHN (b. Blowfield 1843, 21st April; d. Lyndhurst 1912, 1st November). Painted animals and domestic subjects. *coll.* Edinburgh N.G. of Scotland 'Callum', a wiry-haired terrier, and dead rat, S&D 1895. *exhib.* R.A. (20); B.I. (1); S.S. (51); N.W.C.S. (3); G.G. (1); V.E. (12). R.A. 1875, 'Foxhound Whelps'; 1877, 'Foxhounds on the Benches'; 1880, 'Hounds at Rest'; 1900, 'Hawking'.

ENNION, Dr. ERIC A. R. (living artist). Exhibited at Arthur Ackermann & Son, water-colours of birds, notably waders. Includes wild life in his works, also an illustrator.

ETTY, WILLIAM, R.A. (b. York 1787, d. there 1849). Spent most of his time in London. Studied R.A. Schools. Visited Venice in 1822. *coll.* Leicester A.G., 'The Bowman'. *exhib.* York, Etty Centenary Exhibition, 1949 (42). Illus. in Leicester catalogue 1958.

EVANS, WILLIAM (of Eton) (b. Eton 1798, 4th December; d. there 1877, 31st December). Painted principally landscapes. Master of Design at Eton. *exhib.* O.W.C.S. (264). *auct.* Christie's, 25/26th April 1940, A. N. Gilbey Collection. 'Eton Eyot', gentleman fishing, with a companion in a gown beside him. Eton College in background.

EVANS (op. 1774). Wales. *exhib.* F. S. Landscape with Dead Game.

EYRE, JOHN (op. 1877–1910). London address. *exhib.* R.A. (9); S.S. (14); N.W.C.S. (5), 'Domestic'. R.A. 1882, 'The Angler and Little Fish'; 1910, 'Anglers'.

FAED, JAMES, Junior (op. 1880–1902). Edinburgh and London addresses. Painted mostly landscapes and some animals. *exhib.* R.A. (6). 1870, 'The Gamekeeper's Daughter'; 1872, 'Dead Game'; 1880, 'The Monarchs of the Park'.

FAED, JOHN, R.S.A. (b. 1819, d. 1902; b. Burley Mill, Kirkcudbrightshire, 1820, d. 1902, 22nd October, Benezit). *exhib.* R.A. (40); B.I. (4); S.S. (77); V.E. (8). *auct.* Sotheby's, 11th November 1964, 'An Archery Contest at Haddon Hall', S&D (18) '68.

FAIRBAIRN, THOMAS, R.S.W. (b. Campsie, Stirlingshire, 1820; d. 1884). Pupil of Andrew Donaldson. Painted mostly in water-colours. *coll.* Glasgow A.G., 'A Leafy Glade – On the Kelvin in 1860', with angler, S&D 1860.

FAIRBONE, J. (op. 1794–1798). London address. *exhib.* R.A. (18), 'Figures'. R.A. 1797, 'A Skittleground'.

FAIRCLOUGH, WILLIAM (living artist, b. 1907, 13th June). Head of the School of Art, Kingston-on-Thames. Painter and etcher. *exhib.* R.A. 1954, 'Henley Regatta'; 1964, 'Racing Rudders, Venice'.

FAIRLIE, HENRY (op. 1876). *auct.* Christie's, 24th January 1964, 'The Hampton Court–Staines Coach at Full Gallop', water-colour, S&D 1876.

FANNER, ALICE (MRS. TAITE) (b. 1865, d. 1930). Studied Slade School, London, and Paris. Residing Datchet 1911; London 1912–1918; Burnham-on-Crouch 1920–1930. Painted yacht racing, regatta scenes, smacks trawling, and kindred subjects. *coll.* Birmingham A.G., 'Yachts Racing in the Solent'; 'Yachts Racing in Bad Weather, Burnham-on-Crouch'; Kingston-on-Thames A.G., 'Luffing off Burnham-on-Crouch. *exhib.* R.A. 1908–1930.

FARLEY, WILLIAM (op. 1936). Bury St. Edmunds address. *exhib.* R.A. 1936, 'Galloway Races at Buckingham'.

FARQUHARSON, JOSEPH, R.A. (b. 1846, d. 1935). Landscape painter. Shaw Sparrow, 'Angling in British Art', mentions a picture, 'Salmon Fishing on the Dee'. *exhib.* R.A. (37); G.G. (3); V.E. (19), 'Domestic'.

FARQUHARSON, DAVID, A.R.A., A.R.S.A. (b. Blairgowrie, Perthshire, 1839; d. Birnam, Perthshire, 1907). Apprenticed to a decorator. Removed to Edinburgh c. 1872 to study landscape painting. From 1886 to 1894 lived in London, then at Sennen Cove, Penzance. *coll.* Glasgow A.G., 'The Wayside, Loch Maree', a gamekeeper exercising his kennel, S&D 1879. P.O.U., 'Angling in Scotland 1879' *repr.* 'Angling in British Art', Shaw Sparrow, 1923. *auct.* Christie's, 23rd/30th May 1913. McCulloch Collection, 'The Salmon River'.

FAULKNER, C. (op. 1874–1875). At Fareham. *exhib.* S.S. (1). *exhib.* Parker Gallery, London, 1964, 'Leaving Covert'; 'Gone Away'.

FAULKNER, J. (op. 1832). *exhib.* B.I. 1832, 'Hawking Party'.

FEARNSIDE, WILLIAM (op. 1791–1801). Landscape and sporting painter. *exhib.* R.A. 1791–1801; also N.W.C.S. (water-colours).

FELLOWS, W. M. (William Dorset, Benezit) (op. 1792–1825). An etcher and aquatinter of shooting, coaching and horses, some after his own works.

FEREY, EDMOND (op. 1879). *auct.* Sotheby's, 2nd December 1959, 'A Skating Party on a Frozen River', S&D '79.

FERNELEY, CLAUDE LORRAINE (b. 1822, d. Elgin Lodge, Melton Mowbray, 1891, 15th October). Son of John and Sarah Ferneley. *coll.* Leicester Museum and A.G. (7); Major Guy Paget (the late) (3). *exhib.* R.A. (1); V.E. (3); R.A. 1868, Horses. *repr.* 'Sporting Pictures of England', Guy Paget, 1945, colour plate; 'A Meet of the Quorn at Kirby Gate', water-colour. *lit.* 'The Melton Mowbray of John Ferneley', Guy Paget; 'A Book of Sporting Painters', Shaw Sparrow.

***FERNELEY, JOHN E.** (b. 1782; baptized at Thrussington, Leicestershire, 27th May 1782; d. Melton Mowbray 1860, 3rd June, aged 78). Son of William and Ann Ferneley, being the youngest of six children of a wheelwright. Married Sarah Kettle at Thrussington Parish Church on 14th November 1809. Went to Ireland with his bride after the marriage. Had four sons, John, Reuben (or Reubens), William, and Claude Lorraine by his first wife. Apprenticed to his father as a wheelwright till 21 years of age. In 1803 decided to be an artist and was encouraged by the Duke of Rutland. Three years later began to exhibit at the R.A. Went to Dover in 1804 and remained some time painting for the officers at the garrison—the Leicestershire Militia was stationed at Dover under its Colonel, the Duke of Rutland. Left Dover in 1805 and joined Ben Marshall. Painted for Assheton Smith, the Master of the Quorn. Shaw Sparrow having reproduced the marriage certificate showing the date 14th November 1809, later says 'six years after his arrival in London young Ferneley married and went for his first professional trip to Ireland'. If he left Dover in 1805 and he married six years later, this would be 1811, two years after his actual marriage. Ferneley's first wife died in 1836. He had gone to reside at Melton Mowbray in 1814 and remained there throughout his life. He married a second time, Ann Allan, who died in 1853. There was one son by this marriage, named Charles. Shaw Sparrow has shown beyond doubt that there is no such person as 'John E. Ferneley'. The artist was 'John Ferneley'. *coll.* Hull, Ferens A.G. (1); Leicester, M. and A.G. (4); London, Tate Gallery (1); Worthing, M. and A.G. (1); Major the Hon. Henry R. Broughton (2); Lady Everard (1); Lord Exeter (1); Sir Richard Bellingham Graham (1); Capt. W. H. Lambton (1); Hubert Langley (1); Sir Reginald Macdonald-Buchanan (12); Mr. and Mrs. Paul Mellon, U.S.A. (2); Lt.-Col. Ririd Myddelton, M.V.O., D.L., J.P. (1); J. N. T. North (1); Major Guy Paget (the late) (16 paintings) (8 pencil drawings); The Earl of Sefton (1); Sizergh Castle Collection (2); Miss A. Smith (1); Lt.-Col. A. W. Smith (1); Charles H. Thieriot, New York (4). *exhib.* R.A. (22); B.I. (4); S.S. (13); V.E. (5). *repr.* 'A Book of Sporting Painters', Shaw Sparrow; 'Sporting Pictures of England', Guy Paget, 1945; 'The Melton Mowbray of John Ferneley', Guy Paget. *lit.* 'The Melton Mowbray of John Ferneley', Guy Paget, 1931; 'A Book of Sporting Painters', Shaw Sparrow.

***FERNELEY, JOHN, Junior** (b. 1815 (?) d. Leeds 1862, 10th September). Eldest son of John Ferneley. Lived at 7 Barrack Street, Hulme, Manchester (Shaw Sparrow). Migrated to York (Major Guy Paget). Died of apoplexy in Leeds Infirmary. Death certificate says 'aged 44 years'. If born in 1815 he would have been 47 years of age. Difficult to separate his work from that of his father, though he mostly signed John Ferneley as against his father's J. Ferneley. It has been suggested that the son may have had a second christian name, beginning with 'E', and this would account for 'John E. Ferneley'. Apparently the son did not contribute to any exhibitions. *coll.* Major Guy Paget (the late), 'A Hunter', signed 'John Ferneley Jnr. 1850'. *exhib.* Preston 1943. P.O.U., 'Eglington', a hunter, property of R. J. Lambton, in Lambton Park. *repr.* 'New Sporting Magazine', Vol. 7, 1834, p. 69. 'Portrait of John Hunnun, R. J. Lambton's first Whipper-In'. *repr.* 'New Sporting Magazine', Vol. 5, May 1833. *lit.* 'A Book of Sporting Painters', Shaw Sparrow. 'The Melton Mowbray of John Ferneley', Guy Paget.

FERNELEY, SARAH (b. 1812 d. 1903). Daughter of John Ferneley, Senior. Painted a few sporting paintings.

FIDLER, HARRY, R.O.I., R.B.A. (b. Teffont, Wilts.). Educated Herkomer School. Living at Stoke, Andover, in 1934. Painter in oils. *exhib.* R.A. (5); R.A. 1891, 'Victimised by Golf'; 'Hark! Hark! the Dogs do Bark!'

FIELD, H. C. (op. 1811–1836). *exhib.* R.A. (11); S.S. (6), 'Sculpture' (Graves).

FIELDING, NEWTON LIMBIRD (Newton Smith Fielding – Christie's) (b. Huntingdon 1799, d. Paris 1856). Son of Nathan Theodore Fielding. Instructor to family of King Louis Philippe of France. Lived and died in France. Painter and lithographer of sporting subjects. *coll.* London, V. and A. Museum; A. N. Gilbey Collection (since sold). *exhib.* V.E. (12), Sporting. *repr.* 'Angling in British Art', Shaw Sparrow.

FIELDING, THALES (b. 1793, d. London 1837). Third son of N. T. Fielding. Drawing Master at the Royal Military College, Woolwich. Painted landscapes, some with sporting interest. Worked in Paris and England. Associate of the Old Water Colour Society. Graves gives 'Thales Henry Adolphus Fielding' and not Thales on his own. *exhib.* R.A. (18); B.I. (21); S.S. (27); O.W.C.S. (88); B.I. 1817, 'Landscapes with Hunters'.

FINNIE, JOHN, R.B.A., A.R.E. (b. Aberdeen 1829, d. Liverpool 1907, 27th February). Painter and etcher. *coll.* Liverpool, Walker A.G., 'The Angler' (drawing). *exhib.* R.A. (36); B.I. (6); S.S. (44); N.W.C.S. (3); G.G. (1); V.E. (17). Hon. Mention Salon des Artistes Francais 1896.

FISHER, Miss HELENA (op. 1891–1903). Addlestone address. *exhib.* R.A. (2); S.S. (1); V.E. (4). R.A. 1891, 'Rabbits'; 1903, 'A Mighty Hunter'.

FISHER, S. MELTON, R.A. (b. Herne Hill 1861, d. 1939, 5th September). Painter of portraits. *coll.* Liverpool, Walker A.G., 'The Chess Players'. *exhib.* R.A. (24); S.S. (3); G.G. (6); N.G. (3); V.E. (24).

FITZGERALD, CLAUDE J. (op. 1893–1912). Chiswick, London, address. *exhib.* R.A. 1912, 'The Hunt'; V.E. (1), 'Still-life' (Graves).

FOLKARD, R. W. (op. 1844). *auct.* Sotheby's, 25th March 1964 (135), 'A Bay Hunter in a Stable', S&D 1844.

FONTAINE, T. S. LA (*see* LA FONTAINE, THOMAS SHERWOOD)

FORBES, ALEXANDER, A.R.S.A. (b. 1802, d. 1839). Well known in his day for paintings of horses and dogs.

FORREST, W. S. (op. 1840–1866). Greenhithe address. Two sepia vignettes of Angling sold as by 'W. Forrest', Christie's, 25/26th April 1940, A. N. Gilbey Collection. *exhib.* R.A. (3); B.I. (2); S.S. (17); R.A. 1847, 'A Spaniel's Head'; 1848, 'Head of a Harrier'.

FORRESTER, ALFRED HENRY (*see* ALFRED CROWQUILL)

FORSTER, P. (op. 1845–1858) (b. & d. Coldstream, Berwickshire). *exhib.* R.A. (1); B.I. (2); S.S. (1). R.A. 1845, 'The Leading Hound'.

FOSTER, MYLES BIRKET, R.W.S. (b. North Shields 1825, d. Weybridge 1899). Worked under Peter Landells, the wood engraver. Drew for 'Illustrated London News', etc. Painter of landscapes and rustic subjects in water-colour. *coll.* London, Tate Gallery, 'Eel Bucks'. *exhib.* R.A. (16); S.S. (2); O.W.C.S. (332); V.E. (3). R.A. 1876, 'A Peep at the Hounds'. *auct.* Christie's, A. N. Gilbey Collection, 25/26th April 1940, 'Children Fishing' and 'Two Studies of Fish'.

FOTHERGILL, GEORGE ALGERNON, M.B., C.M. (Edin.) (b. Leamington 1868, d. 1945). Educated Leamington, Uppingham and Edinburgh University. Water-colour painter, pen, ink and pencil artist; painter on pottery; auto-lithographer; book plate designer and experimenter in collotype and tri-colour process printing. *coll.* Darlington, Preston. *exhib.* Dudley, Leeds; R.S.A.; Walker A.G. Liverpool; 'Jockey Club Stakes 1925' owned by Mr. M. G. M. Kidson of Eton College.

FOWLES, A. W. (19th century). *auct.* Bonham's, London, 19th March 1964, 'Yacht Race'.

FOX, C. L. (Mrs.) (*see* HOLLAMS)

FOX, EDWARD or **E. M.** (op. 1813–1864). Brighton address. Painted in oils and water-colours. *exhib.* R.A. (28); B.I. (11); S.S. (2). R.A. 1818, 'Boys Fishing'. *auct.* Christie's, 12th October 1962, 'Mares and Foals in a Wooded Pasture', S&D 1864.

FOX, M. (op. 1847). A Bay Racehorse standing in a Landscape, S&D 1847, sold at Christie's 30th October 1964 (141).

FRAIN, R. *repr.* 'Angling in British Art', Shaw Sparrow, p. 191; 'Rob o' the Trows, Fisherman'. Engraved by C. Cousens.

FRANCIA, FRANCOIS LOUIS THOMAS (b. 1772 Calais, d. there 1839). A French artist who came to London at an early age. Member and Secretary of the Associated Artists in Water Colour. Returned to Calais 1817 and instructed R. P. Bonington. *exhib.* R.A. (85); V.E. (116). R.A. 1805, 'Stables at Tichfield House'.

FRANCIS, W. (op. 1822–1824). Painter of animals. *exhib.* B.I. 1824, 'Horses'.

FRANKLAND, Sir ROBERT, Bt., or FRANKLAND-RUSSELL (1837) (b. 1784, d. 1849). Painter and etcher of sporting subjects. M.P. for Thirsk 1815–1834. High Sheriff of Yorkshire 1838. Married Louisa Anne Murray, daughter of the Bishop of St. David's. Became Sir Robert Frankland-Russell 1837. No original paintings or drawings by Frankland have been discovered according to Shaw Sparrow. *repr.* Six Hunting Prints by and after Frankland published 1811: 'Going along at a slapping pace'; 'Topping a flight of rails and coming well into the next field'; 'Charging an ox fence'; 'Going in and out clever'; 'Facing a brook'; 'Swishing at a rasper'. Four Hunting subjects after Frankland published by Charles Turner 1813–1814:'Heading the fox'; 'Thrown out'; 'Taking a lead' – 'Craning'; 'The Southern Hounds or hunting in its infancy'. Eight Shooting prints after Frankland, engraved by Woodman and C. Turner, published Cambridge 1813. 'Indispensable Accomplishments', eight coloured etchings, published H. Humphrey 1811. 'Angling in British Art', Shaw Sparrow, colour plates facing p. 137 and 174.

FRASER, ALEXANDER, R.S.A. (b. Woodcockdale, near Linlithgow, 1828; d. Musselburgh 1899). Taught by his father, an amateur artist; later studied at the School of Design, Edinburgh. Painted landscapes, some with sporting interest. *coll.* Glasgow A.G., 'View in Cadzow Forest – Woodcutters and Sportsmen with Dogs'; 'The Salmon Trap'. *exhib.* R.A. (11); B.I. (1); S.S. (8); V.E. (4).

FRASER, ALEXANDER, A.R.S.A. (op. 1810–1859). Edinburgh address. *exhib.* R.A. (32); B.I. (97); S.S. (37); V.E. (10). R.A. exhibits included: 1814, 'Snipe Shooting'; 1818, 'A Fortunate Sportsman'; 1829, 'A Sportsman'; 1832, 'A Falconer'; 1833, 'A Highland Sportsman'.

FREEMAN, JAMES EDWARD (b. 1808, d. 1884). 'Portrait of a Boy with Two Ponies and Two King Charles Spaniels in a Landscape', signed and inscribed 'Fulford'. *exhib.* Ackermann's Gallery 1964.

FRITH, WILLIAM POWELL, R.A. (b. Studley, Yorkshire, 1819, 9th January; d. London 1909, 2nd November). Well-known painter of portraits and figure subjects. *coll.* London, Tate Gallery, 'The Derby Day'. *exhib.* R.A. (136); B.I. (13); S.S. (13); G.G. (1); V.E. (9). R.A. 1873, 'English Archers'; 1878, 'Ascot'. *auct.* Christie's, London, 16th October 1964, 'A Racehorse', S&D 1841.

FRY, ROGER ELIOT (b. Highgate, London, 1866; d. London 1944). Took degree at Cambridge. Visited Italy and studied at Julian's in Paris. Again in Italy 1894. Lecturer and writer on Art. Founded Omega Workshops in London. Slade Professor in 1934. *coll.* Preston H.M. and A.G., 'A Game of Bowls'.

FRY, JOSEPH, Junior (op. 1828). *coll.* Capt. Evelyn Barclay, 'The Last Red Deer in Epping Forest taken in garden at Upton in 1828. Hunted by Mr. Rounding'. Exhibited Norwich 1950.

FRY, WILLIAM THOMAS (b. London 1789, d. 1843). Painter and engraver of sporting subjects. *exhib.* S.S. (13), 'Engraving'.

FRYER, WILLIAM. Unknown sporting painter. 'A Huntsman with Harriers' shown in Oscar and Peter Johnson's 'Sport and the Horse' exhibition, June 1969 (no. 24).

FULLER, J. T. 'Deer stalking in the Highlands' signed with monogram, inscribed and dated 1866, sold at Sotheby's 13th July 1966.

FULTON, DAVID, R.S.W. (b. Glasgow 1848, d. there 1930). Studied Glasgow School of Art. *coll.* Glasgow A.G., 'By the Burnside – Boy "guddling" Trout'. *exhib.* R.A. (1).

FULTON, SAM (b. Glasgow 1855, 26th April). Animal painter, principally dogs. *coll.* Glasgow A.G., 'Foxhounds'.

FURNISS, HARRY (b. Wexford 1854, 26th March; d. 1925). Black-and-white artist and caricaturist. *repr.* 'The Picture of Cricket', John Arlott, 1955; W. G. Grace, 'A Century of Grace', by Furniss in 'How's That', Arrowsmith, 1895; 'English Inns', Thomas Burke, 1943–1947; 'The Meet Outside the Village Inn', pen drawing, in collection of Her Majesty the Queen.

FURSE, CHARLES WELLINGTON, A.R.A. (b. Staines 1868, 13th January; d. London 1904, 16th October). Portrait painter. *coll.* F. S. Oliver, 'Mr. and Mrs. F. S. Oliver Angling in Norway about 1902' *exhib.* R.A. (9); S.S. (1); G.G. (1); N.G. (4); V.E. (2). R.A. 1897, 'Foxhunting'; 'Master of Hounds'; 'John

Laurance, Master of Llangibby Foxhounds'; 'J. Blandy Jenkins, Master of Llanharran Foxhounds'. *repr.* 'Angling in British Art', Shaw Sparrow, p. 64.

FUSSELL, JOSEPH (op. 1820–1845). One of a family of painters, including a younger Joseph (b. Birmingham 1818, d. Point Loma, California, U.S.A., 1912, 6th May); Alexander F.; Frederick Ralph F. *exhib.* R.A. (24); B.I. (17); S.S. (8); N.W.C.S. (1). Exhibited pictures included: R.A. 1822, 'Bulls Fighting'; 1837, 'Chess Players'; B.I. 1825, 'Hunting'; 1828, 'Dead Game'; 1830, 'Watering Place'; 1831, 'The Fisherman'.

GAINSBOROUGH, THOMAS, R.A. (b. Sudbury, Suffolk, 1727; baptized 14th May; d. London 1788, 2nd August). Painter of portraits, landscapes and dogs. *coll.* London, Tate Gallery (2); Lt.-Col. Sir Edmund Bacon, Bt. (1); The Earl of Inchcape (1); Major Guy Paget (the late) (1); Lord Templemore (1). *repr.* 'Animal Painting in England', Basil Taylor, pls. 29, 30; 'A Book of Sporting Painters', Shaw Sparrow, p. 56.

GALE, BENJAMIN (op. 1741–1832). Painter of cattle at Hull. Also painted marines. Drawing master at Hull. Did not exhibit.

GARLAND, HENRY (op. 1854–1890). Winchester address. *coll.* Lord's (1). *exhib.* R.A. (30); B.I. (12); S.S. (67); N.W.C.S. (1); V.E. (13), 'Domestic'.

GARRARD, E. (op. 1793). Knightsbridge address. *exhib.* R.A. (7), 'Landscape'. R.A. 1793, 'Portrait of a Horse' and 'Portrait of Saltram'.

***GARRARD, GEORGE, A.R.A.** (b. 1760, 31st May; d. Brompton 1826, 8th October). Pupil of S. Gilpin and R.A. Schools. Painter and sculptor. Married daughter of Sawrey Gilpin (1733–1807); Samuel Whitbread, the brewer, was his patron. *coll.* Lt.-Col. J. L. B. Leicester-Warren (1); Mr. and Mrs. Paul Mellon, U.S.A. (1); Sir Joshua Rowley, Bt. (1); S. H. Whitbread Collection (2). *exhib.* R.A. (215); B.I. (14); S.S. (9). *repr.* 'A Book of Sporting Painters', Shaw Sparrow.

GARRARD, R. H., Junior (op. 1814). Son of George Garrard, A.R.A. Knightsbridge address. *exhib.* R.A. 1814, 'Portrait of Well-Known Hunter Bred nr. Worcester', the property of S. Shepherd.

GARRATT, SAM (b. Barwell, Leics.; living in 1934). Formerly a bootmaker. Painter of landscapes, marines and street scenes, etc. Educated Leicester School of Art. *exhib.* R.A. 1914, 'Coursing on the Dorset Downs'.

GAUDIER-BRZESKA, HENRI (b. 1891, d. 1915). *coll.* Bedford, Cecil Higgins, Mus. (1); London, Tate Gallery, pen-and-ink sketches, 'A Wolf'; 'A Dog'; 'Man on a Horse'. Others of a Lion, a Tiger, Leopard, Puma, Bison, Vultures.

GEAR, J. (op. 1815–1821). Marine painter to the Duke of Sussex. Aquatinted after his own works two sets of prints of angling, coursing, fox-hunting and shooting. *exhib.* R.A. (4), 'Seapieces'.

GEORGE, W. PETTITT (op. 1852–1854). Brethwaite address. *exhib.* B.I. (1); S.S. (8), 'Landscape', some with fishing interest.

GERICAULT, JEAN LOUIS ANDRE THEODORE (b. Rouen 1791, d. 1824). Pupil of Carl Vernet and Guerin. Painted horses, etc. Visited England 1820–1822. Made many lithographs of horses and scenes of the poverty in London streets. Painted two pictures of the Derby.

GESSNER, JOHANN CONRAD (b. Zurich 1764, 2nd October; d. there 1826, 8th May). Studied Dresden Academy. Visited Italy 1787. Came to England 1796 and returned to Zurich in 1804. Learned lithography from Senefelder. *coll.* London, V. and A. Museum (4 drawings); British Museum (1). *exhib.* R.A. (24), in 1797, 'Horses frightened by Lightning'; 'A Bear Hunt'; 'A Farriery'; 'Hunting'; 1802, 'Hunting'.

GIBB, T. H. (op. 1885). 'Otter Hunting on the Esk', S&D 1885, sold at Sotheby's 28th October 1964 (184).

GIBBS, J. F. (op. 1854–1858). *exhib.* B.I. (4), Sporting.

GIFFORD, JOHN. 'Gun Dogs and dead game in a wooded Landscape' was sold at Christie's 16th October 1964 and 'A Pony with three sporting dogs and dead game' on 22nd January 1965.

GILBERT, JOSEPH FRANCIS (b. 1792, d. 1855). Resided at Chichester. Shaw Sparrow gives his name as 'John', Grant and Graves 'Joseph'. Exhibited from Portsmouth address. His painting of 'Goodwood Racecourse' was engraved. *exhib.* R.A. (6); B.I. (5); S.S. (12); V.E. (5), 'Landscape'.

GILBERT, Sir JOHN, R.A. (b. Blackheath 1817, 21st July; d. 1897, 5th October). Pupil of George Lance. *coll.* London, Guildhall A.G., 'Landscape with Hunting Party'; Preston, H. M. and A.G., 'Stage Coach of Last Century', signed 1855; illustrated in catalogue of Newsham Bequest 1884. P.O.U. 'After the Hunt'.

GILES, Major GODFREY DOUGLAS (b. Newmarket 1857, 8th November; d.). Painter of military and battle subjects, possibly some sporting. In army in India. Visited Paris. Benezit gives name as 'Geoffrey Douglas'. *exhib.* R.A. (5); S.S. (1); G.G. (2); V.E. (1); Salon 1885.

GILES, J. D. Mentioned by Shaw Sparrow. No details given.

GILES, JAMES WILLIAM, R.S.A. (b. Glasgow 1801, 4th January; d. Aberdeen 1870, 6th October). Resident in Aberdeen and Edinburgh. Said to have visited Italy with his relative John West Giles. *exhib.* R.A. (2); B.I. (80); S.S. (13), 'Landscape'. *auct.* Christie's, 25/26th April 1940, A. N. Gilbey Collection, 'Three Young Anglers Fishing in a Highland River', S&D 1830. Shaw Sparrow mentions the following pictures untraced: 'A Day's Fishing 1840'; 'The Angler's Evening 1844'; 'The Rod 1846'; 'Playing a Fish on the Findhorn 1853'; 'The Pet Pool 1856'; 'Good Sport, Salmonidae of Scotland 1863'; 'Salmon Pool at Kinloch Leven 1865'.

GILES, JOHN WEST (op. 1830–1864). Painter and lithographer residing Aberdeen. Visited Rome with James William Giles. *exhib.* R.A. (6); B.I. (5); S.S. (9). R.A. 1848, 'Hounds at Fault'.

GILL, CHARLES (op. 1772–1819). Working at Sir Joshua Reynolds. Painted portraits, etc. *exhib.* R.A. (14), 'Portraits'. In R.A. 1781, 'Portrait of Spanish Dog and Terrier'; 'Portrait of Indian Greyhound'; 'Portrait of a Foxdog'.

GILL, EDMUND, EDWYN or **EDWIN** (op. 1810–1835). These are probably the same man. Ackermann's had three coaching paintings signed Edmd Gill dated 1835. There are also a set of very rare hunting prints engraved by J. Pollard in 1819 after E. Gill Esq. *exhib.* R.A. (1), 1810, 'Evening, Wearied Sportsmen'. *auct.* Christie's, A. N. Gilbey Collection, 25/26th April 1940, 'An Angling Party' and 'Anglers Refreshing', humorous figure subjects, a pair, S&D 1812.

GILL, E. W. (op. 1843–1868). Hereford address. Painted portraits, still-life, and sport. *exhib.* R.A. (16); B.I. (3); S.S. (1). His 1847, 1851, 1854 and 1855 R.A. exhibits were all dead game-birds. *repr.* 'Foxhunt—The Death Postponed', colour plate, 'British Sporting Artists', Shaw Sparrow. *auct.* Sotheby's, 29th July 1964, 'James M. Hopton with his Gun and Dogs at Dulas, c. 1845'.

GILL, F. T. (op. 1847). London address. *exhib.* B.I. (1), Hunting Scene.

GILLARD, W. (op. 1850–1856). Working at Liverpool, Chester, London, and Dublin. *coll.* Dr. H. J. Taylor (the late), 'Dead Game', *exhib.* Preston H.M. and A.G. 1943; 'Spaniel and Dead Game', *exhib.* Preston H.M. and A.G. 1943. *repr* in catalogue.

GILLETT, G. (op. 1862–1871). Melton Mowbray address. *exhib.* B.I. (7); S.S. (1), Sporting.

GILLRAY, JAMES (b. Chelsea 1757, d. London 1815, buried St. James's, Piccadilly, 7th June). Caricaturist, some with angling interest. *repr.* 'Angling in British Art', Shaw Sparrow. 'Sheridan's Fishing Party', p. 143.

GILPIN, SAWREY, R.A., F.S.A. (b. Carlisle 1733, d. Brompton 1807). Pupil of Samuel Scott. Early patron was the Duke of Cumberland. President Incorporated Society of Artists 1774. Painted horses, dogs, hunting subjects, and some historical pieces. His daughter married George Garrard, the animal painter. One of his sons was a drawing master and water-colour painter. *coll.* Cambridge, Fitzwilliam Museum (1); London, R.A. (1); City of York A.G. (1); H.M. The Queen (7); The Earl of Albemarle (1); Sir Maurice Bromley-Wilson, Bt. (the late) (1); Lord Emlyn (1); Lord Exeter (1); Mrs. Merian Leader (1); Mr. and Mrs. Paul Mellon, U.S.A. (2); Sir Clive Milnes-Coates (1); Major S. Whitbread (1). *exhib.* R.A. (36); S.A. (83); B.I. (1). *repr.* 'Sporting Pictures of England', Guy Paget, 1945; 'Apollo', April 1963. *lit.* Pilkington's 'A General Dictionary of Painters'; 'William Gilpin and Samuel Rogers', Sidney Barbier.

GLASCOTT, S. (Glasscott—Shaw Sparrow) (op. 1833–1852). Brighton address. *exhib.* R.A. (1); B.I. (1); S.S. (16); V.E. (1), 'Sporting'.

GLENDENNING, A. A. (op. 1891). *auct.* Sotheby's, 11th November 1964 (118), 'Anglers by a Mountain Waterfall', S&D (18) '91.

GLINDONI, HENRY GILLARD, A.R.W.S. (b. London 1852, d.). Water-colour painter. *exhib.* London and Liverpool. R.A. (29); S.S. (71); O.W.C.S. (51); V.E. (23), 'Figures'. *auct.* Christie's, 21st July 1961 (16), 'The Lump of Sugar', water-colour, S&D 1883.

GODDARD, GEORGE BOUVERIE (b. Wiltshire 1832, d. Brook Green, London, 1886). Working in London 1849; Salisbury 1851; London 1857. *exhib.* R.A. (24); S.S. (3); G.G. (1); V.E. (6). R.A. 1856, 'Hunters', property of D. Morrison; 1857, 'Eric', a Skye Terrier, property of the Hon. Mrs. Sidney Herbert, Wilton House; 'Favourite', property of Alfred Morrison, High Sheriff of Wilts.; 1868, 'Home to Die, An Afternoon Foxhunt' with the Cotswolds; 1869, 'Gone to Ground'; 1875, 'Lord Wolverton's Bloodhounds'; 1876, 'Colt Hunting in the New Forest'.

GOLD (op. 1782). *exhib.* F.S. (2), Horses and a Dog.

***GOOCH, THOMAS** (b. 1750, d. 1802) (Grant, op. 1777–1802). Pupil of Sawrey Gilpin in 1777. Lived in London and retired in 1802 to Lyndhurst in the New Forest. Painted mostly animals and vehicles. *coll.* Major Sir Reginald Macdonald-Buchanan (1); Mr. and Mrs. Paul Mellon, U.S.A. *exhib.* R.A. (76); S.A. (4); F.S. (1). *lit.* Grant, 'Old English Landscape Painters', Vol. 4, p. 293, fig. 307.

GOOD, JOHN WILLIS (op. 1870–1873). A sculptor. The following R.A. exhibits are possibly paintings: R.A. 1870, 'Putting Hounds into Cover'; 1873, 'Prince of Wales', a celebrated Clydesdale horse, property of Lawrence Drew; 'Before the Race'; 'After the Race'.

GOOD, THOMAS SWORD (b. Berwick-on-Tweed 1789, d. 1872). In London in 1822–23. Painted landscape, fishermen and humorous subjects. *coll.* Fitzwilliam Museum (3); Nottingham A.G. (1); Tate Gallery (3); V. and A. Museum (1). *exhib.* R.A. (19); B.I. (43); S.S. (2). *lit.* 'English Art in Public Galleries', 1888 (a memoir); Grant, 'Old English Landscape Painters', Vol. 7, p. 609.

GOODE, JOHN (op. 1835). Adderbury address. *exhib.* S.S. (2), 'Sporting'.

GOODE, W. E. (op. 1845–1866). Adderbury address. *exhib.* B.I. (4); S.S. (4). The exhibits at B.I. included, in 1864, 'Otter Hunting'; 1865, 'Boys Ferretting Rabbits'; 1866, 'Otter Hounds'.

GORDON, GODFREY JERVIS, 'Jan', R.B.A. (b. Finchampstead 1882, 11th March; d. 1944). Painter, etcher, lithographer, writer, and art critic. Educated Marlborough. *exhib.* Preston H.M. and A.G., 'British Sporting Paintings' 1943: 'They Still Play Bowls'; 'Snooker at the old "Savage" '; 'The Mark'.

GOULDSMITH, HARRIOT (*see* MRS. ARNOLD)

GRANT, A. (op. 1786–1789). His painting, 'Royal Hunt at Windsor', engraved by S. Fores 1786. *exhib.* R.A. (2), 'Landscape'.

GRANT, DUNCAN (b. Rothiermurchus, Invernesshire, 1885; living). *coll.* London, Tate Gallery, 'Football 1911'.

GRANT, Sir FRANCIS, P.R.A. (b. 1803, d. 1878; b. Kilgraston 1810, Benezit, others Edinburgh 1803, d. Melton Mowbray 1878). Some say London. A portrait painter, many with sporting interest. The Glasgow Art Gallery catalogue 1935 gives his birthplace as Kilgraston, Perthshire, and says he died at Melton Mowbray. *coll.* J.Campbell of Saddel (1); Earl of Cromer (1); Viscount Errington (1); Earl of Kintore (1); Major Sir Reginald Macdonald-Buchanan (1); David Baird Newbyth (1); The Duke of Rutland (1); The Hon. Mrs. G. Walsh (1). *exhib.* R.A. (253); B.I. (7); S.S. (9); G.G. (3), 'Portraits'. *repr.* 'Hunt Breakfast scene at Melton', in colour.

GRAY (op. 1783). London address. A George Gray (b. 1758, d. 1819) visited Poland and North America. *exhib.* F.S. (4), two of Horses, one of Fowls, and a Landscape.

GRAY, H. BARNARD (Graves and Grant), F. Barnard (Shaw Sparrow) (op. 1844–1871). London address. *exhib.* R.A. (18); B.I. (41); S.S. (36); V.E. (53), 'Sporting'. The exhibits at the R.A. included: 1845, 'Retriever and Pheasant'; 1851, 'Retrieving'; 1857, 'A Favourite Trout Stream'.

GREAVES, WALTER (b. Chelsea 1846, d. London 1930). Son of a Thames-side boatman. Adopted as protegé by Whistler. *coll.* London, Tate Gallery, 'Hammersmith Bridge on Boat Race Day', c. 1862. *repr.* 'English Painting', Mark Roskill, colour plate. *exhib.* Goupil Gallery, London, 1911.

GREEN, AARON (op. 1863–1871). An Alfred H. Green, painter of animals, was working at Birmingham 1844–1862, and an Amos Green, c. 1760, d. 1807, was in Birmingham 1764 and later in Bath. *coll.* Hanley Stoke-on-Trent, A.G. and M., 'Derby Day', signed 'Epsom Down 1863, A. Green, 1871'.

GREEN, ROLAND, F.Z.S. (b. Rainham, Kent, 1896, 9th January; living). Well known for his water-colours of game-birds and wild fowl. Executed large frieze in oils for Lord Desborough's shooting lodge. Also illustrator of many bird books. *exhib.* Frequent one-man shows at Ackermann's Galleries, London.

GREEN, STEPHEN (op. 1956). London address. *exhib.* R.A. 1956, 'Eights at Putney'.

GREGORY, EDWARD JOHN, R.A. (b. Southampton 1850, d. Marlow 1909). Studied at South Kensington Schools. *coll.* Lady Lever Art Gallery, Port Sunlight, 'Boulter's Lock, Sunday Afternoon', painted 1895. *exhib.* R.A. 1897; Paris 1900; Glasgow 1901; St. Louis 1904. *coll.* C. J. Galloway, 1905. Water-colour study for the painting in same collection.

GRIERSON, CHARLES MacIVER, R.I. (b. Queenstown, N. Ireland, 1864, 8th December; d.). Exhibitor at R.A., R.H.A., R.I., P.S. *exhib.* R.A. 1893, 'A Game of Marbles'.

GRIFFIER, ROBERT (b. London 1688, d. 1750). Son and pupil of John Griffier, Senior. Painted landscape, hunting and hawking subjects.

GRIFFITHS, JOHN (op. 1869–1904). Newtown, Montgomeryshire, address. Visited India. In Bombay 1869–1893. *exhib.* R.A. 1904, 'Black Buck Hunting in India: the Kill'.

GRIMSTONE, E. (op. 1837–1879). London address. *exhib.* R.A. 1840, 'Bloodhounds and Whelps'; 1841, 'Return from the Chase'; 1843, 'The Dying Hound'; 'Pike'; 1853, 'The Death of "Grafton", a Celebrated Bloodhound'.

GUNTON, W. (op. 1829). *exhib.* S.S. (3), Dogs with Birds of Sport.

GUERIN, Mrs. WILLIAM COLLINGS LUKIS DE, formerly Miss Anna Maria Edmonds (op. 1875–1885). London and Folkestone addresses. *exhib.* R.A. 1875, Partridges; 1876–1880, Flowers.

HACKERT, JOHANN GOTTLIEB (op. 1771–1791). London address and Rome. *exhib.* S.A. (40); R.A. (9), 'Landscape'; R.A. 1773, 'Four Hounds'.

HADLEY, W. H. (op. 1874–1876). Liverpool address. *exhib.* R.A. (2); V.E. (5), 'Landscape'; R.A. 1876, 'A Trout Stream'.

HAGHE, LOUIS, P.R.I. (b. Tournai 1806, 17th March; d. Stockwell 1885, 9th March). A Belgian artist; came to London 1823. Painted water-colours and produced lithographs, including angling subjects, after Charles Landseer. President of the New Water Colour Society 1873. *coll.* V. and A. Museum (22); British Museum (3); Manchester.

HAIGH, A. G. (b. 1870; d. 1962). Painted racehorses, also many of the famous Hunts. A number of his works are at the National Stud.

HALFPENNY, JOSEPH (b. 1748, d. 1811). *exhib.* Frank T. Sabin, London. 'Edward Constable and his Brother Francis Constable of Burton Constable, Yorkshire, Boar Hunting', water-colour. Also painted Angling subjects.

HALL, CLIFFORD (b. 1904, 24th January; living). Portrait, figure and landscape painter. Studied R.A. Schools and Paris. *coll.* Brooklyn, Museum of Fine Art, U.S.A.; London, V. and A. Museum. *auct.* 'A Bull goring a Bull-fighter', sold at Christie's 9th June 1961, S&D (19) 55.

***HALL, HARRY** (op. 1838–1886). Sporting and portrait painter working in London and Newmarket. Well known for his faithful portraits of hunters and thoroughbreds, often varied with incidents of shooting, poaching, ferreting, etc. *coll.* Burnley A.G. (oil, S&D 1861); Cheltenham A.G. (oil, S&D 1861); Major The Hon. H. R. Broughton (oil); Lord Exeter (3 oils); Major Sir Reginald Macdonald-Buchanan (1); Mr. and Mrs. Paul Mellon (oil, S&D 1846); N. C. Selway (1); Charles H. Thieriot, New York (four since sold). *exhib.* R.A. (11); B.I. (17); R.S.B.A. (26); V.E. (1).

HALL, SYDNEY PRIOR (op. 1874–1893). London address. *exhib.* R.A. (7); G.G. (14); N.G. (4); V.E. (21), 'Historical'. R.A. 1878, 'Prince of Wales with the Gaekwar of Baroda witnessing the Elephant Fight at Baroda, Nov. 19, 1875'; 1899, 'Mr. Gladstone playing his evening Game of Backgammon with his Son the Rev. Stephen Gladstone at the Rectory, Hawarden'.

HAMILTON, CHARLES (op. 1831–1867). Kensworth address. *exhib.* R.A. (12); B.I. (22); S.S. (12); V.E. (1). The following sporting paintings were included, at R.A. 1832, 'Persian Sportsman'; 1835, 'The Falconer's Boy'; 1837, 'Robert Oldaker, Huntsman to T. G. S. Sebright, with Horses and Hounds'; 1838, 'The Kensworth Harriers'; B.I. 1833, 'Italian Stable'; 1836, 'French Post Horses'; 1838, 'Hawking'; 1839, 'Persian and Greyhound'.

HAMILTON-RENWICK, LIONEL (b. Warkworth, Northumberland, 1919; living at Upend, near Newmarket). Painter of racehorses and equestrian portraits. *coll.* H.M. The Queen; H.R.H. The Princess Royal; H.H. The Maharajah of Jaipur; H.H. Sultan Mahommed Bey (2); Mrs. Brotherton (2); Mrs. A. Elphinstone (2); Sebastien de Ferranti (2); Mrs. De Havilland; John Ismay ('Santa Claus', 1964 Derby winner) and 2 others; Lord and Lady Hemphill; Commander and Mrs. King, M.F.H. (3); Mrs. Hugh Leggatt (3); Sir Reginald and Lady Macdonald-Buchanan; Mr. and Mrs. Mullion ('Ragusa'); John Olin ('Noblesse'); Countess Chevreau D'Antrigues (2); Count Sielern (2); Hon. Richard Stanley (2); John Straker; Dorian Williams, M.F.H. (2). *exhib.* Fores Gallery; Frost & Reed Ltd.; Walker Galleries.

HAMILTON, WILLIAM, R.A. (b. Chelsea 1751, d. London 1801). London address. *exhib.* R.A. (82), 'Mythological'. *auct.* Christie's, A. N. Gilbey Collection, 25/26th April 1940, 'Summer—A Fishing Scene', S&D 1796, engraved by P. W. Tomkins; 'Children Playing at Hoops, engraved by R. S. Marcuard. *repr.* 'Angling in British Art', Shaw Sparrow; 'Angling and Boudoir Idealism', p. 144; 'Return from Coursing', engraved by A. Cardon 1803.

HANCOCK, CHARLES (b. Marlborough 1795, d. 1868). Sporting painter working at Marlborough, Reading, Tattersalls, London, and Brompton. *coll.* Glasgow A.G. (1); London, Tate Gallery (1); Major The Hon. Henry R. Broughton (1); Major Sir Reginald Macdonald-Buchanan (1); Major Guy Paget (1). *exhib.* R.A. (23); B.I. (55); S.S. (47); N.W.C.S. (9); V.E. (12).

HAND, THOMAS (op. 1790, d. 1804). Pupil of George Morland. *exhib.* S.A. (1); R.A. (21), 'Landscape'. R.A. 1794, 'Interior of a Stable'; 1796, 'Drawing a Cover'; 1801, 'Four Pictures of Fox Hunting'; 1802, 'First Shot in September'; 'Drawing a Cover in Northamptonshire'.

HANKES, J. F. (op. 1838–1859). London address. *exhib.* R.A. (19); B.I. (5); S.S. (9), 'Scriptural'. R.A. 1855, 'Angling'.

HARDCASTLE, Miss CHARLOTTE (op. 1852–1866). London address. *exhib.* R.A. (9); B.I. (4); S.S. (12);, 'Still-life'. R.A. 1855, 'Snipes'; 1856, 'Pheasants'; 1864, 'A Teal'; 1866, 'A Plover'.

HARDING, JAMES DUFFIELD, R.W.S. (b. Deptford 1798, d. Barnes 1863; Grant says b. 1797). Son of an artist. Studied under Samuel Prout. Painted in oils, water-colours, and produced lithographs. *coll.* Glasgow A.G., 'Highland River in Spate—Trout Fishing'. *exhib.* R.A. (35); B.I. (8); S.S. (17); O.W.C.S. (143); V.E. (5); R.A. 1844, 'Anglers on the Loire'. *lit.* Grant's Dictionary.

HARDMAN, Mrs. THOMAS (EMMA LOUISE) (op. 1888–1934). Northaw, Herts., and Potter's Bar addresses. Wife of Thomas Hawthorn Hardman, an artist. *exhib.* R.A. (2); S.S. (7); N.W.C.S. (3), 'Flowers'. Included at R.A. 1902, 'Wild Fowl Shooting, an Anxious Moment'.

HARDMAN, J. (op. 1812). *exhib.* R.A. (2), Horses.

HARDY, CHARLES (op. 1815). Drew title page, 'Trophies of Angling' for 'The Angler's Guide', 1815.

***HARDY, HEYWOOD, A.R.W.S., R.E.** (op. 1861–1903). Painted in oils and water-colours, some with sport and angling interest. 'At the Cross Roads', signed, and 'The Stirrup Cup', signed, were auctioned at Sotheby's 11th November 1964. *exhib.* R.A. (31); B.I. (9); S.S. (16); O.W.C.S. (7); G.G. (22); N.G. (5); V.E. (62), 'Animals'. Included in R.A. 1893, 'Grouse Shooting'.

***HARDY, JAMES, Junior, R.I.** (b. 1832, d. 1889). Bristol address. *coll.* Nuneaton A.G. ('Man, three dogs, gun and game in landscape', S&D 1874); Tryon Gallery, London ('The Keeper's Boy', S&D 1868). *repr.* 'Country Life', 26th September 1963, coloured cover. *exhib.* R.A. (9); B.I. (8); S.S. (46); N.W.C.S. (28); V.E. (28), 'Domestic'. The R.A. exhibits included, 1871, 'Gillie on the Look Out'; 1872, 'Tying up the Game'; 1873, 'Hillman with Deer Hounds'; 1874, 'The English Gamekeeper'; 1875, 'Waiting to collect the Game'; 1885, 'On the Moors'; and 1886, 'Setters and Scotch Game'.

HARGITT, EDWARD, R.I. (op. 1835–1895). Edinburgh and London addresses. Pupil of H. MacCulloch· *exhib.* R.A. (19); B.I. (11); S.S. (1); N.W.C.S. (255); V.E. (53), 'Landscape', some with angling interest· R.A. 1853, 'Park Scene with Fallow Deer; 1881, 'Early Morning in a Deer Forest'.

HARLAND, J. S. His 'Scarborough Steeplechase' acquatinted by J. Harris.

HARPER, THOMAS. A 'T. Harper', London, 1817–1843, exhibited 19 portraits at the R.A. *auct.* Christie's, A. N. Gilbey Collection, 25/26th April 1940, 'Joseph Hornsby Fishing', water-colour.

HARRISON, CLAUDE, A.R.C.A. (b. Leyland 1922, 31st March). Educated Hutton Grammar School. Studied art at Preston Art School (1938–1940); Liverpool (1940–1941); Royal College of Art, London (1947–1949). Works in oil, egg tempera, and pen and wash. Paints conversation pieces and imaginative landscapes. Fabric designer for Morton Sundour Fabrics. *exhib.* R.A. 1955, 'The Anglers'.

***HARRISON, J. C.** (b. Tidworth, Wiltshire, 1898). Started drawing at about six years of age and lived in British Columbia from 1912–1915. Later studied and sketched bird life, learning anatomy from practice of taxidermy. After demobilization at end of 1914–1918 War he studied at Slade School of Art. Visited Scotland regularly and observed the Golden Eagles. Illustrated 'Days with the Golden Eagle', by Seton Gordon. Went to Iceland in 1938 to study bird life and landscape. Wrote and illustrated 'Bird Portraits' and illustrated 'Pheasants of the World', by Jean Delacour, both published by 'Country Life'. At present engaged on illustrations for 'The Birds of Prey of the World', to be published by 'Country Life'. Toured South Africa on three occasions, visiting the Rhodesias, Nyasaland, and Portuguese East Africa. Has lived for many years in Norfolk, painting the rare birds of the Broads and game-birds. *exhib.* The Tryon Gallery, London.

HARVEY, Sir GEORGE, P.R.S.A. (b. St. Ninians, near Stirling, 1806, d. 1876). Began as a bookseller's apprentice. In 1823 moved to Edinburgh, spending two years at the Trustees' Academy. President of the Royal Scottish Academy 1864. *coll.* Edinburgh, National Gallery of Scotland, 'The Bowlers', S&D 1850. Exhibited R.A. 1850, engraved by W. H. Simmons 1866; 'The Curlers', study for the large painting exhibited R.S.A. 1835. *exhib.* R.A. (22); B.I. (1); S.S. (2), 'Historical'. *repr.* 'Angling in British Art', Shaw Sparrow, 'The Rev. Dr. Guthrie angling on Loch Lee', oil, p. 68.

HARWOOD, EDWARD (b. Clonnell 1814, d.). Rugby address. *exhib.* R.A. (1) 1859, 'Winter Scene at Rugby School—Game at Football: 'a Match'.

HASSELL, JOHN (Graves and Grant); **HASSALL** (Shaw Sparrow) (b. 1767, d. 1825, London). Painter and engraver, working in water-colour. *exhib.* R.A. (20); V.E. (1), 'Landscape'. R.A. 1797, 'Salmon Leap at Kennearth, Cardiganshire'.

HAUGH, GEORGE (op. 1777–1818). Doncaster address. *exhib.* R.A. (11); B.I. (9), 'Landscape'. Ackermann Gallery, London, 1930, 'Portrait of Kate, Countess of Effingham, Shooting, 1787'.

HAVELL, EDMUND (op. 1840–1890). A sporting artist, his work includes a painting of the 'Beaufort Hunt'. He also painted with W. H. Hopkins (op. 1853–1890) 'John Hammond's "Laureate" with jockey up, standing on a racecourse, with figures and other racehorses beyond', S&D 1890, sold at Christie's 30th October 1964. Grant's Dictionary of Landscape Painters gives op. 1814–1847. Member of a painter family of six, with them resided at Reading. Painting chiefly in oil. *exhib.* R.A. (4); B.I. (4); R.S.B.A. (2). *coll.* Bristol A.G.; another was in the Hutchinson Sporting Gallery.

HAVELL, GEORGE (op. 1826–1833). Reading and Oxford addresses. His picture, 'The Blenheim leaving Star Hotel, Oxford' was engraved by F. J. Havell. *exhib.* R.A. (4); B.I. (1); S.S. (5), 'Interiors'. R.A. 1833, 'Foxes Disputing a Prize'.

HAVELL, WILLIAM, R.W.S. (b. Reading 1782, 9th February; d. Kensington 1857, 16th December; buried Kensal Green). Son of a drawing master. Visited China and India (1817–1825). *exhib.* R.A. (103); B.I. (42); S.S. (32); O.W.C.S. (154), 'Landscape'. *auct.* Christie's, A. N. Gilbey Collection, 25/26th April 1940, 'Lady and Gentleman Fishing', water-colour.

HAWKINS, WATERHOUSE (op. 1832–1841). London address. *exhib.* R.A. (5); B.I. (4); S.S. (16); N.W.C.S. (1), 'Sporting'. R.A. 1833, 'A Perch'; 'A Chevin or Chub'; 1839, 'Wounded Pheasant'; 1840, 'A Flemish Pheasant'.

HAYCOCK, WASHINGTON (op. 1862–1864). London address. *exhib.* S.S. (5), 'Sporting'.

HAYDON, W. and LOCKE, J. Locke probably a member of a family of painters of Norbury (op. 1812). *auct.* Sotheby's, 2nd March 1960 (172), 'King Charles Spaniels with a gun in a landscape'.

HAYES, MICHAEL ANGELO, R.H.A. (b. Waterford 1820, 25th July; d. Dublin 1877, 31st December). Son of Edward Hayes. 'Car Driving in the South of Ireland', six pictures, engraved by J. Harris 1836. If date is correct, the artist was only 16 years of age at the time. *exhib.* R.A. (1); S.S. (2); N.W.C.S. (35); V.E. (3), 'Military'.

HAYLLAR, JAMES, R.B.A. (b. Chichester 1829, 3rd January; d.). Studied with F. S. Cary at the R.A. Afterwards worked in Italy. Exhibited last at the R.A. in 1893, from an address at Wallingford. The Misses E., J., and K. Hayllar exhibited at the R.A. in 1893 from the same address. *coll.* M.C.C. Gallery, Lord's, 'A Cricketer'; Nottingham A.G. (2). *exhib.* R.A. (58); B.I. (23); S.S. (217); N.W.C.S. (5); V.E. (64), 'Figures'.

***HAYMAN, FRANCIS, R.A.** (b. Exeter 1708, d. London 1776, 2nd February). Pupil of Robert Brown. Illustrator and painter of conversation and other pictures. *coll.* M.C.C. Gallery, London, 'A Cricket Match 1743'. *repr.* Grant, Vol. 2, pl. 45.

HAYTER, JOHN (b. London 1800, d. 1891). Son of Charles Hayter. *exhib.* R.A. (129); B.I. (26); S.S. (30); O.W.C.S. (2), 'Portraits'. R.A. 1815, 'The Cricketer—portrait of Master E. Landseer'. Artist only 15 years of age at the time.

HAYTLEY, E. (op. 1752). A portrait of a sportsman with a dog, dated 1752. *exhib.* Spink's, London.

HAZLEHURST, E. (op. 1815). His picture, 'Knutsford Racecourse', aquatinted by R. G. Reeve 1815.

HEAPHY, THOMAS, R.B.A. (op. 1797–1873). London address. Member of the Old Water Colour Society. *exhib.* R.A. (60); B.I. (9); S.S. (14); O.W.C.S. (42); N.W.C.S. (8), 'Portraits'. R.A. 1812, 'Heron Shooting'; 1813, 'Trout, Grayling, Crayfish, etc.'.

HEARNE, THOMAS, F.S.A. (b. Brinkworth 1744, d. London 1817, 13th April). Studied under Woolett, the engraver. Visited West Indies with Lord Lavington. London again 1777. *exhib.* S.A. (42); F.S. (12); R.A. (24), 'Landscape'. *repr.* 'Shooting', 'Coursing', 'Angling', 'Fox-hunting', engraved by W. Bryon 1810.

HEATH, HENRY, Junior (c. 1850). Published 'Angling Reminiscences' with five plates London c. 1850. The following were lithographed: 'Barbel Fishing at Twickenham'; 'Roach Fishing at Broxbourne'; 'Perch Fishing at Teddington'; 'Jack Fishing at Lea Bridge'. *lit.* 'Angling in British Art', Shaw Sparrow.

HEATH, JAMES, A.R.A. (b. London 1757, 19th April; d. there 1834, 15th November). An engraver *exhib.* S.A. (3); R.A. (26), 'Engraving', angling interest.

HEATH, WILLIAM (b. 1785, d. Hampstead 1840, 7th April). Painted coaching scenes at Windsor, engraved 1827. Made sketches which he lithographed of Wild Sports of Scotland, Island of Islay. Otter Hunting and Stag Hunting. *coll.* The Lord Fairhaven (2). *repr.* 'Angling in British Art', Shaw Sparrow. Fishing drawing for lithograph, p. 113. *lit.* 'Windsor Castle thro's three Centuries', Bunt, p. 66 (Lewis, 1949).

HEMSLEY, WILLIAM, R.B.A. (b. London 1817, d. 1906). *exhib.* R.A. (20); B.I. (28); S.S. (163); N.W.C.S. (1); V.E. (30), 'Domestic'. *auct.* 'The Start of the Race', sold at Christie's 9th October, 1964.

HEMY, CHARLES NAPIER, R.A. (b. Newcastle on Tyne 1841, 24th May; d. Falmouth 1917). Studied School of Art, Newcastle. Painter of marines and sea fishing.

HENDERSON, CHARLES COOPER (b. Chertsey 1803, 14th January; d. Lower Hallford-on-Thames 1877). Painter of coaching scenes in oils and water-colours. *coll.* Bath, Victoria A.G. (2), 'The Bristol to London Coach'; 'The Leeds to London Coach'; Preston H.M. and A.G. (3); Major Sir Reginald Macdonald-Buchanan (57); Major Guy Paget (the late) (1). *exhib.* R.A. (2).

HENDERSON, ELSIE MARIAN (b. 1880, d.). Sculptor, lithographer, mainly wild animal subjects. London address. *coll.* London, Tate Gallery, 'Three Studies of Leopards', B. Chalk; 'A Tiger', B. Chalk.

HENDERSON, JOSEPH, R.S.W. (b. Stanley, Perthshire, 1832, 10th June; d. Ballantrae 1908, 17th July). Studied Trustees' Academy, Edinburgh. Settled in Glasgow in 1852. Painted portraits and marines. *coll.* Glasgow A.G., Sea-piece, 'Boys fishing from a Rock', S&D 1876.

HENDRIE, ROBERT (op. 1867–1868). Eynsford address. *exhib.* R.A. (1); V.E. (1). R.A. 1868, 'Cub-hunting—Noon at Lullingstone'.

HENRY, EDWARD L. (b. 1841, 12th January; d.). Studied New York and Philadelphia Academy In Paris, pupil of R. Fleury and B. Constant. Exhibited from London address. Member of National Academy of America. *exhib.* R.A. (1), 'Black and Tan 1879'; S.S. (2).

HENWOOD, THOMAS (op. 1842), an example by this artist is to be seen in the M.C.C. Gallery, Lord's Cricket Ground, London.

***HERBERT, E. B.** (or **HERBERTE** (b. early 19th century). An English sporting painter. Born during the early part of the 19th century, a period in which fox-hunting was at its height. There were, therefore, many sporting painters and engravers working at this time, among them J. F. Herring, Senior, who helped influence Herbert in his early years. One can also see in his work the style of Widdas. Though he rarely exhibited, he always found patrons for his work, which is certainly well regarded. It is interesting to note that one of his pictures was sold for two hundred dollars in New York in 1946. Signed and dated 1875, 1879 and 1881 paintings, have sold at both Christies and Sotheby's in recent years. Another S&D 1860 sold at Sotheby's 11th May 1966.

HERKOMER, Sir HUBERT, R.A., A.R.W.S., R.I. (b. 1849, d. 1914). A water-colour, 'Got Him!' an angling subject mentioned by Shaw Sparrow. *exhib.* R.A. (87); O.W.C.S. (4); S.S. (2); N.W.C.S. (47); G.G. (45); N.G. (17); V.E. (45), 'Figures'.

***HERRING, BENJAMIN, Senior** (b. 1806, d. 1830). Was a brother of J. F. Herring, Senior, and may have been the Benjamin Herring who married Susanna King in 1826 (26th October) at St. George's, Hanover Square. About eight of his paintings have come on the market, dated c. 1820. One, a copy of Ben Marshall's 'Longwaist', S&D 1827. *coll.* Charles H. Thieriot, New York (two S&D 1827 and 1829). *lit.* 'British Sporting Painters', Shaw Sparrow, 1922.

HERRING, BENJAMIN, Junior (b. 1830, d. 1871). Son of the Elder J. F. Herring. Exhibited from a Tonbridge address 1861–1863. *exhib.* B.I. (4); S.S. (2). B.I. 1861, 'The Cowshed'; 1863, 'The Meeting at the Stile'. His 'Hippia', winner of the 1867 Oaks, is S&D 1867.

HERRING, CHARLES (b. 1828, d. 1856, 1st June). Son of the Elder J. F. Herring. Died aged 28 at Meopham Park, Tonbridge, from malignant scarlet fever. *exhib.* S.S. (1), 'Animals'.

HERRING, JOHN FREDERICK, Junior (op. 1860, d. London 1907, 6th March). Son and pupil of J. F. Herring. Painted many water-colours of field sports. *exhib.* R.A. (3); B.I. (10); S.S. (53); V.E. (4). R.A. 1864, 'Horses and Poultry'; 'Horses, Pigs, etc.'; 1868, 'Horses and Poultry'.

***HERRING, JOHN FREDERICK, Senior** (b. Surrey 1795, d. Tunbridge Wells, 1865, 23rd September). Started as a coach painter and studied under Abraham Cooper and Sawrey Gilpin. London 1818, Lancaster 1826, Doncaster 1830, then London again. Often difficult to distinguish his work from that of his son. *coll.* Aberdeen A.G. (2); Burnley A.G. (one S&D 1850); Cambridge, Fitzwilliam Museum (1, water-colour); Doncaster A.G. (3, one painted aged 20); Dunedin A.G., New Zealand (1); Glasgow A.G. (2); Leamington Spa A.G. (1); Leeds A.G. (1); Leicester A.G. (1 S&D 1854); Liverpool, Walker A.G. (1); London, Guildhall A.G. (1); Tate Gallery (1); V. and A. Museum (1); Nottingham A.G. (2, one S&D 1858); Wolverhamtpon A.G. (3); H.M. The Queen (1); Major The Hon. Henry R. Broughton (3); Lieut. J. S. Clarke, U.S.A. (1); Lord Exeter (1); Lord Fisher (1 S&D 1834); Major Sir Reginald Macdonald-Buchanan (18); Mrs. F. G. McNab (1 S&D 1849); Mrs. Leader (1); Mr. and Mrs. Paul Mellon, U.S.A. (3, one S&D 1826 and one S&D 1833); R. H. Saunders (2 S&D 1839); Chas. H. Thieriot, New York (7). *exhib.* R.A. (8); *repr.* 'Sporting Pictures of England', by Guy Paget, p. 34; 'A Book of Sporting Painters', by Shaw Sparrow, pp. 139, 184, and 185; 'Sporting Magazine, Vol. 6, 1824; 'British Sporting Artists', Shaw Sparrow; 'Lord Woolavington's Collection of Paintings', Sir Theodore Cook, 1927.

HICKIN, GEORGE (op. 1858–1877). Greenwich address. *exhib.* R.A. (7); B.I. (6); S.S. (24); V.E. (26), 'Still Life'. R.A. 1858, 'A Mallard and Snipe'; 1859, 'Dead Game'; 1862, 'Wild Ducks'.

HIGTON, T. (op. 1801–1815). London address. Chiefly a painter of sporting dogs and horses. *exhib.* R.A. (15), including R.A. 1801, 'Horses Going to Water'; 1808, 'Portrait of a Dog, property of Lord Sedley'; 1809, 'Portrait of a Dog'; 1810, 'Portrait of a Dog, property of the Earl of Warwick'; 1811, 'Farriery'; 1812, ' "Crab", a favourite Terrier'; 1813, 'Dogs at Ampthill Park'.

HILL, J. C. (op. 1862). *auct.* Christie's, 28th July 1961, 'A Chestnut Horse standing by a Wall', S&D 1862.

HILL, JAMES JOHN, R.B.A. (b. Birmingham 1811, d. Highgate 1882). *exhib.* R.A. (10); B.I. (5); S.S. (122), 'Rustic Figures'. R.A. 1858, 'A Fisher Boy'. *auct.* Christie's, 25/26th April 1940, A. N. Gilbey Collection, 'The Punt—Children Fishing', S&D 1854. Exhibited R.A. 1855.

HILL, ROWLAND HENRY (b. Halifax 1873, 3rd March; d.). Oil- and water-colour painter. The M.C.C. Gallery, Lord's Cricket Ground, London, have seven pictures by a Roland Hill (op. 1889–1890), probably the same? *exhib.* R.A. (2), 'Architecture'.

HILLS, ROBERT (b. Islington 1769; d. 17 Golden Square, St. James's, London, 1844, 14th May); buried Kensal Green. Pupil of John Gresse. Painter and etcher. *coll.* Cambridge, Fitzwilliam Museum, 38 animal studies. *exhib.* R.A. (44); B.I. (2); O.W.C.S. (600). R.A. 1813, 'Asses'; 1816, 'Fallow Deer'; 1817, 'A Stag and Hind'; 1820, 'The Wounded Stag'; 1821, 'Fallow Deer in Knowle Park'; 'Red Deer'; 1822, 'Red Deer'.

HILTON, T., of York (op. 1805). Racehorse 'Haphazard' by him engraved by J. Whessel 1805.

HILTON, WILLIAM, R.A. (b. Lincoln 1786, 3rd June; d. London 1839, 30th December). Son and pupil of W. Hilton. 'Pike Fishing' and 'A Trout Angler' engraved by H. R. Cook after Hilton. *exhib.* R.A. (31); B.I. (20); S.S. (1), 'Scriptural'. R.A. 1822, 'The Calydonian Hunt'.

HINCKS, S. C. (op. 1858–1867). Bagshot address. *exhib.* B.I. (7); S.S. (2). B.I. 1858, 'The Cover Side'; 1861, 'Deer Stalking in the Highlands'; 1862, 'Time to Start'; 1866, 'Pet Fawns'.

HIXON, WILLIAM J. (op. 1827–1856). *exhib.* R.A. (4); B.I. (10); S.S. (13); V.E. (26), 'Cattle'. R.A. 1856, 'An Arabian Horse in a Farrier's Shop'; B.I., 'Going to the Chase'; 'Oliver Cromwell on Horseback'.

HOBDAY, H. H. (op. 1830). Birmingham. Shaw Sparrow mentions pictures of 'A Dancing Dog' and 'Young Anglers'. *exhib.* R.A. (1); B.I. (4); S.S. (5), 'Sporting'.

HODGES, WALTER PARRY (b. 1760, d. 1845, aged 85). Receiver-General of the County of Dorset. Family name was Parry. Took name of Hodges at request in will of uncle. Apparently did not exhibit in the exhibitions. Known by engravings after his works. 'Hare Hunting, Ware Turnips!', engraved by R. G. Reeve 1836; *repr.* in colour I.C.I. Plastics Division Calendar 1959; 'Beaufort Hunt', nine paintings in water-colour, varnished, sold 1928, bought by Spink & Son; 'Chase and Death of the Roebuck', engraved by R. G. Reeve 1834; 'Yellowham Wood and The Cocktails Done', engraved by Alken. *lit.* 'The Field', 25th October 1923.

HODGINS, HENRY (op. 1778, d. 1796). Cricketing Scene. At Lord's.

HODGSON, R. (op. 1780–1787). A painting of a Fighting Cock was in the Hutchinson Collection.

HODGSON, W. (op. 1838–1841). *exhib.* R.A. (3). R.A. 1838, 'Portrait of a Pony property of the Earl, of Erroll'; 1841, 'Cora, Favourite Dog, property of the Hon. C. A. Murray'; 'Punch, a Horse, property of the Rev. Douglas Veitch'.

HOFLAND, THOMAS CHRISTOPHER (b. Worksop 1777, d. Leamington 1843, 3rd January). Pupil of John R. Rathbone. At Derby; London 1811. Visited Italy. Living at Kew 1799–1806. Drew plants at Kew Gardens. Wrote and illustrated the 'Angler's Guide' 1839. *coll.* Commander Robert T. Bower, R.N., 'Grouse Shooting', exhibited Preston 1943. *exhib.* R.A. (72); B.I. (141); S.S. (118); V.E. (8), 'Landscape'. *repr.* 'Angling in British Art', Shaw Sparrow, 'Trout Fishing in Lock Awe', colour plate, p. 169.

HOGARTH, WILLIAM (b. London 1697, 10th November; d. there 1764 (25th October). Apprenticed to a goldsmith and studied engraving. Also studied St. Martin's Lane Academy. Painted groups and conversation pieces. Married the daughter of Sir James Thornhill painted and engraved moral subjects. Visited Paris 1743 and 1748. *coll.* P.O.U., 'The Pascall Family with Mr. Pascall Angling'. *repr.* 'Angling in British Art', Shaw Sparrow, colour plate, p. 200.

HOLD, ABEL (op. 1849–1871). Bromley address, previously Barnsley. *exhib.* R.A. (16) B.I. (1); S.S. (1). R.A. 1850, 'Black Grouse, Woodcock and Snipes'; 1852, 'Study of Game and Dogs'; 1854, 'Red Grouse, Mallard, Woodcock'; 'Pheasants, Hare, Partridge, etc.'; 1863, 'High Bred Pheasants, Woodcock and Hare'; 1867, 'Red Grouse, Ducks and Snipes; 1871, 'Dead Snipe'.

HOLIDAY, GILBERT JOSEPH (b. London 1879, January; d. 1938/9). Living at East Moseley 1936. Studied R.A. Schools. Painted pictures of hunting, polo matches and soldiering. Died from a fall with the Woolwich Drag and wounds received in the first World War. *auct.* 'The Huntsman', sold at Sotheby's 6th October 1960. *exhib.* R.A., R.I., P.S., and Sporting Gallery. *lit.* 'Sporting Pictures of England', by Guy Paget.

HOLLAMS, F. M. (MRS. C. L. FOX). Horse portraits. Clients include the Hon. Edward Lascelles, Earl Beatty, Earl of Sefton, Lord Cornwallis. *exhib.* Ackermann's Galleries, London, 1934, loan exhibition, mainly horse portraits. Painter allegedly of 3,000 horse portraits.

HOLLINS, JOHN, A.R.A. (b. Birmingham 1798, 1st January; d. London 1855, 7th March). *exhib.* R.A. (101); B.I. (35); S.S. (6); N.W.C.S. (1), 'Historical'. R.A. 1853, 'Gillies and a Young Heron'; 'Grouse Shooting—Bridge of Carr, Invernesshire, with Portraits of M. T. Bass, M.P., his Gamekeeper and Gillies'; 1854, 'Salmon Fishing on Loch Awe' (with F. R. Lee, R.A.).

HOLT, J. (op. 1828–1863). Painter of views and pictures of sport. *exhib.* R.A. (2); R.S.B.A. (17).

HOLYOAKE, WILLIAM, R.B.A. 'Derby Day at Epsom', one of a pair, one signed, sold at Sotheby's 13th July 1966.

HONE, NATHANIEL (b. 1718, d. 1784), painted portraits of sportsmen.

HOOK, JAMES CLARKE, R.A. (b. London 1819, 21st November; d. Churt, Surrey, 1907, 14th April). Studied R.A. Schools. *exhib.* R.A. (161); B.I. (8); S.S. (1); G.G. (1); V.E. (3), 'Sea-pieces'. R.A. 1871, 'Salmon Trappers, Norway'; 1873, 'Fishing by Proxy'; 1877, 'He Shot a Fine Shoot'; 1886, 'The Salmon Pool'; 1887, 'Tickling Trout'; 1889, 'The Fowler's Pool'; 1900, 'A Surrey Trout Stream'. *repr.* 'Angling in British Art', Shaw Sparrow, colour plate p. 48; 'A Wily Angler watching his Red Float'.

HOPKINS, WILLIAM H. (op. 1853–1890; d. 1892, 18th October). Keynsham, Bath, address. He collaborated with Edmund Havell in a sporting painting. *exhib.* R.A. (37); B.I. (21); S.S. (24); V.E. (21), 'Sporting'. R.A. 1864, 'Guy Mannering and Ghillie Cullum, Favourite Hunters of H.R.H. the Prince Consort'; 1868, 'Late in the Grousing Season'; 1874, 'A Hunting we will Go'; 1876, 'Her Majesty's Buckhounds, etc. (Figures by Edmund Havell)'; 1877, 'A Holloa Forward and Killed in the Open'; 1879, 'Forrard Away'; 1890, 'The Fitzwilliam Hounds'.

HORLOR, GEORGE W. (op. 1849–1891). Cheltenham address, later Birmingham and Brentford. *coll.* Cheltenham A.G., 'Portraits of Favourites, Cheltenham 1851', S&D 1891; 'Arthur Edwin May, M.P., in dress of Cheltenham Stag Hounds of which he was Master 1860, with horse and hounds', S&D 1852. *exhib.* R.A. (19); B.I. (35); S.S. (33); V.E. (7), 'Animals'. His B.I. exhibits included, 1853, 'The Keeper's Home'; 1858, 'The Pride of the Moors'; 1860, 'Black Game'; 'Grouse Shooting'; 1861, 'Setters on the Moor'; 1862, 'Ready for Sport'. The R.A. exhibits, including 1854, 'Collie Dog and Rabbit'; 1855, 'A Day's Sport in Perthshire'; 1856, 'The Shepherd's Dogs'; 1859, 'Highland Sport'; 1863, 'Highland Sport'; 'Sporting Dogs'; 1864, 'Return from the Moors'; 1865, 'Denizens of the Moors'; 1866, 'Wild Duck Shooting'; 1890, 'A Shooting Pony'.

HOWARD, FRANK (b. London 1805, d. Liverpool 1866, 29th June). Son and pupil of Henry Howard and Lawrence. Painted portraits, etc. His 'The Derby 1833' was aquatinted by E. Duncan. *exhib.* R.A. (43); B.I. (26); S.S. (9), 'Mythological'. The B.I. exhibit for 1831 was 'Numidian Lion Hunt', and in 1832 'Lion Hunt'. *repr.* 'Game and Wild Animals of Southern Africa', 1840.

HOWE, B. A. (op. 1844–1857). London address. *exhib.* S.S. (3), 'Sporting'.

HOWE, JAMES (b. Stirling 1780, 30th August; d. Edinburgh 1836, 11th July). John Bell, art dealer, of Aberdeen had a 'Hunting Scene' ex Carberry Towers Collection. Reproduced in 'Country Life' 28th September 1961 (advert.). Engraved 'Foxhunting' and 'Racing', by Lizars after Howe. 'Mr. Fleming of Barochan Castle with John Anderson, one of the last of the old Scottish Falconers and William Harvey, his Assistant Falconer'. Mezzotint by Charles Turner after Howe.

HOWELL, PETER (b. 1932, living). At age of 8 used to ride out with the Hon. George Lambton's string. Leaving school spent some time in a racing yard at Lambourn. Rose during racing career as a National Hunt Jockey. During this time drew extensively, mainly equestrian subjects. In 1969 moved to Cornwall to paint full-time. First exhibited at Wadebridge, then at Newmarket. Then Ackermann's became his sole agent and his first London exhibition was held under their auspices in 1972. Now living on the Norfolk Broads. Recently one of his works 'The Eighth Pole, Aiken Training Track' was shown in New York by Criswick Associates.

HOWITT, SAMUEL (b. c. 1765, d. London 1822). A prolific and excellent painter and etcher of animals and sporting scenes. *coll.* Birmingham A.G. (2); London, V. and A. Museum (49 drawings); National Art Collections Fund (a Stag Hunt); Manchester, Whitworth A.G. (Otter Hunting); Preston H.M. and A.G. (collection of etchings); Gilbert Davis (1). *exhib.* R.A. 1784, 'A Hunting Piece'; 1793, 'Jacques and the Deer'; 'A Fox Hunt'; 1800, 'A Deer'. *repr.* 'Angling in British Art' (Shaw Sparrow), p. 162; 'Sporting Pictures of England' (Guy Paget), p. 30; 'Field Sports of the East', 1807; Orme's 'British Field Sports' (1807–8); 'British Sportsman' (1812). *lit.* 'Book of British Etching' (Shaw Sparrow).

HUBBARD, B. (op. 1839–1864). Louth address. Painted horses and dogs, usually with portraits of their owners. *exhib.* R.A. (7); these included in 1839 'Bob, a favourite Pony, property of J. D. Naull'; 'Bustle, a favourite Spaniel, property of Philip Meredith', in 1842; 'Nimrod, a favourite pony, property of Rev. William Wright, Rector of Healing, Lincs., in 1864'.

HUBBARD, W. (op. 1867). Crayford address. *coll.* Lord's (1). *exhib.* B.I. (1); S.S. (4), 'Flowers'.

HUDSON, THOMAS (b. Devonshire 1701; d. Twickenham 1779, 26th January). Son-in-law of Jonathan Richardson. Portrait painting in 1733. In London 1741. Had as a pupil Sir Joshua Reynolds (1741–1743). *coll.* London, M.C.C. Gallery, Lords (2); Leicester A.G. (1).

HUGGINS, WILLIAM (b. Liverpool 1820; d. Chester 1884, 25th February). At New Ferry, Cheshire, and Liverpool 1842–1862. Chester 1863. Animal painter. *coll.* Liverpool, Walker A.G. (31); Preston, H.M. and A.G. (4); Lady Ascroft (1). *exhib.* R.A. (31); 1854, 'A Foraging Party'; 'Thomas Gorton, Master of the Holcombe Hunt'; B.I. (8); R.S.B.A. (1).

HUGHES, WILLIAM (b. Lanarkshire 1842; d. Brighton 1901, 18th December). Pupil of Lance and William Hunt. Painted flowers, fruit and game, including 'A Sport in the Olden Time' (R.A. 1875). *exhib.* R.A. (30); B.I. (8); S.S. (71); G.G. (31); V.E. (21).

HULK, WILLIAM F. (op. 1875–1898). *exhib.* R.A. (45); S.S. (43); N.W.C.S. (13); V.E. (29), 'Cattle'. No sporting pictures in R.A.

HULL, EDWARD (op. 1823 – 1877). London address. Painter and lithographer. Produced lithographs of Hunting, Coaching, etc. *exhib.* R.A. (7); S.S. (18), 'Domestic'. No sporting in R.A.

HUME, Mrs. THOMAS O. (*née* MISS EDITH DUNN) (op. 1862–1892). Painted fishing subjects. *exhib.* as Dunn from Worcester 1862–1867; B.I. (3); S.S. (4); V.E. (6); as Hume from London, R.A. (32); S.S. (14); N.W.C.S. (3); G.G. (2); V.E. (22), 'Domestic'. R.A. 1874, 'Fishing on the Old Pier Head'; 1876, 'Unhooking the Fish'; 1880, 'Just Landed'; 1884, 'Fisher Children'.

HUNT, CECIL ARTHUR, M.A., LL.B., V.P.R.W.S. (b. Torquay 1873, living 1964). Landscape painter in oil- and water-colour. *coll.* Huddersfield A.G., 'A Difficult Approach'.

HUNT, WALTER (op. 1881–1910). London address. *coll.* London, Tate Gallery, 'The Dog in the Manger', Chantrey Purchase. *exhib.* R.A. (19), 'Animals', including R.A. 1888, 'Otter Hunting—the Find'; 1894, 'Bolting the Otter'; 1896, 'Off the Scent'; 1901, 'Breaking Cover'; 1910, 'Otter Hounds in Full cry'.

HUNT, WILLIAM HENRY (b. London 1790, 28th March; d. there 1864, 10th February). Pupil of John Varley, painter of figures, flowers, and still-life. *coll.* Lord's (1). *auct.* 'A Duck Decoy' (Sotheby's, 11th September 1964).

HUNTER, COLIN, A.R.A., R.I., R.S.W. (b. Glasgow 1841, 16th July; d. London 1904, 24th September). Painter of fishing subjects and marines. *exhib.* R.A. (67); S.S. (1); N.W.C.S. (1); G.G. (1); N.G. (8); V.E. (14), 'Sea-pieces' R.A. 1874, 'Salmon Stake-nets'; 1885, 'Salmon Fishers'; 'The Girl who Baits the Line'; 1886, 'Summer Fishing'; 1903, 'Salmon Fishers'.

HUNTER, ROBERT (op. 1790). A fine portrait of sportsman with gun and dog is reported by Messrs. Arthur Ackermann & Son.

HUTCHISON, Sir WILLIAM O., Hon.R.A., R.S.A., R.P., Hon.LL.D., P.R.S.A. (1950–1959) (b. Kirkcaldy 1889, 2nd July; living). Educated Rugby. Studied Edinburgh College of Art. Portrait and landscape painter. *exhib* R.A. 1933, 'Derby Day'.

***IBBETSON, JULIUS CAESAR** (b. Fulneek, Leeds, 1759, 29th December; d. Masham 1817, 13th October). Apprenticed to a ship painter at Hull. Went to London 1777. Visited China 1788. Painted landscapes in oils and water-colours, some sporting. *coll.* Geoffrey Agnew, 'Winter Skating; Hyde Park', *exhib.* R.A. 1796; Leeds A.G., 'A Phaeton in a Thunderstorm'; Lt.-Colonel J. L. B. Leicester-Warren, 'Bull Baiting'; Mr. and Mrs. Paul Mellon, 'Departure of a Coach', S&D 1792; Charles H. Thieriot, New York, 'Bird Shooting'; Birmingham A.G., 'An Ass Race', S&D 1792. *lit.* 'Julius Caesar Ibbetson', by R. M. Clay, 1948. Woodcock, Pheasant, Partridge, Snipe and Duck Shooting subjects were aquatinted by Robert Dodd after Ibbetson.

INCE, JOSEPH MURRAY (b. Presteign 1806, d. there 1859, 24th September). Pupil of David Cox. Resided in Cambridge for some time. Some works may have angling interest. *exhib.* R.A. (16); B.I. (23); S.S. (137); N.W.C.S. (9); V.E. (12), 'Landscape'.

INGALTON, WILLIAM (b. Worplesdon 1794, d. Clever 1866. Resident chiefly at Eton. At age of 30 became a professional architect. *exhib.* R.A. (9); B.I. (19); S.S. (5), 'Landscape'. R.A. 1817, 'The Skittle Players'; B.I. 1817, 'The Game of Putt'.

INGPEN, A. W. (op. 1830–1838). Canterbury address. *exhib.* R.A. (8); B.I. (2); S.S. (6). R.A. 1834, 'Portrait of a Hackney'; 1835, 'Emerald, a Hunter'; 1836, 'A Hawking Party'; 'Mameluke, Derby Winner 1827'; 1837, 'Hunting Sketches'; 1838, 'Forester, a Favourite Carriage Horse'; B.I. 1833, 'Two Hounds'.

INSKIPP, JAMES (b. 1790, d. 1868). Godalming address. Exhibited from London address. Visited Italy. *exhib.* R.A. (24); B.I. (83); S.S. (56), 'Figures'. R.A. 1822, 'A Favourite Dog, property of H. Ansley'; 1823, 'Game'; 'Wild Fowl'. *repr.* 'Angling in British Art', Shaw Sparrow, colour plate, p. 94.

IRELAND, THOMAS (op. 1881–1903). *exhib.* R.A. (19); S.S. (19); N.W.C.S. (7); G.G. (7); N.G. (10); V.E. (19), 'Landscape. R.A. 1889, 'The Gentle Craft'; 1902, 'A Dorsetshire Trout Stream'.

JACKSON, FREDERICK WILLIAM, R.B.A. (b. Middleton, Manchester, 1859; d.). Pupil of J. Lefebvre and Boulanger in Paris. Visited Capri, Venice, Florence and Rome. *exhib.* R.A. (19); S.S. (13); V.E. (5). R.A. 1896, 'Winter Fishing'; 1899, 'The Return from Line Fishing'.

JACKSON, G. (op. 1833–1844). 'Two Pointers', signed G. Jackson, Jr., dated 1833, was sold by Ackermann's. A S&D 1837 painting of 'Bobby a Bay Stallion' was formerly in the possession of a Mr. A. J. Groom. *exhib.* R.A. (1), 1844, 'Dead Game'. *repr.* 'A Book of Sporting Painters', Shaw Sparrow, 1931; 'Hunters at Grass, a Roan and a Dappled Grey', dated 1839, p. 176, then at Ehrich Galleries, New York.

JACOBS, JOHN (op. 1816–1864). *exhib.* R.A. (7); B.I. (8); S.S. (16), 'Landscape'. R.A. 1819, 'Fallow Deer'; B.I. 1853, 'The Boar Hunt'.

JAGGER, CHARLES (b. Bath 1770, d. there 1827). *coll.* Major E. H. Evans Lombe, 'Thomas Browne Evans with two Pointers, Shooting', water-colour, exhibted Norwich 1950.

JAMES, (op. 1776–1783). Peterborough address. *exhib.* F.S. (11), one of angling.

JAMES, J. DEARMAN (op. 1864). *exhib.* B.I. 1864, 'Two sheep dogs'.

JAMES, ROBERT (op. 1841–1851). Nottingham address. *coll.* Lord's (1). *exhib.* R.A. (4); B.I. (1), 'Figures'.

JOHN, Sir AUGUSTUS EDWIN, O.M., R.A. (b. Tenby, 1878, 4th January; d. Fordingbridge 1961, 31st October). Studied at the Slade School. Teaching at Liverpool 1901–2. Visited France. Portrait and decorative painter. *repr.* 'Some Drawings of the English School', Campbell Dodgson, C.B.E., 'Study of a Whippet'.

JOHNSON, CHARLES EDWARD, R.I. (b. Stockport 1832, d. Richmond 1913). *coll.* Rochdale A.G. 'Hunt in the Midlands'. *exhib.* R.A. (71); B.I. (4); S.S. (6); N.W.C.S. (22); G.G. (3); N.G. (2); V.E. (36), 'Landscape'. R.A. exhibits included, 1875, 'The Horse Dealer'; 1881, 'The Wounded Stag'; 1886, 'Cub Hunting in the Midlands'; 1896, 'Bringing Home the Stag'; 1903, 'The Home of the Red Deer'.

JOHNSON, DORIS CROME. Mentioned by Guy Paget, 'Sporting Pictures of England', as a modern sporting artist.

JOHNSON, F. (op. 1791–1797). Croydon address. *exhib.* S.A. (3); R.A. (1); R.A. 1797, 'Snipes'.

JOHNSON, HENRY (op. 1824–1847). Married Ferneley's eldest daughter Sarah (1812–1903). Painted figures, etc. Painted some Egyptian scenes. *coll.* National Portrait Gallery, London (portrait of John Ferneley), S&D 1838. *exhib.* R.A. (12); B.I. (9); S.S. (12), 'Figures'.

JOHNSON, HERBERT (b. London 1848, d. 1906). *exhib.* R.A. (11); S.S. (16); V.E. (6), 'Domestic'. R.A. 1879, 'An Incident in the Prince of Wales's Tour in India, Afternoon Sport'; 1883, 'Tiger Shooting in the Terai 1876'; 1887, 'Young Anglers'.

JONES, ADRIAN (b. 1845, d. 1938). Portrait of the racehorse 'Sheen' auctioned by Shakespear, McTurk & Graham at Ashby Folville, Leicester, 29th November 1973.

JONES, CHARLES, A.R.S.A., R.C.A. (b. Barnham 1836, d. 1892). *exhib.* R.A. (12); B.I. (12); S.S. (61); N.W.C.S. (10); V.E. (6), 'Cattle'. R.A. 1867, 'The Head of the Drove'; 'Red Deer'; 1870, 'Scene in a Deer Forest'; 1871, 'The Combat, Scene in Forest of Glen Tanar'; 1872, 'An Early Morning's Chase'; 1883, ' "Alarmed", the First of October'; B.I. 1867, 'Red Deer Alarmed on the Moor at Rannock'.

JONES, GEORGE, R.A. (b. London 1786, d. 1869). Son of John Jones, an engraver. Studied R.A. Schools. Librarian and Keeper of the Royal Academy. Visited Holland, Switzerland, Germany, France and Italy. *exhib.* R.A. (221); B.I. (141); S.S. (1); O.W.C.S. (5), 'Landscapes'. R.A. exhibits consist of military and battle subjects. B.I. 1835, 'Horse Race at Rome'.

JONES, H. F. A pair of Coaching Scenes by Day and Night were sold at Sotheby's 2nd December 1959, both signed.

JONES, PAUL (op. 1858). 'A Huntsman Holding His Charger with two Dogs', S&D 1858, was sold at Christie's 13th October 1961.

JONES, RICHARD (b. 1767, d. 1840). Reading and London addresses. Four Coursing subjects were engraved by Chas. Turner for 'Ackermann's Repository of Arts', 1821. *coll.* Lord Yarborough, 'Brocklesby Betty', Racing Mare, 1825, possibly after Tillemans. *exhib.* R.A. (11); R.A. 1818, 'Portrait of "Bull Emperor", property of G. Dodd'; 1819, 'Portrait of "Carlo", a Celebrated Old Pointer'; 1820, 'The Death—Portraits of a Favourite Horse and Greyhounds'; 'Soho!'; 'Portraits of Greyhounds'; 'Portraits of Favourite Setters, property of J. N. Paxton'. *auct.* Christie's, 25/26th April 1940, A. N. Gilbey Collection. 'An Angler standing on the banks of the Thames in Eton Playing Fields with roach-pole in his hand and his dog lying beside his fishing gear. Windsor Castle in background'.

JONES, SAMUEL JOHN EGBERT (op. 1820–1845). London address but very little known of him. Many of his pictures of Horses, Shooting, Royal Mails, were engraved by Fellows, Himeley, C. Hunt, G. Hunt, Pyall and W. R. Smart. *coll.* The Hon. David Astor, 'Huntsman Shooting Birds'; Charles H. Thieriot, New York (2, 1 since sold). *exhib.* R.A. (14 'portraits and landscapes'); B.I. (14); S.S. (19); Preston A.G. 1943, 'A Shooting Scene'. *lit.* 'The British Racehorse' (Summer issue 1972. Vol. 24, No. 2, pp. 160–167).

JONES, WILLIAM (op. 1798–1860). Graves lists five William or W. Jones; none, however, exhibited Sporting or Angling subjects. W. Jones, an Irish artist, painted angling subjects 1744–1745. Much too early to be the above. *exhib.* 'Paintings of English Life', Rutland Gallery, London, June-July 1963, No. 3 'Pike Fishing' *auct.* Five paintings catalogued as by William Jones were sold in the A. N. Gilbey Collection at Christie's 25/26th April 1940, they are: 'May Fly Fishing, S&D 1832; 'An Angler Fishing for Pike and Perch'; 'Roach Fishing'; 'Pike Fishing'; 'Fly Fishing' *all repr.* 'Angling in British Art' *lit.* 'Angling in British Art', Shaw Sparrow.

***JONES, W.** (op. 1744–1745). An Irish artist. His 'Salmon Leap at Leixlip' engraved by Giles King 1744–1745.

JOSI, CHARLES (op. 1827–1851). London address. Member of Society of British Artists. *exhib.* R.A. (9); B.I. (12); S.S. (53). R.A. 1838, 'Study of a Horse'; 1843, 'The Bay Arab presented to William the Fourth by the Imam of Muscat'; 1845, 'Spaniels, property of Charles Barclay'; 1847, 'Beagles'; B.I. 1831, 'A Favourite Mare'; 1845, 'Stray Hounds'; 1846, 'Beagles'; 'Skye Terriers'.

JOY, THOMAS MUSGROVE (b. Boughton Monchelsea, Maidstone, 1812; d. 1866, 7th April). Pupil of Drummond. Painted portraits, etc. *exhib.* R.A. (67); B.I. (82); S.S. (50); N.W.C.S. (1). R.A. 1831, 'The Young Poacher'; 1838, 'After a Good Day's Sport in Glen Esk, Forfarshire'; B.I. 1836, 'Hawking'; 1851, 'Going out to Ride'.

***JOYNER, J.** (op. 1825–1833). Relative and resident with M. Joyner, exhibited landscapes and worked mainly around London. A 'Partridge Shooting', S&D 1832, was exhibited in the Galleries of Frost & Reed Ltd. *exhib.* R.A. (1); B.I. (1); S.S. (1).

JURY, JULIUS (b. Konikow 1821, 30th July; d. after 1870). Painted fish and fishing subjects. *exhib.* R.A. (1); B.I. (4); S.S. (4), 'Figures'. *repr.* 'The Fisherman's Magazine', 1864, colour plates.

JUTSUM, HENRY (b. London 1816, d. there 1869, 3rd March). Pupil of James Stark. Painted landscapes in oils and water-colours, some with sporting interest. *exhib.* R.A. (68); B.I. (75); S.S. (19); N.W.C.S. (34); V.E. (7). R.A. 1845, 'The Deer Park at Bolton Abbey, Yorks.'; 1847, 'Going out to the Chase'; 'Returning from the Chase'; 1848, 'A Trout Stream'; 1864, 'The Salmon Pool'.

KEATING, Mrs. R. H. (op. 1863). Ventnor address. Member of the Society of Lady Artists. *exhib.* B.I. (2), 'Sporting'.

KEELING, E. J. (op. 1861). *coll.* Major Sir Reginald Macdonald-Buchanan (1). *auct.* Sotheby's, 26th February 1964 (178), 'Two Pointers with a Sportsman in Moorland Setting', S&D 1861.

KEENE, CHARLES SAMUEL (b. Hornsey 1823, 10th August; d. London 1891, 4th January). Black-and-white artist, caricaturist and painter in oils and water-colours. Also etched a number of plates. Contributor of 'Punch'. *exhib.* V.E. (26). *auct.* 'The Hunt', Sotheby's, 4th November 1964. *repr.* 'Angling in British Art', Shaw Sparrow, 'In Flagrante', 'Punch' drawing, p. 89; 'Extraordinary Take of Twin Salmon', p. 90; 'There's Many a Slip', 'Punch' drawing, p. 91. *lit.* 'Charles Keene', Frank L. Emanuel P.C.C., No. 14, 1935, pl. xi, 'Lord Suffield on a Horse'.

KEMM, ROBERT (op. 1874–1885). *coll.* 'The Bullfight', sold Christie's 9th October 1964. *exhib.* S.S. (13), 'Figures'.

KEMP-WELCH, LUCY ELIZABETH (b. Bournemouth 1869, b. 1860, 20th June, Benezit; d. Bushey, Herts., 1958). Studied at the Herkomer School, Bushey. *coll.* Tate Gallery, London, 'Colt Hunting in the New Forest', exhibited R.A. 1897; Melbourne A.G., Australia, 'Horses Bathing in the Sea'. *exhib.* R.A. 1905, 'Mixed Company at a Race Meeting'.

***KENNEY, JOHN T.** (b. 1911, 16th May; living). Studied Leicester College of Art. Living in Leicestershire. Painter of sporting scenes, hunting, racing, polo, equestrian portraits, and book illustration. True sense of the action of hunting pictures. Hunts with Fernie and Quorn and painted many scenes with them. *exhib.* Ackermann's Gallery, London; Gadsby Gallery, Leicester.

KENNION, EDWARD (b. Liverpool 1744, 15th January; d. London 1809, 14th April). Painted landscapes, some with angling interest. Published 'Elements of Landscape'. *coll.* London, V. and A. Museum, 'Landscape with Fisherman'.

KERSGILL, T. C. (op. 1846). Painter of coaches, horses, etc.

KIDD, WILLIAM, R.S.A. (b. Edinburgh 1796, d. London 1863). Apprenticed to James Howe, animal painter. Went to London and painted chiefly pictures of Scottish domestic life. *coll.* Edinburgh, N.G. of Scotland. *exhib.* R.A. (33); B.I. (68); S.S. (88). *repr.* 'The Poacher detected', S&D 1818, engraved by Lupton 1826.

KILBURNE, GEORGE GOODWIN, R.B.A., R.I. (b. Norfolk 1839, 24th July; d. London 1924, September). Pupil of the Dalziel's. *coll.* Leger Galleries, London, 'The Spill', exhibited Preston 1943. *exhib.* R.A. (19); S.S. (32); V.E. (15). R.A. 1887, 'For a Hunting we will go'; 'Ancient Sport'; 1888, 'At The Meet'; 1900, 'Gamblers'. *auct.* Christie's, 5th February 1965, 'A Village Cricket Match', S&D 1894.

KILLINGBECK, BENJAMIN (op. 1769–1789). London address. A noted Animal and Sporting painter and engraver. *exhib.* S.A. (12); F.S. (28); R.A. (11). S.A. 1777, ' "Solon", a Horse belonging to the Marquis of Rockingham'; 1778, 'Earl of Eglinton's Horse, "Highlander" '; 1783, 'Portraits of Gentlemen Shooting'; 'Racehorse "Highflier" '; 'Brood Mares, belonging to the late Marquis of Rockingham'; F.S. 1771, 'Groom holding his Master's Horse'; R.A. 1776, 'An Arabian Horse, property of the Marquis of Rockingham'; 1779, ' "Dorimant", property of Lord Ossory'; 1780, ' "Cannibal", a Racehorse'; 1781, 'Portrait of a Hound'; 1784, 'Portrait of a Horse belonging to Lord Stawell'; 1785, 'A Hare'; 1786, 'A Brace of Partridges'; 1788, 'A Brace of Partridges'; 1789, 'A Woodcock'.

KINCH, H. (op. 1811–1824). *exhib.* R.A. (17). R.A. 1811, 'A Member of the Hambledon Hunt'; 1814, 'Horses'; 1815, 'A Group of Forest Horses'; 1817, 'A Portrait of a Pony'; 1818, 'Portraits of Horses'; 1820, 'Portraits of a Hunting Mare and Hackney'; 1821, 'Portrait of a Little Mare, property of Major Harris'; 1822, 'Going to Cover'; 1823, 'Portrait of Favourite Hackney, property of G. Battye'; 'Portrait of a Hunter'; 1824, 'Portrait of a Horse bred in Italy, property of G. Poore'.

KING, JOHN (Living). Paints sporting subjects. *exhib.* The Tryon Gallery, London. 'The Last Fence'.

KING, MEADE. Mentioned by Guy Paget as a modern sporting painter, 'Sporting Pictures of England'.

KING, WILLIAM GUNNING (b. London 1859, 2nd September; d.). Painter of cattle in landscapes, etc. Drew for 'Punch'. *coll.* Newport A.G., 'Thrown'; Sydney H. Paviere, (Angling drawing). *repr.* Bibby's Calendars. *exhib.* R.A. 1894.

KNELLER, Sir GODFREY, Bart. (b. Lubeck 1646, 8th August; d. London 1723, October). *coll.* The Duke of Grafton, 'Charles Somerset, Marquess of Worcester, with Spaniels, Gun and dead Bird', exhibited Norwich 1950; The Renaissance Gallery, Philadelphia, U.S.A., 'Deer Hunting', S&D 1712. *repr.* 'A Book of Sporting Painters', by Shaw Sparrow, p. 57.

KNIGHT, A. ROWLAND (op. 1810–1840). Sporting painter, especially of Angling. Two examples were in the Hutchinson Sporting Gallery. *auct.* Christie's, 25/26th April 1940, A. N. Gilbey Collection, 'Study of Fish on a Bank'.

KNIGHT, WILLIAM HENRY (b. Newburg 1823, 26th September; d. London 1863, 31st July). *exhib.* R.A. (29); B.I. (17); S.S. (8); V.E. (2), 'Domestic'. R.A. 1846, 'Boys Playing at Draughts'; 1854, 'A Game of Base-ball'; 'A Card Party'; 1856, 'Playing the First Card'; 1859, 'In Training for the Derby'.

KNIGHT, Dame LAURA, R.A., R.W.S., R.E., Hon.LL.D. (b. 1877; living London). Studied Nottingham School of Art and South Kensington. Bronze, Silver, and Gold Medals. Painted circus scenes and gypsies on Epsom Downs. Married Harold Knight, R.A., in 1903. She was the daughter of Charles Johnson. Wrote 'Oil Paint and Grease Paint', 1936, and 'A Proper Circus Omie', 1962. *coll.* London, British Museum; Tate Gallery; V. and A. Museum. *exhib.* R.A. (from 1903). *repr.* 'Colour Magazine', February 1922. 'Between the Rounds' (Boxing match).

KNYFF, LEONARD (b. Haarlem 1650, 10th August; d. London 1721). Apart from paintings of gentlemen's seats, he is also recorded as a painter of fowls and dogs. Knyff was employed to paint animal pieces by Lord Irwin, now in possession of the Earl of Halifax. *coll.* Leeds, City Art Gallery, 'Portrait of Arthur,3rd Viscount Irwin, standing in a landscape, loading a gun, with pointer carrying a dead pheasant. Several birds and a group of dead game'; ex collection of Earl of Halifax, presented to Leeds 1948. *lit.* 'Old English Landscape Painters', Grant, Vol. 1, p. 69.

LADBROOKE, ROBERT (b. 1770, d. Norwich 1842). With Crome formed the Norwich Society of Artists in 1803. Painted landscapes in oils and water-colours. Published 'Views of the Churches of Norfolk', 1843, lithographs. *coll.* W. T. F. Jarrold, 'Foundry Bridge, Norwich, with castle in distance and man fishing from bank, exhibited in Norwich 1927. P.O.U., 'Park Scene with background of unkennelling of a pack of hounds see Shaw Sparrow, 'A Book of Sporting Painters'. *exhib.* R.A. (5); B.I. (8), 'Landscapes'.

LA FONTAINE, THOMAS SHERWOOD (b. 1915, 21st December; living in Wiltshire). Paints varied sporting subjects, racing, hunting, polo. Painted portrait of 'Sweet Solera'; 'Captain H. M. Gosling, M.F.H., on horseback, with hound'; 'H.H. The Maharanee of Jaipur on horseback'. Successful in painting children and family groups with horse. *exhib.* Ackermann's Galleries, London, 1962. *repr.* 'The Meet of the Beaufort Hunt at Easton Grey' and 'The Lindsay Arabs' as prints.

LAMBERT, E. F. (op. 1823–1846). London address. *exhib.* R.A. (15); S.S. (7), 'Historical'. R.A. 1827, 'Pheasants'; 1829, 'A Sportsman's Visit'; 1841, 'John Gilpin'.

LAMBERT, JAMES (b. Eastbourne 1725, d. 1788), of Lewes. His landscapes always enlivened by cattle or sheep. Much employed with portraits of animals. *exhib.* S.A. (17); F.S. (30); R.A. (7), 'Landscape'. R.A. 1774, 'Mr. Bakewell's Famous Ram'; 1777, 'Two Landscapes with Cattle'.

LAMBERT, J. W. (op. 1822–1851). Carshalton address. Animal and sporting painter. *exhib.* R.A. (9); B.I. (4); S.S. (11), 'Sporting'. R.A. 1836, 'The Surrey Foxhounds Breaking Cover'; B.I. 1823, 'Shooting Pony and Pointer'; 1839, 'Sheep Washing'.

LANCE, GEORGE (b. Little Easton, Essex, 1802; d. Sunnyside, near Birkenhead, 1864). Pupil of Haydon and R.A. Schools. Painted fruit, flowers, portraits, and sporting subjects in oils and water-colours. *exhib.* R.A. (38); B.I. (135); S.S. (48); N.W.C.S. (14), 'Fruit'. R.A. 1838, 'Game'; 'The Stricken Mallard'; B.I. 1840, 'A Game Piece'; 1842, 'The Young Falconer'.

LANDSEER, CHARLES, R.A. (b. 1799, d. 1879). Son of John Landseer. *coll.* London, Tate Gallery, 'Bloodhound and Pups'. *exhib.* R.A. (73); B.I. (26); S.S. (11), 'Historical'. R.A. 1840, 'The Tired Huntsman'; B.I. 1828, 'The Tyrolese Hunter'; 1835, 'Highlander Siezed by a Bloodhound'; 1838, 'Two Puppies and a Kitten'.

***LANDSEER, Sir EDWIN HENRY, R.A.** (b. London 1802, d. 1873, buried in St. Paul's). Son of John Landseer, A.R.A., an engraver. Student at R.A. Schools. In 1824 settled at St. John's Wood, which remained his home for life. Made many journeys to the Highlands. *coll.* Bath, Victoria A.G. (1); Birmingham, Museum and A.G. (1); Burnley, Towneley Hall, Museum and A.G. (1); Bury A.G. (1); Cambridge, Fitzwilliam Museum (6); Liverpool, Walker A.G. (3); London, Tate Gallery (9); Preston, H.M. and A.G. (1); Sheffield A.G. (3); Nicholas Argenti (1); John Dewar & Sons (1); Miss FitzWygram (1); Pierre Jeannerat (1); Major Sir Reginald Macdonald-Buchanan (3); Henry P. McSchenny (1); Nettlefold Collection (1); Mr. and Mrs. R. Richards (1); Lord Somerleyton (1). *exhib.* R.A. (43). *repr.* 'Angling in British Art', Shaw Sparrow; 'Days and Nights of Salmon Fishing', W. Scrope, 1843. *lit.* 'Country Life', 16th March 1961, 'Rediscovery of Landseer', Denys Sutton.

LANDSEER, THOMAS, A.R.A. (b. 1795, d. 1880). Painter and engraver. Son of John Landseer. *exhib.* R.A. (35); B.I. (2); S.S. (2); N.W.C.S. (4), 'Engraving'. R.A. 1867, 'Lion Hunting'.

LANE, THEODORE (op. 1800–1830). London address. *coll.* London, Tate Gallery, 'The Gouty Angler', S&D 1828. *exhib.* R.A. (7); B.I. (7); S.S. (3), 'Domestic'. R.A. 1816, 'Portrait of a Dog'. *repr.* I.C.I. Plastics Division Calendar 1959, colour plate, 'Rackets', engraved by George Hunt.

LAPORTE, GEORGE HENRY (b. 1799 at Hanover, Grant and Cundall; Shaw Sparrow says he was 71 when he died in 1873, making his birth 1802; he died at 13 Norfolk Square, Paddington). Member of the N.W.C.S. Painted animals, figures and hunting subjects in oils and water-colours. Animal painter to the Duke of Cumberland, contributed 43 plates to the 'Old Sporting Magazine'. Exhibited R.A. 1821 when aged 22. *coll.* R. G. Cave (1). *exhib.* R.A. (9); B.I. (21); S.S. (18).

LAROON, MARCELLUS, Junior (b. 1679, d. 1774; d. 1772, Grant). Son of Marcellus Laroon. Officer in the army of Marlborough, actor and artist. *coll.* London, Tate Gallery, 'Hunting Party'.

LASCELLES, THOMAS W. (op. 1885–1891). Cookham Dene address. *exhib.* R.A. (6); S.S. (2), 'Domestic'. R.A. 1887, 'The Little Angler'.

LATHAM, MOLLY M. (living artist). Painter of sporting subjects. *exhib.* Ackermann's, London, 1938.

LAVERY, Sir JOHN, R.A., R.S.A. (b. 1856, d. 1941). Portrait and figure painter. *coll.* London, Tate Gallery, 'The Golf Course, North Berwick'; 'The Jockey's Dressing Room at Ascot'; 'The Chess Players'. M. de Saint-Marceaux, 'Les Deux Pecheurs', exhibited Salon 1883. *exhib.* R.A. 1886, 'The Tennis Match'.

LAWRENCE, R. (op. 1793–1814). Painter and sculptor. Veterinary surgeon in Birmingham. *exhib.* R.A. (5); R.A. 1793, 'Portraits of Two Horses at the Veterinary College'; 1807, 'A Stag Swimming'; 'Portrait of Celebrated Durham Ox'; 1814, 'Portrait of a Hunter, property of Lord Middleton'.

LAWSON, ALEXANDER (op. 1899). Wolverhampton address. *exhib.* R.A. 1899, 'Home from Fishing'.

LAWSON, CECIL GORDON (b. Salop 1849, Cundall; b. Wellington, Shropshire, Benezit; b. 1851, V. and A. Museum catalogue). London and Haslemere addresses. Landscape painter. Some landscapes with anglers. Son of W. Lawson, portrait painter. Came to London 1861.

LEADER, BENJAMIN WILLIAMS, R.A. (b. 1831, d. 1923). Changed his name from Williams. Landscape painter. Many of his pictures have angling interest. *exhib.* Arthur Tooth & Son, London, 'The River Llugwy at Bettws-y-Coed' (with Angler). *repr.* 'Angling in British Art', Shaw Sparrow, p. 18.

LEE, FREDERICK RICHARD, R.A. (b. Barnstaple 1798, d. South Africa 1879). Was at one time in the Army. Studied at R.A. Schools. Painted landscapes and still-life. *exhib.* R.A. (171); B.I. (131); S.S. (24), 'Landscape'. R.A. exhibits included, 1834, 'Throwing a Casting Net'; 1836, 'The Salmon Trap'; 1840, 'Caper Caille, Blackcock, Grouse and Ptarmigan'; 'Deer and Heron'; 1853, 'The Poacher, Scene on a Highland River'; 1853, 'The Poacher, Scene on a Highland River'; 1854, 'The Fisherman's Haunt'; 'Salmon Fishing on the River Awe with portraits'; 1863, 'Where the Trout Lie'; 1864, 'A Salmon Cruive on the River Awe'; 'Trimmer fishing Where the Jack Lie'; 1866, 'Jolly Anglers'; 1867, 'Salmon Poachers Discovered'; B.I. 1840, 'Wood Scene with Gamekeepers'; 1841, 'Eagle and Blackcock in a Highland Glen'. *repr.* Houghton Fishing Club Annuals.

LEE, PERCY M. (op. 1935). 'A Basset Hound', S&D 1935 sold at Sotheby's 12th March 1965 (160).

LEECH, JOHN (b. 1817; d. 1864, 29th October). Caricaturist and illustrator. Produced a number of large coloured woodcuts of Hunting, Racing, and other sports. Examples are in the H.M. and A.G., Preston, and Rufford Old Hall, Rufford, Lancs. *repr.* 'Angling in British Art', Shaw Sparrow; 'Angling Adventures of Mr. Briggs—Mr. Briggs practises with his running Tackle'; 'Triumphant Success of Mr. Briggs'; sketch of Angler for 'Punch' woodcut, 4th July 1863, pl. 13.

LEES, CHARLES, R.S.A. (b. 1800, d. 1880). *coll.* Col. P. J. Blair, D.S.O. (1). *exhib.* R.A. (6); B.I. (5); S.S. (1), 'Historical'. *repr.* 'Curling in Scotland', 1853, engraved by John le Comte.

LEIVERS, WILLIAM (op. 1779). An amateur. *exhib.* R.A. (3), Dogs; A Leveret; Two Mice, in 1779.

LEJEUNE, HENRY, A.R.A. (b. 1819, d. 1894). *coll.* Wolverhampton A.G. (2); *exhib.* R.A. (83); B.I. (21); S.S. (3); V.E. (1), 'Scriptural'. R.A. 1851, 'Archers'; 'Anglers'; 1865, 'Young Warreners'; 1882, 'Little Angler'.

LEMAN, Miss ALICIA J. (op. 1891). Putney address. *exhib.* R.A. (1), 'Spotting a Winner', 1891.

LEVICK, RUBY (op. 1898–1901). Chiswick address. A sculptor who possibly painted. *exhib.* R.A. 1898, 'Wrestlers—a group'; 1900, 'Fisherman hauling in a Net'; 'Boys Fishing'; 1901, 'Rugby Football Group'.

LEWIN, G. A. E. Painter of portraits of horses, etc.

LEWIN, S. A painting, 'The Fisherman', S&D '96, sold at Christie's 22nd January 1960 (160). A 'Stephen Lewin' London exhibit 1890–1908, V.E. (3), 'Domestic' and an 'S. Lewin' exhibited architecture from Boston at R.A. 1852–62.

LEWIS, CHARLES JAMES, R.I. (b. London 1830–36; d. there 1892, 28th February). Painted domestic and angling subjects. *coll.* W. Sheppard, 'Young Anglers'. *exhib.* R.A. (49); B.I. (26); S.S. (43); N.W.C.S. (72); N.G. (1); V.E. (187), 'Domestic'.

LEWIS, JOHN (op. 1762–1776). Director of the Society of Artists. Painted portraits, still-life and sporting subjects. *exhib.* S.A. (11).

LEWIS, JOHN FREDERICK, R.A., R.W.S., H.R.S.A. (b. London 1805, d. and buried Walton-on-Thames 1876). Son of F. C. Lewis, engraver. President of the O.W.C.S. *coll.* London, Tate Gallery, 'Buck Shooting in Windsor Great Park. *exhib.* R.A. (82); B.I. (25); S.S. (5); O.W.C.S. (100), 'Animals'. R.A. 1829 'An Enraged Hound'; 'Two Foxhounds in the Pack of J. C. Bulteel'; 'A King Charles Spaniel belonging to the Countess of Morley'; 1830, 'An Old Gamekeeper'; B.I. 1824, 'Gamekeepers Deer Shooting'; 1826, 'Group of His Majesty's Staghounds'; 1827, 'Foresters stalking Deer'; 'Deer Shooting in Windsor Park'; 1829, 'The Trout Stream'. *auct.* Christie's, 25/26th April 1940, A. N. Gilbey Collection, 'Sir Edwin Landseer Fishing'. *repr.* 'Angling in British Art', Shaw Sparrow, colour plate, p. 88.

LINDSAY, TOM (b. Glasgow 1882, 8th February; d.). Animal painter and etcher. Studied Glasgow School of Art.

LINNELL, JOHN (b. Bloomsbury 1792, d. Redhill 1882). Pupil of John Varley and R.A. Schools. Painted miniatures and portraits, later landscapes in oils. *exhib.* R.A. (177); B.I. (92); N.W.C.S. (53). B.I. 1852, 'Boar Hunt in England—Olden Time'. *repr.* 'The Compleat Angler', 2 vols, 1893.

LLEWELLYN, Sir WILLIAM, P.R.A. (b. 1863, d. 1941). Painted portraits. *coll.* London, Tate Gallery, 'Sailing at Blakeney'.

LLOYD, EDWARD (op. 1866). A Shropshire artist painting hunting subjects. Arthur Ackermann & Son report having had a painting of 'Two Hunters and Groom', S&D 1866, and inscribed 'Ellesmere, 1st June'.

LLOYD, IVESTER. Mentioned by Guy Paget, 'Sporting Pictures of England'.

LLOYD, W. STUART (op. 1875–1902). London and Burnham Park, Sussex, addresses. *exhib.* R.A. 1875–1902. R.A. 1883, 'Wild Duck Shooting'; 1894, 'Salmon Fishing, Christchurch Bay'.

***LODER, JAMES, of Bath** (op. 1820–1857). Bath address. Well known and esteemed in his day. *coll.* Major Sir Reginald Macdonald-Buchanan (1); Charles H. Thieriot, New York (three sporting subjects since sold). *repr.* 'Favourite Cob Harnessed', aquatint by G. Hunt, 1820; 'William Long on Milkman with Hounds', aquatint by G. Hunt 1857.

LODGE, GEORGE E. (b. 1860, d. 1954). London address. Painter and falconer. Provided many illustrations for 'The Gun at Home and Abroad', 4 vols., 1912–1915. *exhib.* R.A. (7); S.S. (3); V.E. (8), 'Domestic'. Sports Exhibition 1893. R.A. 1881, 'Peregrines'; 1888, 'Peregrines'; 1890, 'Wild Duck', the Tryon Gallery, London, April 1965. *repr.* 'The Compleat Angler', 1893.

LOGSDAIL, WILLIAM (op. 1877–1904). Lincoln. London 1888; Venice 1897; London 1903. Portrait and figure painter. *coll.* Liverpool, Walker Art Gallery, 'Eve of the Regatta'

LOMAX, JOHN ARTHUR, R.B.A. (b. Manchester 1857; d. 1923, 13th December). Didsbury address. Studied Munich Academy. Worked in London for a time. Painted genre. *exhib.* R.A. (17); S.S. (26); N.W.C.S. (1); V.E. (12), 'Domestic'.

LONG, JOHN, Junior (op. 1827). A sporting scene, S&D 1827, inscribed on reverse 'Emma Mary Long, given to her by her affectionate father with her pony—was shot 1836', was sold at Sotheby's 6th November 1963.

LONGBOTTOM, ROBERT J. (op. 1830–1845). London address. *exhib.* R.A. (10); B.I. (5); S.S. (14); N.W.C.S. (3). R.A. 1830, 'Portrait of a Favourite Setter'; 1831, 'Interior with Horses'; 1832, 'Portrait of a Setter'; 1834, 'Horses, a Study'.

LORAINE-SMITH (*see* SMITH, CHARLES LORAINE)

LORIMER, JOHN HENRY, R.S.A., R.S.W. (op. 1878–1899). Edinburgh address. *exhib.* R.A. (21); N.W.C.S. (2); G.G. (2); N.G. (6); V.E. (15), 'Domestic'. R.A. 1886, 'Boy and Dogs'.

LOVEGROVE, H. (op. 1829–1844). London address. Painting fish, also landscape. *exhib.* R.A. (1); B.I. (2); S.S. (10), 'Fish'. B.I. 1843, 'Perch caught in the Thames near Marlow'.

LOWRY, LAURENCE STEPHEN, A.R.A. (b. Manchester 1887, 1st November; living). Painter of Industrial Street Scenes. *auct.* Sotheby's, 15th April 1964, 'After the Match'.

LUARD, LOWES DALBIAC (1872–1944). Painter of horses. Lived and worked a great deal in France. *coll.* Birmingham A.G. (1); *exhib.* R.A. (4), 'Historical'; Birmingham A.G., Luard Memorial Exhibition, 1946).

LUCAS, H. F. LUCAS. Mentioned by Guy Paget, 'Sporting Pictures of England'. *coll.* Major Sir Reginald Macdonald-Buchanan (1).

LUCAS, JOHN TEMPLETON (op. 1860–1875). *exhib.* R.A. (7); B.I. (13); S.S. (36), 'Domestic'. B.I. 1860, 'An Angler preparing for a Day's Sport'.

LUCAS, RALPH W. (op. 1821–1862). Blackheath address. *exhib.* R.A. (44); B.I. (12); S.S. (19); N.W.C.S. (2), 'Landscape'. B.I. 1847, 'Trout Fishing'.

LUDLOW, HENRY STEPHEN (op. 1888–1903). London address. *exhib.* R.A. (8); V.E. (1), 'Domestic'. R.A. 1891, 'A Trout Stream, S. Wales'; 1901, 'Playing a Trout'; 1902, 'Fishing the Shallows'.

LUKER, WILLIAM, R.B.A. (b. London 1867, living c. 1934). Bebington, Cheshire, address. Painted equestrian portraits, among general subjects. His works included portraits of the racehorses 'Security and Foal', also 'Double Chance', *exhib.* R.A. (57); B.I. (29); S.S. (127); V.E. (28), 'Eastern'. His R.A. exhibited pictures included, 1852, 'Deer Stalkers with favourite Pony and Deer Hound'; 1853, 'Retriever and Spaniels, property of T. M. Goodlake; 1871, 'The Haunt of the Fallow Deer'.

LUMSDAINE, LEESA SANDYS (Living). Exhibited at The Tryon Gallery, London. 'Gold Cup Winners 1964'.

LUNY, THOMAS (b. 1758, d. 1837). London address. In Navy until 1820. Painted mostly sea battles. *exhib.* S.A. (3); F.S. (1); R.A. (29); B.I. (2), 'Sea Battles'. *exhib.* Rutland Gallery, London, 'Fisherman in a River Estuary', S&D 1835; 'Paintings of English Life', June-July 1963.

LUTYENS, CHARLES AUGUSTUS HENRY (op. 1860–1900). London address. *coll.* Burnley, Towneley Museum and A.G., 'The Meet'. *exhib.* R.A. (41); B.I. (11); S.S. (1); G.G. (1); V.E. (1), 'Sporting'. R.A. 1867, 'Hog Hunting'; 1871, 'Don't Put Trimmer in till the Squire calls the Hounds Away'; 1875, 'The Marquis of Ailesbury's "Adventuriere" '; 'Mr. S. Crawfurd's "Gang Forward" '; 'Earl of Lonsdale's "King Lud" '; 1877, ' "Doncaster", the Derby Winner, 1873, property of the Duke of Westminster'; 1878, 'Major Browne and Northumberland Hounds'; 1900, 'Hunting Scene'; B.I. 1860–67, 'A Horse Grazing'; 'A Prize Colt'; 'Hunting Picture'.

LYCETT, J., 19th century. Did not exhibit. Shaw Sparrow says sporting pictures by him had been seen.

***LYNE, MICHAEL** (b. 1912, Herefordshire; living). Son of a parson and a direct descendant of John Bacon, R.A. Wild animals and their haunts were his absorbing interest from his youngest days. When he had his own pony, hounds and hunting became the breath of life. Started drawing animals at the age of 4. Published his first book, 'Horses, Hounds and Country' at the age of 26. Second book destroyed in bombing of London while being printed. Hunted a pack of beagles himself for a number of years. Since the war commissions have taken him all over the United Kingdom and to the United States, painting scenes of the famous hunts in the Southern States. *coll.* Messrs. Frost & Reed Ltd., London, 'Cantering to the Start'; 'The Pytchley-Returning to Hanging Houghton', signed. *exhib.* Frost & Reed, London (one-man show October 1964). *repr.* 'Horses, Hounds and Country'.

LYON, DAVID (op. 1774). London address. *exhib.* F.S. (2), 1774, 'Dogs and Horses' *auct.* Sotheby's, 29th July 1964, 'A Huntsman on Horseback with his Dogs'; 'A Sportsman with a Dog coursing a Hare'.

MACBETH, ROBERT WALKER, R.A., R.I., R.E., R.W.S., R.O.I. (b. 1848, d. 1910). London address. Painter and engraver. *exhib.* R.A. (70); O.W.C.S. (42); N.W.C.S. (4); G.G. (23); N.G. (8); V.E. (76). R.A. 1891, 'Badminton in the Studio'; 1892, 'Hunting with the Devon and Somerset Staghounds'; 1899, 'Favourites of the Hunt'; 1900, 'Favourites of the Hunt'; 1903, 'Lunch at a Coursing Meet'. *auct.* Christie's, 23/30th May 1913, No. 162, 'The Miller's Daughter—A Girl seated on bank of stream preparing a fishing line, a dog at her side'.

MACALLUM, HAMILTON (b. Kames, Argyllshire, 1841; d. Beer, South Devon, 1896). Studied R.A. Schools. *exhib.* R.A. (21); S.S. (13); N.W.C.S. (28); G.G. (9); N.G. (7); V.E. (95), 'Sea-Pieces'. *repr.* 'Angling in British Art', Shaw Sparrow, 'Landing a Big 'Un', dated 1870, p. 40. *auct.* Christie's, 23rd/30th May 1913, No. 72, McCulloch Collection. 'High, Low, Jack and the Game', group of fishermen playing cards.

McEWEN, R. (op. 1822). A picture, 'Salmon Fishing', was in the Hutchinson Collection.

MACLEOD, JOHN (d. 1872). Edinburgh address. Painted animals, horses and dogs.

McLEOD, JULIET (b. Ashley Green, Bucks., 1917, 25th December; living). Studied painting and sculpture Paris 1933. Apprenticed to Lynwood Palmer 1933–1939. Painter of famous race horses, Derby and other classic winners, etc. *coll.* The National Stud (Mr. Peter Burrell); Mr. and Mrs. Noel Murless; the late Sir Victor and Lady Sassoon; Mdme Andre Marriotti; H.H. the late Prince Aly Khan; the late Prince Abdullilah of Iraq; Mr. Adrian Thorpe; Mrs. A. Wightman; Mrs. V. Hue-Williams; the late Colonel B. Hornung. *exhib.* Ackermann's Gallery 1947; Fores Gallery 1953. *repr.* 'A Hundred Horses', 1960.

McTAGGART, WILLIAM, R.S.A., V.P.R.S.W. (b. Campbeltown 1835, d. Broomieknowe 1910). Studied Trustees' Academy, Edinburgh. Visited Paris when a student and the Continent later. *coll.* National Gallery of Scotland, Edinburgh, 'The Young Fishers'. S&D 1876 *repr.* 'Angling in British Art', Shaw Sparrow, p. 40, as 'The Little Anglers'.

MACWHIRTER, JOHN, R.A., A.R.S.A. (b. Slateford, near Edinburgh; d. London 1911). Studied under R. S. Lauder at the Trustees' Academy. Painted landscapes. *exhib.* R.A. (78); N.W.C.S. (11); G.G. (5); N.G. (2); V.E. (25), 'Landscape'. R.A. 1891, 'Home of the Trout'. *repr.* 'Angling in British Art', Shaw Sparrow, p. 79; 'A Young Celt Angling in the Isle of Skye'.

***MAGGS, J. C.** (b. Bath 1819; died there 1896, 3rd November). One of the English Coaching School Lived all his life in Bath. His studio was at No. 34 Gay Street. Son of a furniture japanner. Maggs founded and ran a successful School of Painting in Bath and possessed one of the best libraries on coaching and driving subjects. His work, which was accomplished during the mid-19th century, just as the old coaches were fast disappearing, was widely exhibited and sought after. Bath was ideally placed as an important coaching junction in the West Country. His patrons included H.M. Queen Victoria, the Duke of Beaufort, and the Earl of Abergavenny. Not mentioned by Shaw Sparrow. *exhib.* Preston, 1943, 'Changing Horses at the Plough, Hotel, Cheltenham', S&D 1879. *auct.* Sotheby's, 29th July 1964, 'The Bath, Taunton and Exeter Coach', S&D Bath 1877. Christie's, 16th October 1964, 'Catching the Stage', S&D 1877.

MAGUIRE, J. (op. c. 1825). Arthur Ackermann & Son exhibited a painting of 'Two pointers with gentlemen shooting in a cornfield', signed but not dated.

MAIDEN, JOSEPH (b. Bury, Lancs., 1813; d. 1843, 26th November). Animal and portrait painter. *lit.* 'Art and Artists in Lancashire and Cheshire', J. H. Nodal.

MAILE, J. (op. 1824). *exhib.* S.S. (3), 'Sporting'.

MALBON, WILLIAM (op. 1834–1848). A Sheffield artist, principally engaged in painting figures and animals into other artists' professional landscapes. Resided in Pomona Street, Sheffield in 1869, according to an inscription of an oil titled 'The Sherwood Rangers' in the Graves A.G., Sheffield. *coll.* Sheffield A.G. (3), 'Winter scene with skaters'; 'Dog and Hare'; The Sherwood Rangers; Nottingham A.G. (2), a 'Market' and a 'Farmyard'. *exhib.* S.S. (1), 'Sporting'.

MALING, S. (op. 1726). *exhib.* Rutland Gallery, London, 'English Sporting Life', April 1960, No. 18; 'Huntsman and a Pack of Harriers—Village in the distance', S&D 1726.

MARLOW, WILLIAM (b. Southwark 1740; d. Twickenham 1813, 14th January). Pupil of Samuel Scott. Studied in France and Italy 1765–1768. *exhib.* S.A. (125); F.S. (2); R.A. (25). *auct.* Christie's, 25/26th April 1940, A. N. Gilbey Collection, 'A Scene beside an extensive lake in a Park with figures fishing'.

MARSH, ARTHUR H., A.R.W.S., R.B.A. (op. 1865–1896). London address. *exhib.* R.A. (16); S.S. (3); O.W.C.S. (108); G.G. (1); V.E. (11). R.A. 1870, 'Baiting the Lines'; 1873, 'The Salmon Fishers'.

***MARSHALL, BENJAMIN** (b. Seagrave, Leicestershire, 1768, 8th November; d. London 1835, 24th July). Fifth child of Charles and Elizabeth Marshall. Pupil of L. F. Abbott, the portrait painter. Generally rated second to George Stubbs in Sporting Art. His patrons were numerous: The Prince Regent, The Duke and Duchess of Devonshire, Lord Hartington, Lord Sondes, the Margravine of Ansbach, whose horses were painted in 1797, and many others. Went to London 1771 and later to Newmarket 1812. After the death of his daughter returned to London. Met with a severe accident when his coach overturned in 1819. His works declined in popularity in his latter years, so much so that in the William Mellish sale of 1831 examples of his made only a few pounds. After his death his estate realized a mere £200. His portrait was painted by John E. Ferneley in 1824 (Macdonald-Buchanan collection). The majority of his works are of racing rather than hunting. *coll.* London. Tate Gallery (1); National Sporting Club (1); Sir Alfred H. Aykroyd, Bt. (1); Viscount Bearsted (1); Stephen C. Clarke, Junior (1); Sir Michael Culme-Seymour, Bt. (3); Capt. J. W. H. Goddard (3); Q. E. Gurney (1); The Earl of Jersey (2); Major Sir Reginald Macdonald-Buchanan (14); Mr. and Mrs. Paul Mellon, U.S.A. (5); Mr. V. R. Pochin (1); H.M. The Queen (6); Earl of Scarborough (1); Charles H. Thieriot, New York (1). *exhib.* Denys Sutton says Marshall 'never submitted his sporting works' to the Royal Academy. This is hardly correct as will be seen from the following list of R.A. exhibits: 1800, ' "Diamond", belonging to J. Cookson'; 'Portrait of Capt. Ricketts with his Horse and Hounds'; 1808, 'Portrait of a Foreign Nobleman and His Horse'; 1810, 'Portrait of a Favourite Horse, the property of Lord Deerhurst'; 'A well-known Horse, the property of T. O. Hunter'; 1812, 'A Game Cock'; 'The Trimmed Cock'; 1819, ' "Fanny", the property of R. Jones'. *lit.* 'The Art of Ben Marshall', Denys Sutton, 'Country Life', Vol. CX, No. 2864, 7th December 1951.

MARSHALL, JOHN (op. 1840–1896). London address. *exhib.* R.A. (8); S.S. (17). R.A. 1848, ' "The Curate", a Famous Steeple-chaser, the property of George Brettle'.

MARSHALL, LAMBERT (b. 1810, d. 1870). Youngest son of Ben Marshall and much influenced by his father's style. *coll.* An example was in Hutchinson Sporting Gallery (now dispersed). *exhib.* B.I. (1); S.S. (1), 'Sporting'. B.I., 'Badger Baiters'. *repr.* Twenty-five works engraved for the 'Sporting Magazine'. 'Country Life', 15th February 1962, coloured cover; 'The Bull Ring Snug', c. 1840.

MARSHALL, WILLIAM ELSTOB (op. 1859–1881). London and Edinburgh addresses. *exhib.* R.A. (8); B.I. (5); S.S. (18); V.E. (9). R.A. 1861, 'The Old Keeper'.

***MARTIN, A. ANSON** (op. 1840–1861). Painted fine quality coaching and hunting scenes. Undoubtedly the same as A. A. Martin. A fine coaching piece bearing the signatures of Anson Martin and Charles Cooper Henderson's evidence of some collaboration. The 'Bedale Hunt' engraved by Simmons and published 1842.

MARTIN, HENRY HARRISON (op. 1847–1882). London address. *exhib.* R.A. (10); B.I. (20); S.S. (56), 'Figures'. R.A. 1858, 'At the Bull Fight'; 1864, 'For the Bull Fight'.

MARTIN, SYLVESTER (op. 1869–1871). A S&D 1871 painting, ' "Brighton", winner of the Ulverston Open Hunt Steeplechase of 1870, owner up', sold at Christie's 21st July 1961 (111). *exhib.* Rutland Gallery, London, 'Paintings in English Life', 1963, exhibited, a pair of 'The Meet', S&D 1869.

MARTINDALE, G. (c. 1820). One painting of 'Cheltenham Coach on the Road', signed but not dated, passed through the Galleries of Arthur Ackermann & Son. Grant's Dictionary of British Landscape Painters notes an uninitialled 'Martindale' exhibiting in 1782 a landscape at the Free Society of Artists.

MARTINEZ, F. E. (op. 1910). Two paintings of 'setters' were shown by Arthur Ackermann & Son at their Galleries.

MASON, GEORGE HEMMING, A.R.A. (b. 1818, d. 1872). Visited the Continent and Italy. His picture, 'Young Anglers', was etched by Waltner. *exhib.* R.A. (25); V.E. (12), 'Landscape'.

MASON, WILLIAM (b. Kingston-upon-Hull 1724, 12th December; d. Aston 1797, 7th April). *exhib.* R.A. (3). R.A. 1783, 'A Country Town in Race-time'; 1786, 'A Review'.

MASSEY, F. E. (op. 1871). *auct.* Christie's, 14th December 1928, Capt. Tatton Sale, 'Huntsman and Hounds', 1871.

MEADOWS, JOSEPH KENNY (b. Cardinganshire 1790, 1st November; d. 1874, August). Illustrator for 'Punch' and 'Illustrated London News'. Two of his pictures were in the Hutchinson Collection. *exhib.* R.A. (1); S.S. (4), 'Portraits'.

MEARNS, A. (op. 1855–1864). Lewisham address. *exhib.* B.I. (4); S.S. (2), 'Sporting'.

MEASE, J. (op. 1797–1798). London address. *exhib.* R.A. (2). R.A. 1797, 'Portrait of a Hunter'; 'Portrait of Mr. Sheridan's Horse "Billy" '.

MEDLEY, SAMUEL (b. Liverpool 1769, 22nd March; d. 1857, 10th August). Animal, landscape and portrait painter. *exhib.* R.A. (28), Portraits and Scriptural. *lit.* 'Art and Artists in Lancs. and Cheshire', J. H. Nodal.

MELCHIOR, WILHELM (b. Nymphenbourg 1817, 25th July; d. Munich 1860, 9th September). Painter and lithographer. *coll.* Munich, 'View of Hunters and Dogs overtaking the Fox'. *exhib.* R.A. (3); B.I. (1).; R.A., Still-life and landscape; B.I., 'A Fox' and 'Still-life'.

MELVILLE, ARTHUR, R.W.S., A.R.S.A. (b. Loanhead of Guthrie, Forfarshire, 1855; d. Whitley, Surrey, 1904). Self-taught. Later studied in Paris and Graž. Visited Egypt, India, and Persia 1881–1882. Associated with Glasgow Group for some years in Scotland. Settled in London and visited Spain and Morocco with Sir Frank Brangwyn, R.A. *coll.* Aberdeen A.G.; Edinburgh, National Gallery of Scotland; Glasgow A.G.; Leeds A.G.; Liverpool, Walker A.G.; London, British Museum; V. and A. Museum; Paris, Musee d'art Moderne; Preston, H.M. and A.G.; Miss M. Elliot, Alastair McEwen; Marion Melville; J. H. Pillman. *lit.* 'Arthur Melville', by Agnes Mackay (with catalogue of 442 pictures), 1951.

MELVILLE, HARDEN S. (op. 1837–1879). *exhib.* R.A. (6); B.I. (10); S.S. (17), 'Domestic'. R.A. 1841, 'Study of a Bloodhound'.

MERRY, D. *exhib.* 'Head of a Dog', Preston A.G., 1943.

METHUEN, Lord, R.A., R.W.S., Hon.A.R.I.B.A., F.S.A. (b. 1886, 29th September; living). *exhib.* R.A. 1953, 'Badminton Olympic Trials'.

MEYER, M. (op. 1834). *exhib.* R.A. 1834, 'Game'.

MILES, W. (op. 1841). *exhib.* B.I. 1841, 'A Horse'.

MILLAIS, H. RAOUL (living). Sporting artist. Has painted portraits of many of the leading racehorses, also paints very attractive small racing, hunting, mare and foal subjects. Grandson of Sir John Everett Millais, P.R.A. Now lives most of the year in Spain. *coll.* H.H. the late Prince Ali Khan; Major Sir Reginald Macdonald-Buchanan (2). *repr.* 'Connoisseur', April 1962, advert. *exhib.* Ackermann Gallery.

MILLAR, JAMES (b. c. 1735; d. Handsworth, Birmingham, 1805). Painted portraits, historical subjects, landscape and horses and dogs, etc. Living at Birmingham addresses. Offered when Christ Church, Birmingham, was to be built to paint an altar-piece valued £100, but did not live to perform this task. Ackermann's had a portrait of a Hunter with owner and dog, S&D 1787. *exhib.* R.A. (6) between 1784–1790; S.A. (1), 'A Lady at confession'. *coll.* Birmingham A.G. (3), all portraits; Mr. and Mrs. Paul Mellon, U.S.A. (1), a family group.

MILLER, JOHN (op. 1761–1785). Westminster address. Painted portraits, historical, biblical, flowers, landscape, sporting. *exhib.* S.A. (51); F.S. (2); R.A. (7), 'Engraving'. R.A. 1782, 'Landscape with Fox Basking'; 'A Gentleman Springing Game'. Graves lists eight 'John Millers'.

MILLER, J. S. (op. 1767). *exhib.* S.A. (3), 'Landscape'. A landscape with two foxes may be by this artist.

MILLER, ROY C. (b. Chorlton-cum-Hardy 1938, 8th September; living). *coll.* Rochdale A.G., 'The Field from Above' (Horse Racing).

MITCHELL, J. A. (op. 1826–1832). *exhib.* R.A. (1), 1832, 'Historical' *exhib.* Knoedler & Co. Ltd., London, 'Preparing for the Hunt', S&D 1826, exhibited Preston A.G. 1943.

MOLE, JOHN HENRY, V.P.R.I. (b. Alnwick 1814; d. 1886, 13th December). Studied Newcastle. *exhib.* R.A. (11); B.I. (1); S.S. (5); N.W.C.S. (679); G.G. (4); V.E. (12), 'Figures'. *auct.* Christie's, 25/26th April 1940, A. N. Gilbey Collection. 'Two Scottish Children Fishing in a Stream in a Highland Landscape, water-colour, S&D 1861.

MONTGAANT or **MONTAGAANT** (op. 1783). London address. *exhib.* F.S. (1), 'Sporting'.

MOORE, HENRY, R.A., R.B.A. (b. York 1831, d. Margate 1895). Son of William Moore, a portrait painter, brother of Albert Moore. In 1853 went to London with his brother. Started as a landscape painter but later turned to the sea. *coll.* V. and A. Museum, London, 'Strath Fillan, Perthshire, with a Leaping Salmon'. *repr.* 'Angling in British Art', Shaw Sparrow, p. 41; Glasgow A.G., 'St. Alban's Race'.

MOORE, JOHN (op. 1954). Hawkhurst, Kent, address. *exhib.* R.A. 1954, 'Fisherman'.

MOORE, W. (op. 1830–1856). London address. *exhib.* B.I. (1); S.S. (5), 'Sporting'.

MORGAN, FRED (FREDERICK), R.O.I. (op. 1865–1916). Aylesbury, London, and Broadstairs addresses. Painted figures and domestic scenes. *exhib.* R.A. 1865–1916, 'H.M. Queen Alexandria, Her Grandchildren and Dogs' (1902) (the dogs by T. Blinks); 'Thirsty Calves' (1905); 'Wagon and Horses' (1913).

MORGAN, JOHN, R.B.A. (b. London 1823, d. Hastings 1886). M. Bernard, London, exhibited a 'The Fight' (two young boys about to fight, surrounded by their friends and onlookers. Some of the boys with bats and stumps. In field a cricket match is seen.) S&D 1869. *exhib.* R.A. (66); B.I. (26); S.S. (114); V.E. (17), 'Domestic'.

***MORLAND, GEORGE CHARLES** (b. London 1763, 26th June; d. there 1804, 29th October). Son of Henry Robert Morland and Jane Lacam. Painter and etcher. *coll.* Birmingham A.G. (1); Cambridge, Fitzwilliam Museum (7); Edinburgh, National Gallery (1); Leamington A.G. and Museum (1); London, Tate Gallery (1); V. and A. Museum (1); Preston, H.M. and A.G. (1); Mrs. J. P. Arkwrith (1); Major the Hon. H. R. Broughton (1); Lt.-Col. Sir Edmund Bacon, Bt. (1); Col. Ralph S. Clarke (1); Miss F. Foster (2); Henry Keevil (1); Col. J. G. Lowther (5); Major Sir Reginald Macdonald-Buchanan (1); Mr. and Mrs. Paul Mellon (2). *exhib.* R.A. (38); S.A. (34); F.S. (33), 'Animals'. *repr.* 'Sporting Pictures of England', Guy Paget.

MORLEY, E. (op. 1832). Salisbury address. *exhib.* B.I. 1832, 'Dogs'.

MORLEY, GEORGE (op. 1832–1860). London address. Painted animals, his portraits of horses and dogs being in great request by Queen Victoria and others of the Royal Family. Also by officers for pictures of their charges. Three works were in the Hutchinson Sporting Gallery. *exhib.* R.A. (40); B.I. (2).

MORLEY, HENRY (b. Nottingham 1869, 29th December; d.). Studied Paris. Painted animals and landscape. Graves gives 'H. Morley', op. 1837–1853. *exhib.* R.A. (1); S.S. (7), 'Cattle'.

MORLEY, ROBERT, R.B.A. (b. London 1857, 20th July; d.). London address. Living Frensham, Farnham in 1919, Langford, Glos., 1934. Painted animals, figures and landscapes. Educated Slade School. *exhib.* R.A. (5); S.S. (30); V.E. (14). R.A. 1892, 'Lions'; 1893, 'A Ducking'.

MORLEY, W. S. (op. 1845). An amateur. *exhib.* R.A. (1), 'A Retriever'.

MORRELL, R. J. (op. 1839). London address. *exhib.* R.A. 1839, ' "Fuss", Portrait of a Skye Terrier'.

MORRIS, ALFRED (op. 1853–1873). Deptford address. *exhib.* R.A. (2); B.I. (17); S.S. (14); V.E. (1), 'Sporting'. R.A. exhibits were landscapes.

MORRIS, J. W. (op. 1866–1867). London address. *exhib.* B.I. (3), 'Sporting'.

MORRIS, W. WALKER (op. 1850–1867). Greenwich address. *exhib.* R.A. (7); B.I. (14); S.S. (12), 'Sporting'. R.A. 1856, 'The Gamekeeper's Son'.

MORSHEAD, Miss ARMINELL (b. Tavistock, Devon; op. 1920–1934). Painter in oil, water-colour, and etcher of horses, polo subjects, and equestrian portraits. Educated Slade and R.C.A. Schools. Works include 'Changing Ponies'; 'Midwick Country Club, Calif.'; 'Canadian Timber Team'; 'New Forest Stag Hounds'. *exhib.* R.A. 1920, 'Foxhounds'.

MULLER, DANIEL (op. 1863–1878). Putney address. *exhib.* R.A. (4); B.I. (4); S.S. (16), 'Sporting'.

MULLER, WILLIAM JAMES (b. Bristol 1812; d. there 1845, 8th September). Pupil of J. B. Pyne. Painted landscapes, oils and water-colours. 1833, Europe; 1838, Greece and Egypt; 1843, Lycia; 1844, London. *coll.* London, Tate Gallery, 'Sketch for the Eel-pots at Goring', water-colour; Preston, H.M. and A.G. 'Scene in Wales with man fishing', illustrated in Newsham Bequest Catalogue 1884. *exhib.* R.A. (17); B.I.(14); S.S. (9), 'Landscape'. *lit.* 'Life and Art of William James Muller', by C. G. E. Bunt (Lewis, 1948).

MULREADY, WILLIAM, R.A. (b. Ennis, Ireland, 1786, 1st April; d. London 1863, 7th July). Studied R.A. Schools. *coll.* Sir Ralph and Lady Clarke, Haldimand Collection, 'Sleeping Lad with Hound', water-colour; exhibited Towner Art Gallery, Eastbourne, 1963. *exhib.* R.A. (77); B.I. (5); S.S. (1), 'Figures'. R.A. 1808, 'The Dead Hare'; 1811, 'Horses Baiting'; 1813, 'Boys Playing Cricket'; 1814, 'Boys Fishing'; 1831, 'A Sailing Match'; 1848, 'Shepherd Boy and Dog'.

MUNDY, W. (op. 1814). *coll.* P.O.U. 'Landscape with Hounds', signed 'W. Mundy' and dated 1814. Ex. Dalton Hall Collection. Exhibited Preston H.M. and A.G. 1955. Illustrated in catalogue Picture Book, No. 5.

***MUNNINGS, Sir ALFRED J., K.C.V.O., P.P.R.A., R.W.S., Hon.LL.D.** (b. 1879, 8th October; d. 1959, 17th July). Son of John Munnings. *coll.* Aberdeen, A.G. (1); Birmingham, A.G. (1); Liverpool, Walker A.G. (1); London, Tate Gallery (2); Manchester City, A.G. (1); Preston H.M. and A.G. (3); Stoke-on-Trent, Hanley Museum and A.G. (1); Yale University A.G., U.S.A. (1); J. Mitchell Chapman, California (1); Lord Fairhaven (1); Major Sir Reginald Macdonald-Buchanan (1); Miss E. M. Woods (7). *exhib.* R.A. (114). *lit.* Chamont, M., 'Modern Painting in England', 1937, fig. 51; Munnings, 'Second Burst', pp. 281–282.

MURDOCH, W. G. BURN-. Illustrated angling studies by Andrew Land. Author of 'Modern Whaling and Bear Hunting'. *repr.* 'Angling in British Art', Shaw Sparrow, p. 82; 'Fishing by Lantern Light', oil; 'Salmon Spearing in Scotland', body colour.

MURRAY, Sir DAVID, R.A., P.R.W.S., LL.D. (b. Glasgow 1849, d. London 1934). Commenced in the counting house of a local firm. Studied Glasgow School of Art. Went to London 1883. *exhib.* R.A. 1875–1904. R.A. 1880, 'The Trawl Net, Loch Fyne'; 1892, 'A Duck Shooter'; 1895, 'The Angler'.

MURRAY, W. (op. 1848). A picture by this name is included in the collection of the M.C.C. Gallery, Lord's Cricket Ground, London. Quite probably William Murray (op. 1800–1807) in following entry.

MURRAY, WILLIAM (op. 1800–1807). Scottish artist. Arthur Ackermann & Son have had a series of small, fine quality paintings of hound and dog subjects dated as above.

NASMYTH, ALEXANDER (b. Edinburgh 1758, 9th September; d. there 1840, 10th April). Member of Society of British Artists. *exhib.* R.A. (9); B.I. (18); S.S. (3), 'Landscape'; 'The Nasmyth Family' Exhibition at Lowndes Lodge Gallery, London, Oscar and Peter Johnson, May-June 1964; 'Fishing near the Falls of Tummel', S&D 1811, collection of Lord Elphinstone.

NASMYTH, PATRICK (b. Edinburgh 1787, 7th January; d. Lambeth 1831, 17th August). Son and pupil of Alexander Nasmyth. Member of the Society of British Artists. *exhib.* R.A. (20); B.I. (78); S.S. (23); 'The Nasmyth Family' Exhibition at Lowndes Lodge Gallery, London, Oscar and Peter Johnson, May-June 1964; 'Angler's Nook', S&D 1821, colour plate in catalogue; 'Salmon River'.

***NEALE, E.** (op. 1850–1910). Spent much of his life in the countryside of Scotland painting wild birds and animals. Ornithologist and painter. *exhib.* R.A. (1); B.I. (6); S.S. (9); V.E. (9); Frost & Reed Ltd., London, 'Ptarmigan', S&D 1895 (P.O.U.).

NEDHAM, WILLIAM (op. 1823–1836). Working in Leicestershire, thought to have come from Syston and to have been a pupil of Ferneley (?). *coll.* Leicester A.G., 'Horse and Rider', S&D 1836; Major Guy Paget, 'Dick Burton and Hounds', S&D 1826, Leicester; Mr. V. R. Pochin, 'Favourite Hunter of Mr. Pochin, of Barkby, and Groom', S&D 1823. *lit.* 'Book of Sporting Painters', by Shaw Sparrow, p. 226, who says 'Needham'.

NETTLESHIP, JOHN TRIVETT (op. 1874–1901). London address. *exhib.* R.A. (20); S.S. (1); N.W.C.S. (3); G.G. (9); N.G. (7); V.E. (20), 'Animals'. R.A. 1881, 'A Cheetah Hunt'; 1891, 'An Angler'.

NEW, EDMUND HORT, Hon.M.A., Hon.A.R.I.B.A. (b. Evesham 1871; d. Oxford 1931, 3rd February). Black-and-white artist and illustrator. *exhib.* R.A. 1903, Illustrations. *repr.* 'Angling in British Art', Shaw Sparrow; 'Statue of Izaak Walton in Winchester Cathedral', p. 24; 'Carp'; 'Trout'; 'Pike Rising to Take a Small Fish'; 'A Pike on the Prowl'; 'Salmon'; 'Salmon Trout'; 'A Tailpiece'.

NEWHOUSE, C. B. (b. c. 1805, d. 1877). Known for coaching subjects, some of which were engraved between 1832–1845. Also some Military scenes and equestrian portraits. Several coaching subjects in water-colour have been on the market in recent years. *coll.* Major Sir Reginald and Lady Macdonald Buchanan.

NEWTON, C. F. (op. 1826). London address. *exhib.* R.A. (1), 1826, 'Portrait of a Fast-Trotting Mare'.

NICHOLLS, GEORGE F. (op. 1913). Oxford address. *exhib.* R.A. 1913, 'Hunting'.

NICHOLSON, FRANCIS (b. Pickering, Yorks., 1753, 14th November; d. London 1844, 6th March). Studied at Scarborough. Working at Whitby, Knaresborough, Ripon and London. Painted landscapes, principally in water-colours. *exhib.* S.A. (6); R.A. (11); S.S. (1); O.W.C.S. (279); V.E. (21), 'Landscape'. *repr.* 'Angling in British Art', Shaw Sparrow; 'Salmon Fishing', p. 141; sold Christie's 25/26th April 1940, A. N. Gilbey Collection, as 'A Cascade in Wensley Dale'; exhibited R.A. 1789, No. 333.

NICOL, ERSKINE, A.R.A., R.S.A. (b. Leith 1825, 3rd July; d. Feltham 1904, 9th March). Studied at the Trustees' Academy, Edinburgh. Worked for a time as drawing master at the Leith Academy. Went to Dublin, where he remained for several years. Returned to Edinburgh and finally settled in England. *coll.* Glasgow A.G. (1); Sheffield A.G. (1); Mrs. Malcolm, Harrow (1). *exhib.* R.A. (53); B.I. (6), 'Domestic'.

NIEMANN, EDMUND JOHN (b. Islington 1813; d. Brixton 1876, 15th April). *exhib.* R.A. (29); B.I. (45); S.S. (40); V.E. (63), 'Landscape'. R.A. 1846, 'Biting Time' and 'The Fisher of the Solitudes'. *auct.* Christie's, 25/26th April 1940, A. N. Gilbey Collection: 'A View of a Mill near Trefiw, North Wales, with an angler fishing from the rocks in the foreground'; 'Angling on the Thames at Cookham', S&D 1862; 'An Angler seated on a rocky bank in the Highlands'. Graves has confused the names: he gives 'Niemann, Edmund John' and 'Niemann, Edward H., 1863–1867'. Nottingham A.G. exhibited 41 works in 1878. He left a son, Ernest, also a landscape painter.

NIGHTINGALE, R. (op. 1873). Possibly known as Robert Nightingale. A 'redivivus' six-year-old winner of the Warwick Steeple Chase, 1871 was exhibited in Middleburg, Virginia.

NIGHTINGALE, ROBERT (b. 1815, d. 1895). Maldon address. *exhib.* R.A. (4); S.S. (25), 'Sporting'. R.A. exhibits were Portrait, Fruit, and Landscape.

NISBET, NOEL, R.I. (Mrs. H. Bush) (b. Harrow 1887, 30th December). Working 1938 from Wimbledon address. *exhib.* R.A. 1928, 'Return from the Hunt'.

NISBETT, M. (op. 1843). In this year he showed two animal subjects at the R.A. and a landscape at the B.I.

NOBLE, JOHN SARGEANT, R.B.A. (b. 1848, d. 1896). Studied R.A. Schools. *coll.* London, V. and A. Museum, 'Foxhounds and Pups', Birmingham A.G. (2). *exhib.* R.A. (46); S.S. (96); V.E. (1), 'Sporting'. Showing at R.A. in 1876, 'Otter Hounds'; 1877, 'The Sportsman's Friends'; 1878, 'The Otter's Stronghold'; 1880, 'The Keeper's Bothie'; 1881, 'Sportsman's Friends'; 'Selling a Three-year-old'; 1883, 'Watching the Stalkers'; 'Otter Hunting—Full Cry'; 1888, 'Waiting with the Ponies'; 'Highland Sport'; 1890, 'Digging out the Otter'.

***NODDER, R. P.** (op. 1793–1820). London address. Painted animals, birds, flowers, and sporting. Probably related to, if not the same as, F. P. Nodder, a flower painter and designer in human hair, who worked from 1773–1788. *exhib.* R.A. (27), 'Sporting'. The R.A. exhibits included, 1793, 'Portrait of a Dog'; 'Portrait of a Horse'; 'Portrait of a favourite Dog'; 1797, 'Portrait of a Greyhound'; 'Portraits of Spaniels'; 'Portrait of a Mare'; 1798, 'The Sportsman's Refreshment'; 1799, 'Portrait of a Pointer Bitch'; 1811, 'Death of a Fox'; 'A Setter'; 1813, 'Study of a Fox'; 1815, ' "Hollyhock", a Pony'; ' "Tippoo", a celebrated Pony'; 1816, 'Riding School Exercise'; 'The affrighted Horse'; 1819, 'Shooting Pony with Pointers'; 1820, 'A Fox's Head'.

NORTHCOTE, JAMES, R.A. (b. Plymouth 1746, 22nd October; d. London 1831, 13th July). Pupil of Reynolds. Painted portraits and historical subjects. *exhib.* R.A. (229); B.I. (22); S.S. (15), 'Historical'. R.A. 1783, 'Beggars with Dancing Dogs'; 1798, 'Portrait of a Dog'; 1804, 'Tiger Hunting'; 1806, 'Buck Hunting in the Forest of Bowland with portrait of Robert Shaw, aged 84, Keeper to T. L. Parker'; 1807, 'Chess Players'; 'Portrait of a Favourite Dog, in possession of J. Robinson'; 1813, 'Lion Hunting'; B.I. 1808, 'A Dog and a Hawk'; 'A Dog with a Brood of Ducks'. *engr.* 'Grouse Shooters', by George Dawe; 'Sportsman's Dog', by S. W. Reynolds.

NOVICE, GEORGE W. (op. 1824–1833). London address. Painter of mixed subjects, including birds. *exhib.* R.A. (3); B.I. (4); S.S. (5), 'Still-life'. R.A. 1833, 'A Fisherman'.

NOVICE, W. F. (op. 1828–1829). London address. Relative of George W. and resident with him. Painted animals. *exhib.* R.A. (2), 1828, 'A Dog's Head'; 1829, 'A Study of a Dog's Head'.

OAKES, JOHN WRIGHT, A.R.A., H.R.S.A. (b. near Middlewich, Cheshire, 1820; d. Kensington 1887; buried Brompton). Educated at Liverpool. Associate of Liverpool Academy 1847, Member 1850, Secretary 1853–1854, retired 1859. Went to London 1859. Painted landscapes. *exhib.* R.A. (90); B.I. (28); S.S. (11); N.W.C.S. (3); V.E. (23). R.A. 1877, 'Line Fishing on the South Coast'.

OAKLEY, OCTAVIUS (b. 1800, April; d. Bayswater, London, 1867, 1st March). Worked in Derby and Leamington. Painted in oils and water-colours, 'gypsies, gleaners, fisher boys' (Grant). *exhib.* R.A. (30); S.S. (1); O.W.C.S. (221), 'Portraits'.

O'CONNOR, JOHN, R.I., R.H.A. (1830–1889). London address. An Irish artist said to have been a scene painter. *exhib.* R.A. (28); B.I. (6); S.S. (26); N.W.C.S. (12); G.G. (29); V.E. (42), 'Landscape'. R.A. 1874, 'The Last of the Old Horse'.

OLDMEADOW, F. A. (op. 1840–1851). Bushey address. Worked for the Duke of Westminster at Moor Park. *exhib.* R.A. (6). R.A. 1840, ' "Touchstone", the property of the Marquess of Westminster'; 1841, ' "Banker" and "Maid of Honour", Brood Mares, property of the Marquess of Westminster'; 1844, 'The Arabian and His Horse'; 1847, 'Portrait of "Brunette", a Celebrated Steeple-chase Horse, the property of J. J. Preston'.

OLIVER, ARCHER JAMES, A.R.A. (op. 1791–1841). London address. *exhib.* R.A. 1791–1841, 'Portraits'. R.A. 1827, 'Portraits of a Lady and a Favourite Spaniel' (2); 1829, 'Dead Game'; 1832, 'Portrait of a Little Girl and Spaniel'.

ORME, DANIEL (1766 (?)–1832 (?)). Said to have been born in Manchester. An engraver and miniature painter, his coloured prints of sporting subjects are of value.

ORMSBY, V. (op. 1870–1886). London Address. Painted fruit, etc. *exhib.* Rutland Gallery, London, 'Paintings of English Life', June-July 1963; 'The Promenade, S&D 1876. Men and women with umbrellas up, lining promenade, watching yacht racing; illustrated in catalogue.

OSBORNE, WILLIAM (1823–1901). 'The Ward Hunt' in the National Gallery of Ireland, Dublin. *repr.* Apollo, October 1966.

OVENDEN, T. (op. 1817–1832). London address. Painter solely of fish, in landscape. *exhib.* R.A. (4), 'Fish'. R.A. 1817, 'Group of Freshwater Fish'; 1830, 'Group of Freshwater Fish'; 1832, 'A Chub, Trout, Pike and Gudgeon'.

OVEREND, WILLIAM (op. 1845–1855). Painting of racehorse, 'Dandy Jim', at Doncaster.

PAGET, H. M., R.B.A. (op. 1874–1894). London address. Painter and illustrator. *exhib.* R.A. (18); S.S. (4); G.G. (3); V.E. (7), 'Sporting'. R.A. 1894, 'A Boxing Contest'.

***PALMER, LYNWOOD** (b. Lynwood 1868, January; d. 1939). Third son of Canon Palmer. Educated King's College, London. Educated for the Diplomatic Service. Always a lover of horses, Lynwood ran away to Canada and roughed it, ranching and horse-breaking. Devoted spare time to drawing and painting, and his work sold well in Montreal. Obtained commission from a prominent horse owner in Canada to paint his horses. Went to U.S.A. and settled in New York. Returned to England after a lapse of eleven years. He was chosen to paint for King Edward VII, his horse 'Minoru' (winner of the Derby). George V commanded a portrait of 'Scuttle'. Also painted for the Jockey Club a picture of 'Limelight', which they presented to George V. *coll.* Belfast, Ulster Museum (1); Boodle's Club, London (5); Doncaster Museum and A.G. (1); Major Sir Reginald Macdonald-Buchanan (4); Major Guy Paget (the late) (1). *exhib.* Allendale Exhibition of Sporting Pictures, 1931.

PARDON, JAMES (op. 1800–1850). Canterbury address. *coll.* 'Rice Wynne on His Hunter', exhibited Preston 1943; P.O.U. *exhib.* R.A. (13); S.S. (5), 'Miniatures'.

PARKER, H. PERLEE ('Smuggler Parker') (b. Devonport 1795, 15th March; b. Plymouth 1795, Benezit; d. London 1873, 11th November). Removed early in life to Newcastle and made a name as a painter of the sea and coast. About 1840 appointed drawing master at Wesley College, Sheffield. Left for London c. 1845. His pictures of fishermen and smugglers were numerous. Also painted subject pictures and inland views in Scotland and the Lakes. The Hutchinson Gallery of Sporting Pictures included an oil. *coll.* London, V. and A. (1); Newcastle, Laing A.G. (2); Sheffield A.G., 'A Game of Cricket'. *exhib.* R.A. (23); B.I. (40); S.S. (23); N.W.C.S. (4); V.E. (61), 'Historical'. *auct.* Sotheby's, 5th February 1964 (184), 'The Disputed Shot'.

PARRIS, EDMUND THOMAS (b. London 1793, 3rd June; d. there 1873, 17th November). Studied R.A. Schools. Painted flowers, fruit, history and angling. *exhib.* R.A. (26); B.I. (36); S.S. (18); N.W.C.S. (5); V.E. (1), 'Historical' *auct.* Christie's, 25/26th April 1940, A. N. Gilbey Collection. 'A Young Lady and Gentleman Fishing in a Stream at the bottom of an ornamental garden'.

PARROTT, WILLIAM (b. Overley 1813, October; d. 1869, Benezit and Grant; Graves gives him as exhibiting as late as 1875). Pupil of Pye. Visited Paris, Italy, Germany, Brittany, and Normandy. A picture of 'Henley Regatta' was in the Hutchinson Sporting Gallery. He also painted a 'Derby Day', S&D 1864. *auct.* Christie's, 25/26th April 1940, A. N. Gilbey Collection, 'Fishing at Hampstead'.

PASMORE, JOHN (op. 1830–1845). London address. Painted animals and birds. *exhib.* R.A. (11); B.I. (3); S.S. (3), 'Domestic'. R.A. 1845, 'Portrait of a Highland Sheep Dog, property of the Dowager Countess of Dunmore'.

PASMORE, JOHN F. (op. 1841–1866). London address. *exhib.* R.A. (30); B.I. (23); S.S. (11); V.E. (26), 'Domestic'. His R.A. exhibits included 'Study of Trout' (1842); 'Head of a Favourite Pointer' (1843); 'The Shooting Pony' (1847); 'Portrait of a Dog' (1852); 'The Old Sportsman' (1862).

PATON, WALLER HUGH, R.S.A., R.S.W. (b. 1828, d. Edinburgh 1895). Brother of Sir Noel Paton. *exhib.* R.A. (15); N.W.C.S. (4); V.E. (17), 'Landscape'. R.A. 1863, 'Salmon Fishing on the Tay'; 1867, 'Deer Forest in Skye—Summer Moonlight'.

PATRICK, JAMES McINTOSH, R.S.A., R.O.I., A.R.E. (b. Dundee 1907, 4th February; living). Studied Glasgow School of Art. Painter in oil and water-colour, also etcher. *coll.* Aberdeen A.G.; Cape Town, N.G. of South Africa; Dundee A.G.; Hull, Ferens A.G., 'A hunt setting out from an Exmoor Farm in a snow landscape'; London, British Museum; Tate Gallery; Pittsburgh, Carnegie Institute; Port Sunlight, Lady Lever A.G.

PAUL, Sir JOHN DEAN, First Baronet (b. 1775, d. 1852). Banker in the firm of Snow, Paul and Paul, closed in 1855. Amateur artist and member of the Melton Hunting circle. *coll.* Leicester A.G., 'Greyhound in a Landscape, pair, both S&D 1858. *exhib.* R.A. (20), 'Landscape'. Engravings, 'A Trip to Melton Mowbray'; 'A Trip to Brighton' (four plates); 'Hunting in Leicestershire'. *auct.* Sotheby's, 20th May 1964, 'Park Mount'; 'Rosebud', Bay Racehorses in Stables, a pair.

PAYNE, CHARLES J. ('Snaffles'). Painter and illustrator. Now over 80 years of age. Works include 'Osses and Obstacles'; 'The Grand National'; 'The Gent in Ratcatcher', etc. *repr.* 'Sunday Telegraph', 15th March 1964, 'The Worst View in Europe—Grand National 1901, Arthur Nightingale on Grudon, the Winner'.

PEALE, T. R. (Titian) (b. 1800, d. 1885). 'A Canyon with Anglers Fishing above a Waterfall' was sold at Sotheby's 18th December 1963.

***PEARCE, STEPHEN** (b. 1819; d. London 1904, 31st January). Prolific painter of portraits, in which he had many highly placed sitters. Attached to the Queen's Mews, he also painted portraits of the Royal Stud. A few landscapes, one in Rome, were done by him. Many of his equestrian portraits and scenes of hunting include well-painted landscapes. *exhib.* R.A. (92); B.I. (3); G.G. (1), 'Portraits'.

PEEL, JAMES, R.B.A. (b. Newcastle 1811, 1st July; d. Reading 1906, 28th January). Pupil of A. Dalziel, London, 1840. *coll.* London, V. and A. Museum, 'Fox Covers in North Devon'. *exhib.* R.A. (69); B.I. (37); S.S. (248); V.E. (149), 'Landscape'.

PELHAM, JAMES, Junior (b. Saffron Walden, Essex, 1840; d. Blundellsands 1906). Resided in Liverpool. Member of Liverpool Academy and Secretary for many years. Treasurer and Secretary to the Old Liverpool Sketching Club. *coll.* Liverpool, Walker A.G., 'A Young Angler', drawing. *exhib.* R.A. (1); G.G. (1); V.E. (3), 'Landscape'.

PENNY, EDWARD, R.A. (b. 1714, d. 1791). Professor of Painting at the Royal Academy. *exhib.* S.A. (10); R.A. (21), 'Portraits'. R.A. 1779, 'The Return from the Chase'.

PERCY, SIDNEY RICHARD—SYDNEY RICHARD WILLIAM (b. 1821; d. Sutton 1886, 13th April). A painting, 'Wooded River Landscape with figures, fishing, etc.' sold at Christie's 22nd January 1965 (73), illustrated in catalogue.

PETTIE, JOHN, R.A., H.R.S.A. (b. Edinburgh 1839, d. Hastings 1893). Studied Trustees' Academy. Went to London in 1862. Painted historical subjects and a few angling subjects. Shaw Sparrow, 'Angling in British Art', mentions a picture of Fly Fishing.

PETTIT, ALFRED (op. 1850–1871). 'The Evening Mail, Grasmere', S&D 1856 inscribed, sold at Sotheby's 13th July 1966.

PHIPPS, J. (op. 1838). *coll.* Hanley, A. G., Stoke-on-Trent, 'York Racecourse', signed. *exhib.* R.A. (1); S.S. (1), 'Buildings'.

PINE, ROBERT EDGE (op. 1766). 'Portrait of Young Sportsman' (green and brown costume, holding a gun in left hand, two hounds beside him). S&D 1766. *auct.* Sotheby's 7th June 1965 (156).

PITTARO, CHARLES (op. 1881). London. May be same as 'Pittara, Carlo', (b. Turin 1836; d. 1890, 25th October), painter of animals. *exhib.* V.E. (1), 'Sporting'.

PITT, R. (op. 1796). Exhibiting a painting of a 'Kingfisher' at the R.A. in this year.

PITTS, FREDERICK (op. 1856–1882). London address. *exhib.* R.A. (3), 'Wild Herbage'; B.I. (2); S.S. (6), 'Sporting'.

POCOCK, INNES (op. 1852). London address. A William Innes Pocock was b. Bristol 1783, d. Reading 1836, 13th March, and may have been a relative. *exhib.* B.I. (1); 'Sporting'. *coll.* Reading Museum and A.G., 'Master of the Berkshire Hounds', S&D 1844.

POINGDESTRE, CHARLES H. (b. Jersey, op. 1849; d. London 1905, 26th October). Resident in Italy, where he painted in and around the marble quarries of Carrara. President of the British Academy in Rome. *exhib.* R.A. (24), no sporting; B.I. (2); S.S. (2); N.W.C.S. (9); G.G. (1); N.G. (2); V.E. (10), 'Sporting'.

POINGDESTRE, W. W. (op. 1856). London address. *exhib.* B.I. (1), 1856, 'Animals'.

***POLLARD, JAMES** (b. 1792; d. Chelsea 1867, 15th October, aged 75 years; b. 1797, Grant and Benezit; d. 1859, Benezit; b. 1772, Paget). Son and pupil of Robert Pollard. Painter of sporting and coaching subjects and engraver. *coll.* Major The Hon. Henry R. Broughton (4); Major Sir Reginald Macdonald-Buchanan (6); Lord's (1); Mr. and Mrs. Paul Mellon (4); Harry J. Peters, Jr., New York (4); Mr. N. C. Selway (20); Charles H. Thieriot, New York (6). *exhib.* R.A.; B.I. *repr.* 'A Book of Sporting Painters', Shaw Sparrow; 'Country Life', 20th October 1955; I.C.I. Plastics Division Calendar 1959. *lit.* 'Animal Painters', Sir Walter Gilbey, Bt., Vol. II; 'A Book of Sporting Painters' and 'Angling in British Art', Shaw Sparrow; 'The Regency Road', N. C. Selway, London, 1957; 'James Pollard', N. C. Selway, Leigh-on-Sea, 1965.

POLLARD, ROBERT (b. Newcastle-on-Tyne 1755; d. London 1838, 23rd May). Father of James Pollard. Went to London from Newcastle in 1780. Engraved his own works. *repr.* 'Angling in British Art', Shaw Sparrow, p. 128; 'The Contemplative Boy's Recreation' (Fishing), designed and engraved by R. Pollard. *exhib.* F.S. (2), 'Landscape'. *lit.* 'A Book of Sporting Painters' and 'Angling in British Art', Shaw Sparrow.

POLLARD, SAMUEL (op. mid 19th century). Unknown other than by a water colour 'A Carriage Accident' shown in Oscar and Peter Johnson's 'Sport and the Horse' exhibition, June 1969 (no. 37).

POWER, HAROLD S. (op. 1911–1912). London address. *exhib.* R.A. 1911, 'Stag Hunting'; 1912, 'A Fox Hunt in the Midlands'.

***PRADES, A. F. DE** or **PRAEDES** (op. 1844–1883). Living at 8 Southampton Street, Fitzroy Square, London. A sporting painter of limited output and consequently rare. *exhib.* R.A. (2); B.I. (6); S.S. (4), 'Sporting'. *repr.* 'Nat Langham, the Jockey', published by J. Moore, 1853, and one other later, a colour aquatint of the racehorse 'Nancy', is also known. *auct.* 'Begum' and 'Rob Roy'; studies of the heads of hunters in their stables, a pair, both S&D 1883, sold at Sotheby's 28th October 1964, No. 154.

PRINGLE, W. (op. 1842). There is also a W. J. Pringle (op. 1826–27) *exhib.* B.I. (1); S.S. (3), 'Dramatic'. *coll.* Birmingham A.G., 'The Stourbridge-Birmingham Royal Mail Coach Passing Quinton Toll Gate', S&D 1842.

PROUT, MARGARET FISHER, A.R.A., R.W.S., R.W.A. (b. Chelsea 1881; d. St. Leonards-on-Sea 1963). Daughter of Mark Fisher, R.A. Married J. A. Prout. Studied at the Slade School. *exhib.* R.A. 1955, 'The Fisherman'; 1961, 'The Angler'.

PULLER, JOHN ANTHONY (op. 1821–1867). London address. *exhib.* R.A. (43); B.I. (53); S.S. (82), 'Domestic'. R.A. 1845, 'Young Anglers'; 1850, 'Tittlebat Fishers'; 1853, 'Young Anglers'.

PYBOURNE, THOMAS (b. 1708). *coll.* Ackermann's Gallery, 'Flying Childers'. *repr.* Book of Sporting Painters.

PYNE, WILLIAM HENRY, R.W.S. (b. London 1769; d. there 1843, 29th May). Son of a leather seller. Landscape painter in water-colours and author. *exhib.* R.A. (22); O.W.C.S. (58), 'Landscape'. R.A. 1796, 'Anglers'. *auct.* Christie's, 25/26th April 1940, A. N. Gilbey Collection, 'A View near Whitby with anglers beside a stream', S&D 1790.

QUADRONE, JEAN B. (op. 1887–1888). London address. *exhib.* R.A. 1887, 'Morning of the Chase'.

QUIGLEY, D. (d. 1764, 28th April). Working in Dublin. *coll.* 'Carriage Match at Newmarket', ex. Hutchinson Sporting Gallery. *exhib.* Rutland Gallery, London; 'English Sporting Life', April 1960; 'Curragh of Kildare Races, 28th April 1764, signed and inscribed; illustrated in catalogue, pl. 7.

RACKHAM, ARTHUR, R.W.S. (b. 1867, d. 1939). Water-colour painter and illustrator. *coll.* London, V. and A. Museum, 'Isaak Walton reclining against a Fence', pen and water-colour, illustration for 'The Compleat Angler'. *exhib.* R.A. (10); S.S. (4); N.W.C.S. (2), 'Landscape'; Leicester Galleries, London, December 1935, 'One-Man'.

RAEBURN, Sir HENRY, R.A. (b. Stockbridge 1756, 4th March; d. 1823, 8th July). Portrait painter. *coll.* National Gallery of Scotland, Edinburgh, 'Henry Raeburn on a Grey Pony'; 'Study of a Dog'; National Gallery, London, 'Lt.-Col. Bryce McMurdo with Fishing Rod'; *repr.* colour plate, 'English Painting', Mark Roskill, 1959. *exhib.* R.A. (53), 'Portraits'.

RAFTER, H. (op. 1856). Coventry address. *exhib.* V.E. (1), 'Sporting'.

RANKIN, GEORGE. 'Grouse Flying' signed, sold at Sotheby's 11th May 1966.

RAVEN, SAMUEL (b. Birmingham 1775; d. 1847, 10th December). A panel,'Old English Fighting Dogs', S&D 1800, was sold at Sotheby's 11th November 1964 (84). All paintings seen have been small panels: hunting, shooting, etc.; also painted boxes, etc. Fine quality.

***READE, JOHN R.** (op. 1773–1783). Bedford address. *exhib.* M.C.C. Gallery, Lord's, 'A Cricket Match'. *exhib.* R.A. (2); S.A. (31). R.A. exhibits were 'Dead Game'. *lit.* Grant, Old English Landscape Painters', Vol. 3, p. 229; 'The Farrington Diaries', 1935.

REDFARN, W. B. (op. 1869–1870). Cambridge address. *exhib.* S.S. (1); V.E. (3), 'Sporting'.

REDWORTH, WILLIAM JOSIAH, P.S. (b. Slough, Bucks, 1873, 9th March; d. c. 1947). Painted in oils, water-colours, and pastel, mostly landscape, but included portraits of horses. Four oils inscribed 'Lucy', 'Commotion', 'Sunbeam', and 'Seagull', S&D 1909, were sold at Christie's 24th January 1964.

***REED, GEORGE** (op. 1823). Possibly son of Thomas Reed, farmer, of Clench Street, High Halstow, Kent, who died in 1849. His sister was Harriet Reed. Will, probate records for the Rochester diocese—*vide* County Archivist, Kent County Council, Maidstone. High Halstow is about 22 miles from the Cudham Hills. *exhib.* Lowndes Gallery, London, Oscar and Peter Johnson Ltd., 'Mr. T. Reed and Mr. T. Squires with Pointers on Cudham Hills, Kent', S&D 1823.

REID, JOHN ROBERTSON (b. Edinburgh 1851, d. 1926). Apprenticed to a firm of house painters. Studied R.A. Schools. Settled at Shere, Surrey. Painted principally coast scenes. *coll.* London, Tate Gallery, 'A Country Cricket Match, Sussex', S&D 1878; Glasgow A.G., 'Sons of the Sea' (six boys, sons of fishermen, and a dog; two boys fish with rods). *exhib.* R.A. (29); S.S. (52); N.W.C.S. (1); G.G. (23); N.G. (5); V.E. (30) 'Domestic'. *repr.* 'Angling in British Art', Shaw Sparrow; 'Glen Ashdale, Arran', p. 75 exhibited R.A. 1910; 'Lord Selborn, Angling', p. 80.

***REINAGLE, PHILIP, R.A.** (b. 1749; d. Chelsea 1833, 27th November). One of a family of twelve artists. He was of Hungarian origin, his family emigrating to England in 1745 as supporters of the Young Pretender. Pupil of Allan Ramsay in Scotland. Went to London in 1769. Painted portraits, animals, still-life, landscape, and birds, etc. Married Jane Austin, spinster, at Marylebone Church, London, 24th July 1771. *coll.* London, V. and A. Museum (1); Sheffield A.G. (1); Sir Maurice Bromley Wilson, Bt. (the late) (1); Lt. John S. Clarke, U.S.A. (1); Lytham Hall, Lancs. (2); Mrs. Stroyan (1). *exhib.* R.A. (114); B.I. (138); S.S. (1), 'Landscape'. *lit.* 'A Book of Sporting Painters' and 'Angling in British Art', Shaw Sparrow.

REINAGLE, P. A. (op. 1804–1811). Son of Philip Reinagle. *exhib.* R.A. (6); B.I. (4), 'Horses'. R.A. 1804, 'Portrait of a Horse'; 1811, 'Portrait of "Young Woodpecker", a Celebrated Horse, property of J. Claridge'; 'Portrait of "Robin Hood", a Celebrated Horse, property of J. Claridge'.

REINAGLE, RAMSAY RICHARD (b. 1775, 19th March; baptized 16th April at St. James's, Piccadilly; d. 1862). Son of Philip and Jane Reinagle. Married Oriana Bullfinch at St. Marylebone Church, 10th June 1801. Visited Italy. Resigned from R.A. 1848. *exhib.* R.A. (244); B.I. (51); S.S. (2); O.W.C.S. (67), 'Landscape'.

REINHARDT, W. (op. 1868). 'A Fox Standing in a Winter Landscape', S&D 1868, sold at Sotheby's 11th May 1966.

REYNOLDS, FRANK, R.I. (b. London 1876, 13th February; living 1950). Illustrator and sometime Manager of 'Punch', to which he contributed. *exhib.* B.I. (2); S.S. (2), 'Figures'. *repr.* 'Angling in British Art', Shaw Sparrow, p. ix, 'No bites and No Mascot', drawing for 'Punch'.

REYNOLDS, Sir JOSHUA, P.R.A. (b. Plympton St. Maurice, Devon, 1723; d. 1792). Son of the head-master of the Grammar School. Pupil of Hudson in 1740 in London. Returned to Devonshire. Renowned for his portraits, sometimes with fine landscape backgrounds. His 'Colonel Acland and Lord Sydney as Archers in a Woody Glade' bring him within the sphere of this volume, plus several of groups hunting. *coll.* Leicester A.G.; Mrs. H. Meynell (portrait of Hugo Meynell, known as 'Father of English Foxhunting').

RHODES, F. R. (op. 1841–1843). Handsworth, Staffs., and Birmingham addresses. *exhib.* R.A. (5); B.I., (1). R.A. 1841, 'Pheasant Shooting'.

RHODES, JOSEPH (b. 1782, d. 1855). A native of Leeds who was for a short time at the R.A. Schools in London. Returned to Leeds 1811, where he is said to have supplied every type of subject that clients desired—landscape, architectural, flowers, fruit, history, etc. *coll.* Leeds A.G. (10). *exhib.* B.I. (2), 'Landscape'.

RIBBLESDALE, THOMAS, 4th Baron (op. 1892). London address. *exhib.* N.G. (1), 'Sporting'.

RICHARDS, CHARLES (op. 1854–1857). Keynsham address. *exhib.* R.A. (4); B.I. (4); S.S. (7); V.E. (6); 'Sporting'.

RICHARDS, RICHARD PETER (b. Liverpool 1839; d. at Pisa, Italy, 1877). *coll.* Liverpool, Walker A.G., 'Fishing', water-colour. *exhib.* R.A. (11); B.I. (1); S.S. (3); V.E. (2), 'Sea-pieces'.

RICHARDSON, GEORGE (b. 1808, d. 1840). Son of T. M. Richardson. Working in Newcastle. *coll.* 'A Moorland Scene with Highlanders Shooting Deer', body colour. Signed with monogram. *exhib.* B.I. (6); N.W.C.S.

RICHARDSON, THOMAS MILES, Junior, R.S.A. (b. Newcastle 1813; d. London 1890, 5th January). Son and pupil of T. M. Richardson. Visited France, Switzerland, Italy, and Germany. *auct.* Christie's, 9th June 1961 (44), 'Trout Fishing, Glen Falloch', water- and body-colour, S&D 1857.

RICKETS, CHARLES ROBERT (op. 1868–1879). London address. *coll.* Royal Thames Yacht Club, 'Ocean Match from Nore to Dover for Queen's Cup, June 1874'. *exhib.* R.A. (7); S.S. (3); V.E. (2), 'Sea-pieces'.

RICKMAN, PHILIP (op. 1930's). Water-colour painter of game-birds and wildfowl. Exhibited annually at the Greatorex Gallery. His picture titles included 'Startled Blackgame'; 'Evening in the coverts'; 'Mallard Coming In', etc.

RITCHIE, JOHN (op. 1858–1875). London address. A painting, 'Cricket at Hambledon, Sussex', S&D 1855, is at Lord's. *exhib.* R.A. (18); B.I. (9); S.S. (12), 'Figures'.

RIVIERE, BRITON, R.A. (b. London 1840, d. there 1920). Studied at Cheltenham College, where his father was drawing master. Painted animals and sometimes these had a sporting interest.

ROBERTS, A. (op. 1793). London address. *exhib.* R.A. (1), 'Portrait of a Sportsman'.

ROBERTS (op. 1771–1777). Dublin address. *exhib.* S.A. (1); F.S. (2), 'Sporting'.

ROBERTS, JAMES (op. 1708–1755). Executed forty portraits of famous horses which were engraved by his brother Henry. They published 'The Sportsman's Pocket Companion', c. 1760.

ROBERTS, SAMUEL (op. 1778–1824). London address. *exhib.* R.A. (4), 'Still-life'. Fish, Hares, and Mallards.

ROBERTS, WILLIAM, A.R.A. (b. London 1895, living). *coll.* Tate Gallery, 'Cantering to the Post'. *exhib.* R.A. 1964, 'The Bicycle Lesson'; 'The Lake—Rowing'; Contemporary Art Society. Arts Council Gallery, London, 1964, 'Boxing Match'.

ROBINSON, W. HEATH (b. Hornsey 1872, 31st May; d.). Artist and caricaturist. *repr.* 'Angling in British Art', Shaw Sparrow; 'Mr. Spodnoodle and a Friend hook and land the same fish and quarrel' from 'The Spodnoodle Papers', 1923; 'Mr. Spodnoodle and his Friend divide the fish unequally and return home joyous with the spirit of Compromise'.

ROBSON, R. (op. c. 1840). A hunting scene, 'Breaking Cover', signed but not dated, was exhibited at Ackermann's Galleries, London.

ROE, ROBERT HENRY (op. 1846–1868). Resided in Scotland and later worked in London and Cambridge. Painting scenery and sporting incidents, with careful delineation of animals and birds. *exhib.* R.A. (10); B.I. (11); S.S. (16); R.A. 1852, 'A Highland Shooting Party'; 1853, 'The Tired Stag'; 'A Highland Keeper Waiting for Shot at an Eagle'.

ROGERS, J. (op. 1842). A painting, 'Sir John Malcolm's Arabian "Sultan" in a landscape with two other horses', signed 'Deptford', sold at Christie's 20th November 1964 (159). Graves gives a 'J. Rogers' London exhibition 1838–1864, 'Figures', R.A. (3); B.I. (1); S.S. (6).

ROGERSON, J. A water-colour 'The Bristol to London Stage Coach' shown in Oscar and Peter Johnson's 'Sport and the Horse' exhibition June 1969 (no. 39).

ROLFE, ALEXANDER F. (op. 1839–1871). London address. One of a family of four artists all painting fish and angling subjects. *exhib.* B.I. (6); S.S. (52); V.E. (40), 'Fish'. B.I. 1863, 'Salmon Fishing on River Usk'; 1864, 'First Woodcock of the Season'; 'Salmon Fishing on the Usk, South Wales'; 1865, 'Dead Game'. *auct.* Christie's, 25/26th April 1940, A. N. Gilbey Collection. 'Two Anglers Playing a Pike', S&D 1857; 'The Catch—The Duke of Hamilton standing by the Artist, who kneels with a trout in his hands', S&D 1868.

ROLFE, Mrs. A. F. (op. 1866). London address. Wife of Alexander F. Rolfe. *exhib.* S.S. (1), 'Sporting'.

ROLFE, EDMUND (op. 1830–1847). Painted fish and birds. *exhib.* R.A. (1); B.I. (6); S.S. (5), 'Still-life'.

ROLFE, F. (op. 1849–1853). London address. Painted fish. *exhib.* B.I. (2); S.S. (4), 'Fish'.

ROLFE, HENRY LEONIDES (op. 1847–1881). Painted fish and angling subjects. *exhib.* R.A. (16); B.I. (23); S.S. (92); V.E. (40). R.A. 1847, 'Study of Tench and Dace'; 1852, 'The Last Landed'; 1854, 'A Morning's Sport on the Usk'; 1855, 'Study of Carp'; 'Study of Trout'; 1859, 'Study of Trout'; 1866, 'A Good Day's Sport'; 1873, 'Perch, Roach and Dace'.

ROMNEY, GEORGE (b. 1734, Beckside, Dalton-in-Furness; d. Kendal 1802). Apprenticed to Charles Steele. Went to London 1762. Spent two years in Italy. Returned to London 1775. *coll.* The Hon. Mrs. R. White, 'Master Pelham out Partridge Shooting' (painted 1786–1787). *exhib.* Sabin Galleries, London. 'Dicky Barnard with a favourite pointer' (1785–1786). *repr.* 'Connoisseur' advert. June 1963. *lit.* 'Memoirs of George Romney', 1830, p. 165, by Rev. J. Romney.

ROPE, GEORGE T. (op. 1876–1885). Wickham address. *exhib.* R.A. (2); S.S. (1), 'Sporting'. R.A. 1877, 'Field Mice'; 1885, 'Harvest Mice'.

***ROPER, RICHARD** (or **THOMAS**) (op. 1749–1765). Painter of portraits and sporting subjects. The earliest extant of sporting interest is dated 1749. E. Edwards ('Anecdotes') wrote 'sufficient to satisfy the gentle men of the turf and stable'. His portraits of horses are not ill done; some maybe by another of the name, for the Christian name is variously recorded and there may have been two painters. Roper exhibited at S.A. (3); F.S. (9). 'Saddled Chestnut with Groom, Huntsman and Hounds Outside a Stable' S&D 1762, was exhibited at Ackermann's Gallery, London, October/November 1965 (no. 24).

ROSA, GWILYM (op. 1856). *coll.* Lord Fairhaven, 'Portrait of Charles Davis, Her Majesty's Huntsman, Windsor, 1856'. Charles Davis was the father of Richard Barrett Davis, the well-known sporting painter.

ROSE, GERARD DE, R.B.A., A.R.C.A. (b. Accrington 1920; living). Painted many pictures of wrestlers. *coll.* Rochdale A.G., 'Wrestlers', oil.

***ROSS, JAMES** (op. 1729–1821 (?)). Possibly working in Gloucester, Hereford and Worcester. Grant gives a 'James Ross(e)? 1745–1821' and 'James Ross'. The latter painted a large hunting scene dated 1738 (see illustration). Graves gives a 'James Ross, Worcester', exhibiting an architectural subject at the R.A. 1791. *exhib.* Messrs. Leggatt Bros., London (c. 1930). Four paintings of the Beaufort Hunt. *lit.* Grant, 'The Old English Landscape Painters', Vol. 3, p. 191.

ROSS, THOMAS (op. 1730–1745). At Gloucester. A Sporting party outside a Mansion (24 × 29 in.) is known. Thought to be of the same family as James Ross (op. 1729–1821). *lit.* Grant, 'Old English Landscape Painters', Vol. 3, p. 190, fig. 184.

ROTH, GEORGE (op. 1810–1815). London address. Painter of fish in landscape. *exhib.* R.A. (5), all of Fish.

ROWLANDSON, G. D. *auct.* 'Going to the Meet', signed, sold Christie's 9th October 1964.

ROWLANDSON, THOMAS (b. London 1756, d. there 1827). Studied at R.A. Schools. Drew caricatures and painted landscape, genre, and sporting subjects in oils and water-colours, also engraved. *coll.* Bedford, Cecil Higgins Museum (2); Birmingham A.G. (3); Doncaster Museum and A.G. (4); Dudley A.G. (1); Liverpool, Walker A.G. (1); London, V. and A. Museum (3); Earl of Besborough (1); Mr. and Mrs. Paul Mellon, U.S.A. (2); Lord Somerleyton (2); the late Sir Robert Witt (1); York, City A.G. (1). *exhib.* R.A. (20); S.A. (4). *repr.* 'The Picture of Cricket', John Arlott, 1955; 'Rural Sports or a Cricket Match Extraordinary, 1811'. *lit.* 'Thomas Rowlandson', A. P. Oppé, 1923; 'Thomas Rowlandson', F. Gordon Roe, 1947.

RUGGLES, W. H. (op. 1833–1846). Lewisham address. *exhib.* R.A. (2); R.A. 1846, 'Portrait of a Favourite Hunting Mare'.

RYOTT, J. R. (c. 1810–c. 1860). A set of four hunting scenes; 'At Cover'; 'Gone to Earth'; 'Full Cry'; 'The Death'; S&D 1846 and inscribed 'Newcastle'. *exhib.* Ackermann's Gallery, London, November 1965.

SADLER, WALTER DENDY (b. Dorking 1854, 12th May; d. St. Ives 1923, 13th November). Studied London and Dusseldorf. *coll.* London, Tate Gallery, 'Thursday—Monks Fishing'. *exhib.* R.A. (35); S.S. (24); G.G. (2); V.E. (26), 'Domestic'. R.A. 1873, 'The Deciding Game'; 1880, 'Thursday'; 1881, 'It's Always the Largest Fish that's Lost'; 1884, 'A Goodly Catch'; 1885, 'Gudgeon Fishing'; 1890, 'The Hunting Morn'.

SALOMAN, A. *auct.* 'A Yacht Race off New Brighton', sold at Christie's 9th November 1962.

SAMBOURNE, LINLEY (op. 1885–1904). London address. Illustrator and caricaturist. *exhib.* R.A. 1896, 'Athlectics' (for 'Punch').

SAMUEL, GEORGE (op. 1785, d. 1824 from fall of wall upon him whilst sketching). *exhib.* R.A. (94); B.I. (54), 'Landscape'. R.A. 1800, 'Pike Pool on the Dove'. Illustrated Walton's 'Angler' 1808, Cotton's Fishing House on the Dove.

SANDBY, PAUL, R.A. (b. Nottingham 1725, d. London 1809). *coll.* Stoke-on-Trent, City A.G., 'Pheasant Shooting'. M.C.C. Gallery, Lord's (1). *exhib.* S.A. (39); F.S. (2); R.A. (125); B.I. (14); Agnew's 91st Annual Exhibition of Water-colour Drawings 1964 'The Fisherman'.

SANDERSON-WELLS, J. S., R.I. (SEE WELLS, J. S. SANDERSON)

SARGENT, JOHN SINGER, R.A. (b. Florence 1856, 12th January; d. London 1925, 15th April). *coll.* Port Sunlight, Lady Lever A.G., 'Portrait of a Young Salmon Fisher, Alec McCulloch'. *exhib.* R.A. (19); G.G. (6); N.G. (7). *repr.* 'Angling in British Art', Shaw Sparrow, two colour plates.

***SARTORIUS, FRANCIS** (b. London 1734; d. there 1804, 5th March). Son of John Sartorius. Painted hunting and racing subjects. *coll.* Viscount Bearsted (1); Mr. and Mrs. S. B. D. Hood (1); Major Sir Reginald Macdonald-Buchanan (2); Mr. and Mrs. Paul Mellon (1); Major Guy Paget (the late) (1); Charles H. Thieriot, New York (3, two since sold). *exhib.* R.A. (12); S.A. (7); F.S. (20), 'Sporting'.

SARTORIUS, JOHN (b. 1700, d. London 1780). Shaw Sparrow says that J. N. Sartorius, Senior, is usually known as John and refers to J. N. Junior as the most noted of the family. This does not tally with Graves 'Royal Academy Exhibitors', where JN. Junior is given as exhibiting only one work at the R.A. *exhib.* S.A. (1); F.S. (62); R.A. (1). R.A. 1780, 'Portrait of a Horse'.

***SARTORIUS, JOHN FRANCIS** (b. London 1775, d. 1830). Eldest son of J. N. Sartorius. Painting more or less in the same tradition and style of the family. *coll.* The late Lord Rootes. *exhib.* R.A. (20); S.S. (4).

SARTORIUS, J. N., Junior (op. 1805). London address. Both Graves and Grant give this. Shaw Sparrow gives the best known of the family as J. N. Junior, but it is thought to be an erroneous attribution; J. N. Junior is in fact the same as John Nost. *exhib.* R.A. 1805, 'Partridge Shooting'.

***SARTORIUS, JOHN NOST** (Shaw Sparrow and Basil Taylor); **NOTT** (Grant) (b. London 1759, 26th May; d. 1828). Son of Francis Sartorius and grandson of John. *coll.* Liverpool, Walker A.G. (2); The Hon. David Astor (5); Mrs. Gwendolen Altha, Milnthorpe (5); Lord Gretton (1); Major Sir Reginald Macdonald-Buchanan (1); Mr. and Mrs. Paul Mellon (2); Sir Joshua Rowley, Bart. (1); Charles H. Thieriot, New York (8, seven since sold). *exhib.* R.A. (78); S.A. (1); F.S. (31).

SCADDAN, R. (op. 1744). An example of the work of this artist is to be seen in the M.C.C. Gallery, Lord's Cricket Ground, London.

SCANLAN, ROBERT R. (op. 1837–1859). *exhib.* R.A. 1837, 'Portraits of "Beauty" and "Star", two of His Majesty's State Horses'; 'Lord Mount Charles and a Favourite Pony'; 'Portrait of "Angelica", property of a Gentleman'; 1840, 'Portrait of Celebrated Steeple-chase Horse, "Lottery", Winner of 12 Races, ridden by Mr. James Mason'; 1841, ' "The Poacher", property of the Earl of Drumlaurig, 2nd Life Guards'; 1846, 'Portrait of Favourite Charger, property of Capt. Isacke'.

SCHALCH, JOHANN JAKOB (b. Schaffhausen 1723, 23rd January; d. Switzerland 1789, 21st August, Benezit; d. 1770, Bryan's; 1769 others). Pupil of Leonhard Schnetzler in Switzerland and Karl Wilhelm Hamilton in Augsburg. In England 1755, and remained eight years. Specialized in architectural landscapes and buildings of historic interest, many being painted in Northern England. In 1763 at The Hague. Spent some years in Holland and returned to Switzerland, where he died. *coll.* S. J. Richards, Stamford, Lincs., 'Fox attacking Rabbit in a landscape'. *repr.* 'Country Life', 8th September 1960. *lit.* 'Country Life'. *exhib.* S.A. (3).

SCHOLDERER, OTTO (b. Frankfort 1834, 25th January; d. there 1902, 25th January). Spent 28 years in London. Putney address. Painted portraits and still-life. *exhib.* R.A. (40); S.S. (7), 'Game'. R.A. 1875, 'Heron and Ducks'; 1886, 'A Man with Game'; 1893, 'Game'.

SCHWANFELDER, CHARLES HENRY (b. Leeds 1773, Bryan's; 1774, 11th January, Benezit; d. 1837). Painted portraits, still-life, and sporting. Animal painter to George IV. *coll.* Leeds City A.G., 'A Pointer and Two Setters'; 'A Setter standing on a Moorland'; 'A Newfoundland Dog standing on a Cliff Top', S&D 1812; 'Horse and Groom'. Also 7 Portraits and 4 Landscapes. *exhib.* R.A. (10) B.I. (6). Those at R.A. included, 1809, 'A Setter Dog'; 1814, ' "Malcolm", an Arabian, property of H.R.H. Prince Regent'; 1815, 'Setters and Pointer'; 1817, 'Portraits of a Favourite Mare and Dogs, property of R. Walker'; 'A Setter and Dead Pheasant'; 1821, 'Portrait of a Sporting Dog'; 1826, 'Moor Game Shooting'; 1835, 'Dogs: a Favourite Pointer, etc.' *auct.* Christie's, 25/26th April 1940, A. N. Gilbey Collection, 'Anglers beside a Rocky Highland River'.

SCHWEICKHARDT, HEINRICH WILHELM (b. 1746, d. London 1797, 8th July). From Brandenburg. Came to England 1786. Director of the Academy at The Hague. Friend of Benjamin West, P.R.A. Produced etchings of animals in 1788. *coll.* London, Guildhall A.G., 'A Skating Scene'. *exhib.* R.A. 1790, 'Ice-piece with Figures Skating'; 'Landscape with Horses'.

SCOTT, PETER MARKHAM (b. 1909, 14th September; living). Son of Captain Scott, R.N. Studied at R.A. Schools. *exhib.* R.A. 1933, 'Grey Geese and Pink Footed Geese'; 1934, 'White-fronted Geese'; 1935, Barnacle Geese in April'; 1936, 'Red-fronted Geese and One Lesser White-front'; 1937, 'Snow Geese and a Blue Goose'. Ackermann's Gallery, one-man shows since 1933.

SCROPE, WILLIAM (b. Castlecoombe, Somerset, 1772; d. 1852, 20th July). Founder and Director of the British Institution. Author of 'Days of Deer Stalking' and 'Days and Nights of Salmon Fishing'. *exhib.* R.A. (6); B.I. (19), 'Landscapes'.

SEAGO, EDWARD BRYAN (b. Norwich 1910, 31st March; living). Animal and landscape painter. Sporting subjects include 'Foxhunter', winner of the Ascot Gold Cup 1933; The Earl of Harewood's 'Alcester'; 'Over the Sticks'; 'Lord Melchett, M.F.H., with Fred Napper and Tedworth Hounds'; 'Derek and Julian, Sons of Lord and Lady Melchett, with their Beagles at Colworth'. *coll.* Earl of Derby (composite picture of six racehorses S&D 1943). *exhib.* R.A. from 1930.

SEVERN, WALTER (b. 1830, d. 1904). Son of Joseph Severn, painter and Consul at Rome. *exhib.* R.A. 1853, 'Herd of Red Deer'; 1855, 'Herds of Red Deer and Fallow Deer in Windsor Park'.

SEXTIE, WILLIAM A. (op. 1848–1880). Marlborough address and London. *exhib.* R.A. (1), 1848, 'A Favourite Hackney, property of the Earl of Granville'. Painted numerous portraits of famous racehorses.

***SEYMOUR, JAMES** (b. London 1702, d. there 1752). Son of James Seymour, a banker, amateur painter, and friend of Lely and Wren. According to Walpole, Seymour was thought even superior to Wootton in drawing a horse, but too idle to apply himself to his profession. Built a considerable reputation for his portraits of horses, racing and hunting subjects. His many patrons included Charles Seymour, 3rd Duke of Somerset, for whom he decorated a room at Petworth; also John Jolliffe, M.P., for whom he painted some 15 paintings. *coll.* London, Brit. Mus (49); Cambridge, Fitzwilliam Museum (10); Plymouth M. and A.G. (2); The Hon. David Astor (5); The Hon. Michael Astor (1); Louis C. G. Clarke (1); Duke of Grafton (1); The Lord Hylton (3); The Earl of Jersey (1); Mr. and Mrs. Paul Mellon (6); The late Major Guy Paget (2); Witt Collection, Courtauld Institute, London (1).

SEYMOUR, ROBERT (b. 1798, d. 1836, 20th April). Caricaturist and painter in water-colour. Committed suicide as result of mental illness. *exhib.* R.A. (1), 1822, 'Historical'. *repr.* 'Angling in British Art', Shaw Sparrow; 'Uncommon Small! Uncommon! Perch though!!' water-colour in M. H. Spielmann Collection.

SHAKESPEARE, PERCY (b. Dudley 1907; killed in action 1943). Painted many local sporting scenes. A number are on permanent loan to the Civil Defence Headquarters, Priory Hall, Priory Road, Dudley. *coll.* Dudley Art Gallery, 'Afternoon at the Ice Rink', oil, exhibited Birmingham 1939 with 11 studies for this work.

SHAW, BYAM JOHN (b. Madra 1872, 13th November; d. London 1919, 26th January). Painter and engraver. *coll.* Lady Lever A.G., Port Sunlight, 'The Regatta'.

SHAW, J. (op. 1851–1853). London address. May be the same as Joshua Shaw (1776–1861). *exhib.* S.S. (2), 'Sporting'.

SHAW, JOSHUA (of Bath) (b. Bellingborough 1776, d. in America 1861). Apprenticed to a country sign writer and later set up in Manchester. Painted flowers, still-life, and animals. *exhib.* R.A. (9); B.I. (22); S.S. (2), 'Cattle'. Many of the landscapes at R.A. include cattle.

SHAW, NEVIL, A.R.C.A., A.R.E. (b. 1915, 15th April; living at Hartlip, Kent). Mainly topographical, but has completed a number of paintings and studies related to fishing, football, and pigeon racing. *exhib.* R.A. 1964, 'Wind, Rain and Fishermen' (618).

SHAW, WILLIAM, F.S.A. (op. 1757–1774). London address. Lived in Mortimer Street, Cavendish Square, where 'he built a large painting room with conveniences to receive the animals from which he painted' (E. Edwards). *exhib.* S.A. (27), 'Sporting'. Frank T. Sabin, London, 'A Racehorse after a Running Match'. *repr.* 'Country Life' advert., 15th December 1960. There is said to be a portrait of 'Blank, property of Lord Ancaster' (1757), in the Rosebery Collection.

SHAYER, C. (op. 1879). Southampton address. *exhib.* S.S. (1), 'Sporting'.

SHAYER, WILLIAM (b. Southampton 1788; d. Shirley, Southampton, 1879). Painted landscapes with groups of cattle and horses. *exhib.* R.A. (6); B.I. (82); S.S. (338), 'Landscape'. R.A. 1824, 'Children Fishing'; 1843, 'The Fisherman's Daughter'.

SHAYER, WILLIAM J. (b. Southampton 1811, 2nd April; d. 1860). Son of William Shayer. Painted animals, coaching and sporting subjects. 'Confidence', a S&D 1840 painting of the celebrated American trotter performing a match in Harness, was until recently in the Charles H. Thieriot collection, New York. *coll.* Glasgow A.G., 'A Shady Pool—Group of Horses stand in a pool under trees with labourer on horseback near'. *exhib.* Leger Galleries, London, 'The Meet' and 'Full Cry', a pair, S&D 1852, were shown 1943, and later at Preston A.G.

SHEPHEARD, GEORGE (b. 1770, d. 1842). *coll.* Lord's, 'Tom Walker', c. 1800, from a sketchbook. *repr.* 'The Picture of Cricket', J. Arlott. *exhib.* R.A. (50); B.I. (3); S.S. (25); O.W.C.S. (1); V.E. (17), 'Landscape'.

SHEPHERD, DAVID (b. 1931, living). Educated Stowe, later under Robin Goodwin. Known for his paintings of aircraft and especially for his paintings of African Game. *exhib.* Tryon Gallery, London. 38 paintings of African Wild Life (October-November 1964).

SHEPHERD, GEORGE SIDNEY (op. 1821–1858). London address. *exhib.* R.A. (17); S.S. (43); N.W.C.S. (223), 'Still-life'. *auct.* Christie's, 25/26th April 1940, A. N. Gilbey Collection, 'An Angler', water-colour, S&D 1842.

SHEPHERD, THOMAS HOSMER (op. 1817–1840). Son of George Shepherd. *exhib.* S.S. (4), 'Landscape'. *auct.* Christie's, 25/26th April 1940, A. N. Gilbey Collection: 'A View of Keswick and Grassdale Pikes with two Anglers', S&D 1852; 'An Angler with his Wife and Child fishing from the bank of a stream'; 'A View of Nuneham House, Oxford, with anglers beside the river'.

SHIRLEY-FOX, JOHN, R.B.A. (b. 1860; d. 1939, 3rd June). Bath address. Painter of portraits, etc. 'Brush and Feather' of 'The Field', author of 'Angling Adventures of an Artist', 1923. *exhib.* Paris Salon 1887; R.A. from 1890. *repr.* 'Angling in British Art', Shaw Sparrow; 'Silhouette of Active Angling', p. 83.

SHRAPNEL, N. H. S. (op. 1849–1850). Gosport address. *exhib.* B.I. (2); S.S. (3), 'Sporting'.

SIBLEY, CHARLES (op. 1826–1847). London address. Painted portraits, game and water-fowl. *exhib.* R.A. (10); B.I. (6); S.S. (8), 'Still-life'. R.A. 1826, 'Dead Game'; 1827, 'Dead Game'; 1834, 'Water Fowl'.

SICKERT, WALTER RICHARD (b. Munich 1860, 31st May; d. 1942, 22nd January). Painter and etcher. *coll.* Birmingham A.G., 'Dieppe Races'. *lit.* 'Sickert', by L. Browse, 1960, p. 90.

SILLEM, CHARLES (op. 1883–1889). London address. *exhib.* R.A. (3); S.S. (3), 'Sporting'. R.A. 1883, 'Rough Terrier and Rats'; 1889, 'A Poacher's Bag'.

***SIMPSON, CHARLES WALTER, R.I., R.O.I.** (b. Camberley 1885, 5th May; d. Alverton, Penzance, 3rd October 1971). Painter of marines, animals, wild bird and sporting scenes. Son of the late Major-General C. R. Simpson, C.B. Paris Salon 1923 (Silver Medal); International Exhibition, Wembley, 1924; San Francisco International Exhibition 1914 (Gold Medal); VIII Olympiad, Paris, 1924 (Gold Medal). Sporting portraits include Major Burnaby, Master of the Quorn; Major Gordon Foster, Master of the Farndale; Lt.-Col. Harry-Llewellyn on 'Fox-hunter'; Pat Smythe on 'Tosca', on 'Flanagan' and on 'Prince Hal'. *coll.* Blackpool; Bournemouth; Derby; Doncaster (2); Dunedin, New Zealand; Gateshead; Newcastle. *exhib.* R.A., R.I., S.M.A. *repr.* 'Leicestershire and its Hunts'; 'The Harboro Country'; 'El Rodeo'; 'Trencher and Kennel'; 'Animal and Bird Painting'; 'The Fields of Home', etc.

SIMPSON, Mrs. F. (op. 1831). Derby address. *exhib.* R.A. (1), 1831, 'Portraits of a Favourite Horse and Greyhound'.

SIMPSON, Sir GEORGE (b. 1792, d. 1860). *coll.* Yale University, U.S.A., 'Buffalo Hunt'; 'Buffalo Resting'.

SIMPSON, H. HARDEY (op. 1885–1888). Bowden address. *exhib.* R.A. (2); S.S. (2), 'Sporting'. R.A. 1888, 'John Jones, Huntsman to the North Cheshire Hounds'.

SIMPSON, J. H. (op. 1877). *exhib.* R.A. (1), 'Just Caught It'.

***SKEAPING, JOHN R., R.A.** (b. Liverpool 1901, 9th June; living). Pupil at R.A. Schools, won Gold Medal 1920. Prix de Rome 1924. One-time Professor of Sculpture, Royal College of Art. Figure and landscape painter, in recent years almost entirely devoted to sporting subjects, racing, trotting, bull-fighting. Sculptor also, including bronzes of horses, bulls, etc. *coll.* Newport, Mon., A.G.; D. Taylor. *exhib.* R.A., the exhibits, 1954–1964, almost entirely sporting.

SLATER, JOSEPH (op. c. 1745–1787). Painter of landscapes with figures. Also 'decorator' of mansions as Mereworth (Lord Despencer's) and Stowe (Duke of Buckingham's). *exhib.* F.S. (5); R.A. (4), 'Portraits'; R.A. 1774, 'Dead Game', tinted drawing. *repr.* I.C.I. Plastics Division Calendar 1959, 'Archery 1789', engraved by J. Heath.

SMIRKE, ROBERT, R.A., F.S.A. (b. Wigton, Carlisle, 1752; d. London 1845, 5th January). Studied R.A. Schools. *exhib.* S.A. (7); R.A. (25); B.I. (1); S.S. (5), 'Historical'. *engr.* 'The Meeting of the Royal Archers in Gwersyllt Park, near Wrexham, 1794'. Aquatint by C. Apostool.

SMITH, —, Junior (op. 1840). London address. *exhib.* R.A. 1840, 'Terrier and Hedgehog'; 'Juno, a Setter'.

SMITH, CHARLES LORAINE (b. 1751, d. 1835). Of Enderby Hall; Sportsman, Poet, Member of Parliament, Musician, Deputy Master of the Quorn. *coll.* Major Guy Paget (the late) (5); Major Sir Reginald Macdonald-Buchanan (1). *exhib.* R.A. (6), 'Sporting'. *repr.* 'Sporting Pictures of England', Guy Paget, p. 18.

SMITH, EDWARD (op. 1773). At Fowey, Cornwall. *auct.* Christie's, 25/26th April 1940, A. N. Gilbey Collection. 'A Group of Ladies and Gentlemen in an Ornamental Garden in front of a Mansion; some holding Fishing Rods'. Inscribed on back of canvas 'Edrd. Smith at Fowey Cornwall 1773 Invt. et pinxt'. Illustrated in catalogue. 'A Party of Ladies and Gentlemen Angling by a Stream in an Ornamental Garden'.

SMITH, GEORGE, of Chichester (b. 1714, d. 1776). Second of a trio of brothers. All painted landscapes. Some could be termed sporting, i.e. 'Duckshooting in Winter', a panel sold at Sotheby's 11th November 1964. *exhib.* R.A. (4); S.A. (2); F.S. (103).

SMITH, GEORGE ARMFIELD (*see also under* ARMFIELD, GEORGE) (op. 1836–1839 under name Smith after 1840 adopted name Armfield). London address. *exhib.* (under above name) R.A. (5); B.I. (2); S.S. (1). R.A. 1796, 'Portrait of a Gentleman Cricketer'; 1799, 'Portrait of a Setter and Spaniel, property of J. Gibbs'; 'Dead Game'.

SMITH, H. C. (op. 1820–1833). London address. Chiefly a sporting painter, portraits of dogs, with game, etc. *exhib.* R.A. (6); B.I. (5); S.S. (7), 'Sporting'. R.A. 1821, 'Portrait of "Major", a Favourite Dog, property of a Gentleman'; '"Carew", a Favourite Pug Dod'; 1822, 'Dead Game'; 1823, 'Game'.

SMITH, J. L. (op. 1832). Painter of horses, an example of his work was shown at the R.S.B.A. in 1832.

SMITH, JOHN RAPHAEL (b. Derby 1752; d. Worcester 1812, 2nd March, Benezit; Shaw Sparrow says Doncaster). Son of Thomas Smith, of Derby. Drew portraits in crayons and water-colour and engraved. Worked in York, Sheffield, Doncaster and London. *auct.* Christie's, 25/26th April 1940, A. N. Gilbey Collection, 'A Party going Fishing at Hampton-on-Thames'. *repr.* 'Angling in British Art', Shaw Sparrow, p. 177; 'Strephon and Phyllis'; 'The Angelic Angler', both designed and engraved by J.R.S.

SMITH, THOMAS, of Derby (b. op. c. 1740; d. Bristol 1767, 12th September, Benezit; others 1769). Father of John Raphael Smith. Forty of his pictures were engraved by Vivares for Boydell and six pictures of horses engraved by Elliott for Boydell. *exhib.* Gooden & Fox, London, 'Borlace the Jockey on "Sultana" ', S&D 1751. *repr.* 'Angling in British Art', Shaw Sparrow; 'Anglers on the Wie in Monsal Dale, near Bakewell, 1743', from the engraving by Vivares after T. Smith.

SMITH, THOMAS (b. Shalden Manor, Alton, Hants., 1790; d. after 1852). Son of Thomas Smith, a farmer and hunting man. The artist hunted with the Hampshire. He was Master of the Hambledon 1825–1829 and 1848–1852; the Craven 1829–1833; the Pytchley 1840–1844. Smith painted the scene of the Hampshire Hunt moving off, from memory. Lady Gage, unbeknown to the artist, had the picture engraved by C. Turner. Smith wrote and illustrated 'The Life of a Fox', 1843, and 'The Diary of a Huntsman'. *repr.* 'Country Life', 11th November 1954, 'A Run with the Craven'. *lit.* Letter from Brig-Gen. J. F. R. Hope, 'Country Life', 10th February 1955.

SMITH, WILLIAM (op. 1813–1859). London address and Shrewsbury, Newport and Ongar. Painted fish, dogs, horses, and other sporting subjects in oil and water-colour. *exhib.* R.A. (32); B.I. (15); S.S. (7); O.W.C.S. (9), 'Sporting'.

SMITH, WILLIAM COLLINGWOOD, R.W.S. (b. Greenwich 1815, d. Brixton Hill 1887). Pupil of J. D. Harding. Member and Librarian of the Old Water Colour Society. Many landscape drawings have angling interest. *coll.* London, V. and A. Museum, 'The Otter's Haunt' and four other drawings. *exhib.* R.A. (32); B.I. (15); S.S. (21); O.W.C.S. (1064), 'Landscape'.

SMYTHE, EDWARD ROBERT (b. Ipswich 1810; d. Bury St. Edmunds 1899). Benezit gives Emily R., which is incorrect. Son of bank manager. Lived and worked almost entirely in East Anglia. *exhib.* R.A. (5), 'Sporting'; B.I. (4); S.S. (4); V.E. (1), 'Domestic'. R.A. 1874, 'Favourite Hounds, property of E. Walter Green, Master of the Suffolk Hounds'; Leggatt Bros., 1960, 'A Horse Fair'; Oscar and Peter Johnson Ltd., Lowndes Lodge Gallery, London, 'The Smythes of Ipswich', November-December 1964, over forty paintings, including 'Grey Pony with a Greyhound'; 'Hunter and Hound'; 'Three Hounds in a Kennel'. Finely illustrated catalogue.

SMYTHE, THOMAS (b. Ipswich 1825, d. there 1907). Brother of Edward Robert. Both painting similar subjects. *exhib.* R.A. and S.S., 1854–1862 (20). Oscar and Peter Johnson Ltd., Lowndes Lodge Gallery, London, 'The Smythes of Ipswich', the examples by Thomas including 'Game Keepers Returning'; 'The Woodland Harriers, 25th October 1862'; 'Breaking in Horses' and 'After the Shoot'.

'SNAFFLES' (*see* CHARLES PAYNE)

SNAPE, MARTIN (op. 1874–1901). Gosport address. *exhib.* R.A. (17); S.S. (1); G.G. (2); V.E. (8), 'Figures' R.A. 1883, 'The Gamekeeper's Museum'; 1894, 'The Ferret Hutch'; 1897, 'Gosport Fair'.

SNOW, J. W. (op. 1832). London address. *exhib.* S.S. (2), 'Sporting'.

SOPER, THOMAS JAMES (op. 1836–1882). London address. Painted landscapes all over the country. *exhib.* R.A. (45); B.I. (48); S.S. (34). R.A. 1844, 'Eel Traps on the Yeo, N. Devon'; 1859, 'Eel Bucks on the Thames'.

SPALDING, C. B. (sometimes given as G. B. or E. B.) (op. 1840–1849). Reading and Brighton addresses. *exhib.* R.A. (5), 'Sporting'. R.A. 1840, ' "Sailor", "Jerry" and "Lottery", Celebrated Steeple-chase Horses, property of John Elmore'; 1843, 'Horses, property of Sir E. Filmer, Bt.'; 1848, 'Horses'; 1849, 'A Forrester'. *auct.* Sotheby's, 29th July 1964, 'Red Stag Monarch following Thomas Nevill home after having been hunted by his Bloodhounds', signed and inscribed on reverse.

SPENCER, JOHN S. (op. 1835–1863). London address. *exhib.* R.A. (1); B.I. (6); S.S. (6), 'Dramatic'. B.I. 1835, 'A Falconer'.

SPENCER, THOMAS (op. 1700–1767). Disciple of James Seymour. *coll.* Mr. and Mrs. Paul Mellon, U.S.A., 'Chestnut Hunter with Groom' (attributed). *exhib.* Messrs. Spink & Son, London, 'A Grey Hunter held by a Boy in Livery', S&D 1767. *repr.* 'A Book of Sporting Painters', Shaw Sparrow.

SPERLING, J. W. (op. 1845–1848). London address. *exhib.* R.A. (3), 'Sporting'. R.A. 1845, 'Grey Stallion, property of H.M. The King of Wurtemburg'.

SPILSBURY, EDGAR ASKE (op. 1800–1828). London address. *exhib.* R.A. (21); B.I. (10), 'Animals'. Included at the R.A., 1800, 'Horses'; 1801, 'Council of Horses'; 1806, 'Wounded Stag'; 'Aged Horses'; 'Bitterns Fighting'; 1807, 'Greyhound'; 1808, 'Boar Hunting'; 1811, 'Portrait of "Rover" '; 1814, 'Horses Greeting a Stranger'.

SPODE, JOHN (op. late 19th century). 'Two Greyhounds and a Dead Hare in a Landscape'; 'Gentleman on Horseback with his Greyhounds and Stonehenge in the Background'; (signed); *exhib.* Ackermann's Gallery, London, 1964.

STANDFUST, G. B. (op. 1844). London address. Painter of dogs. *exhib.* R.A. 1844, ' "Tan", the property of the Hon. Jerrald Dillon'.

STANDISH, W. (op. 1859). London address. *exhib.* B.I. (1), 'Sporting'.

STANNARD, ALFRED (b. Norwich 1806; d. there 1889, 26th January). Painted some angling pictures.

STANNARD, JOSEPH (b. Norwich 1797, 13th September; d. there 1830, 7th December). Studied art with Robert Ladbrooke. E. T. Daniell shared a studio with him in Norwich. Also an etcher. Twenty drawings are in the British Museum. *coll.* Geoffrey F. Buxton, C.B., 'Old Peter, the Huntsman' (lived in St. Augustine's and sold hare skins, etc., exhibited Norwich 1927. *exhib.* B.I. (9); S.S. (4), 'Sea-pieces'.

STARK, ARTHUR JAMES (b. Chelsea 1831, 6th October; d. Nutfield 1902, 29th October). Son of James Stark. Studied under E. Bristow. His wife, R. Isabella Stark, painted still-life. *coll.* Glasgow A.G., 'Pointer and Dead Duck', S&D 1851. Other works in V. and A. Museum, London, and Norwich. *exhib.* R.A. (35); B.I. (33); S.S. (51), 'Landscape'. R.A. 1852, 'A Rest from Sport'; 1853, 'Interior of a Stable'; 1855, 'The Startled Heron'; 1863, 'A Hunter, property of the Duke of Rutland'; 1873, 'The Angler's Nook'.

STARK, JAMES (b. Norwich 1794, 19th November; d. London 1859, 24th March). Pupil of John Crome. *exhib.* R.A. (66); B.I. (136); S.S. (54); O.W.C.S. (10); N.W.C.S. (4), 'Landscape'. R.A. 1841, 'A Trout Stream'; 1842, 'Taking up Eel Pots'; 1843, 'The Game Keeper's Lodge'; 1850, 'Donkey and Foal'.

STEEL, JOHN SYDNEY (op. 1889–1893). London address. *exhib.* R.A. (4); S.S. (5); G.G. (3); V.E. (2), 'Sporting'. R.A. 1889, 'A Hunter of the Past'; 1890, 'Hunting the Irish Elk'; 1892, 'Death of the Master Stag'.

STEELL, DAVID G., A.R.S.A. (op. 1891). Edinburgh address. Son of Gourlay Steell. *exhib.* R.A. (1), 'Sporting'. R.A. 1891, 'Sporting Dogs'; R.S.A. Centenary Exhibition 1926, 'Ptarmigan', illustrated in catalogue, pl. 95.

STEELL, GOURLAY, R.S.A. (b. Edinburgh 1819, 22nd March; d. there 1894 (31st January). Son of John Steell, artist, and brother of Sir John Steell, R.S.A., the sculptor. Trained in the Galleries of the Board of Manufacturers. Animal painter to H.M. Queen Victoria. Curator of the National Gallery of Scotland. Some reference works say STEEL. *coll.* Glasgow A.G., 'The Trysting Place. Two Pointers with a Setter lying at their feet; on one side a heap of red grouse, on the other some dead mountain hares'. *exhib.* R.A. (10), 'Animals'. R.A. 1866, ' "Totty", property of Mr. Crellen, Liverpool'; 1869, 'Gillie and Capercailzie'; 1871, 'Col. Carrick Buchanan on Horse with His Huntsman, J. Squires, and Favourites of his Celebrated Pack of Hounds'; 1873, ' "Drumpellier Pugs", property of Mrs. Carrick Buchanan'; 1874, 'Portraits of three of Her Majesty's Favourite Dogs, "Noble", "Corran" and "Waldermann" '.

STEUART (or **STUART**), **Sir J.** (b. Rome 1779; d. Edinburgh 1849, 27th January). Made drawings of Cavalry, etc.

STEVENS, GEORGE (op. 1810–1864). London address. *exhib.* R.A. (22); B.I. (75); S.S. (246), 'Fruit'. R.A. 1810, 'Dead Hare'; 1814, 'Portrait of a Mare, property of J. Anderson'; 'Rural Sports' (2); 1817, 'A Deer Hunt'; 1822, 'Portrait of a Horse, property of a Gentleman'; 1842 and 1848, 'Dead Game'.

STEWART, F. A. A water-colour titled 'The Meet at Dawn', signed F. A. Stewart, was sold by Messrs. Baverstock at Godalming 27th May 1964.

STILWELL, J., Junior (op. 1849–1855). Tooting address. *exhib.* R.A. (1); B.I. (4); S.S. (2), 'Cattle'. R.A. 1849, 'A Favourite Dog'.

STIRLING-BROWN, A.E.D.G. (op. 1910). *auct.* Three paintings of Polo Ponies, S&D 1910, sold Christie's 24th January 1964.

STONE (A., J., and R.). Three artists, all painting hunting and coaching subjects which have appeared at auction. None are dated. Possibly worked in Europe. Graves records an *Ada* Stone, a painter of still-life, and sixteen others, none with initials 'J.' or 'R.' A set of four hunting scenes exhibited at Ackermann s Gallery in 1964. They were also shown at The Sporting Gallery, Middleburg, Virginia, U.S.A. in the same year.

STOOP, JAN (?) PETER (b. Utrecht 1610, d. 1686). Styled 'Dirk' Stoop, and best known as an etcher of animals, especially horses. Came to England in 1662 and engaged in painting, hunting, battle scenes, etc. His Christian names are variously given, Dirk or Dirck; or Thierry or Rodrigo, this last by which he was known while court painter at Lisbon. *coll.* National Gallery of Ireland, 'Hunting Party'.

STOTT, J. (op. 1828–1830). London address. *exhib.* R.A. (7), 'Sporting'. In R.A. Exhibitors, Graves gives the artist as 'Gem Engraver'. R.A. 1828, 'Tiger at Bay'; 1829, 'Hunting Antelopes'; 'Portrait of a Wolf Dog'; 'Frame with English Sports'.

STRETTON, PHILIP EUSTACE (op. 1884–1901). London address. *exhib.* R.A. (18); S.S. (3); V.E. (8), 'Animals'. R.A. 1884, 'Disturbed'; 1891, 'After the Hunt'; 'Portraits of Setters'; 'The Master of the Hounds'; 1900, 'A Poacher'; 1901, 'The Pet of the Kennel'.

***STUBBS, GEORGE, A.R.A.** (b. Liverpool 1724, 25th August; d. London 1806, 10th July). Son of a currier and leather dresser. Received some instruction from Hamlet Winstanley. In Leeds as a portrait painter in 1744 and York later. Visited Italy, reaching Rome 1754. Returned to Liverpool and left again after his mother's death, 1756. Rented a farmhouse at Horkstow, Lincolnshire, and began work on 'The Anatomy of the Horse', helped by Mary Spencer, who became his constant assistant. Removed to London c. 1759. Died at 24 Somerset Street, Portman Square, and left all his possessions to Mary Spencer. *coll.* Birkenhead A.G. (1); British Association (1); Glasgow University (3); Indianapolis, U.S.A., John Herron Art Institute (1); Ireland, National Gallery (1); Leeds, City A.G. (2); London, British Museum (1); National Gallery (1); R.A. (1); Tate Gallery (3); Liverpool, Walker A.G. (4); Philadelphia, U.S.A., Museum of Art (1); Yale University A.G., U.S.A. (2); Her Majesty the Queen (about 20); Sir Martyn Beckett (1); Castle Howard Collection (1); London Jockey Club (1); Lord Cobham (1); Lt.-Col. J. N. Chaworth-Musters (2); Mr. Odo Cross (1); Mrs. Walter Elliot (1); Sir Raymond and Lady Evershed (1); Earl Fitzwilliam and Trustees of the Wentworth Estates (2); Thomas W. Fitzwilliam (2); Mrs. Katharine T. Gilbey (1); Duke of Grafton (1); Mrs. Muriel Heely (1); Mrs. Edward Hulton (1); Sir Bruce Ingram (the late) (7); Mr. Michael Ingram (1); Mr. Pierre Jeannerat (1); Mrs. Mary Keith (1); Mrs. Leader (1); The Dowager Marchioness of Londonderry (1); Major Sir Reginald Macdonald-Buchanan (4); Major A. E. W. Malcolm (1); Mr. and Mrs. Paul Mellon (22); Earl of Middleton (1); Lord Monson (1); Mrs. Paul Moore, Covent, U.S.A. (1); Mr. and Mrs. A. Moss, Memphis, U.S.A.; Countess Mountbatten (1); National Trust (Ascott Collection), (1); Miss Clara S. Peck (1); Brig.-Gen. Sir Robert Pigot, Bt. (1); Viscount Portman and Trustees of the Tate Gallery (1); Mr. J. V. Rank (2); The Duke and Duchess of Richmond and Gordon (2); Mr. John Robarts (1); Brig. The Baron de Robeck (1); Mr. Anthony De Rothschild (2); Mr. E. J. Rousuck, U.S.A. (1); Royal College of Surgeons (3); Earl Spencer (1); Brig. C. E. Tryon-Wilson, C.B.E., D.S.O. (2); Hon. Nicholas Villiers (1); Mrs. G. F. Weld Blundell (4); Major J. B. Walker (1); Earl of Yarborough (2); The Yorkshire Club (1). *exhib.* R.A. (34). *lit.* 'A Book of Sporting Painters', Shaw Sparrow; 'Memoirs of George Stubbs and Others', Joseph Mayer, 1879; 'Studies', by Sir Walter Gilbey, 1898; 'The Harp of Aeolus', Geoffrey Grigson, 1947; 'Image', No. 3, 1949–50, Basil Taylor; 'Life of Stubbs with catalogue of his work', Basil Taylor; 'George Stubbs' Catalogue of Exhibition', Walker A.G., Liverpool, 1951.

STUART, CHARLES, F.S.A. Exhibited paintings of red deer in Scottish forests at R.A. (1888–1900).

STUART, GILBERT CHARLES (b. America 1755, 3rd December; d. Boston 1828, 9th July). Went to Scotland 1770. Returned to America. Came back to London in 1775. In Dublin 1787–1793. Returned to America. Well-known portrait painter. *exhib.* R.A. 1782, 'Portrait of a Gentleman Skating'.

STUBBS, GEORGE TOWNLEY (op. 1771, d. 1815). Said to have been the natural son of George Stubbs. Painter and engraver. *exhib.* R.A. (1); S.A. (3). R.A. 1782, 'Portrait of an Old Hunter belonging to Mr. Oldmeadow, of West Wickham, Kent'.

STURGESS, JOHN (op. 1875–1884). London address. *exhib.* S.S. (1); V.E. (3), 'Sporting'.

STURGESS, JULIAN (op. 1850). *exhib.* Preston A.G. 1943, 'Scene at Newmarket' (attributed to).

STURGESS, RICHARD (op. 1873). A set of four coaching subjects, one of which S&D 1873. *exhib.* Frost & Reed, London, 1966.

SUHRLANDT, CARL (b. Ludwigslust 1828, 10th July; d. Kochel 1919, 11th February). Pupil of Ary Scheffer in Paris. Visited Copenhagen, Russia and England. *exhib.* S.S. (1), 1884, 'Sporting'.

SULLIVAN, EDMUND JOSEPH, A.R.W.S. (b. London 1869; d. there 1933, 17th April). Illustrator. *repr.* 'Angling in British Art', Shaw Sparrow; 'Use Him as Though you Loved Him', p. 228; 'Go Yourself so far from the Waterside', illustration to 'The Compleat Angler', 1896, p. 84.

SUMMERS, S. N. (op. 1764–1806). Chelmsford address. Portrait and landscape painter. 'Black Jokes'; 'Selling a Horse' and 'The Winchester Coach' all engraved by Hunt. *exhib.* F.S. (1); R.A. (6).

SURTEES, JOHN (op. 1849–1889). London and Newcastle addresses. *exhib.* R.A. 1849, 'Baiting the Line'; 1868, 'A Trout Stream, N. Wales'; 1889, 'A Fishing Day at Rowsley'.

SWAN, C. E. (op. 1893). London address. Painted wild animals. *exhib.* R.A. (1).

SWEBACH, BERNARD EDWARD (b. Paris 1800, 21st August; d. Versailles 1870, 2nd March). Studied School des Beaux Arts 1814. Visited Russia. *exhib.* Messrs. Leggatt Bros., London, 'A Race Meeting in 1819', S&D 1819. *repr.* advert., 'Country Life', 21st July 1960.

TAIT, ARTHUR F. (b. 1819, d. 1905). Sporting artist emigrated to U.S.A. in 1850, becoming a full Academician at the National Academy of Design in 1858. Very fine quality paintings.

TALBOT KELLY (Capt. Richard Barrett, R.I.) (b. Birkenhead 1896, 20th August). Painter of birds, including many sporting. *coll.* Birkenhead.

TALMADGE, GEORGE. *lit.* 'Sporting Pictures of England', Guy Paget.

TALMAGE, ALGERNON, R.A. (b. 1871, d. 1939). *exhib.* R.A. 1917, 'The Bass Fisher'.

TANNER, J. (c. 1800). An imitator of Morland. Dubbed 'The Mohawk from his Indian-like complexion by Morland.

TAPPING, G. (1797–1799). Painter of horses and dogs. *exhib.* R.A. (3), 'Sporting'. R.A. 1797, 'Portrait of a Nobleman's Groom'; 'Portrait of a Setter just finding the Game'.

TASKER, WILLIAM (b. London 1808, 16th April; d. Chester 1852, 1st September). Pupil of Robert Lorris at Chester. Painted chiefly race courses.

TAYLER, ALBERT CHEVALLIER (b. 1862, d. 1925). *exhib.* R.A. (10); S.S. (2); V.E. (16), 'Domestic'. *repr.* 'Angling in British Art', Shaw Sparrow, p. 81; 'Benson on Thames' (boy in boat, fishing; lady seated on bank preparing a meal), exhibited R.A. 1912.

TAYLER, JOHN FREDERICK (b. Boreham Wood, Elstree, 1802; d. West Hampstead 1889, 20th June). Educated Eton and Harrow. Studied Sass's Academy, R.A. Schools, and under Vernet in Paris. Visited Rome. President of the Old Water Colour Society 1858–1871. *coll.* H. K. Foers (1); Accrington, Haworth A.G., 'After the Chase', water-colour; Glasgow A.G., 'The Gamekeeper's Corner', S&D 1865. *exhib.* R.A. (5); B.I. (5). R.A. 1850, 'The Keeper's Daughter'. *auct.* Christie's, 25/26th April 1940, A. N. Gilbey Collection, 'A Dog sitting beside Fishing Tackle and Fish by a Highland Stream'; 'A Caricature of Samuel Prout Angling'.

TAYLOR, STEPHEN (op. 1817–1849). Winchester, Oxford and London addresses. Painted game, animals, and portraits. *exhib.* R.A. (48); B.I. (29); S.S. (42). R.A. works included, 1817, 'Dead Game'; 'A Hawk and Lark'; 'A Dead Woodcock'; 1818, 'Woodcock and Snipe'; 'Teal, Snipe and Land Rail'; 'Brace of Partridges'; 1819, 'Pug Puppies'; 1823, 'Spaniel Puppies'; 1824, 'A Hare Sitting'; 1825, 'A Spaniel Watching Dead Game'; 1830, 'Blenheim Spaniel Puppies'; 1831, 'A Wounded Bittern'; 1837, 'Wild Fowl'.

THATCHER, C. F. (op. 1816–1846). London address. Painted fish, game, rustic, religious and portraits. *exhib.* R.A. (9); B.I. (5). R.A. 1818, 'Dead Game'.

THEOBALD, W. (op. 1817). London address. *exhib.* R.A. (2). R.A. 1817, 'Portrait of a Dog'; 'Portrait of a Dog's Head'.

THIRTLE, JOHN (baptized Norwich 1777, 22nd June; d. Norwich 1839, 30th September). Started as a frame-maker with a shop in Norwich. Devoted spare time to painting in water-colour. Member of the Norwich Society of Artists. Painted miniatures and landscapes. *coll.* W. W. Rex Spelman, 'Two Sketches of Huntsmen', exhibited Norwich 1927. *exhib.* R.A. (1), 'Figures'.

THOMPSON, HARRY (b. , d. 1901). Painter of genre and animals. Studied Paris. Married Ellen Kendall Baker. *coll.* York Castle Museum, 'Hunting Scene', S&D 1893. *exhib.* S.S. (1). Paris, Hon. Mention 1882, Medal 1884, Silver Medal 1889, Universal Exhibition.

THOMPSON, JACOB (of Penrith) (b. Penrith 1806, 28th August; d. Hackthorne 1879, 27th December). Studied R.A. Schools. Returned to Penrith. *exhib.* R.A. 1831–1866. R.A. 1835, 'The Gamekeeper'; 1844, 'Trout'.

THOMPSON, RALPH (Living). Born in Yorkshire, educated Leeds College of Art and Royal College of Art, London. Painter of animals and birds, also an illustrator. Exhibits at The Tryon Gallery, London.

THOMSON, ALFRED REGINALD, R.A. (b. Bangalore, India, 1894; living artist). *exhib.* R.A. 1950, 'Oxford and Cambridge Boat Race 1949'; 1958, 'A Winner of Doggett's Race'; 1961, 'Dinner, Pytcheley Hunt, 1960'.

THOMSON, CLIFTON (*see* TOMSON, J. CLIFTON)

THOMSON, HENRY, R.A. (b. Portsea 1773, 31st July; d. there 1843, 6th April). Visited Paris, Germany, Italy, Rome. *exhib.* R.A. (83); B.I. (3); S.S. (1), 'Mythological'. R.A. 1793, 'A Fisherman'; 1808, 'Trap-ball'; 1809, 'Boys Fishing'.

THOMSON, HUGH (b. Coleraine 1860, 7th June; d. Wandsworth Common 1920, 7th May). Illustrator. *repr.* 'Angling in British Art', Shaw Sparrow, pp. 218, 219 and 221. Illustrations to Walton's 'Angler's Song'.

THOMSON, Rev. JOHN, H.R.S.A. (b. Dailly 1778, 1st September; d. Duddingston 1840, 20th October). *coll.* Glasgow A.G., 'River Scene with Falconer and Falcon'.

***THORBURN, ARCHIBALD** (b. 1860, 31st May; d. Godalming 1935, 9th October). *coll.* Preston, H.M. and A.G., 'Studies of Falcons'; Major Sir Reginald Macdonald-Buchanan, (Five Sporting Birds). *exhib.* R.A. (16); S.S. (1). R.A. pictures included, 1882, 'Black Game'; 'The Twelfth of August'; 'The First of October'; 1888, 'The Covey at Daybreak'; 'Black Game Disturbed'; 1890, 'The Pack at Sunrise'; 1893, 'A Grouse Drive'; 1899, 'The Lost Stag'.

THORBURN, MICHAEL (c. 1862–c. 1934). Painter of game birds. *exhib.* The Tryon Gallery, London, April 1965.

THORN, Miss SARAH ELIZABETH (op. 1842–1846). London address. *exhib.* R.A. 1842–1846. R.A. 1844, 'Portrait of a Spaniel'.

THORNTON, HERBERT (c. 1840). *exhib.* The Parker Gallery, London, 'The Refuge—Fox Sheltering from Hounds'.

THURSTON, JOHN (b. Scarborough 1774; d. Holloway, London, 1822). Painted in water-colour and engraved. Drew book illustrations in pencil and ink. Illustrated rural sports. *exhib.* R.A. (16); O.W.C.S. (5), 'Illustrations'.

***TILLEMANS, PETER** (b. Antwerp 1684; d. Norton, Suffolk, 1734, 5th December; buried Stow Langtoft). Son of a diamond cutter. Came to England 1708. *coll.* The Hon. David Astor, 'Horse Racing', a pair; G. P. Fores, 'The Duke of Kingston in Thoresby Park Shooting with ten of his noted Pointers'. *repr.* 'A Book of Sporting Painters', Shaw Sparrow, colour plate p. 65; Mr. and Mrs. Paul Mellon, U.S.A., 'Charles II and Nell Gwynn at Newmarket Heath'. *repr.* 'Apollo', April 1963, 'Horse Racing at Newmarket: Mr. Jemmet Browne at a Meet'; 'Fox Hunting in a wooded Landscape'. Colonel H. T. S. Patteson, 'Newmarket Heath'. *repr.* 'History of British Water-Colour Painting', by H. M. Cundall, colour plate 7, p. 26. *auct.* Sotheby's, 4th December 1957 (107), 'The Kill—Huntsmen and Hounds gathered round a Hare'.

TINKLER, W. A. (op. 1839). Putney address. Painted a View in Spain, exhibited R.A. 1839. *auct.* Sotheby's, 4th November 1964 (192), 'A Bay Racehorse in a stable', signed. *exhib.* R.A. (1), 'Landscape'.

TOLLEY, EDWARD (or **TOLLY**) (op. 1848–1867). London address. *exhib.* R.A. (9); B.I. (3); S.S. (1); V.E. (9), 'Sporting'. R.A. 1848, 'Portrait of a Famous Hunting Mare'; 1849, 'Study of Horses'; 1857, 'Favourite Hunters at the Cover Side'.

TOMSON, J. CLIFTON (or **THOMSON**) (op. 1775–1843). Nottingham. His patrons included Earl Fitzwilliam. Many of his works reproduced in the *Sporting Magazine*. *coll.* Liverpool, Walker A.G. (1); Nottingham A.G. (1); Lytham Hall Collection (2); C.H. Thieriot, New York (2, one now sold).

TOPOLSKY, FELIKS (b. 1907; living). Cartoonist and illustrator. *coll.* Tate Gallery, London, 'Goodwood, 25–28th July', pastel and wash.

***TOWN, CHARLES** (1781–1854), ('of London'). Not to be confused with Charles Towne. Painted 'The Earth Stopper', S&D 'C. Town 1790'. Ex Worden Hall Collection; exhibited Preston 1943. *coll.* The Lord Fairhaven, 'The Royal Hunt at Windsor', S&D 1827.

TOWNE, CHARLES (b. Wigan 1763; baptized Parish Church 7th July; d. Liverpool 1840, 6th January). Left Wigan 1775 for Leeds. Visited Bolton, Liverpool and Manchester later, in Essex and Oxfordshire; London later. *coll.* Liverpool, Walker A.G. (9); The Hon. David Astor (1); Lady Danson (2); Sir Lionel Earle (1); G. P. Fores (1); Lytham Hall, Lancs. (1); Major Sir Reginald Macdonald-Buchanan (5); Stone Collection (1). *exhib.* R.A. (12); B.I. (1); V.E. (1).

TOWNE, FRANCIS, F.S.A. (b. 1740; d. London 1816, 7th July). Pupil of W. Pars. Painted landscapes in water-colour and some oils, including hunters. *exhib.* S.A. (16); F.S. (3); R.A. (27); B.I. (10).

TOWNLEY, CHARLES (b. London 1746, d. 1800). Painter and engraver of sporting subjects. Studied Florence and Rome. Visited Berlin 1789. *exhib.* S.A. (2); F.S. (21); R.A. (16). R.A. exhibits, portraits and miniatures.

TOWNSHEND, ARTHUR LOUIS (op. 1880–1886). London, Newmarket, and Paris. *exhib.* R.A. (5); V.E. (3). R.A. 1885, ' "Jannette" and Her Foal'; 'The Gem of the Paddocks'; 'A. Bit on Newmarket Heath'.

TOYNBEE, LAWRENCE LEIF (b. London 1922, 21st December; living Oxford). Studied Ruskin School, Oxford, under A. D. Rutherston. *exhib.* R.A. 1964 (2 football subjects). *coll.* Lord's (1).

TRERY, HENRY C. (op. 1849–1854). London address. Painted animals, deer, dogs, etc. *exhib.* R.A. (5); B.I. (1), 'Cattle'. R.A. 1853, 'Study of a Dog's Head'; 1854, 'Red Deer'.

TRICKETT, W. WASDELL. coll. Sir Reginald and Lady Macdonald-Buchanan (3).

TUCK, WILLIAM HENRY (op. 1874–1882). London address. Painted portraits and some sporting, which included three water-colours of 'The Royal Stag Hunt in Windsor Park, 1882'. *coll.* Lord Fairhaven (3). *exhib.* R.A. (1), 'Portraits'.

TUKE, HENRY SCOTT, R.A. (b. 1858, d. 1929). Painted seascapes and sea fishermen. *repr.* 'Angling in British Art' Shaw Sparrow; 'A Summer Evening—Anglers in a Boat', p. 42 exhibited R.A. 1901.

TULLOCH, MAURICE (living). Paints hunting and racing subjects. *exhib.* Tryon Gallery, London.

TUNNARD, J. C. Sporting artist exhibiting at Ackermann's Galleries, London, in the 1930's.

TUNNICLIFFE, CHARLES FREDERICK, R.A. (b. near Macclesfield 1901, 1st December. Living). Painter and etcher of animals, birds and fish. *exhib.* R.A. from 1928; Tryon Gallery, London. (Birds, Beasts and Fishes. November-December 1964. 52 paintings and drawings).

TURBERVILLE, GEORGE (c. 1611). Woodcut from 'The Book of Falconrie and Hawking'. *repr.* 'Sporting Pictures of England', Guy Paget, 1945.

TURK, G. (op. 1875). Painted animals. A 'Stags and Hinds in a thicket', S&D 1875, was sold at Sotheby's 26th February 1964.

***TURNER, F. C.** (1795–1846). London address. Member of Society of British Artists. Painted mostly portraits of horses, shooting subjects, etc. Said to be the father of two other sporting artists. *coll.* Liverpool, Walker A.G. (2); Manchester, City A.G. (1); Major Sir Reginald Macdonald-Buchanan (4); Charles H. Thieriot, New York (2 since sold). *exhib.* R.A. (11); B.I. (23); S.S. (36); V.E. (6). *repr.* 'Twenty Sporting Pictures', W.A.G.

TURNER, G. A. (J. A., Benezit) (op. 1836–1841). London address. *exhib.* R.A. (3); B.I. (1); S.S. (2), 'Sporting'. R.A. 1836, 'Lance and His Dog "Crab" '.

TURNER, H. (op. 1831). *exhib.* S.S. (2), 'Sporting'.

TURNER, J. (op. 1872). *exhib.* R.A. (1), 'Horses'.

TURNER, J. M. W., R.A. (b. London 1775, 23rd April; d. Chelsea 1851, 19th December). *coll.* Tate Gallery, London, 'Yacht Racing on the Solent, No. 2'; 'Yacht Racing on the Solent, No. 3'; 'A Regatta at Cowes'; Wallace Collection, London, 'Grouse Shooting with portraits of the artist's dogs'; 'Woodcock Shooting on the Chiver', S&D 1813. *repr.* 'Pictures and Drawings (illustrations), Wallace Collection Catalogues, p. 188. *exhib.* R.A. (259); B.I. (17); S.S. (7). *repr.* Shaw Sparrow, 'Angling in British Art', illustrated pp. 44 and 45; Bedford; Rievaulx Abbey; Llanberis Lake and Hampton Court Palace, all with anglers.

TURNER, P. (op. 1826). London address. *exhib.* B.I. (1), Angling.

TURNER, WILLIAM, of Oxford (b. Blackbourton, Oxon., 1789, 12th December; d. Woodstock, Oxon., 1862, 7th August). Pupil of John Varley. Member of the Old Water Colour Society. *coll.* Tate Gallery, London, 'Skating'. *exhib.* R.A. (17); B.I. (18); S.S. (3); O.W.C.S. (464), 'Landscapes'.

TURNER, W. A. (op. 1844). *exhib.* R.A. 1844, 'Wild Fowl'.

UGARD, R. 'A Meet at a Country Inn', a signed panel, was sold at Sotheby's 11th November 1964.

UNDERHILL, WILLIAM (op. 1848–1870). London address. *coll.* Birmingham A.G., 'The Poacher', S&D 1859; Wolverhampton A.G. (2). *exhib.* R.A. (13); B.I. (30); S.S. (19); V.E. (23), 'Domestic'. R.A. 1856, 'The Salmon Trap'; 1857, 'The Fisherman's Family'; 1864, 'The Gamekeeper's Daughter'.

UWINS, JAMES (op. 1836–1871). London address. *exhib.* R.A. 1846, 'A Salmon Weir at Lynmouth, N. Devon'.

VIEBURGH, C. G. One painting of a Cricket Match, S&D 1852, is known.

VINCENT, GEORGE (b. Norwich 1796, 27th June; d. 1831). Son of a weaver. Pupil of John Crome. *exhib.* R.A. (9); B.I. (41); S.S. (12); O.W.C.S. (5). *auct.* Christie's, 25/26th April 1940, A. N. Gilbey Collection, 'Anglers in a Punt on the Bure', S&D 1825.

***VINNE, JAN VAN DER** (b. Haarlem 1663, 3rd February; d. there 1721, 1st March). Pupil of Jan Wyck. Came to England 1686 and painted sporting subjects. *repr.* Grant, Vol. 1, pl. 31. *lit.* Grant, Vol. 1, p. 77.

VOLMAR, JOSEPH SYMON (b. Berne 1796, 26th October; d. there 1865, 6th October). Pupil of Horace Vernet. Professor of Painting at Berne. *coll.* R. and M. Richards, Gawsworth Hall, Macclesfield, 'Horses and Groom in a Stable'.

VOSS, F. B. American artist working in first half of this century. Came to England and amongst others painted 'The Beaufort Hunt', which was later reproduced as a print by Ackermann's.

WAGEMAN, MICHAEL ANGELO (op. 1838–1879). Painted portraits, scriptural, animals, and landscape. *exhib.* R.A. (3); B.I. (4); S.S. (17), 'Domestic'. R.A. 1855, 'Study of Dogs'.

WAIN, LOUIS WILLIAM (b. London 1860, 5th August; d. there 1939, 4th July). Studied music till 1879 and then art at West London School of Art. Assistant Master there 1881–2. On staff of 'Illustrated Sporting and Dramatic News' 1882, and 'Illustrated London News' 1886. Visited New York 1907–1910. On staff of 'New York American'. President National Cat Club. Painter of cats, some sport. A pair titled 'Cricket' and 'Tennis' are known. *exhib.* S.S. (1); Brook Street A.G., London.

WALKER, ANTHONY (op. 1771). An engraver who exhibited six engravings at the S.A. 1760–1765. Shaw Sparrow illustrates in 'Angling in British Art' his drawing of 'Gudgeon Fishing, or He's Fairly Hook'd', engraved by T. Wilson, p. 134.

WALKER, FREDERICK, A.R.A. (b. Marylebone, London, 1840; d. St. Fillan's Perthshire, 1875; buried Cookham). Son of a designer of jewellery. Studied Leigh's School and R.A. Schools. Designed book illustrations. Painted subject pictures and landscapes in oils and water-colours. Many landscapes had angling interest, notably 'The Peaceful Thames'. *exhib.* R.A. (8); O.W.C.S. (38); V.E. (4). 'Sports Exhibition' 1890, 'Boy Fishing'.

WALKER, WILLIAM (b. Hackney 1780, d. Sawbridgeworth 1863). Pupil of R. Smirke, R.A. Travelled in the East, making many sketches in Greece. *auct.* Christie's, 25/26th April 1940, A. N. Gilbey Collection, 'Young Anglers Landing a Pike'. *lit.* 'Angling in British Art', Shaw Sparrow, p. 134.

WALKER, W. (op. 1782–1808). London address. Painted portraits and fish. *exhib.* F.S. (5); R.A. (22), 'Portraits'. R.A. 1784, 'Fish'.

WALLACE, HAROLD FRANK, B.A., F.Z.S. (b. 1881, 21st March; living in 1934). Watercolourist and black-and-white artist, landscapes and sporting scenes. Resident in Staffordshire and Inverness, Scotland, his works included fishing subjects and deer stalking. *exhib.* Sporting and Greatorex Galleries, London.

WALLER, Miss E. (op. 1828–1838). Greenwich address. *exhib.* R.A. (5); S.S. (1), 'Sporting'. R.A. 1836, 'Portrait of a Young Lady and a Favourite Spaniel'.

***WALLER, SAMUEL EDMUND** (b. Gloucester 1850, 16th June; d. London 1903, 9th June). Pupil of John Kemp at Gloucester. *coll.* Preston, H.M. and A.G., 'One and Twenty'—a Group of horsemen toasting a Young Squire on the balcony of his Home, exhibited R.A. 1891. *exhib.* R.A. (26); S.S. (2); V.E. (23), 'Domestic'. R.A. 1893, 'The Wedding Gift' (Horses); 1899, 'The Huntsman's Courtship'.

WALLIS, JOSEPH H. (op. 1861–1890). Cardiff address. Graves gives him as an architect. *exhib.* R.A. (6); G.G. (7); N.G. (1), V.E. (12), 'Sporting'. R.A. 1878, 'Mr. John Bagot Scriven's "Kitty" '.

WALLS, WILLIAM, R.S.A., R.S.W. (op. 1891–1901; living 1926). Studied Edinburgh Academy. Living for a time at Dunfermline. *exhib.* R.A. (4). R.A. 1891, 'A Dead Fox'; 1893, 'The Fox's Lair'; 1899, 'The Deer-Stalker's Companions'; 1901, 'Bolting the Otter'; 'Jaguar Stalking'; R.S.A. Centenary Exhibition 1926, 'Pumas Startled'; illustrated in catalogue, pl. 39. *repr.* 'Angling in British Art', Shaw Sparrow, colour plate 16.

WALTER, HENRY (b. London 1786; d. Torquay 1849, 23rd April). Painted genre, animals and landscapes. *exhib.* R.A. (6); B.I. (6); S.S. (2); N.W.C.S. (3), 'Sporting'. R.A. 1846, 'Study of Animals'.

WALTON, FRANK, R.I. (b. London 1840, 10th July; d. Holmbury St. Mary, Dorking, 1928, 23rd January). Pupil at R.A. Schools in 1860. Won Turner Gold Medal for landscapes. Worked around Harrow between 1862 and 1893. President of the Royal Institute of Painters in Water-Colour (R.I.). Painted landscapes. Collaborated with Heywood Hardy in a number of paintings; 'A Steady Shot' and 'The Parson's Holiday', a pair of oils, S&D 1892, are good examples. *coll.* Birmingham; Liverpool; Melbourne, and Cape Town. *exhib.* R.A. (75); B.I. (2); S.S. (9); N.W.C.S. (82); G.G. (11); N.G. (10); V.E. (182).

WALTON, HENRY, F.S.A. (b. Dickleborough 1746, d. London 1813). *exhib.* S.A. (9); R.A. (4); International Art Treasures, V. and A. Museum, London, 1962. *repr.* pl. 30 in catalogue, 'Cricket Scene at Harrow Playing Field'.

WANKLYN, JOAN (living). Studied Central School of Art, London, and Bertram Mills Circus. *coll.* The Foxhunter Inn, Hereford, mural of 'Foxhunter'. *lit.* 'Evening Standard', 26th March 1964, with illustration.

WANOSTROCHT, NICHOLAS—'Felix N' (c. 1845). A Camberwell schoolmaster and cricketer. George Frederic Watts was a pupil at one of his Latin classes and was chosen to illustrate Felix's book, 'Felix on the Bat'. Felix himself later produced a number of oils of cricketers and other portraits. *lit.* 'The Picture of Cricket', John Arlott.

WARD, C. H. (op. 1825–1840). Portrait of the grey Arabian 'Kirkel' signed C.H.W. and inscribed 'Kirkel'. *exhib.* Ackermann's Gallery and The Sporting Gallery, Middleburg, Virginia, U.S.A. in 1964.

WARD, EDWARD MATTHEW, R.A. (b. Pimlico 1816; d. London 1879, 15th January). Studied R.A. Schools. Visited Rome 1836. Studied fresco painting in Munich. Returned to England 1839. *exhib.* R.A. (86); B.I. (16); S.S. (11); V.E. (4), 'Historical'. R.A. 1850, 'Izaak Walton Angling—A Summer's Day on the Banks of the Colne'; 1851, 'John Gilpin Delayed by Customers'. *coll.* London, Guildhall A.G., 'Isaak Walton Angling'.

***WARD, JAMES, R.A.** (b. London 1769, 23rd October; d. Cheshunt 1859, 23rd November). Pupil of J. R. Smith and his brother, William Ward. Painter and engraver. *coll.* Burnley, Towneley Hall M. and A.G. (1); Cambridge, Fitzwilliam Museum (41); London, Tate Gallery (7); Lord Camrose (1); His Excellency The Prince Aly Khan (1); Mr. and Mrs. Paul Mellon, U.S.A. (3); Duke of Northumberland (1); Mr. Denys Sutton (1); Mrs. E. M. Ward (1); Hon. John Ward, M.V.O. (1). *exhib.* R.A. (298); B.I. (91); S.A. (2); S.S. (9). *lit.* Frankau, J., 'William Ward, A.R.A., and James Ward, R.A.', London, 1904; Grundy, C. R., 'James Ward, R.A.', London, 1909; Arts Council, Ward Exhibition catalogue, London, 1960.

WARD, MARTIN THEODORE (b. London 1799; d. York 1874, 13th February). Son of William Ward, R.A. Pupil of Landseer. *coll.* Preston, H.M. and A.G. (1); Commander Robert T. Bower, R.N. (3). *exhib.* R.A. (16); B.I. (18); S.S. (5), 'Sporting'.

WARD, WILLIAM, A.R.A. (b. 1762, d. 1826). Engraver and painter in water-colour. *coll.* Lord's (1).

WARD, VERNON DE BEAUVOIR (b. Hampstead 1905, 12th October; living). Pupil at Slade School. Painter of landscape, figure subjects, birds, flowers, etc. A painting, 'Wildfowl leaving Arran', S&D (19)46, sold at Christie's 22nd January 1965.

WARDLE, ARTHUR, R.I., R.B.C. (b. London 1864; d. 1949, 16th June). *exhib.* R.A. (21); S.S. (29); N.W.C.S. (20); V.E. (27), 'Cattle'. R.A. 1891, 'Panthers Resting'; 1892, 'Deer Stalkers'; 1895, 'Deer Stalkers'; 1896, 'On the Moors—Resting'; 1903, 'Stalkers'; 1904, 'Got Him!!'

WATTS, FREDERICK WILLIAM (b. 1800, d. 1870). Landscape painter. *exhib.* R.A. (76); B.I. (108) S.S. (65). *auct.* Sotheby's, 29th July 1964, 'Sportsmen on a sandy hill, an extensive valley, with a cottage in background'.

WATTS, GEORGE FREDERICK, O.M., R.A., D.C.L., H.R.C.A. (b. London 1817, d. 1904, buried Compton. Studied R.A. Schools and in Florence for four years. Was a pupil at Latin classes held by Felix (Nicholas Wanostrocht). *coll.* M.C.C., Lord's, 'The Cut', drawing. *exhib.* R.A. (126); B.I. (6); S.S. (3); G.G. (84); N.G. (20); V.E. (29), 'Historical'. *repr.* 'Felix on the Bat'; 'The Picture of Cricket', John Arlott, 1955; 'Leg Half-Volley', 1845; 'The Bowler', 1845.

WEATHERBY, R. C. (op. 1948). Penzance address. *exhib.* R.A. 1948, 'The Huntsman'.

WEAVER, J. (op. 1801–1809). London address. *exhib.* R.A. (4), 'Sporting'. R.A. 1808, 'Portrait of a Favourite Mare belonging to Viscountess Anson'; 1809, ' "Bobtail", a Celebrated Carthorse, belonging to J. Powell'. 'A Piebald Hunter in a Landscape' sold at Sotheby's 12th May 1965 (Frank Carlridge).

WEAVER, THOMAS (b. 1774, d. Liverpool 1843). Painter of pedigree cattle, etc. *exhib.* R.A. (4); Rutland Gallery, London, 'Black Greyhound', S&D 1806. *repr.* 'Animal Painting in England', Basil Taylor, pl. 57, 'A White Short-Horned Heifer'. 'Richard Marriott Esq, M.F.H. on his Hunter with Hunt Servants and Hounds'. *exhib.* Ackermann's Gallery, London, October–November 1965 (no. 32). Richard Marriott lived at Marriott Hall, near Braintree, Essex, and was Master of the East Essex, 1842–1867.

WEBB, BYRON (op. 1846–1866). Painter of animals, especially of Highland deer in well-painted scenery. Portraits of horses and scenes of hunting and skating. *exhib.* R.A. (11); B.I. (16); R.S.B.A. (8).

WEBB, CHARLES (b. London 1830, 16th July; d. Dusseldorf 1895, December). Studied Amsterdam, Antwerp and Dusseldorf. *auct.* Christie's, 15th May 1964, 'Card Players'.

WEBB (op. 1844). Melton Mowbray address. *exhib.* R.A. (1). R.A. 1844, ' "Shah-war-Ali", a Thoroughbred Cape Horse, favourite Charger of General Shubrick in India'.

WEBB, E. W. (1805?–1854). London address. Painter of sport and animals. *exhib.* R.A. (1); B.I. (1); V.E. (1), 'Sporting'. R.A. 1850, 'The Captive'.

WEBB, OCTAVIUS (op. 1880–1889). Guildford address. *exhib.* R.A. (5); S.S. (12); G.G. (1); V.E. (4), 'Sporting'. R.A. 1883, 'Clumber Spaniel'; 1888, 'A Member of the Hunt'; 1889, 'Waiting for the Master. pointer and setter'.

***WEBB, WILLIAM** (op. 1819–1850). Tamworth address. Painted animals as well as sporting subjects, including equestrian portraits. *coll.* Mr. and Mrs. Paul Mellon, U.S.A., 'Euphrates', S&D 1825. *exhib.* R.A. (7); B.I. (1), 'Sporting'. R.A. 1819, 'Portraits of Horses, property of F. Lawley'; ' "Duchess", a Lioness, and Whelps'; 1822, 'Dog, property of a Nobleman';1828, 'Portrait of "Gulnare", a celebrated Racing Mare, property of the Duke of Richmond; Ackermann & Son, London, 'The Master of Hounds', reproduced coloured cover, 'Country Life', Christmas Number, 6th December 1962; 'The Pack Working on a Good Scent' (c. 1830).

WEBSTER, THOMAS, R.A. (b. London 1800, 20th March; d. Cranbrook 1886, 23rd September). Painted figures and domestic subjects. Working for a time at Windsor. *coll.* Guildhall A.G., London (2); Lady Lever A.G., Port Sunlight (1). *exhib.* R.A. (83); B.I. (39); S.S. (9), 'Domestic'.

WEBSTER, TOM (b. Bilston, Staffs., 1890, 17th July; d. 1962, 2nd June). Drew sporting caircatures, especially of horses. 'Tishy' is a good example of his sporting caricatures.

WEIGHT, CAREL, C.B.E., A.R.A. (b. 1908, 10th September; living at Battersea 1964). *exhib.* R.A. 1955, 'Football at Fulham'.

WEIR, HARRISON WILLIAM (b. Lewes 1824, 5th May; d. Appledore, Kent, 1906, 3rd January; buried Sevenoaks). Pupil of George Baxter. Drew animal illustrations. Married (1) Anne, eldest daughter of J. F. Herring; (2) Alice Upjohn; (3) Eva Gobell. *exhib.* R.A. (6); B.I. (3); S.S. (5); N.W.C.S. (100); V.E. (2). R.A. 1870, 'Partridges'.

WELLS, J. S. SANDERSON, R.I. (op. 1892–1938). London address. The artist lent the following to the Preston exhibition 1943: 'The Call', exhibited R.A. 1938; 'The Winner'; 'Moving Off from Venniford Cross' 'Waddesdon Cross Roads, Meet of the Bicester Hounds'. *exhib.* S.S. (4), 'Fishing Boats'. R.A. 1895, 'Gone Away'; 1903, 'Gone to Ground'; 1906, 'Rushing the Hill—Derby Day'.

WEST, BENJAMIN, P.R.A. (b. Springfield, U.S.A., 1738; d. London 1820; buried in St. Paul's Cathedral). Went to Italy 1760. Returned to England 1763. Foundation member of the Royal Academy. *exhib.* S.A. (21); R.A. (258); B.I. (32), 'Historical'; Thos. Agnew & Sons Ltd., February-March 1962, 'Cricket on the Village Green'. *auct.* Christie's, 25/26th April 1940, A. N. Gilbey Collection, 'A Party of Gentlemen Fishing from a Punt', S&D 1794; exhibited R.A. 1795.

***WEST, WALDRON** (b. 1904, 25th October; living). Resident in Worcester. Studied Worcester School of Art and with Sir Frank Brangwyn, R.A. Painter of portraits and sporting pictures. *coll.* E. W. R. Uden, 'Major Fanshawe and the North Cotswold Hounds'; 'D. L. Jones, Senior Jockey'. John Young, 'Eric Young holding "Dumbarnie"'; 'Philip Young holding "Falls of Clyde"'; 'Donald Young holding "Border Chief"'. D. L. Jones, 'D. L. Jones, Senior Jockey'; 'Peter Jones wearing racing colours'. W. H. Carr, 'W. H. Carr wearing H.M. the Queen's Racing Silks'.

WESTALL, RICHARD, R.A. (b. Hertford 1765; d. London 1836, 4th December). Landscape painter. *exhib.* R.A. (313); B.I. (70); S.S. (1), 'Historical'. *auct.* Christie's, 25/26th April 1940, A. N. Gilbey Collection, 'A Boy Angling', engraved by W. Nutter; 'A Boy kneeling on the bank of a stream with rough fishing rod and some small Roach beside him', engraved by W. Whessell.

WHEATLEY, FRANCIS, R.A., F.S.A. (b. London 1747; d. 1801, 28th June). Son of a master tailor. Studied Shipley's School and R.A. Schools. Spent some time in Dublin, painting portraits. *coll.* Trustees of Duke of Newcastle, 'The Return from Shooting'. *exhib.* S.A. (45); F.S. (1); R.A. (87). R.A. 1785, 'An Amorous Sportsman'; 1789, 'Portrait of a Nobleman returning from Shooting'; 1790, 'Jaques and the Wounded Stag'. *auct.* Christie's, 25/26th April 1940, A. N. Gilbey Collection, 'Two Young Anglers by a Mountain Stream, S&D 1800. *repr.* 'Angling in British Art', Shaw Sparrow, p. 141. 'A Group of Anglers on a Rocky Bank beside a Mountain Stream', S&D 1783.

WHEELER, ALFRED (b. 1851, d. 1932). Son of John Alfred and painter of sporting subjects, animals and dogs, etc. A painting, 'Ladas' a bay horse, foaled in 1891, by Hampton out of Illuminata by Rossicrucian, is in the Charles H. Theriot Collection, New York. Winner of the Woodcote Stakes, Coventry Stakes, Champagne Stakes, and Middle Park Plate at 2 years, and at 3 years the Two Thousand Guineas, Newmarket Stakes, Derby, and was second in the St. Leger and Eclipse Stakes. The painting inscribed 'Ladas A. Wheeler'. *coll.* Charles H. Thieriot, New York (1). *auct.* Sotheby's, 8th January 1964, 'Steeplechasing', S&D 1896.

WHEELER, ALMIRA (op. 1880). 'The Duke of Beaufort out with the Beaufort', S&D 1880, shown in Oscar and Peter Johnson's Gallery, London, June 1974. *repr.* Country Life, 14th June 1974.

WHEELER, FREDERICK JOHN (b. Bath 1875, d. 1930). Elder son of Alfred and his wife Catherine. Black and white artist and caricaturist. Worked in Bristol and Bath. Grandson of John Alfred Wheeler.

WHEELER, JAMES THOMAS (b. Cheltenham 1849). Elder son of John Alfred Wheeler. Painter mainly of cattle, but the occasional horse.

***WHEELER, JOHN ALFRED** (of Bath) (b. Andoversford, near Cheltenham, 1821; d. Hanwell 1903). Animal painter. Self-taught artist. Joined 2nd Queen's Bays as a youth and became a bandsman. His practical experience with horses in the calvary led him to painting them and other animals. Retiring from the Army, he came to Bath in 1854, where he painted sporting pictures, including hunting scenes and race meetings. His outstanding works were 'The Beaufort Hunt' and 'Meet of the Coaching Club, London', in which all the members with their horses and hounds were portrayed. He was patronised by the aristocracy and many well-known sporting figures. He left Bath for London in 1877. '... (after coming to Bath) he resumed the acquaintance ship of his old comrade-in-arms, Captain Havilland who became adjutant in the North Somerset Yeomanry. Wheeler joined the regiment and was trumpeter for several years at the time Sergt.-Major

Anderson was in the troop and the late Charles Pinkett was Sergeant' (extract from article by George Smith, a personal friend of Wheeler, p. 7, 'Keene's Bath Journal', 17 April 1897. Residences while in Bath: 1858–1863, '15 Northampton St.; 1864–1865, Cypress Cottage, Weston'; 1866–1871, 1 Highbury Place; 1874–1877, 11 Raglan Villas. *coll.* Bath, Victoria Art Gallery, 'An English "Laverick" setter'; 'The Bath Coach', S&D 1863.

WHEELER, WALTER HERBERT (1878–1960). Third son of Alfred. Painter of animals, particularly horses and dogs.

WHEELWRIGHT, J. HADWEN (op. 1834–1849). London address. *exhib.* R.A. (12); B.I. (6); S.S. (7), 'Sporting'. No sporting subjects at R.A.

WHEELWRIGHT, ROLAND (b. Ipswich 1870, d. 1955). Pair of coaching scenes shown in Oscar and Peter Johnson's 'Sport and the Horse' exhibition, June 1969 (no. 55). *coll.* Cheltenham; Preston A.G.

WHEELWRIGHT, W. H. (op. 1872–1880). London address. Painted coaching subjects and interiors. *auct.* Sotheby's, 5th February 1964, 'Preparing the Coach', S&D 1872. *exhib.* V.E. (2), 'Interiors'.

WHESSELL, J. (op. 1802–1823). London address. Painted views and racehorses, possibly the same as the engraver of this name. *exhib.* R.A. (14).

WHISTLER, REX JOHN (b. London 1905, 24th June; killed in action 1944, World War II). Illustrator. *coll.* V. and A. Museum, London. *auct.* 'A Hunting Scene', one of the panels for the decoration of 36 Hill Street, London, was sold at Sotheby's 26th April 1961. *lit.* 'Country Life', 25th March 1939.

WHOOD, ISAAC (b. 1688; d. London 1752, 24th February). Worked for the Duke of Bedford, painting portraits and copying. *coll.* Leicester A.G., 'Two Boys with Greyhounds'.

WHYMPER, CHARLES (op. 1876–1893). Six Angling sketches etched from his drawings by Frank Paton. 'Salmon Fishing', exhibited at 'Sports' Exhibition 1890. *exhib.* R.A. (5); S.S. (1); N.W.C.S. (2); G.G. (1); V.E. (3), 'Landscape'.

WHYMPER, JOSIAH WOOD, R.I. (b. 1813, d. 1903). Resided at Ipswich. Engraved on wood for illustrations. Angling interest in some of his pictures. *exhib.* R.A. (11); S.S. (14); N.W.C.S. (414); G.G. (3); V.E. (3), 'Landscapes'.

WICKSTEAD, I. (or **WICKSTEED**). Probably related to C. F. Wickstead (op. 1790–1846), the son of James Wicksteed (or Wickstead), an engraver (b. 1719; d. London 1791, 11th July), all the family being thus alternatively spelt. There is also Philips Wickstead, the portrait painting pupil of Zoffany.

WIDDAS, JOHN (op. 1802–1858). Resident in Hull. Painted Horses and Dogs.

WIDDAS, RICHARD DODD (op. 1826–1885). Son of John Widdas. Painter of animals and shipping and sporting; a 'The Derby 1870', S&D 1870–1871, was auctioned at Sotheby's 28th October 1964 (81). *coll.* Hull Museum.

WIDGERY, WILLIAM (op. 1866). Exeter address. His 'Poltimore Hunt' was engraved by J. Harris. *exhib.* S.S. (1), 'Landscape'.

WIGHTMAN, THOMAS (b. 1811, d. New York 1888). Painted racing subjects. Until recently a painting, 'Elis, Winner of the St. Leger, 1836', was in the Charles H. Thieriot Collection, New York. This horse was painted by both Herring and Cooper.

WILDMAN, JOHN R. (op. 1823–1839). Painted figures, including one of J. M. W. Turner and Horton Fawkes with two other gentlemen and greyhounds in the grounds of Farnley Hall. *exhib.* R.A. (8); B.I. (4); S.S. (9), 'Figures'.

WILKIE, Sir DAVID, R.A., H.R.S.A. (b. Cults, Fife, 1785, 18th November; d. off Gibraltar 1841, 1st June). *coll.* National Gallery of Scotland, Edinburgh, 'Pitlessie Fair'. *exhib.* R.A. (100); B.I. (12). R.A. 1811, 'Portrait of a Gamekeeper'.

WILKINSON, NORMAN, C.B.E., R.O.I., PP.R.I., H.R.W.S. (b. Cambridge 1878, 24th November; living). Painter of marines and angling subjects and etcher. *repr.* 'Angling in British Art,' Shaw Sparrow; 'Fly Fishing, the Intake Pool, River Spey'; 'Fly Fishing, The Disputed Pool, River Awe, colour plates p. 52.

WILLIAMS, EDWARD (b. 1782; d. Barnes 1855, 24th June). Son of a noted engraver and his wife, a sister of James Ward, R.A. Studied under Ward and then articled himself to a carver and gilder before taking up painting again. Regarded as Father of the Williams family of painters. *exhib.* R.A. (36); B.I. (21); S.S. (38); V.E. (49), 'Landscape'. *repr.* 'Angling in British Art', Shaw Sparrow, colour pl. p. 106; 'Perch Fishing'.

WILLIAMS, EDWARD CHARLES (op. 1839–1865). Son of Edward Williams. *exhib.* R.A. (19); B.I. (23); S.S. (10); V.E. (84), 'Sea-Pieces'. *auct.* Christie's, 25/26th April 1940, A. N. Gilbey Collection, 'A Man Fishing'; 'A Sportsman Firing over Dogs', pair.

WILLIAMS, HENRY (op. 1835–1858). *coll.* Lord's, London (1). *exhib.* R.A. (7); B.I. (19); R.S.B.A. (13).

WILLIAMS, J. M. (op. 1834–1849). London address. Painted landscapes, castles, ruins, birds, and sporting. Visited Waterloo and Antwerp. *exhib.* R.A. (8); B.I. (8); S.S. (9); N.W.C.S. (1), 'Sporting'. R.A. 1840, Ptarmigan and Wood Pigeon'; 1841, 'Wild Ducks'.

WILLIAMS, JAMES T. (op. 1828–1840). London address. *exhib.* R.A. (9); S.S. (10). R.A. 1831, 'Race-horses'; 1833, 'Partridge Shooting'; 1834, 'Indian attacking a Buffalo'.

WILLIAMS, WILLIAM (op. 1758–1792). London and Norwich addresses. Painted landscapes and some hunting pictures. *auct.* Sotheby's, 31st May 1961, 'A Chestnut Hunter held by Groom in a Landscape', S&D 1769; ex collection Lord Berners. *exhib.* R.A. (31), 'Landscape', S:A and FS (18).

WILLIS, EDMUND AYLBURTON (b. Bristol 1808, 12th October; d. Brooklyn, U.S.A., 1899, 3rd February). Painted animals and landscapes.

WILLOUGHBY, W. (presumably of the Hull family). *exhib.* Arthur Ackermann & Son Ltd., London, Racehorse 'Filho Da Puta', with jockey up.

WILLSON, JOHN J. (b. Leeds 1836, 2nd June; d. there 1903). Pupil of Edwin Moore and Richard Waller. *exhib.* V.E. (2), 'Sporting'.

WILSON, ALEXANDER (op. 1803–1846). Long resident in Long Millgate, Manchester. Animal painter. Mentioned by Shaw Sparrow. *lit.* 'Art and Artists in Lancashire and Cheshire', J. H. Nodal.

WILSON, G. A. (op. 1806–1808). *auct.* Sotheby's, 20th May 1964, ' "Roseden", a Bay Racehorse in land-scape setting, S&D Newcastle 1808; winner of Carlisle Steeplechase 1806.

WILSON, RICHARD, R.A. (b. 1714, d. 1782). Renowned as a painter of classical and other landscapes. Not a sporting painter, but the M.C.C. Gallery, Lord's Cricket Ground, have a painting attributed to him titled 'Cricket at Moulsey Hurst', the reverse bears the date 1790. (Wilson died in 1782). *lit.* 'Richard Wilson —The Grand Classic', by Adrian Bury.

WINGFIELD, J. (op. 1791–1798). Painted animals, game, fish and flowers. *exhib.* R.A. (8), including 1791, 'Larks'; 1792, 'Wild Duck and Widgeon'; 1793, 'Pheasants'; 1796, 'Wild Fowl'; 1797, 'Death of a Hare'.

WITHERINGTON, WILLIAM FREDERICK, R.A. (b. London 1785, 25th May; d. there 1865, 10th April). Studied R.A. Schools. *coll.* Liverpool, Walker A.G., 'The Dancing Bear'. *exhib.* R.A. (138); B.I. (62); S.S. (1), 'Domestic'. R.A. 1812, 'Partridges'; 'Going out Coursing'. *auct.* Christie's, 25/26th April 1940, A. N. Gilbey Collection, 'A Group of Cottage Children Fishing from the Bank of a Pond'; engraved by G. H. Phillips'.

WOLF, JOSEPH, R.I. (b. Morz, near Coblenz, 1820; d. London 1899, 20th April). Came to London 1848. Drew illustrations for natural history works and produced lithographs. Member of the New Water Colour Society, painting mostly birds, a great number sporting. *coll.* Preston A.G., 'Stags in landscape' and others'. *exhib.* R.A. (14); B.I. (7); N.W.C.S. (20); V.E. (8), 'Animals'. R.A. 1849, 'Woodcocks Seeking Shelter'; 1850, 'Wild Boar'; 1851, 'The Falcon's Nest'.

***WOLSTENHOLME, DEAN, the Elder** (b. Yorkshire 1757; d. London 1837, 25th October). Died aged 80 at 22 Chadd's Row, Gray's Inn Lane. *coll.* Major Sir Reginald Macdonald-Buchanan (2); Mr. and Mrs. Paul Mellon, 'Lord Glamis and His Staghounds'. *exhib.* R.A. (26), 'Sporting', which included in 1803 'Coursing'; 1804, 'Fox Hunting'; 1805, 'Epping Forest Hunt'; 1806, 'Hounds drawing cover'; 'Hounds running Gallantly into a Fox in View'; 1809, 'The Chase'; 'Digging the Fox from earth'; 'The Leap of the Stag'; 1810, 'Portraits of Horses belonging to a Stage Coach changing at an Inn on the Edmonton Road'; 'Return from Hunting by Moonlight'; 'Portraits of Two Horses and Hunters and hounds stopping to refresh returning from Hunting'; 1813, 'Portrait of an Old Horse, property of C. S. Chauncey'; 'Horse and Dog, property of Mr. Fuller'; 'Pointers belonging to Mr. Chauncey'; 'Mr. Joliffe's Hounds and Horses'; 1819, 'Belfont, a Fast Trotter'; 'Gentleman and Son waiting in Cover—Hounds finding'.

WOLSTENHOLME, DEAN, Junior (b. 1798; d. Highgate 1883, 12th April). Died at 3 High Street, Highgate, London, aged 86. *coll.* Captain Taylor, 'Essex Harriers' *repr.* 'Sporting Pictures of England', Guy Paget, colour plate; 'A Book of Sporting Painters', Shaw Sparrow, p. 176; W. S. Martin, U.S.A., 'Queen Elizabeth Escorted from Hatfield House to Enfield Chase; exhibited B.I. 1831; R.A. 1846. *repr.* 'A Book of Sporting Painters', Shaw Sparrow. *exhib.* R.A. (13); B.I. (10); S.S. (13). R.A. 1818, 'Portrait of "Beach", a Favourite Bitch'; 1819, 'Portrait of Three Horses, property of Wyatt, Esq.'; 1823, 'Portrait of "Harlot", a Favourite Staghound, property of Lord Glamis'; 1824, 'A Favourite Hackney and Dog'; 1825, 'Terriers Ferretting Rabbits'; 1826, ' "Backertrumps", a Favourite Trotter, property of George Wyatt'; 1828, ' "Cope", a Favourite Hunter, property of W. H. Whitbread, M.P.'. *auct.* Christie's, 25/26th April 1940, A. N. Gilbey Collection, 'A Party of Anglers Fishing for Pike and Perch', illustrated in 'Angling in British Art', Shaw Sparrow, p. 15.

WOMBILE, T. W. (WOMBWELL?) (op. 1834–1837). London address. *exhib.* S.S. (4), 'Sporting'.

WOOD, WILLIAM (b. Ipswich 1768; d. London 1809, 15th November). Founder Society of Associated Artists 1808 and President. *coll.* Lord Fairhaven, 'George III returning from Hunting', miniature, S&D 1798.

WOODHOUSE, WILLIAM (b. 1857, d. Morecambe 1939). *coll.* Preston A.G., 'Donkey in Landscape'; 'Horse and Foal'; 'Horse'; 'Snipe', all water-colours. *exhib.* R.A. (2). R.A. 1889, 'Doomed'; 1896, 'Wolves and Wild Boar'.

WOODROUFFE, R. (op. 1835–1854). London address. Painted game-birds and animals, especially deer in the Highlands. *exhib.* R.A. (4); B.I. (4), 'Sporting'. R.A. 1835, 'Dead Game'; 'A Hare and Pheasant'; 1839, 'Dead Game'; 'A Brace of Pheasants, Hare, Woodcock and Snipe'; 1840, 'A Pheasant and Rabbit'.

WOODWARD, THOMAS (b. Pershore, Worcestershire, 1801; d. Worcester 1852, November). Pupil of Abraham Cooper, R.A. *coll.* London, Tate Gallery (1). *exhib.* R.A. (85); B.I. (60); S.S. (15), 'Sporting'.

WOOLCOTT, D. (op. 1828). *exhib.* R.A. 1828 (1), A 'Horse and Groom'.

WOORT, T. W. (op. 1873). 'Partridges on a hillside', S&D 1873, sold at Sotheby's 28th October 1964 (395).

WOOTTON, FRANK (b. Milford, Hants., 1914, 30th July; living). Painter of landscape, animals and sport. His work ranging from a 'Captain R. E. Wallace, Master of the Heythrop, with hounds'; a 'Stampede'; a 'Trumpeter of the Household Cavalry'. Official R.A.F. war artist during Second World War. *exhib.* Ackermann's Gallery, London. 1964 (38 paintings, all sporting); R.A.; R.I., and other Galleries.

***WOOTTON, JOHN** (b. 1678 (?), d. 1765). Pupil and collaborator with Jan Wyck. Worked at Newmarket, drawing racehorses. His patron, the 3rd Duke of Beaufort, helped him to study in Rome. Fine works by him may be seen at Althorp, Longleat, and Welbeck. He also painted hunting and battle pieces, equestrian portraits, and in late life landscape. *coll.* London, Tate Gallery (1); The Hon. Michael Astor (1); Marquis of Bath (1); Duke of Beaufort (1); Major the Hon. H. R. Broughton (2); Brig. W. G. Carr (1); Marquess of Cholmondeley (1); Lord Fairhaven (1); Mrs. D. Hart (1); Jockey Club, Newmarket (1); Mr. A. M. Glen Kidston (2); Mrs. Leader (1); Marquess of Linlithgow (2); Mrs. J. de Lotbiniere (1); Lytham Hall, Lancs. (1); Major Sir Reginald Macdonald-Buchanan (4); Mr. and Mrs. Paul Mellon (7); Lord Monson (1); Major Guy Paget (the late) (5); H.M. The Queen (3); Earl Spencer (1); Lord Shuttleworth, M.C. (1).

WORRALL, J. E. (b. Liverpool 1829, d. there 1913). *exhib.* R.A. (5); S.S. (4), 'Domestic'. Liverpool, Walker A.G., 'An Enthusiastic Fisherman'.

WORTLEY, ARCHIBALD JAMES STUART- (b. 1849, 27th May; d. 1905, 11th October). Pupil of J. E. Millais. Painted portraits and sporting subjects. *coll.* Lord's (1). *exhib.* R.A. (29); G.G. (41); N.G. (2); V.E. (16), 'Sporting'.

***WRIGHT, GEORGE** (b. 1860, d. 1942). Leeds and Oxford addresses, later Rugby. *exhib.* Ackermann & Son Ltd., London, 'Gone Away'; 'The Royal Mail Coach', both exhibited Preston 1943. R.A. 1894, 'Well-earned Rest—Kennels, Bramham Park'; 1897, 'The Fresh Team'; 'Putting in to Draw Cover'; 1898 Coaching'; 1899, 'Meeting the Hounds'; 1901, 'A Fine Hunting Morning'; 'A Meet in the Market Place'; 1903, 'A Check'; 1904, 'Polo at Rugby'; 'Breaking Cover'.

WRIGHT, GILBERT S. (living 1900). Brother of George. London address. *coll.* H. R. Cresner, 'The Welcome Arrival', coach outside an inn, horsemen in distance. *exhib.* R.A. 1900, 'How He Won the V.C.'

WRIGHT, JOHN MASEY (b. Pentonville, London, 1777, 14th October; d. 1866, 13th May). Son of an organ builder. Painted scenery and drew book illustrations. *exhib.* R.A. (9); B.I. (8); S.S. (29); O.W.C.S. (134), 'Historical'; Frank T. Sabin, London, 1959, 'Ascot Heath Races'.

WRIGHT, JOSEPH, A.R.A. (b. Derby 1743, 3rd September; d. there 1797, 29th August). Pupil of Thomas Hudson. *coll.* Mr. and Mrs. R. Richards, Gawsworth Hall, Macclesfield, 'Portrait of Peter Brooke in uniform of Tarporley Hunt Club'. *exhib.* S.A. (43); F.S. (2); R.A. (40), 'Domestic'.

WRIGHT, T. (op. 1750). Painted racehorses and racecourses. *exhib.* Ackermann & Son Ltd., London, 'Gold Cup at Newmarket, 1751'.

***WYCK, JOHN—JAN VAN WIJCK** (b. Haarlem 1640; d. Mortlake 1702, 26th October). Came with his father, a noted artist, to England during the reign of Charles II and remained until his death. Published and illustrated a 'Book on Hunting and Hawking'. *coll.* Ipswich A.G., 'Hawking Party', exhibited Norwich 1950; Lytham Hall, Lancs., 'A Hawking Party'; Mr. and Mrs. Paul Mellon, 'Hare Hunting'; 'A Hunting Party' (drawing). *lit.* Grant, Col. M. H., 'Chronological History of the Old English Landscape Painters (in oil), Vol. 1, pl. 8 (revised edition).

YEATS, JACK BUTLER, R.H.A. (b. 1871). Painter of Ireland. *coll.* Tate Gallery, London, 'Back from the Races'.

YORKE, H. J. (op. 1867). A pair of Coaching scenes S&D 1867 sold at Sotheby's 28th October 1964 (7).

YOUNG, T. (op. 1877). 'A Horse in a Landscape', thus dated, is recorded to this otherwise unknown hand —vide Grant's Dictionary.

ZINKEISEN, ANNA KATRINA (b. Kilereggan 1901, 28th August; living). Studied R.A. Schools. Married Colonel G. R. W. Heseltine. Paints portraits, figures, and romantic subjects, including sport. *auct.* 'The Hunt in Wintertime', sold Sotheby's 8th January 1964. *repr.* 'Medieval English Hunting Scene' (Christmas card).

ZINKEISEN, DORIS CLARE (b. Gareloch; living). Painter, theatrical designer, etc. Sister of Anna Zinkeisen. *exhib.* at R.A., Paris Salon, etc. *repr.* 'Skating in Hyde Park, 1810' (Christmas card).

***ZOFFANY, JOHN, R.A.** (b. Germany 1725, d. 1810). Studied in Italy. Came to England c. 1761. Foundation Member of R.A. Visited India 1783–1789. *coll.* The Earl of Durham, 'Mr. and Mrs. Garrick at Tea entertaining Dr. Johnson and Mr. Bowden at their Chiswick Villa' (A Gentleman Fishing). *repr.* 'A Book of Sporting Painters', Shaw Sparrow; Mrs. Spencer Percival, 'Mr. and Mrs. Burke of Carshalton' (Angling). *repr.* 'Angling in British Art', Shaw Sparrow, p. 176, colour plate; Major Sir Reginald Macdonald-Buchanan, 'Master James Sayer, aged 13, Angling in a Woodland Stream'. *repr.* 'Angling in British Art', Shaw Sparrow, p. 193, colour plate; Lord Tweeddale, 'Col. Mordaunt's Cock Match at Lucknow'. *engr.* 'Tiger Hunting at Chandernagur', by R. Earlom. *exhib.* S.A. (29); F.S. (1); R.A. (42), 'Portraits'.

PLATES

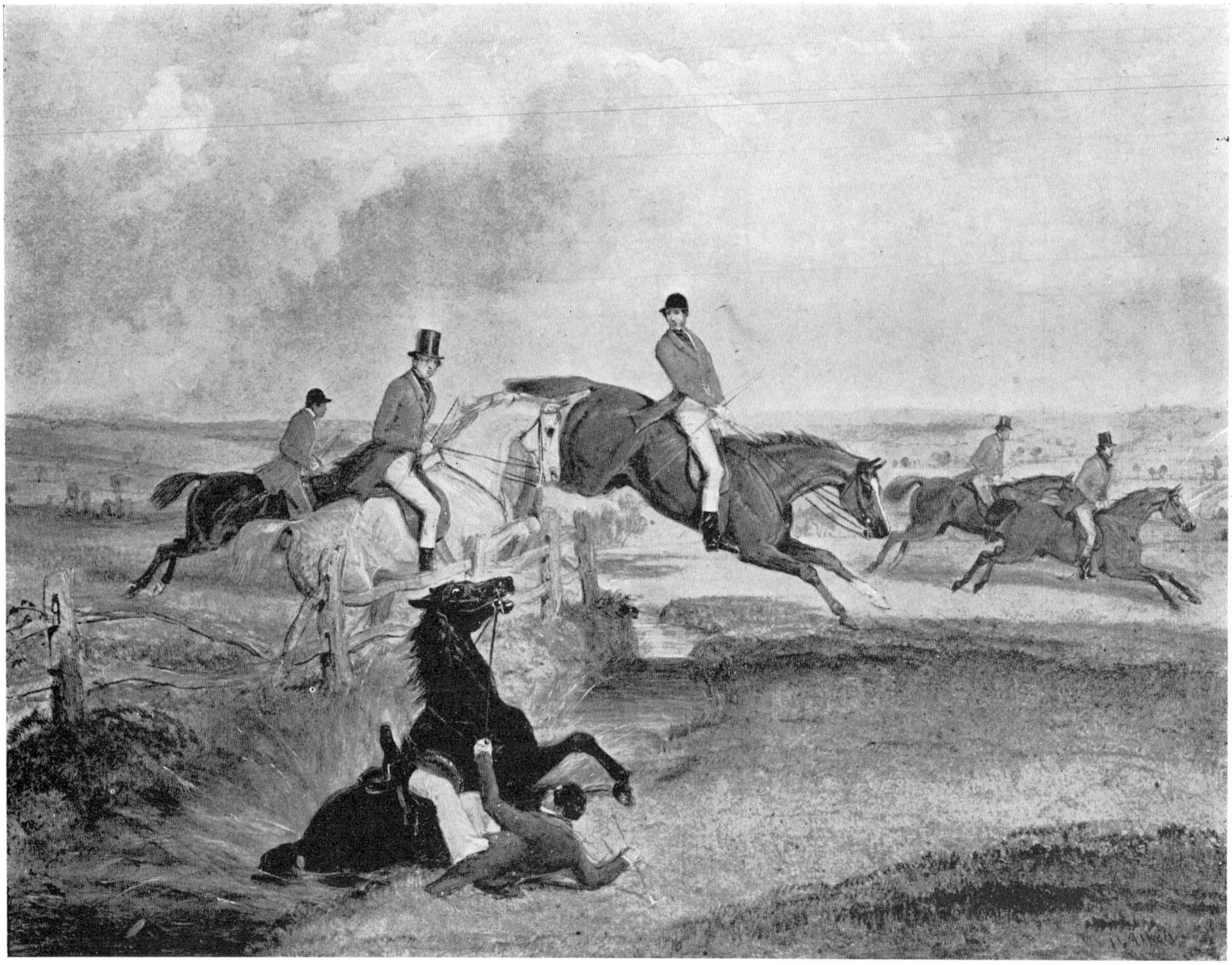

14 × 18 in. HENRY ALKEN, SENIOR. 1785–1851 Signed

One of a set of four Hunting scenes

Courtesy of Messrs. Frost & Reed Ltd., Bristol & London

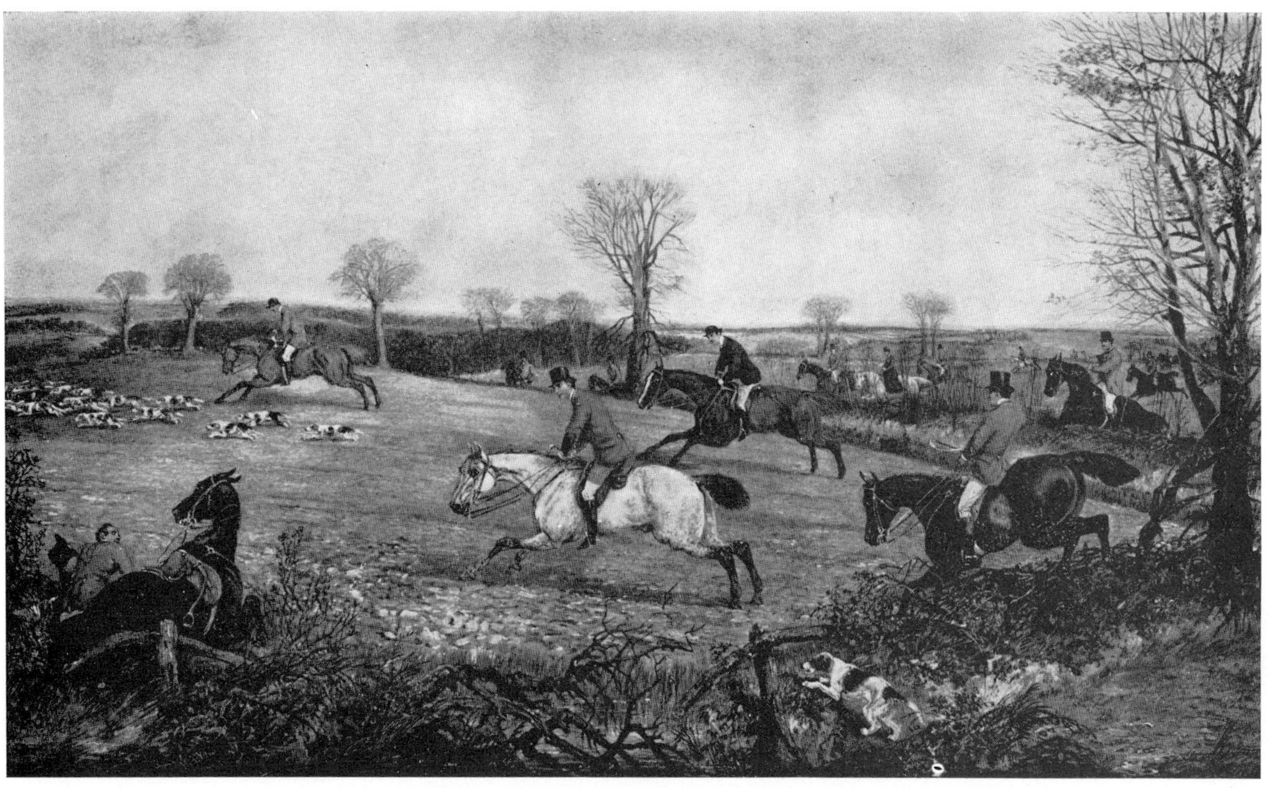

Oil. 18 × 29¾ in. SAMUEL HENRY ALKEN. (called Henry Alken, Junior) 1810–1894 Signed

'Full Cry' from a set of four

Courtesy of Messrs. Frost & Reed Ltd., Bristol & London

PLATE 2

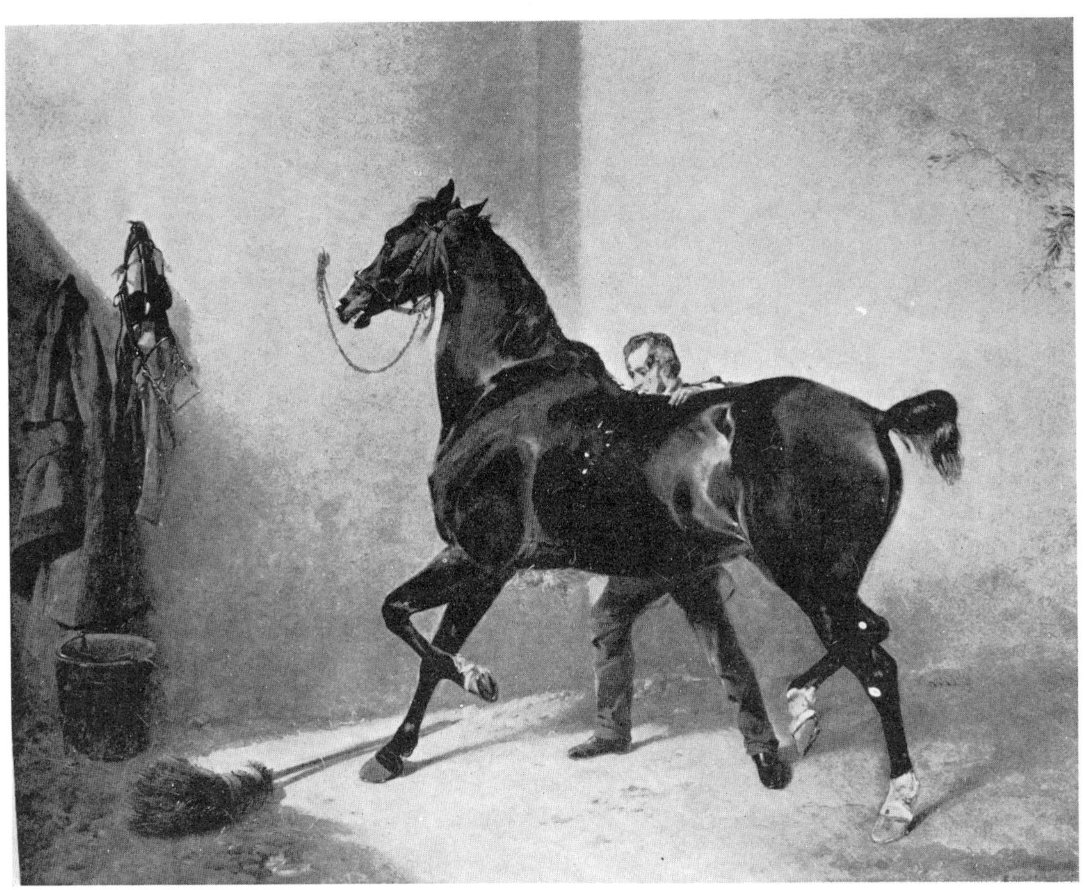

Oil. 27 × 35 in.

RICHARD ANSDELL, R.A. 1815–1885

S & D. 1846

A Stable Scene

Courtesy of Messrs. Frost & Reed Ltd., Bristol & London

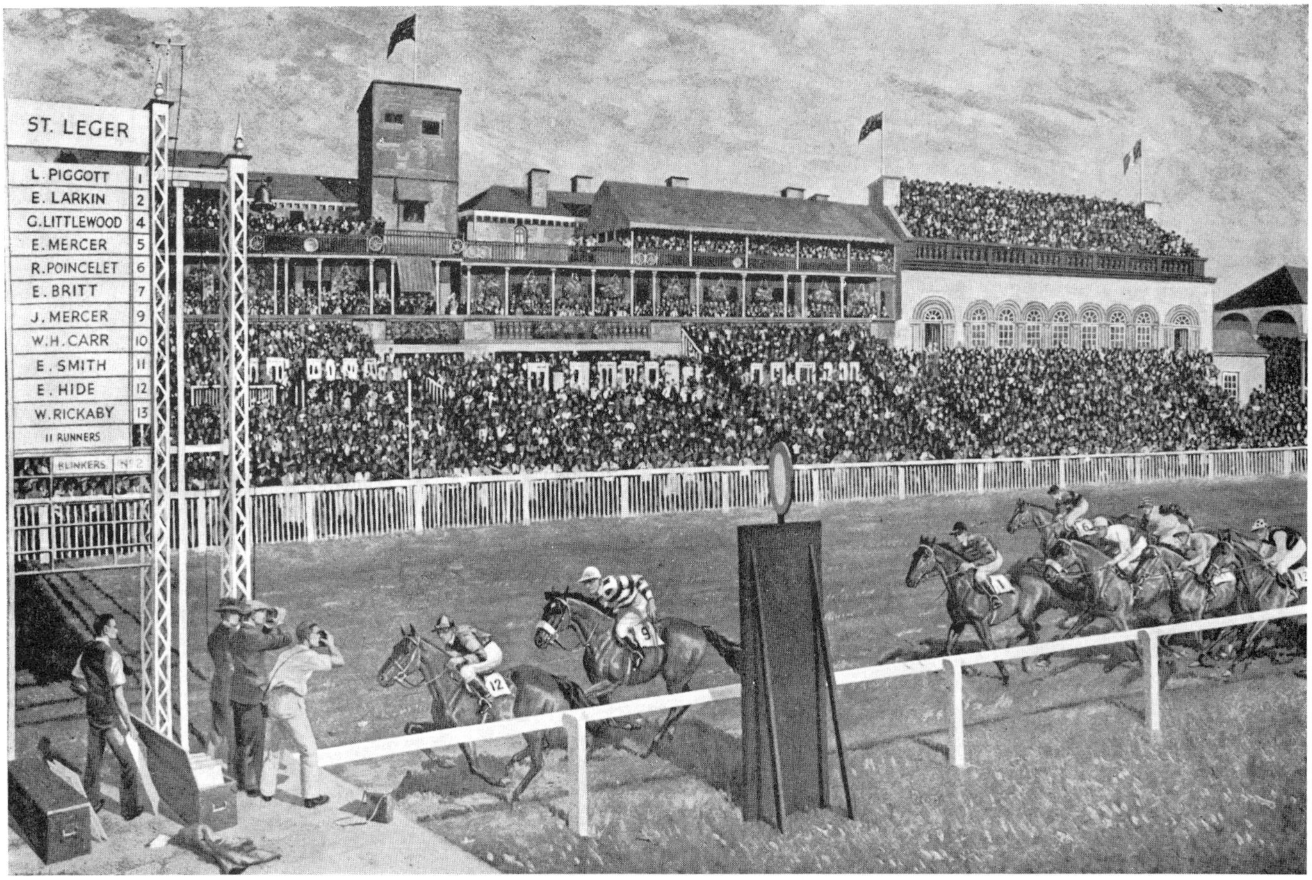

Canvas. $39\frac{1}{2} \times 59\frac{1}{2}$ in.

JOSEPH APPLEYARD. b. 1908

S & D. 1959

'Finish of the St. Leger, 1959'

In the Museum & Art Gallery, Doncaster

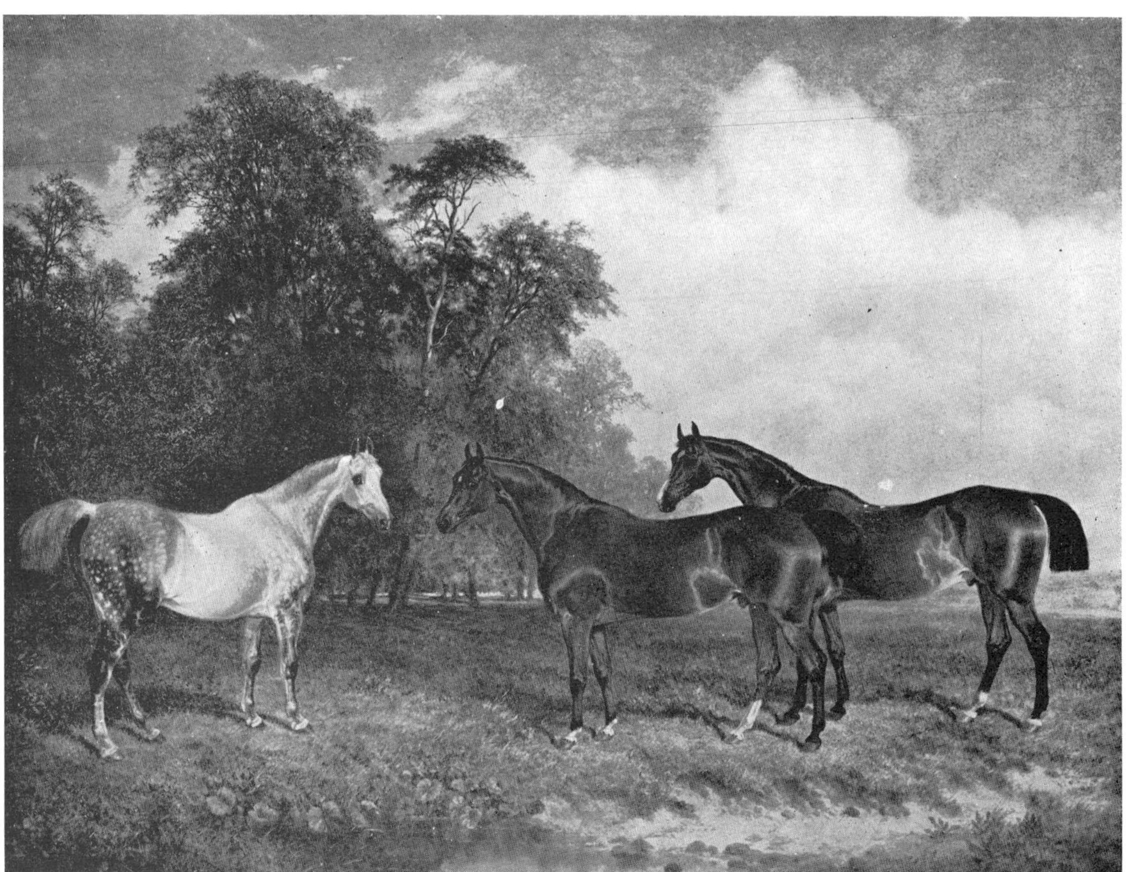

Oil. 33½ × 44 in. JAMES BALDOCK. op. 1867–1887 S & D. 1879

Two Bay Horses & a dappled Grey in a field

Courtesy of Messrs. Frost & Reed Ltd., Bristol & London

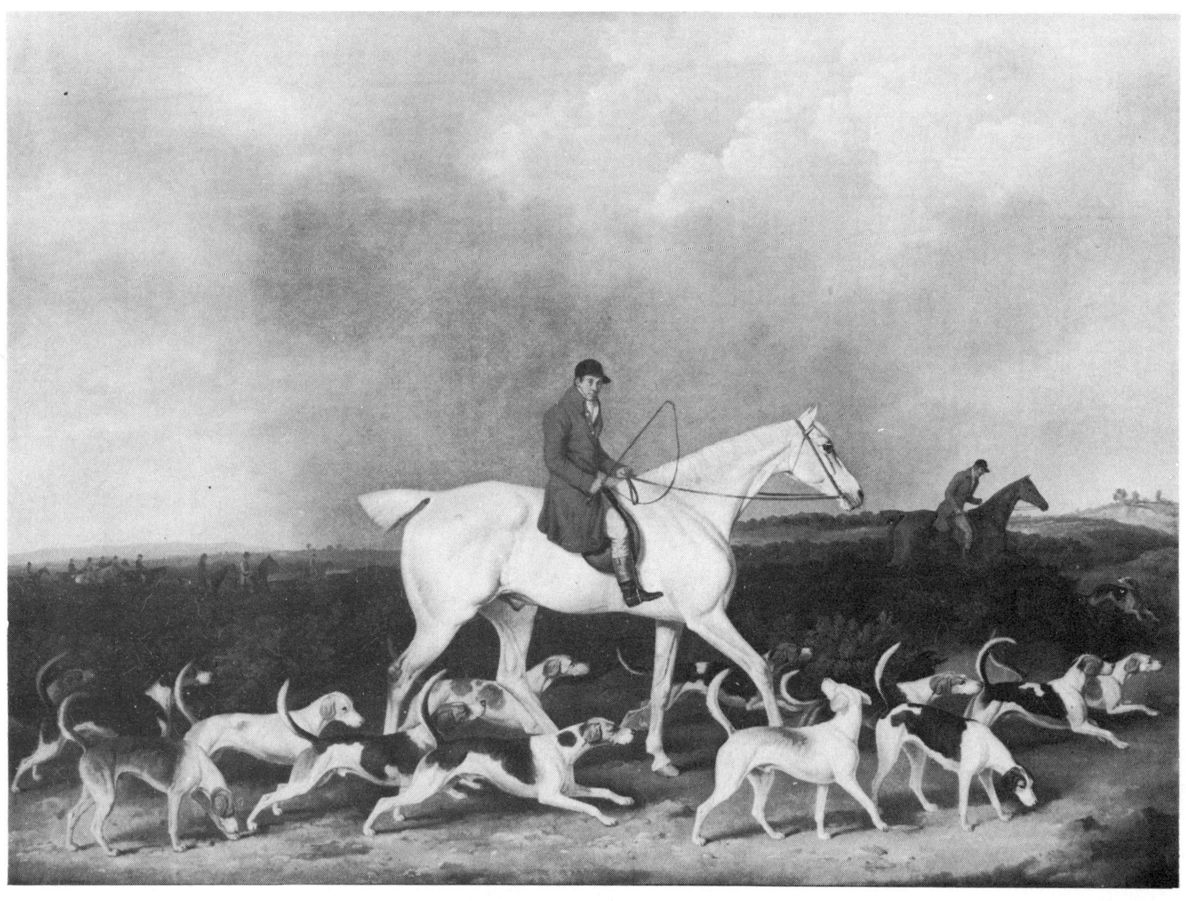

Canvas. 36 × 48 in. JAMES BARENGER. 1780–1831 S & D. 1819

Lord Derby's Staghounds

In the collection of Mr. & Mrs. Paul Mellon

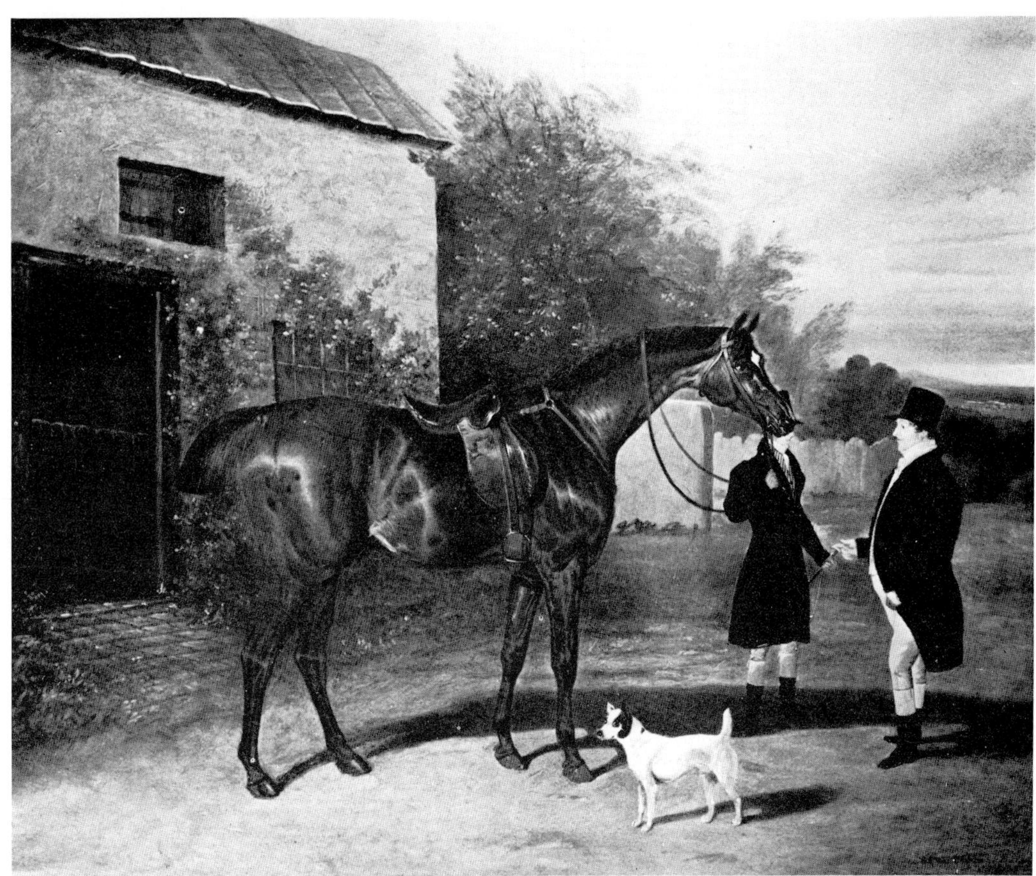

Oil. 24 × 30 in. WILLIAM BARRAUD. 1810–1850
Hunter with owner and groom outside a stable
Courtesy of Messrs. Frost & Reed Ltd., Bristol & London

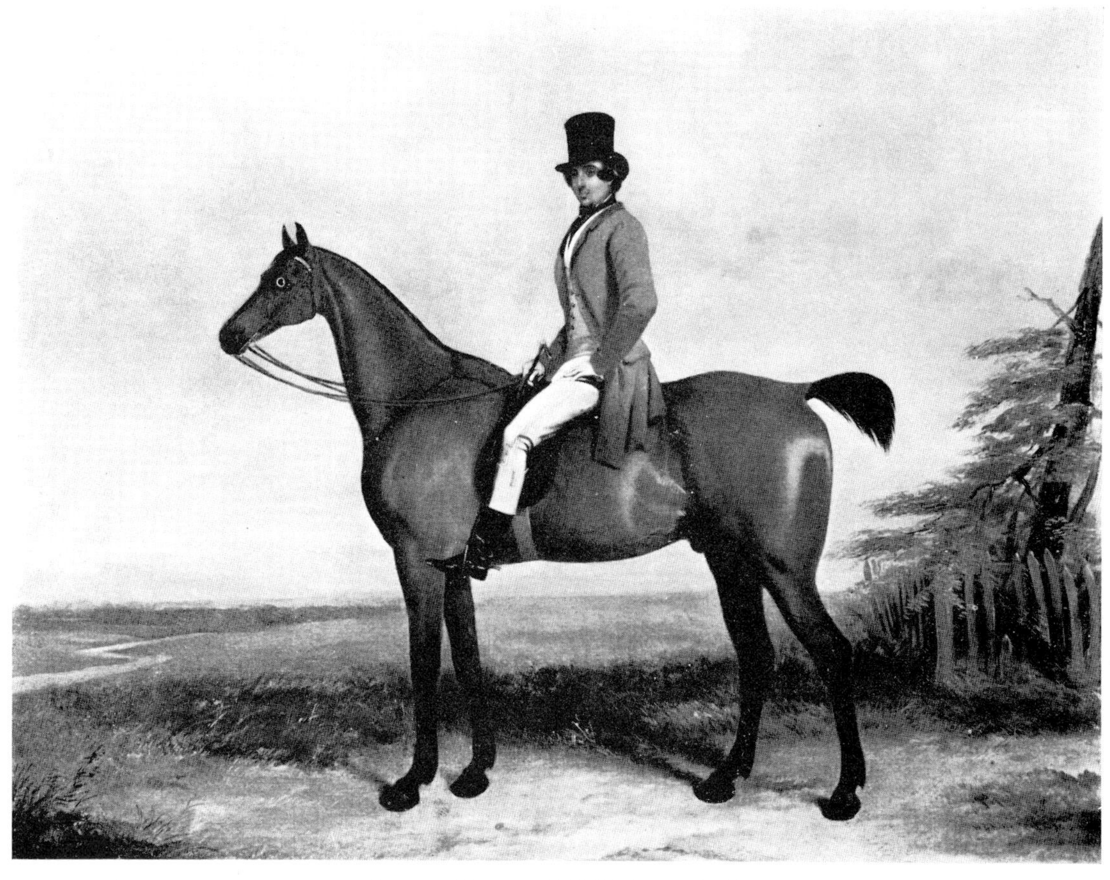

Canvas. 28 × 36 in. WILLIAM and HENRY BARRAUD S & D. 1840
Man in Hunting Pink mounted on his Horse
Courtesy of Messrs. Oscar & Peter Johnson Ltd., London

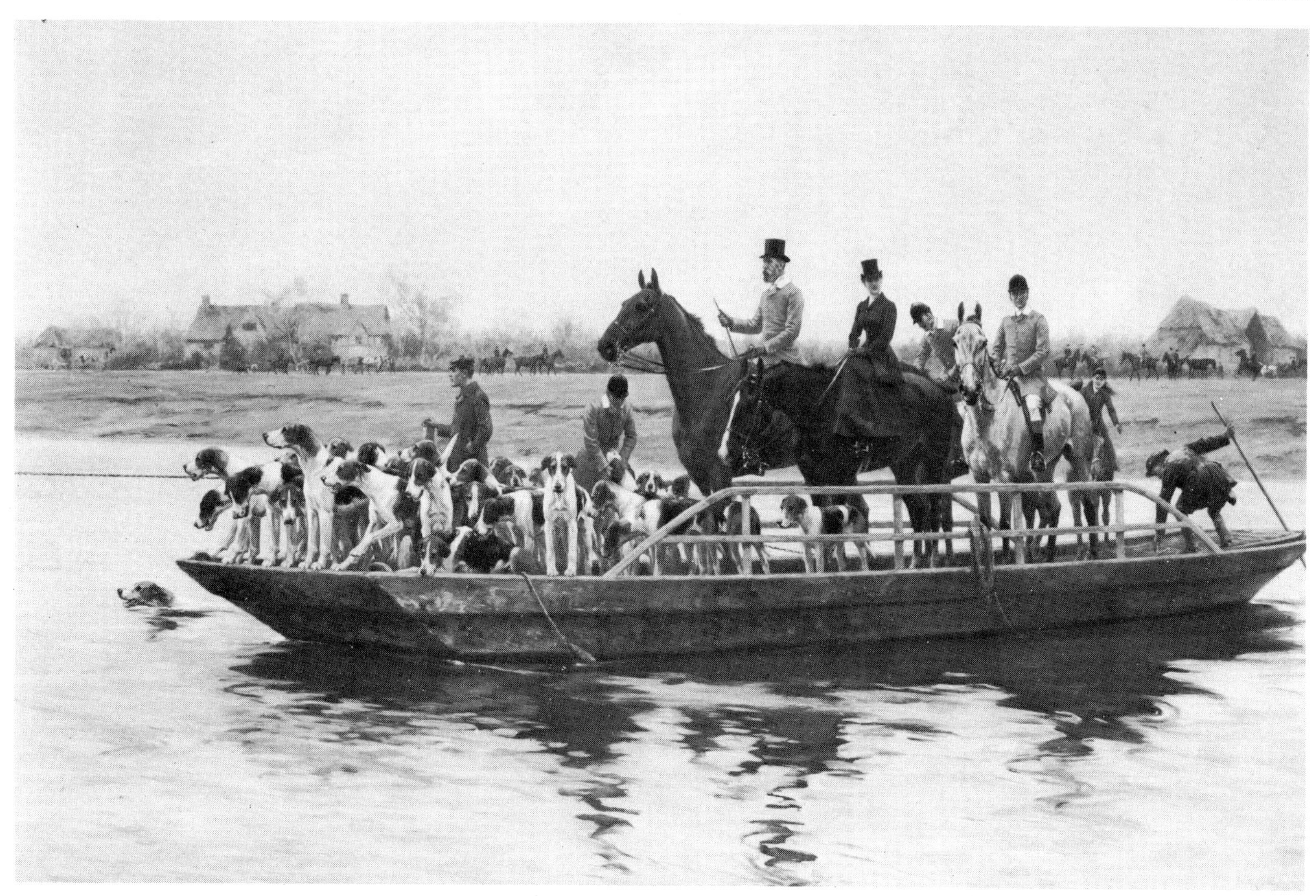

Canvas. 32 × 50 in.

THOMAS BLINKS. 1860–1912
The York & Ainsty Hounds on the Ferry at Newby
Courtesy of Messrs. M. Newman Ltd., London

S & D. 1898

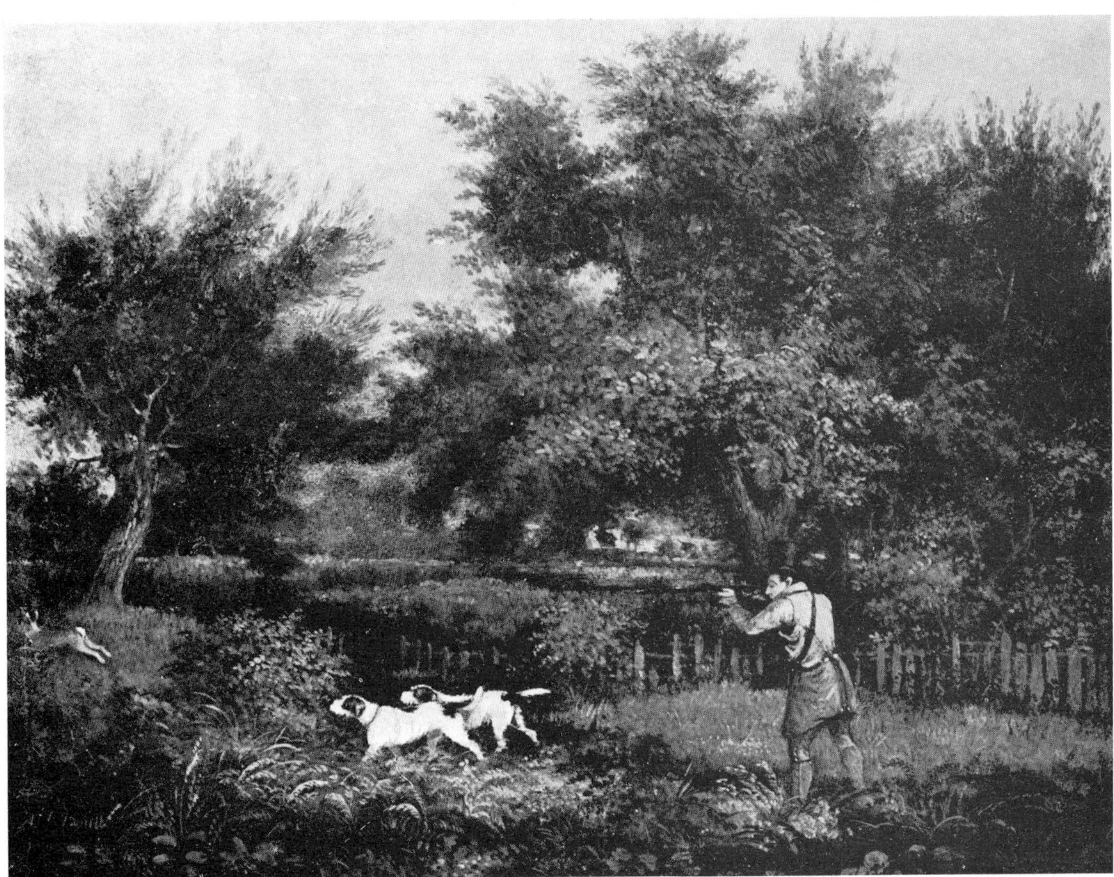

Oil. $12\frac{1}{4} \times 15\frac{3}{4}$ in. A. S. BOULT. op. 1815–1853 Signed

'Shooting scene'

Courtesy of Messrs. Frost & Reed Ltd., Bristol & London

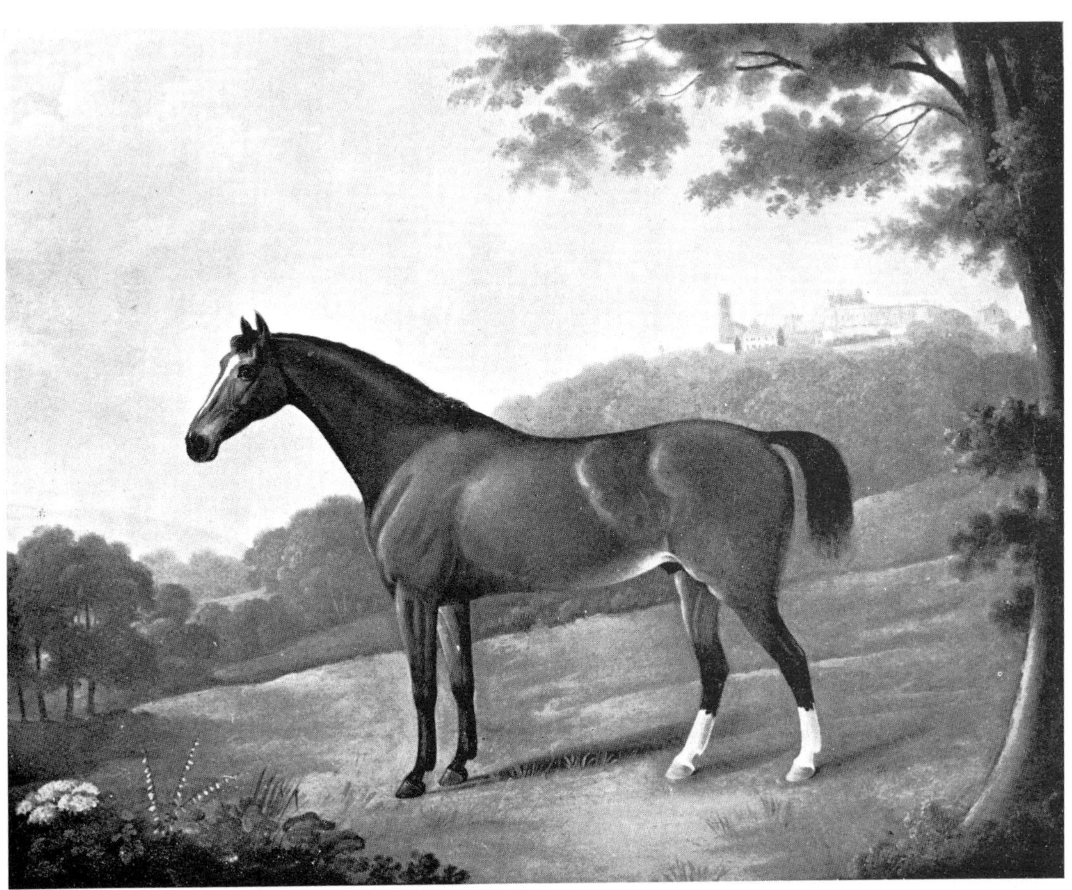

Oil. 24×30 in. JOHN BOULTBEE. c. 1765–1812

A Bay Hunter in a Landscape

Courtesy of Messrs. Frost & Reed Ltd., Bristol & London

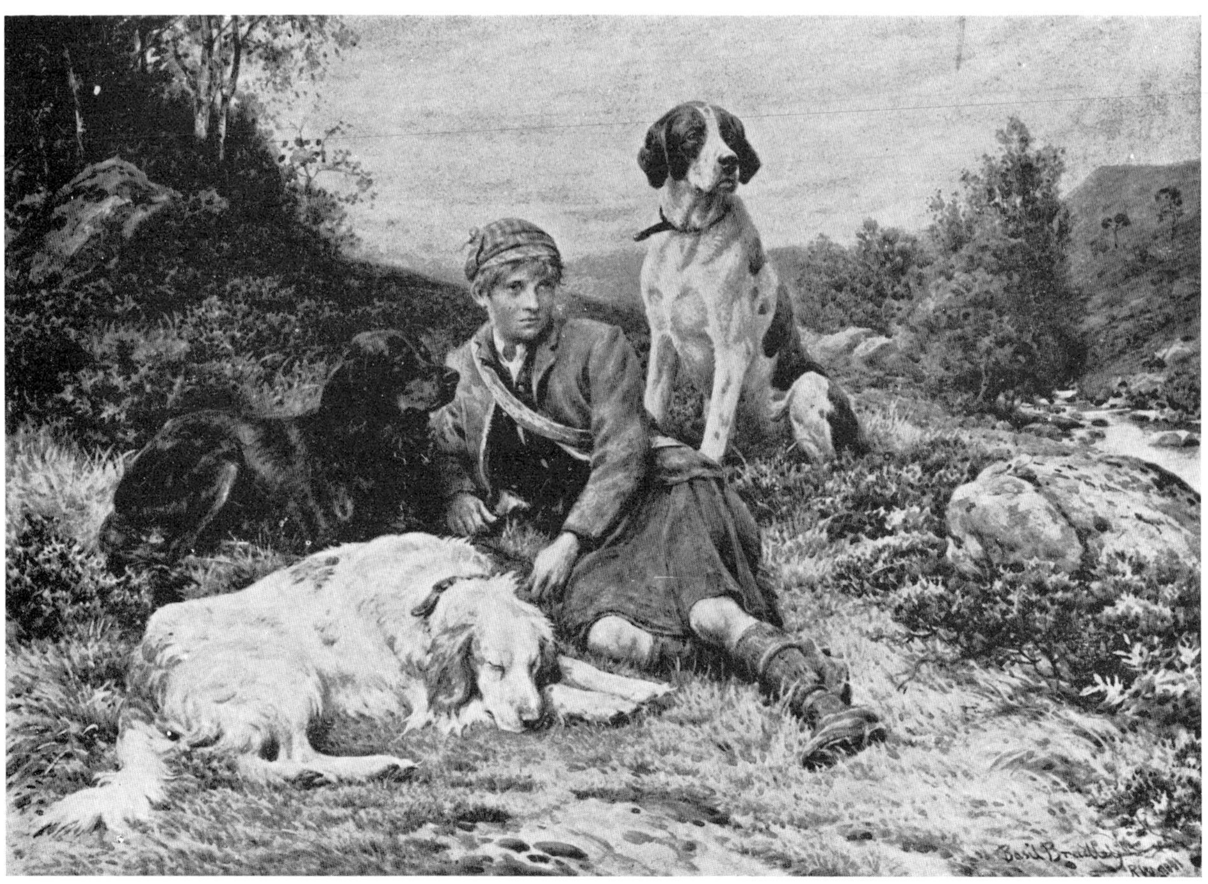

Water colour 15 × 21 in. BASIL BRADLEY, R.W.S. 1842–1904 Signed

'Taking a Rest'

Courtesy of Messrs. Frost & Reed Ltd., Bristol & London

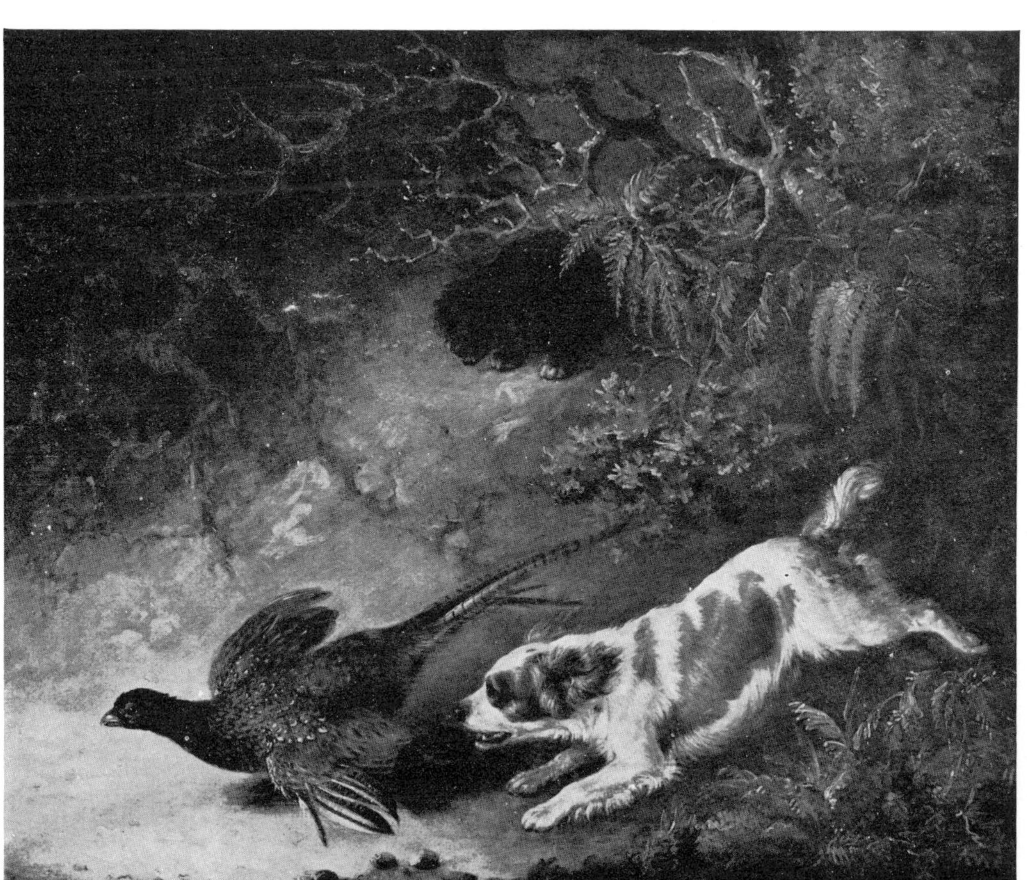

Oil. $19\frac{1}{4} \times 23\frac{1}{2}$ in. EDMUND BRISTOW. 1787–1876 S & D. 1828

'Caught on the ground'

Courtesy of Messrs. Frost & Reed Ltd., Bristol & London

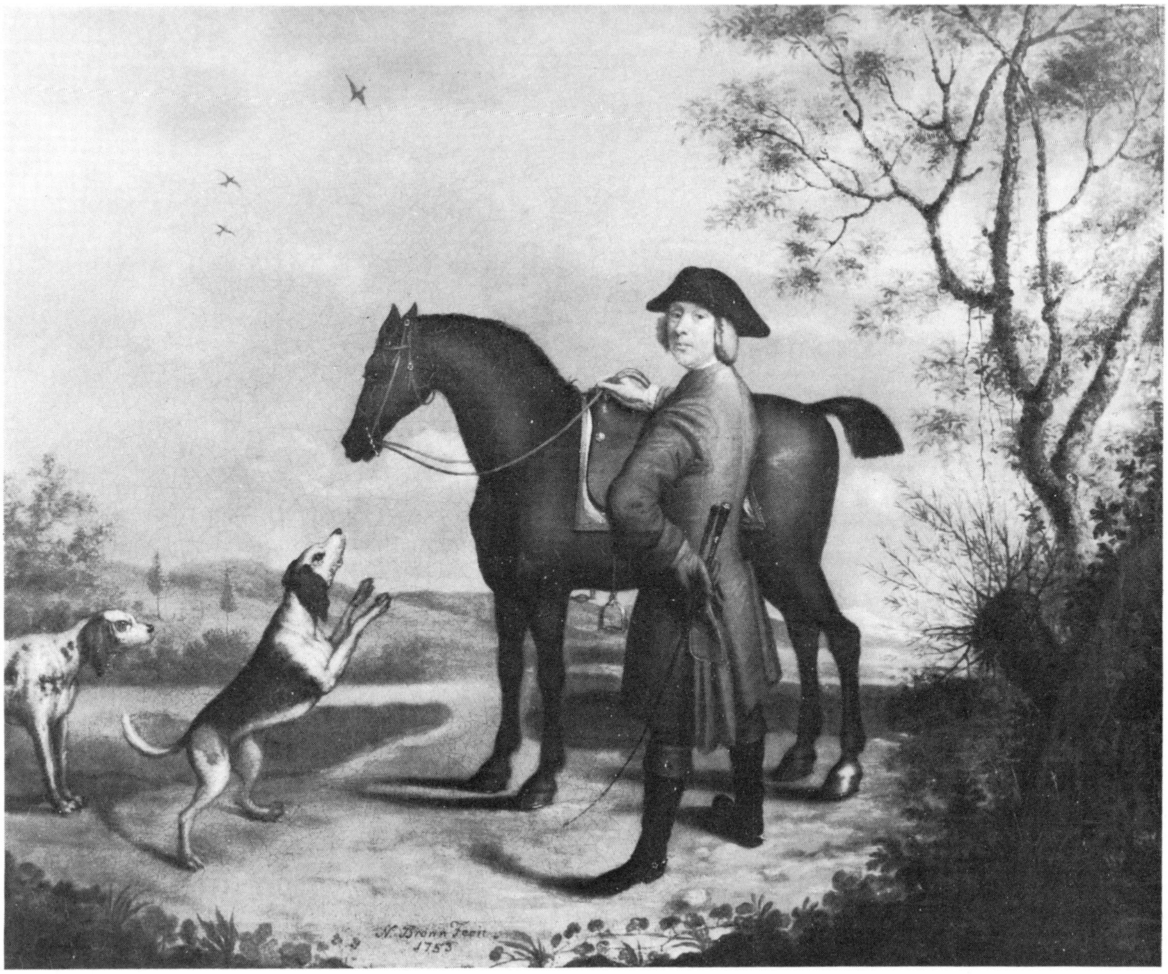

Canvas. 25 × 31 in. | NATHANIEL BROWN. op. 1753–1779 | S & D. 1753

Hunter and Sportsman with Hounds

Courtesy of Messrs. Frank T. Sabin, London

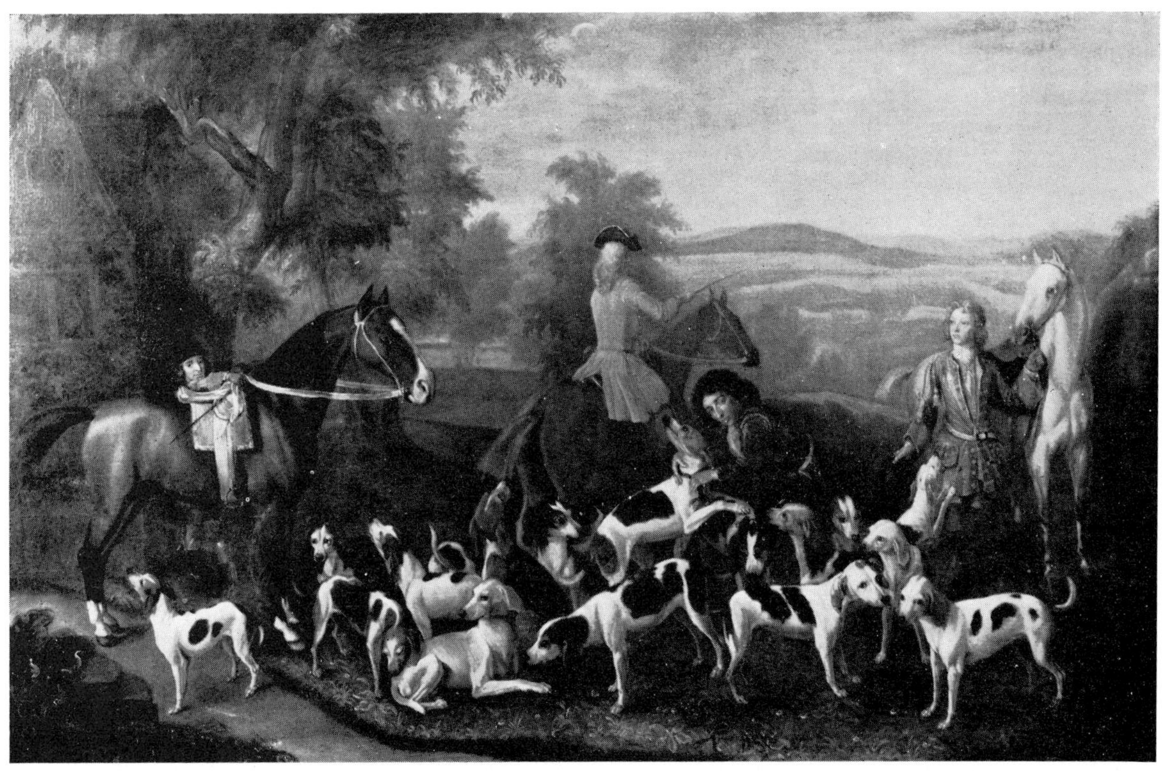

Canvas. 57 × 93 in. | BYNG. op. 1706 | S & D. 1706

Sportsmen with Horses and Hounds

Courtesy of Messrs. St. James's Galleries Ltd., London

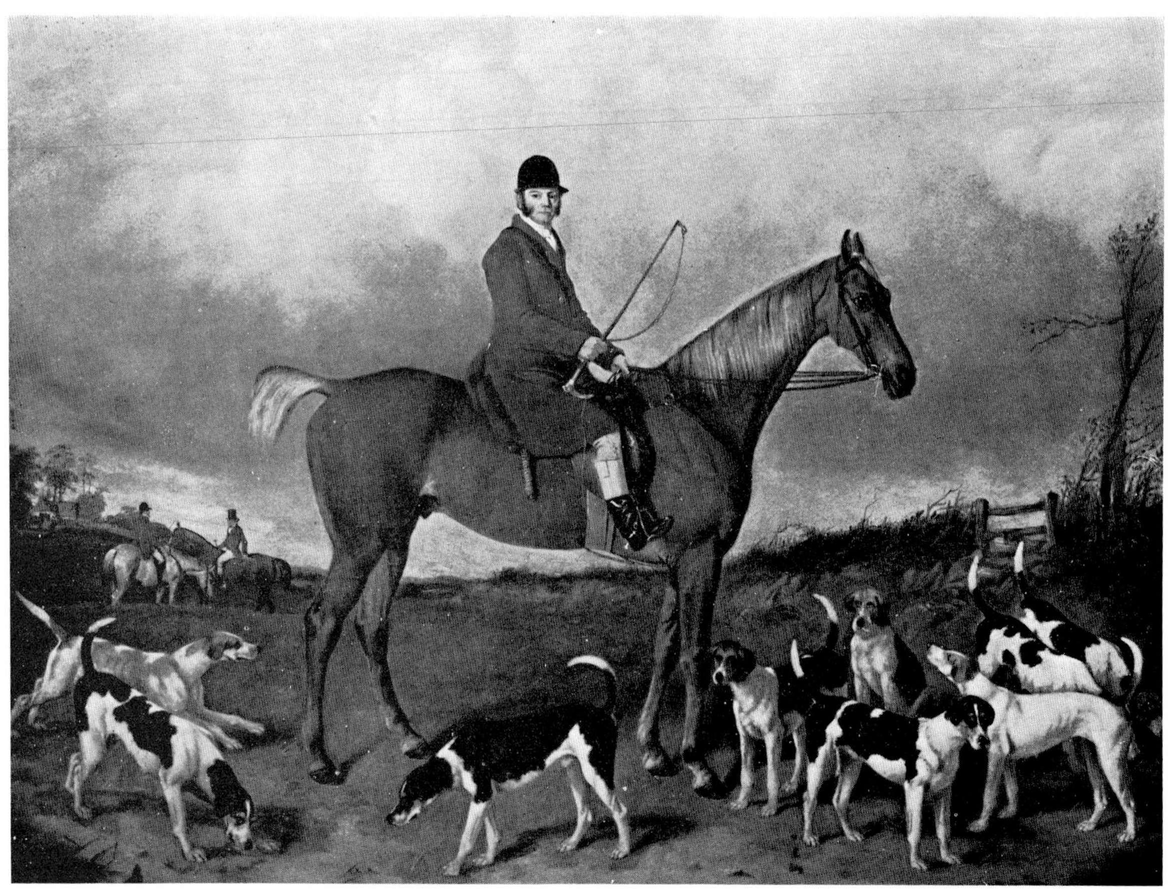

Oil. 28 × 36 in.

HENRY CALVERT. op. 1813–1861
Huntsman & Hounds
Courtesy of Messrs. Frost & Reed Ltd., Bristol & London

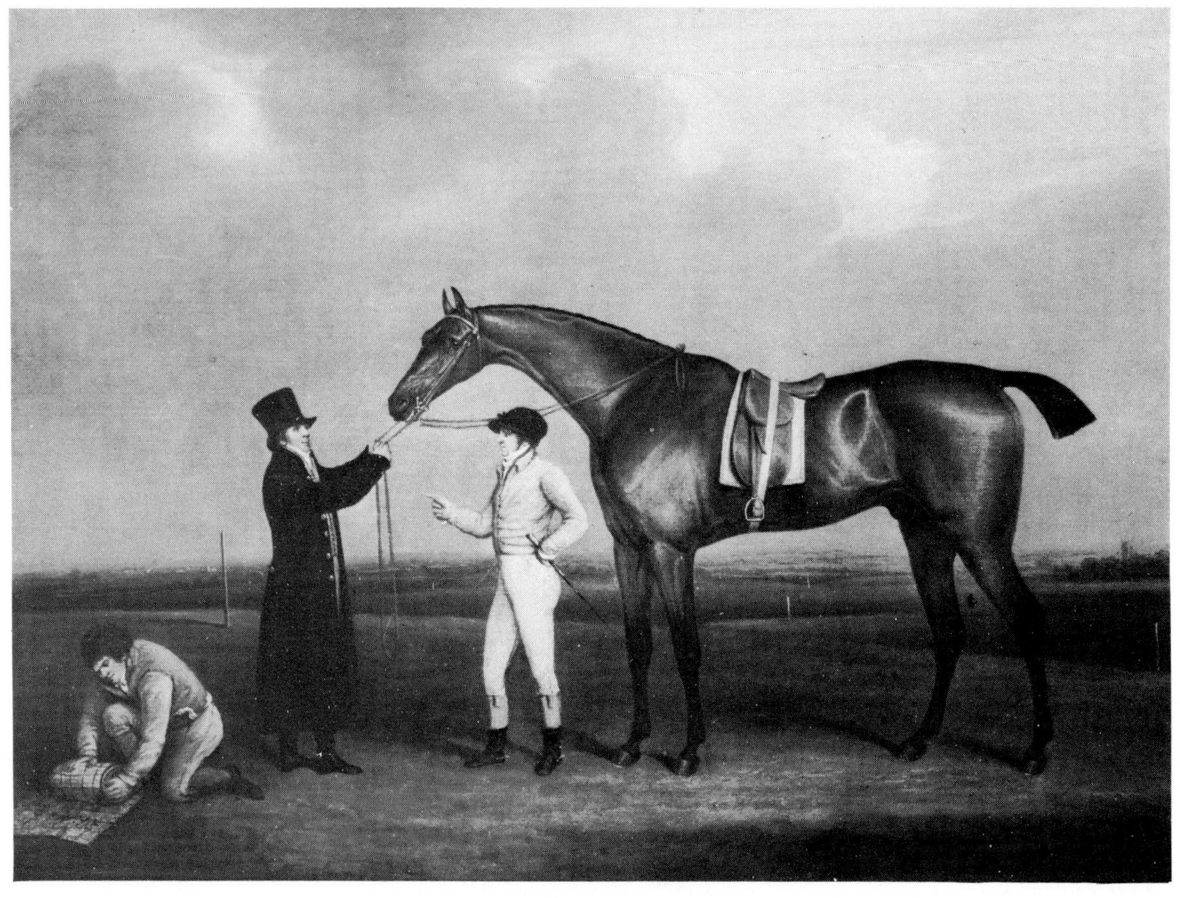

Canvas. 21 × 28½ in.

H. B. CHALON. 1770–1849
'Walton' with jockey, trainer & stable-boy
Courtesy of Berry-Hill Galleries, New York

Signed

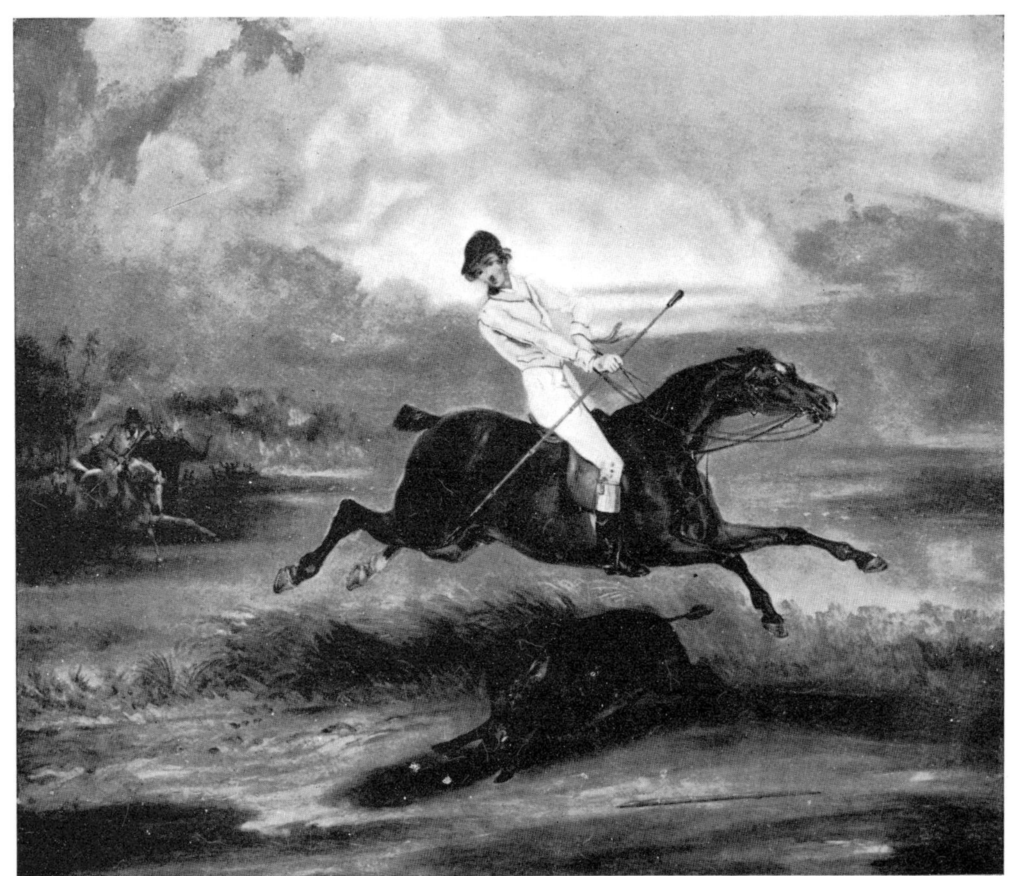

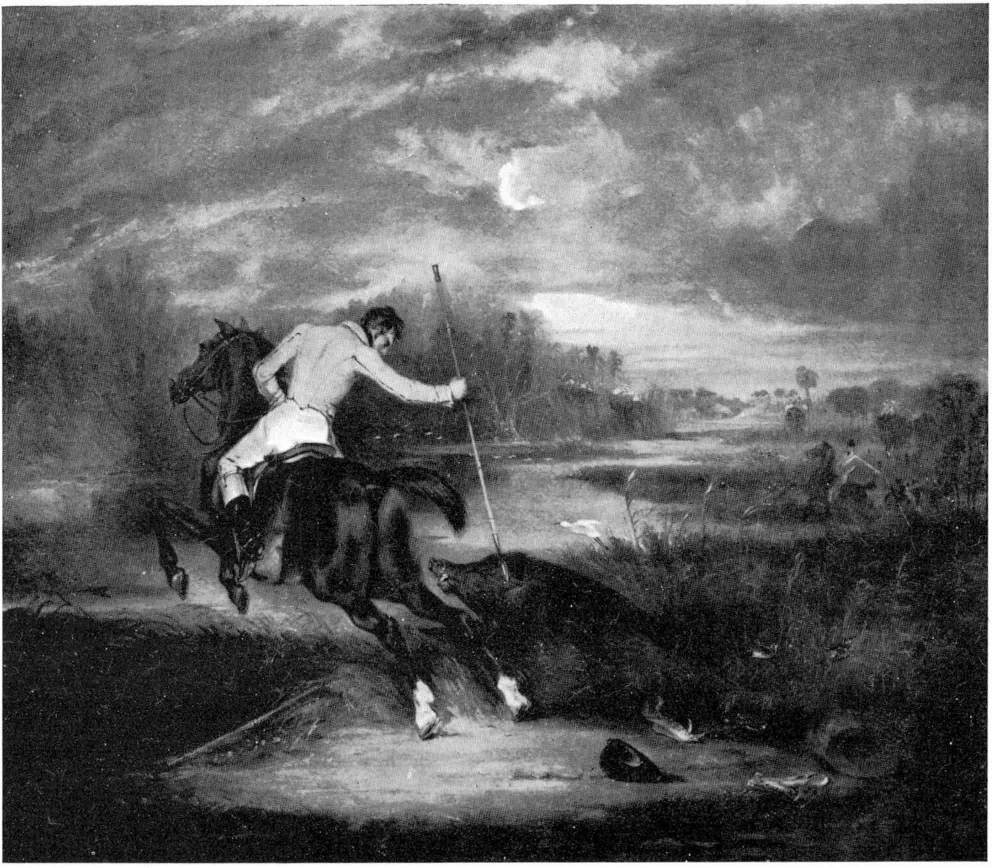

Canvas (pair) 25 × 30 in. GEORGE CHINNERY. 1774–1852 c. 1808–12
Pig-sticking from Horseback
Courtesy of Mr. John Galvin

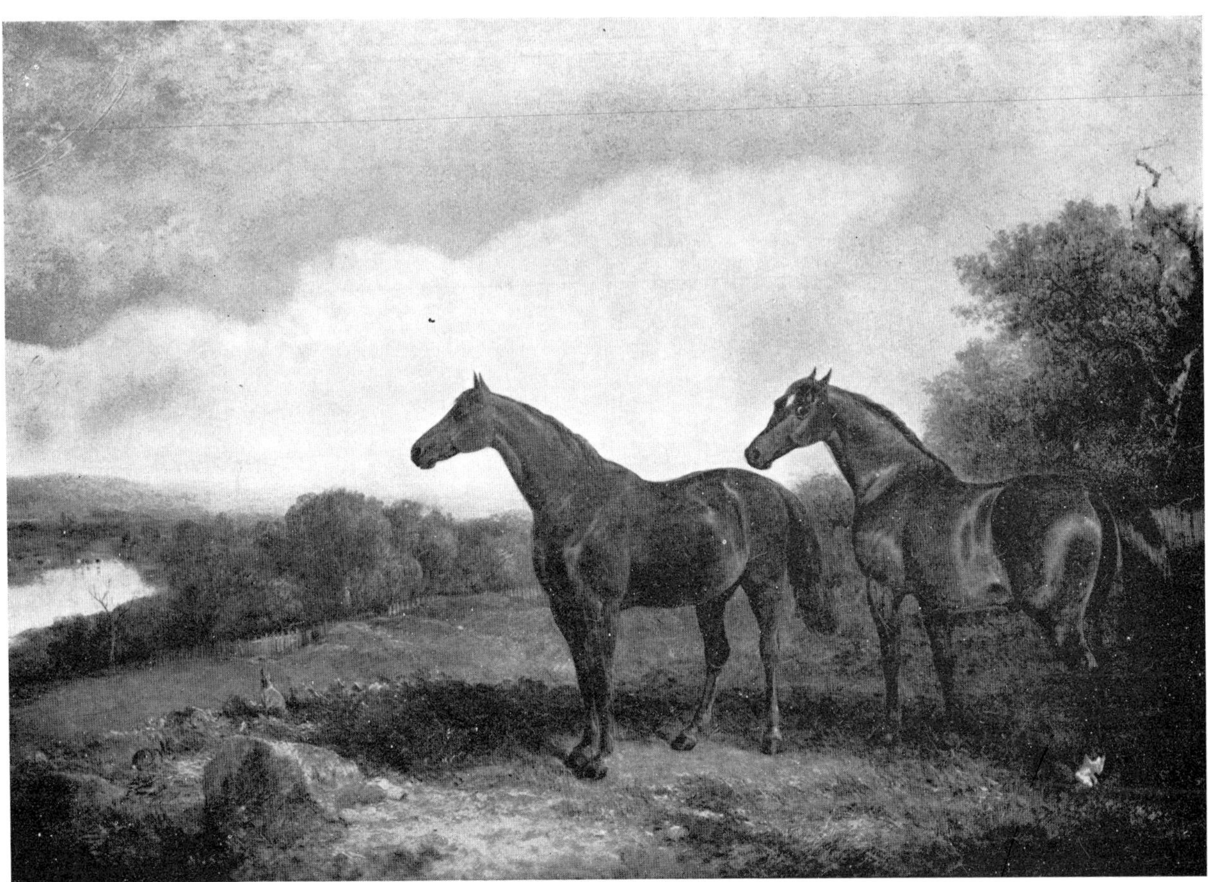

Oil. 24 × 35½ in. GEORGE COLE. 1810–1883 S & D. 1855

Two Chestnut Hunters near a River

Courtesy of Messrs. Frost & Reed Ltd., Bristol & London

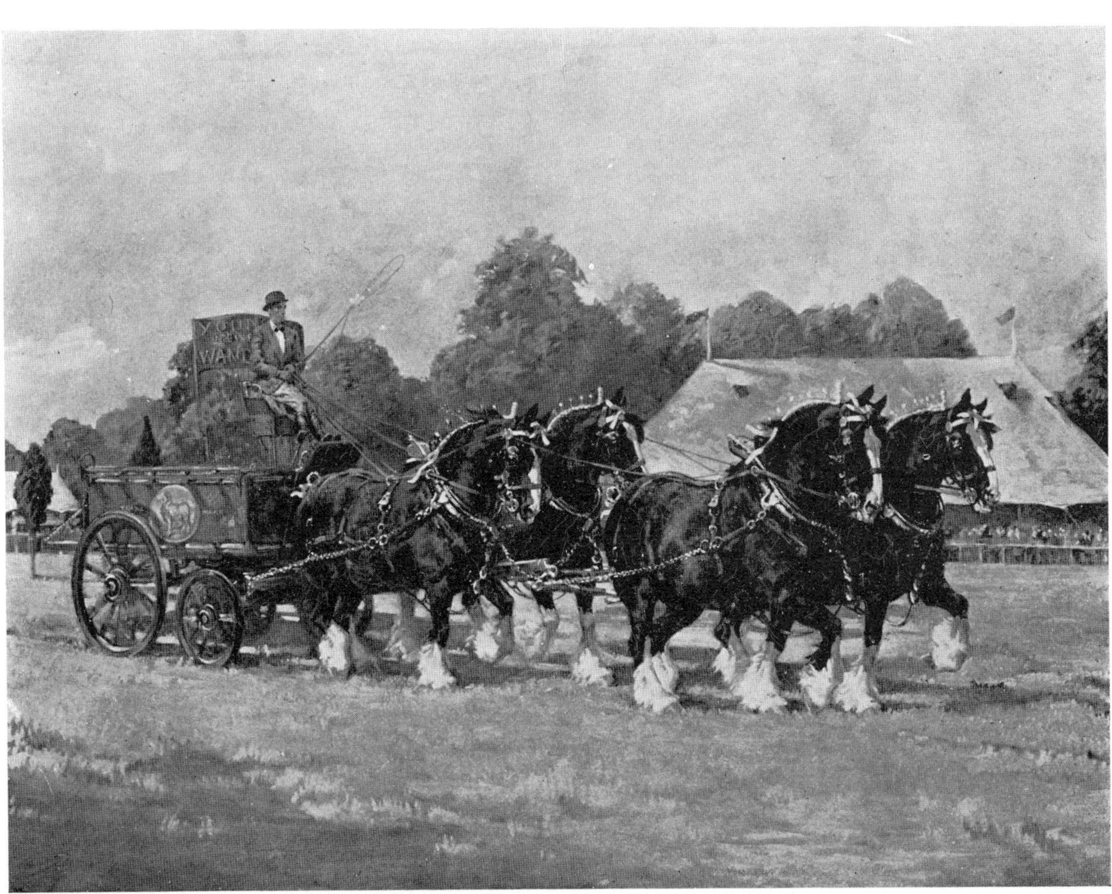

Canvas. 35 × 40 in. NINA COLMORE, M.B.E. b. 1889 Signed

Young's Brewery Champion Team of Shire Horses

Courtesy of Henry Young Esq.

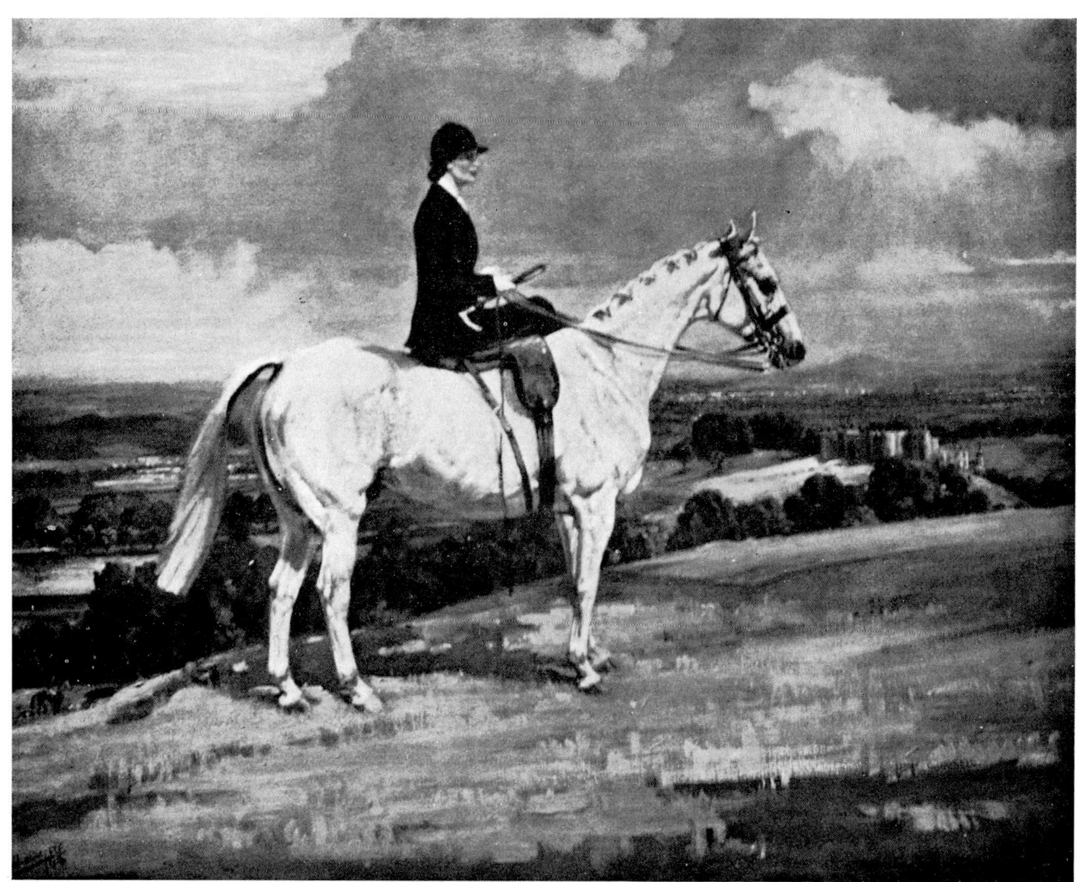

Canvas. 20 × 30 in. NINA COLMORE, M.B.E. b. 1889 S & D. 1946
Lady Margaret Myddelton on 'Shadow' at Chirk Castle, N. Wales
Courtesy of Lady Margaret Myddelton

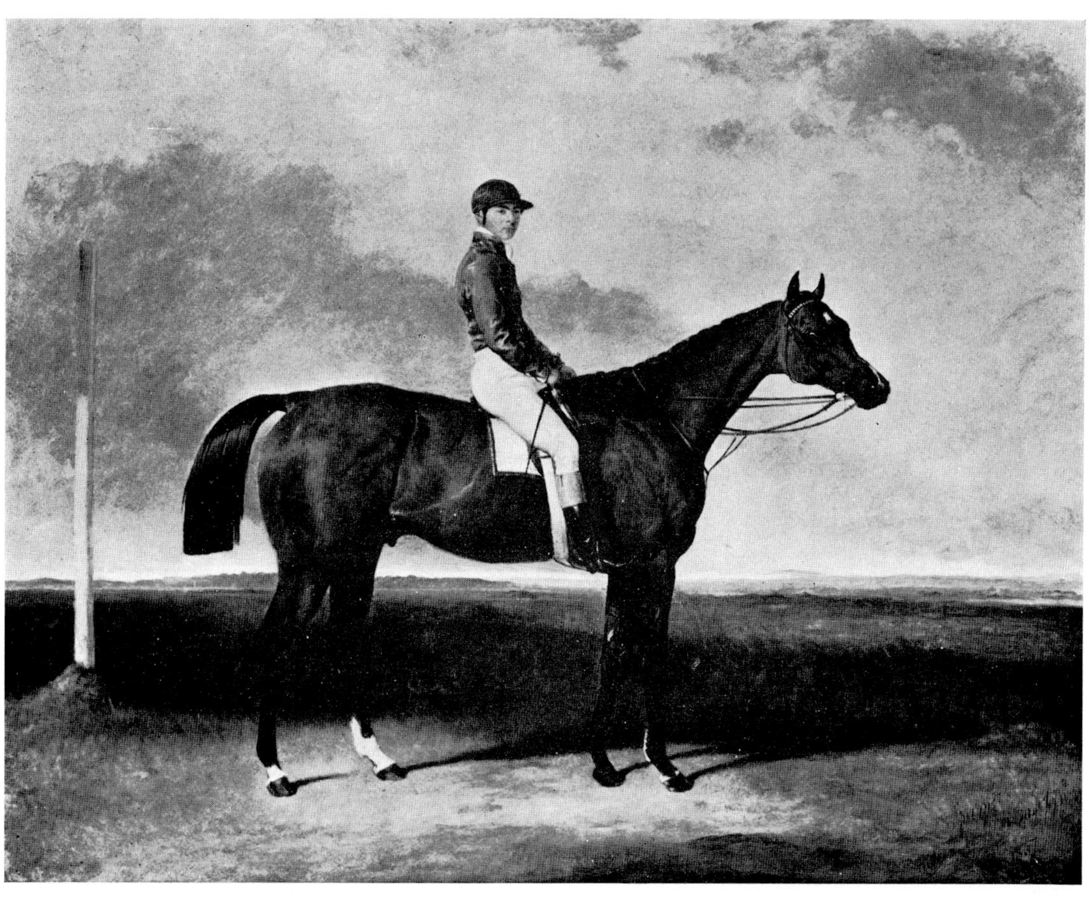

Canvas. 19 × 33½ in. ABRAHAM COOPER. R.A. 1787–1868 S & D. 1837
'Spume' with John Day up
Courtesy of Messrs. Frost & Reed Ltd., Bristol & London

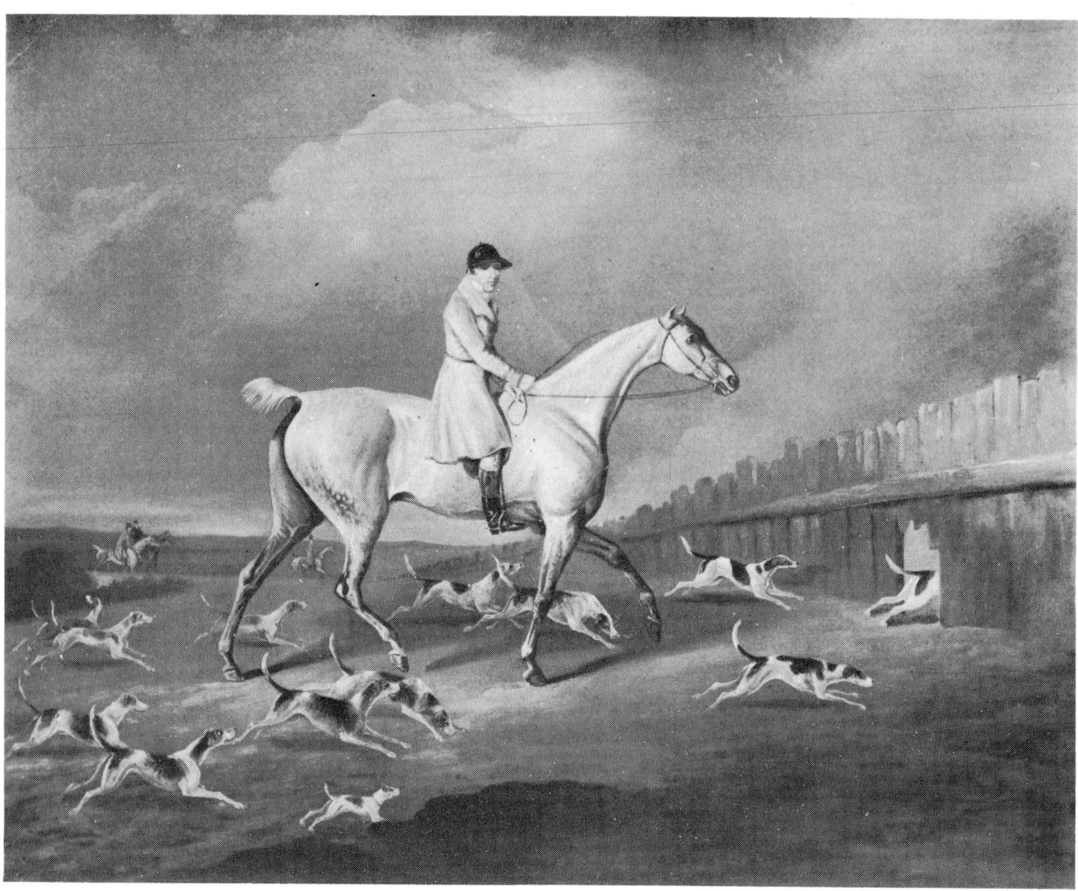

Canvas. 24 × 30 in. EDWIN COOPER. op. 1803–1831 Signed

The Berkeley Hunt

Courtesy of Messrs. Arthur Ackermann & Son, Ltd., London

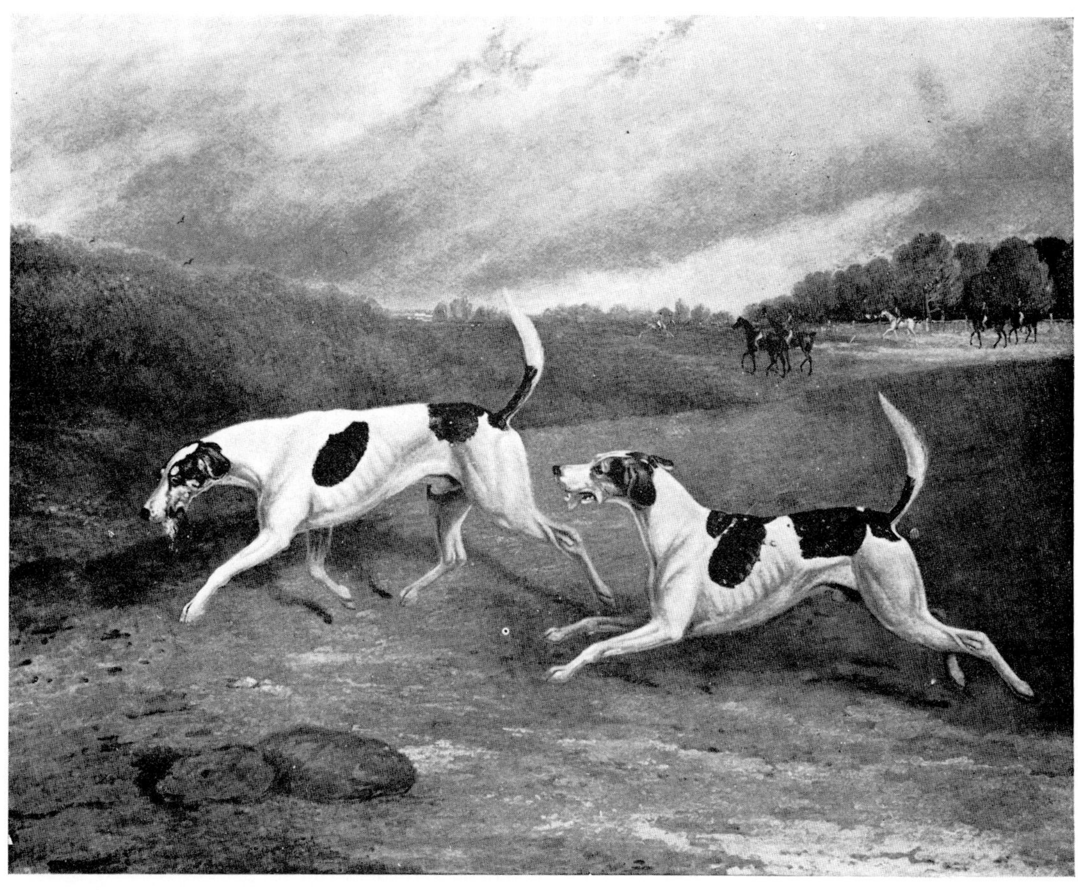

Canvas. 25 × 32 in. EDWIN COOPER, op. 1803–1831 S & D. 1825

Two Hounds in a Landscape

Courtesy of Messrs. Frost & Reed Ltd., Bristol & London

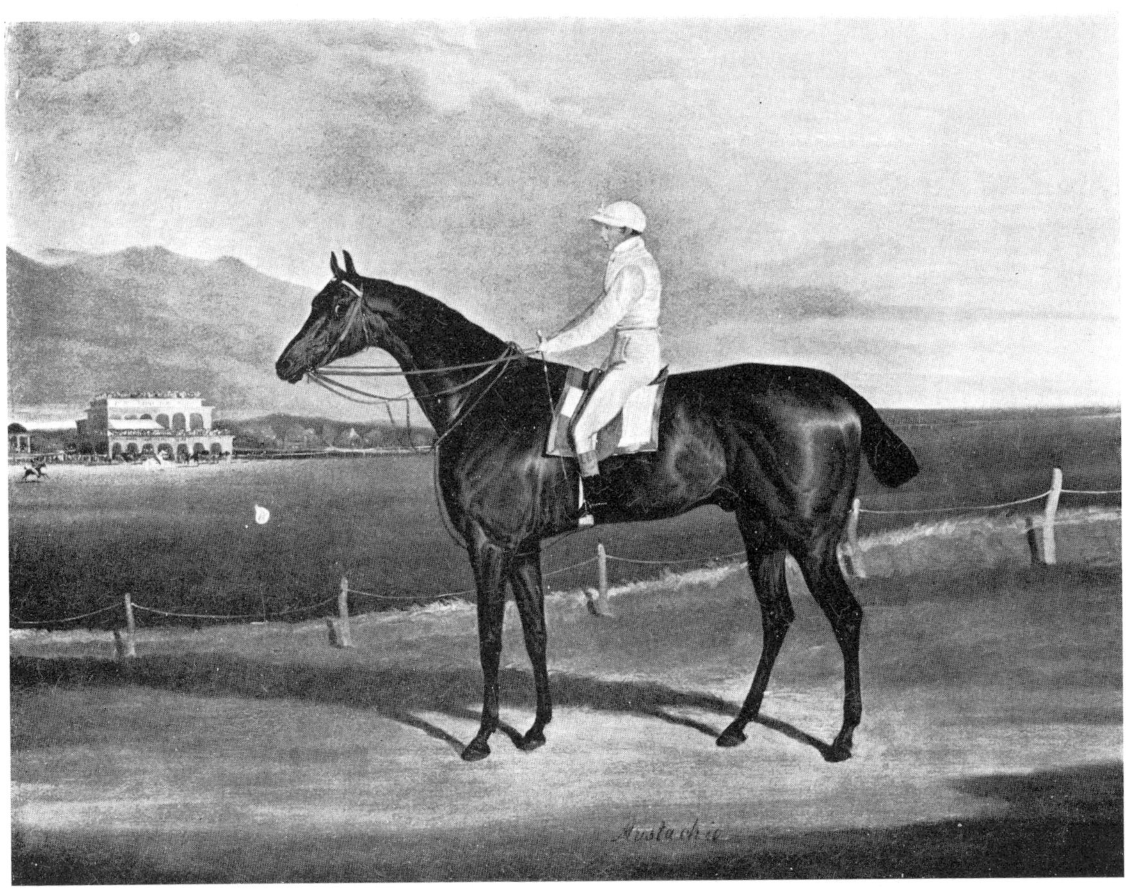

Oil. 26 × 34 in. D. DALBY. op. 1780–1849 Signed

'Mustachio' with Jockey up

Courtesy of Messrs. Frost & Reed Ltd., Bristol & London

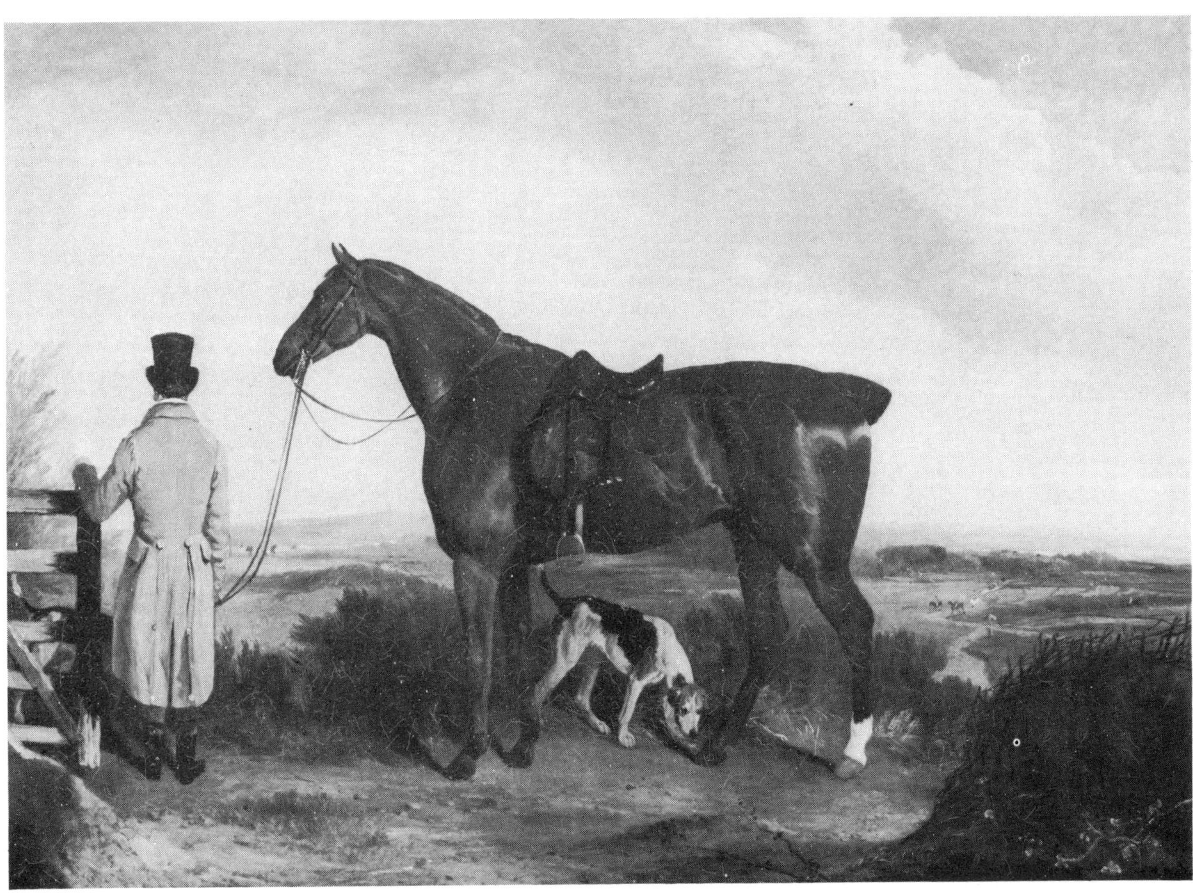

Canvas. $29\frac{1}{2} \times 35\frac{1}{2}$ in. RICHARD BARRETT DAVIS. 1782–1854 S & D. 1829

Sportsman with his Hunter and Hounds

Courtesy of Messrs. Frank T. Sabin, London

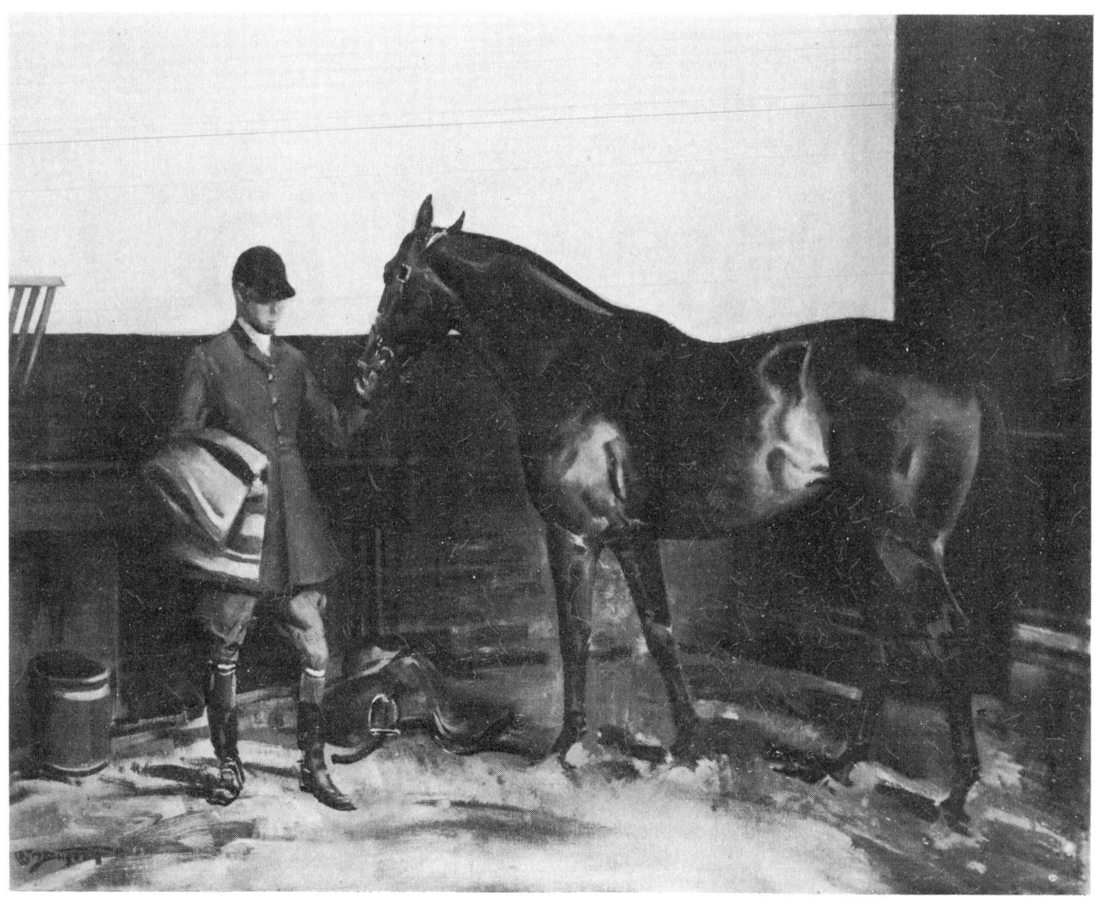

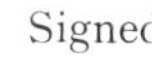

Oil. RICHARD J. M. DUPONT. b. 1920 Signed

Hunting Morning

Courtesy of the Artist

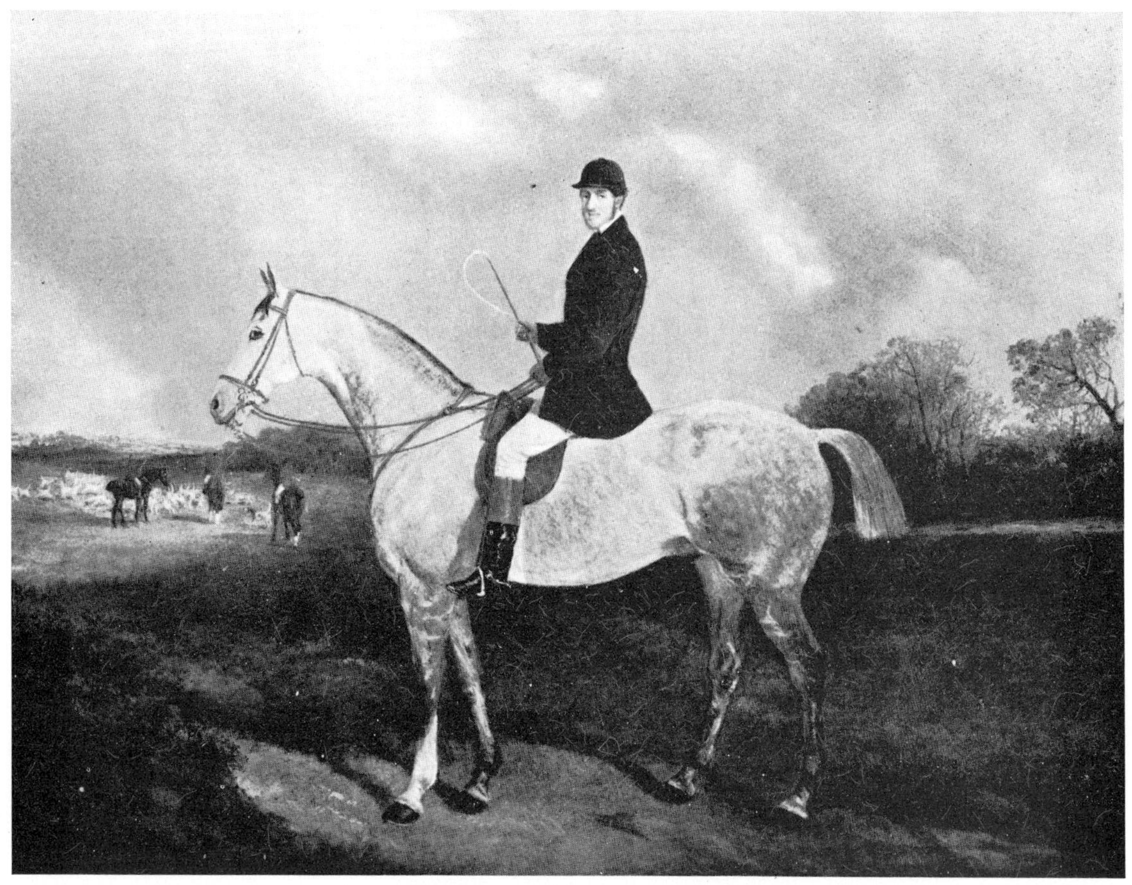

Oil. 20 × 26 in. JOHN DUVAL. op. 1834–1881

Hunting portrait

Courtesy of Messrs. Frost & Reed Ltd., Bristol & London

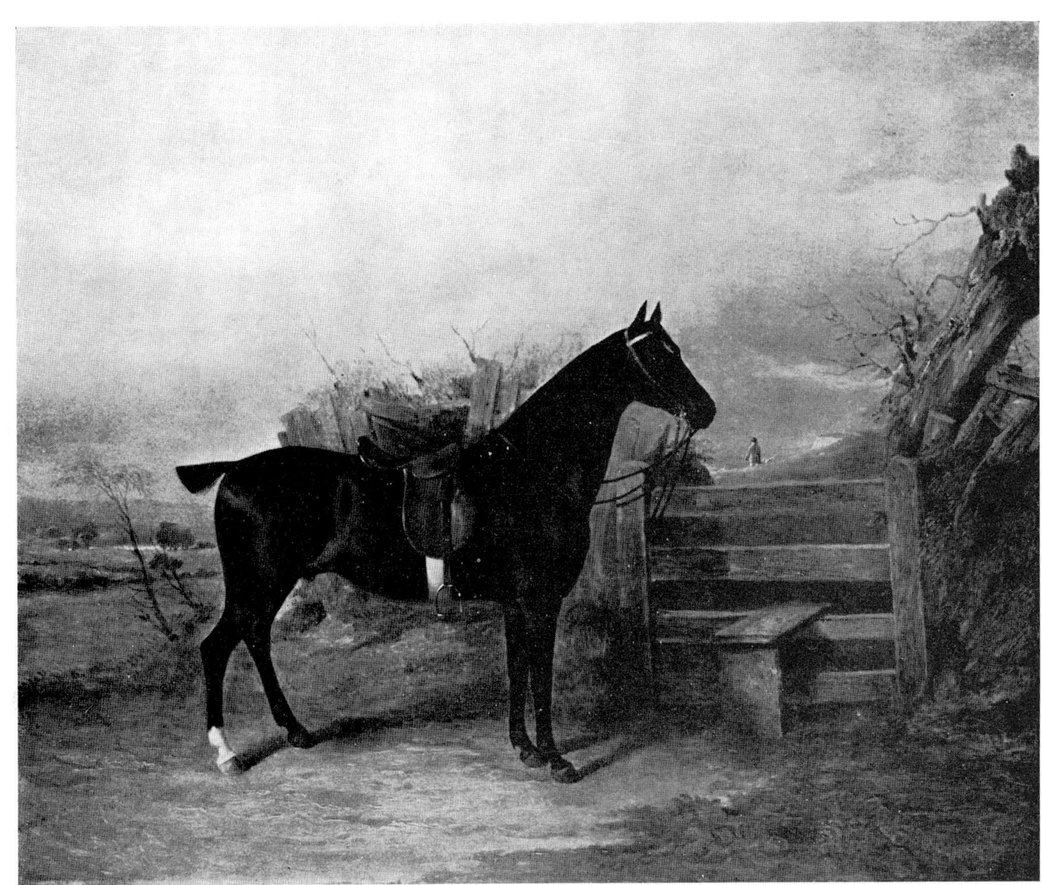

Oil. 25 × 30 in. DANIEL THOMAS EGERTON, R.B.A. op. 1824–1840. d. 1842 Signed
The Bobtailed Hunter. 1820
Courtesy of Messrs. Frost & Reed Ltd., Bristol & London

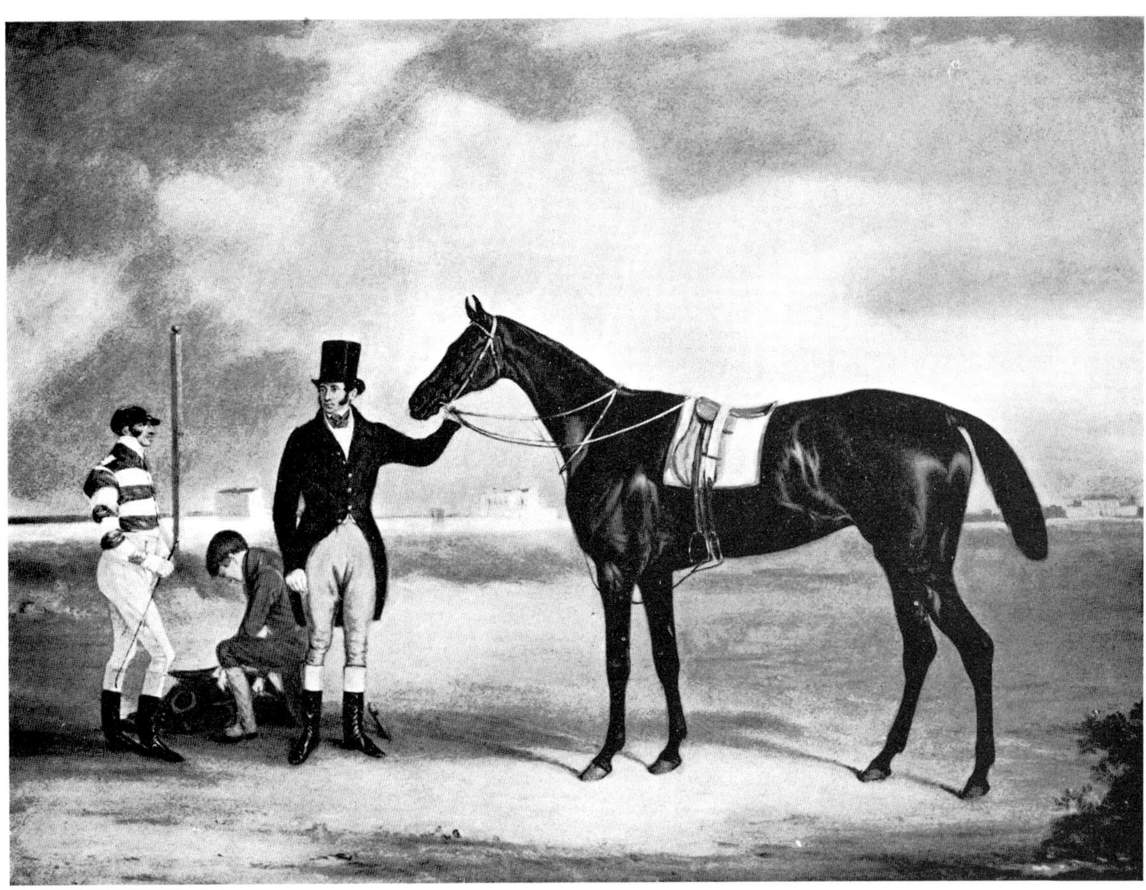

Oil. 32 × 42 in. JOHN E. FERNELEY, SENIOR. 1782–1860
'Pussy' winner of the Oaks 1834, with William Day and his brother John Barnham Day
Courtesy of Messrs. Frost & Reed Ltd., Bristol & London

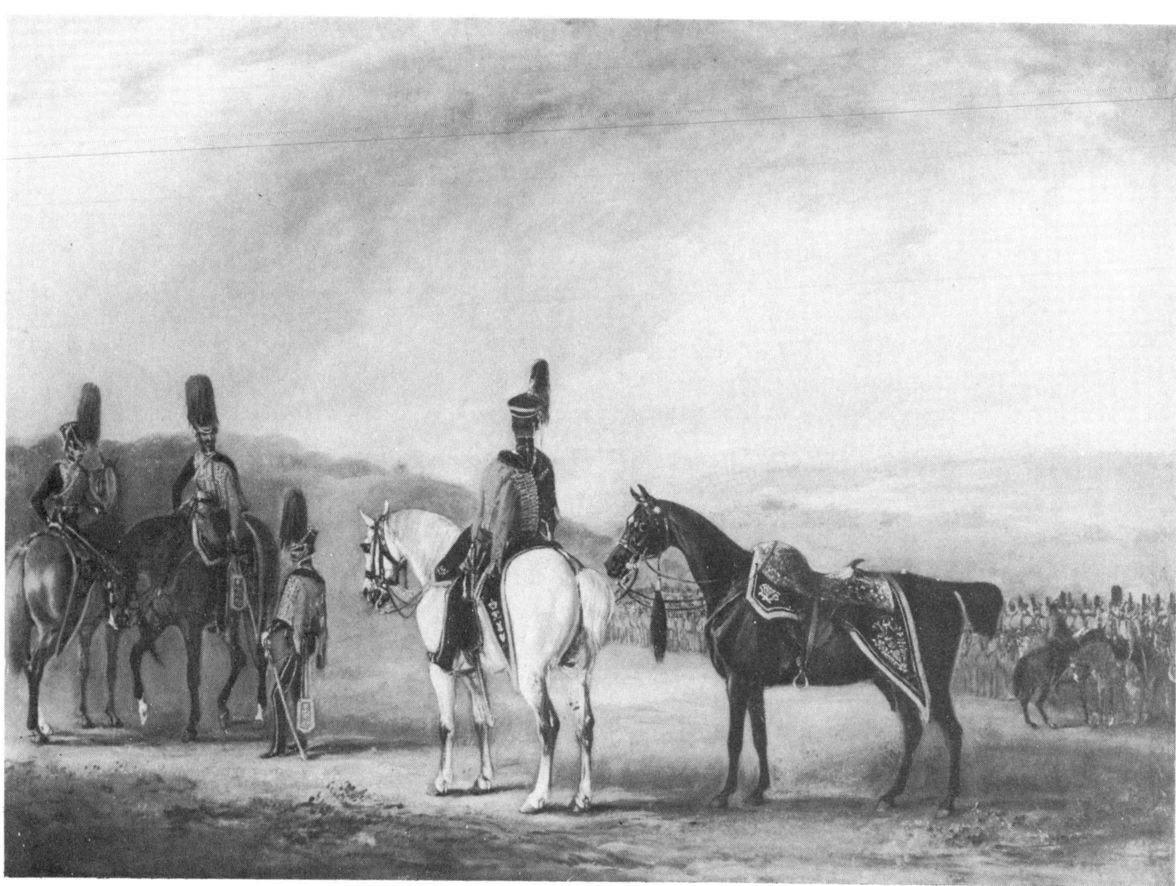

Canvas. $27\frac{3}{4} \times 39$ in.

JOHN FERNELEY, JUNIOR. 1815?–1862
Officers and Troopers of the VIII Hussars
Courtesy of Messrs. Oscar & Peter Johnson Ltd., London

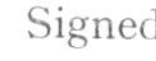
Signed

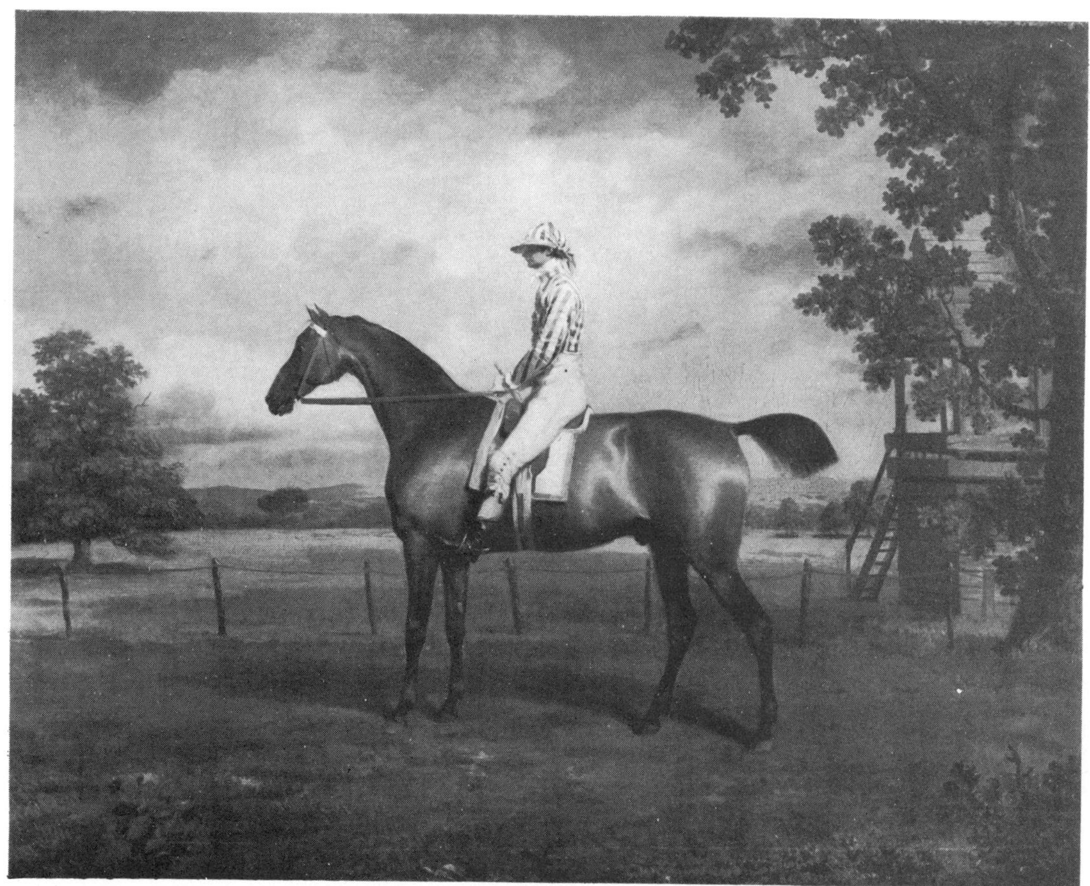

Canvas. $33\frac{1}{2} \times 42\frac{1}{2}$ in.

GEORGE GARRARD, A.R.A. 1760–1826
Racehorse with Jockey up
Courtesy of Mr. & Mrs. Paul Mellon

S & D. 1796

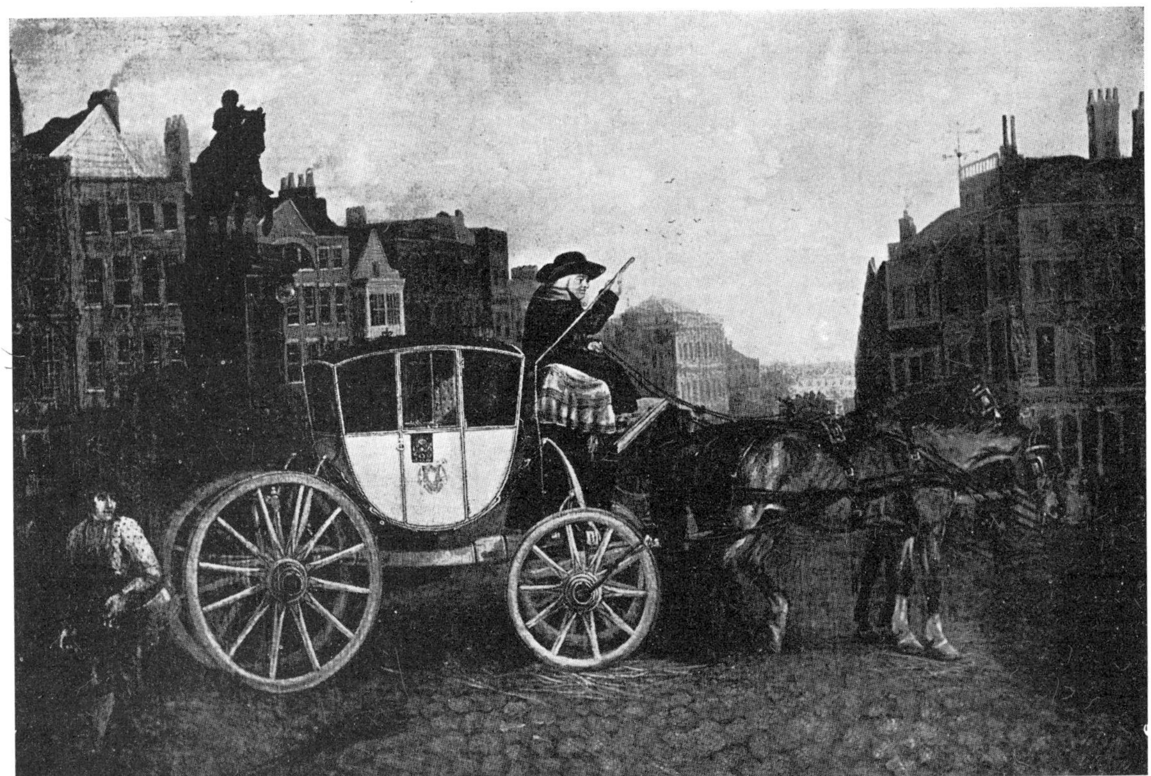

Oil.

T. GOOCH. 1750–1802
Charing Cross, 1795
P.O.U.

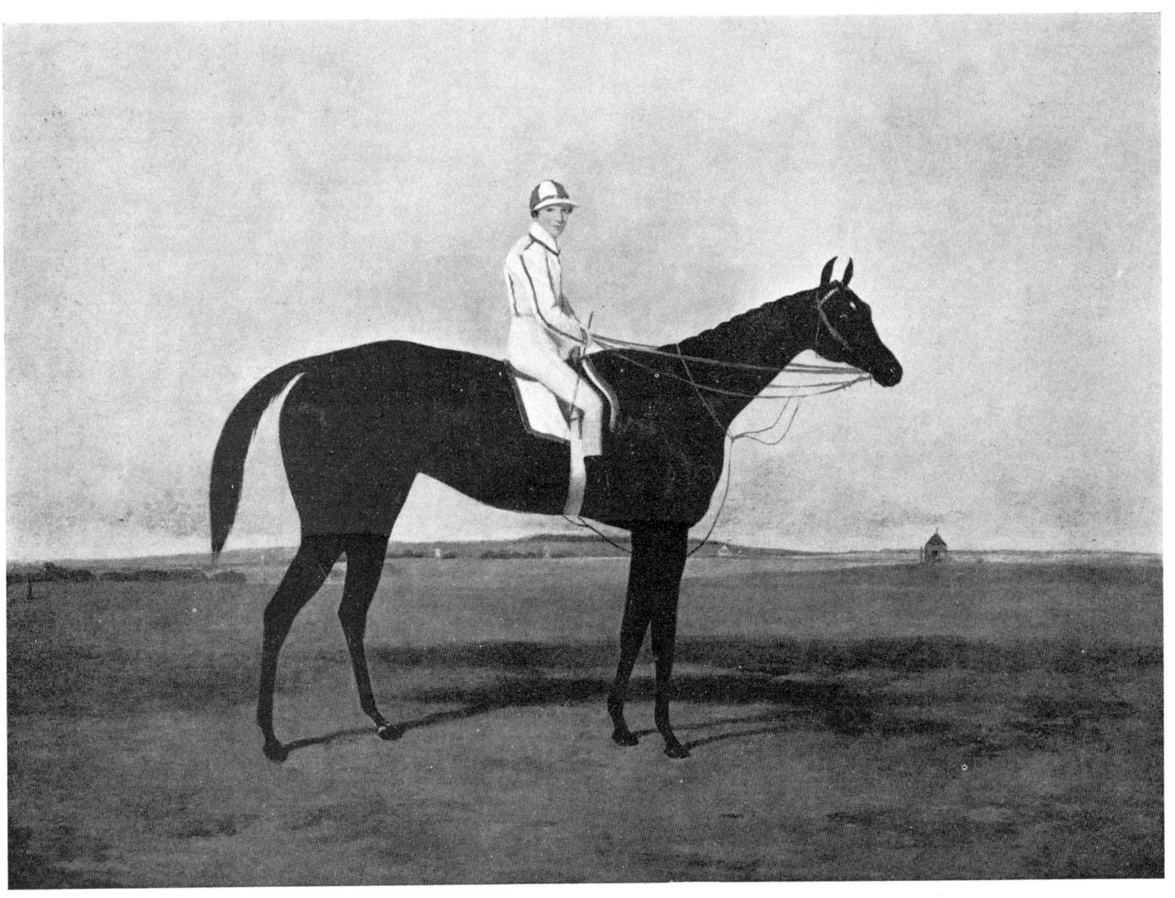

Oil. 22 × 30 in.

HARRY HALL. op. 1838–1886
'Lucky Ashton' with Jockey up
Courtesy of Messrs. Frost & Reed Ltd., Bristol & London

S & D. 1847

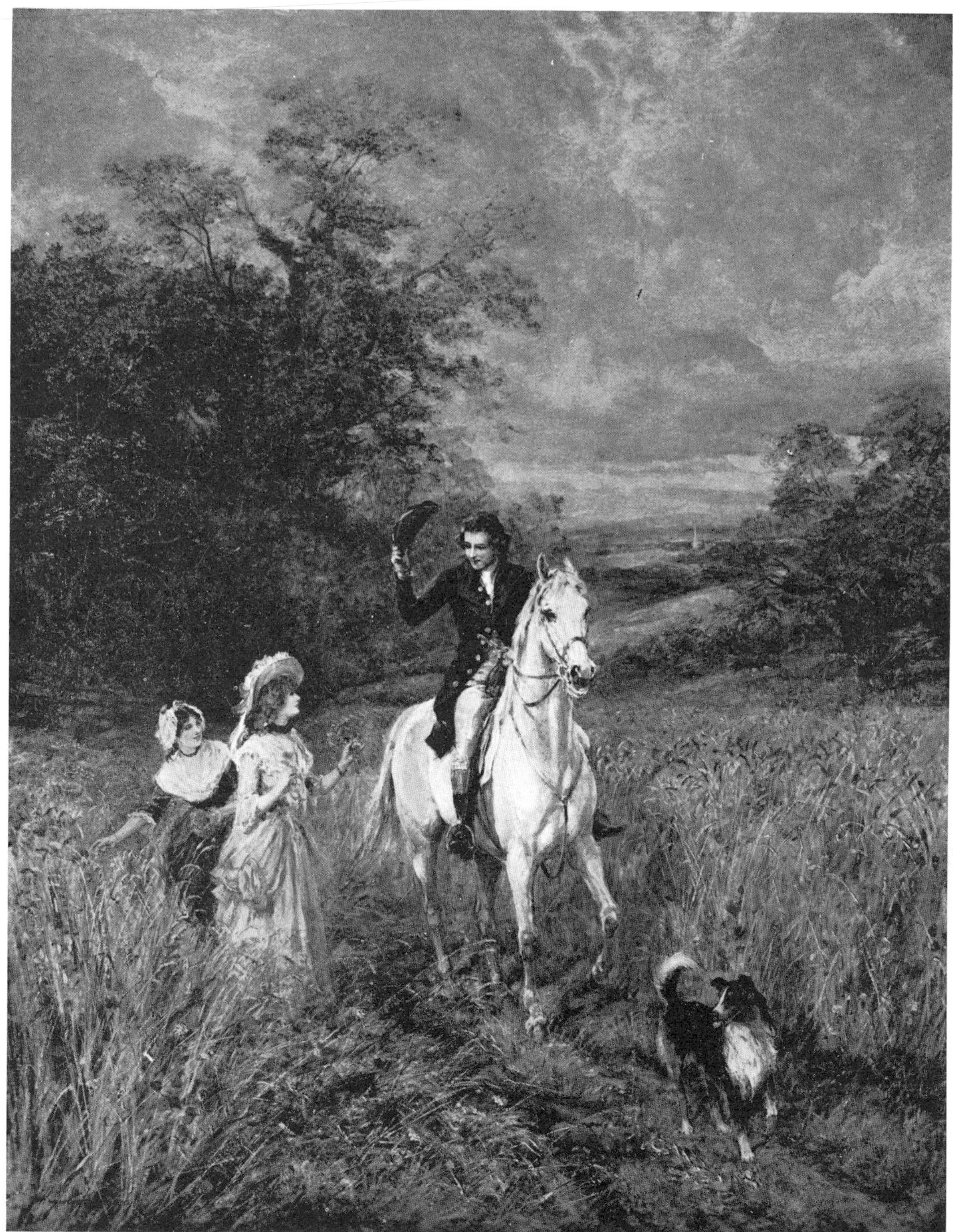

Oil. 35 × 27¾ in. HEYWOOD HARDY, A.R.W.S., R.E. op. 1861–1903 Signed

The Salutation

Courtesy of Messrs. Frost & Reed Ltd., Bristol & London

PLATE 20

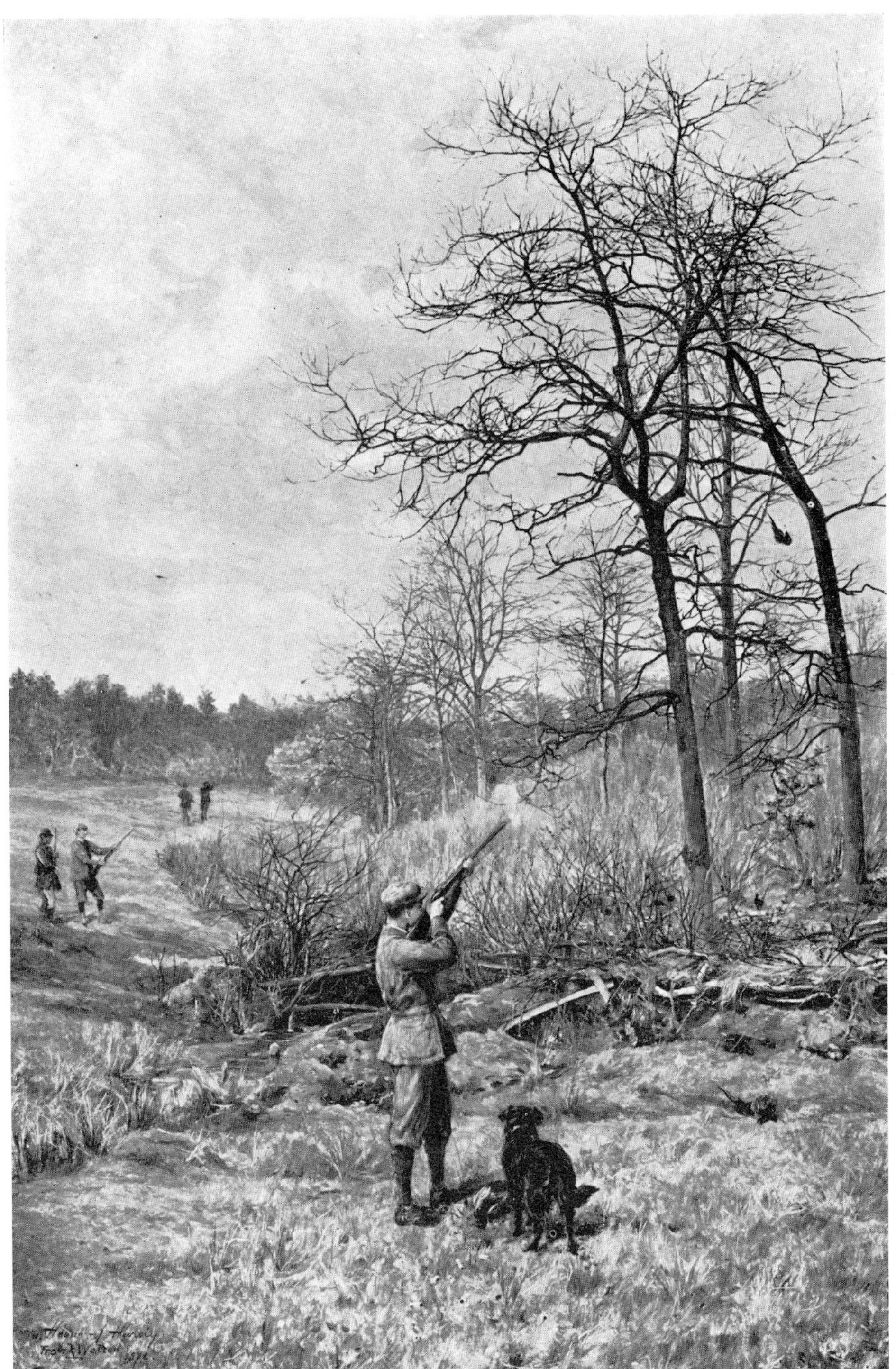

Oil. 35 × 23 in. HEYWOOD HARDY. op. 1861–1903 & FRANK WALTON, 1840–1928 S & D. 1892

A Steady Shot

Courtesy of Messrs. Frost & Reed Ltd., Bristol & London

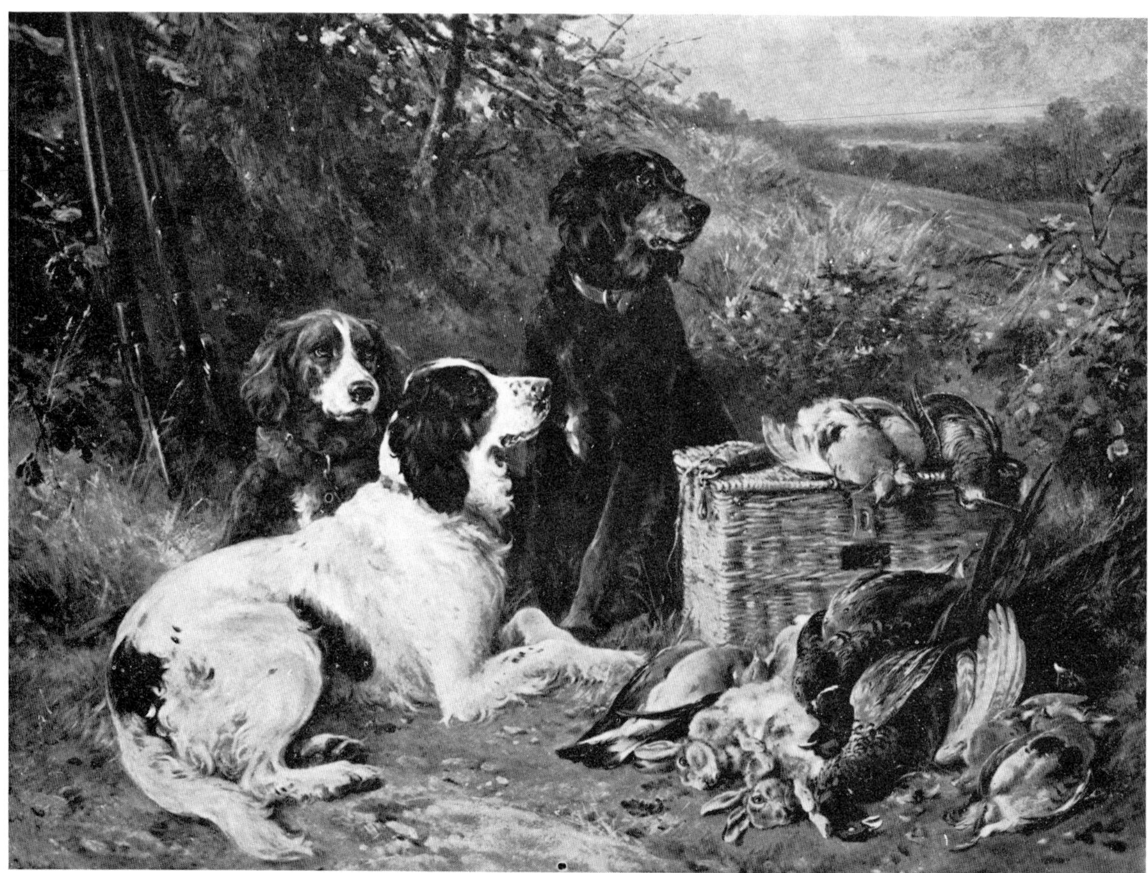

Oil. 26 × 34¾ in.

JAMES HARDY, JUNIOR. 1832–1889
Guarding the morning's bag
Courtesy of Messrs. Frost & Reed Ltd., Bristol & London

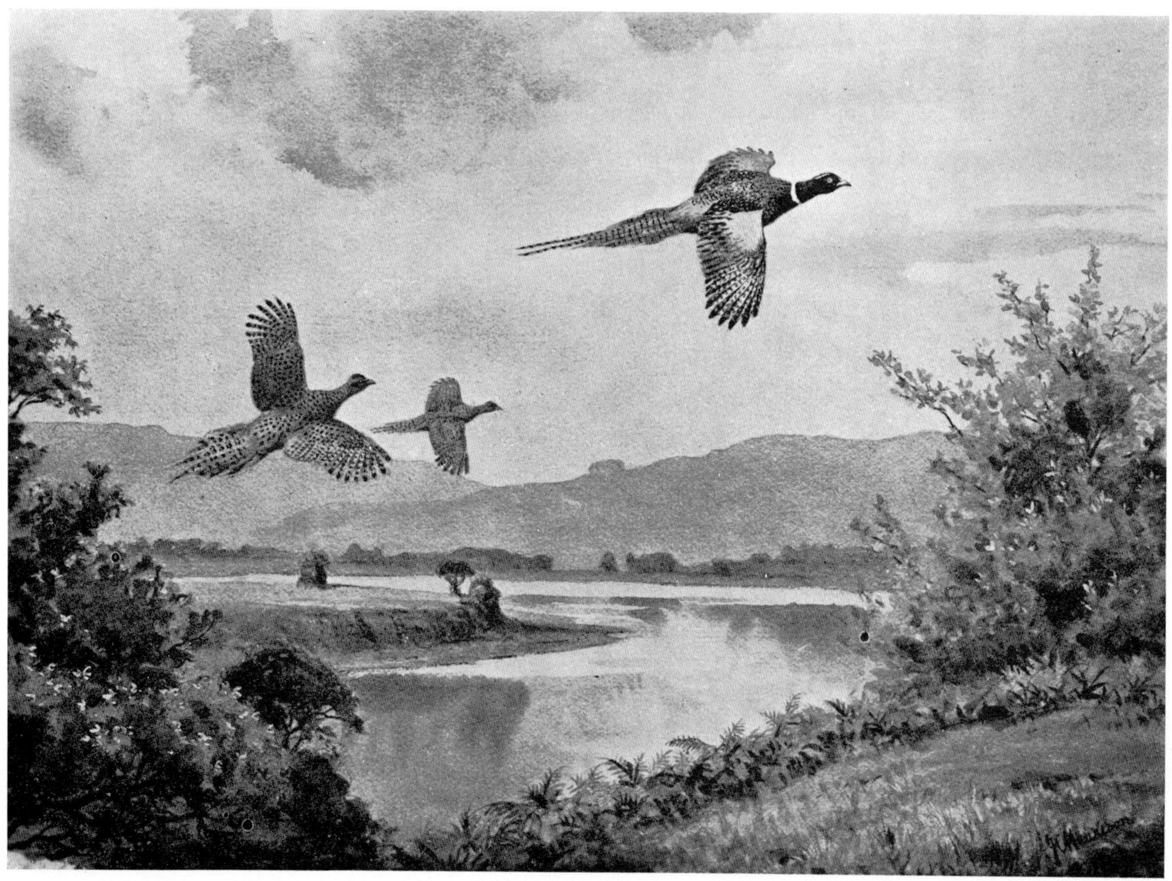

Water-colour 13 × 19 in.

J. C. HARRISON. b. 1898
Pheasant in Galloway, Scotland
Courtesy of Messrs. Frost & Reed Ltd., Bristol & London

Signed

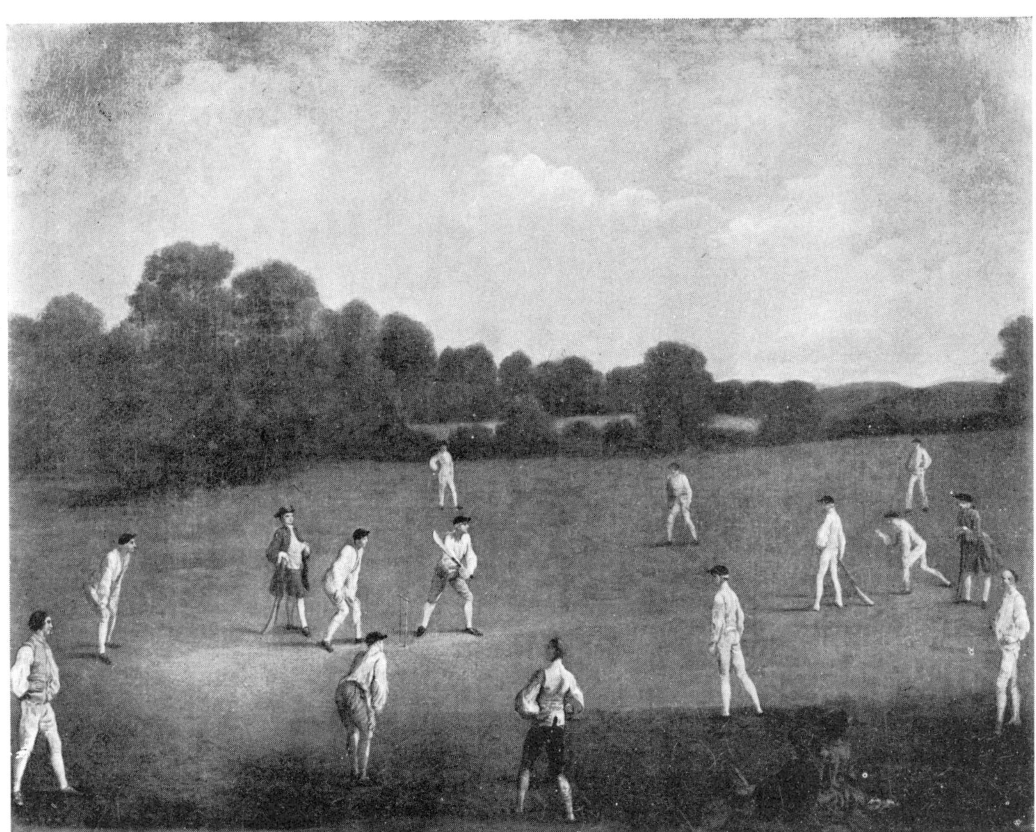

Oil. 25 × 41 in.

FRANCIS HAYMAN, R.A. 1708–1776
A Cricket Match 1743
Courtesy of Marylebone Cricket Club, London

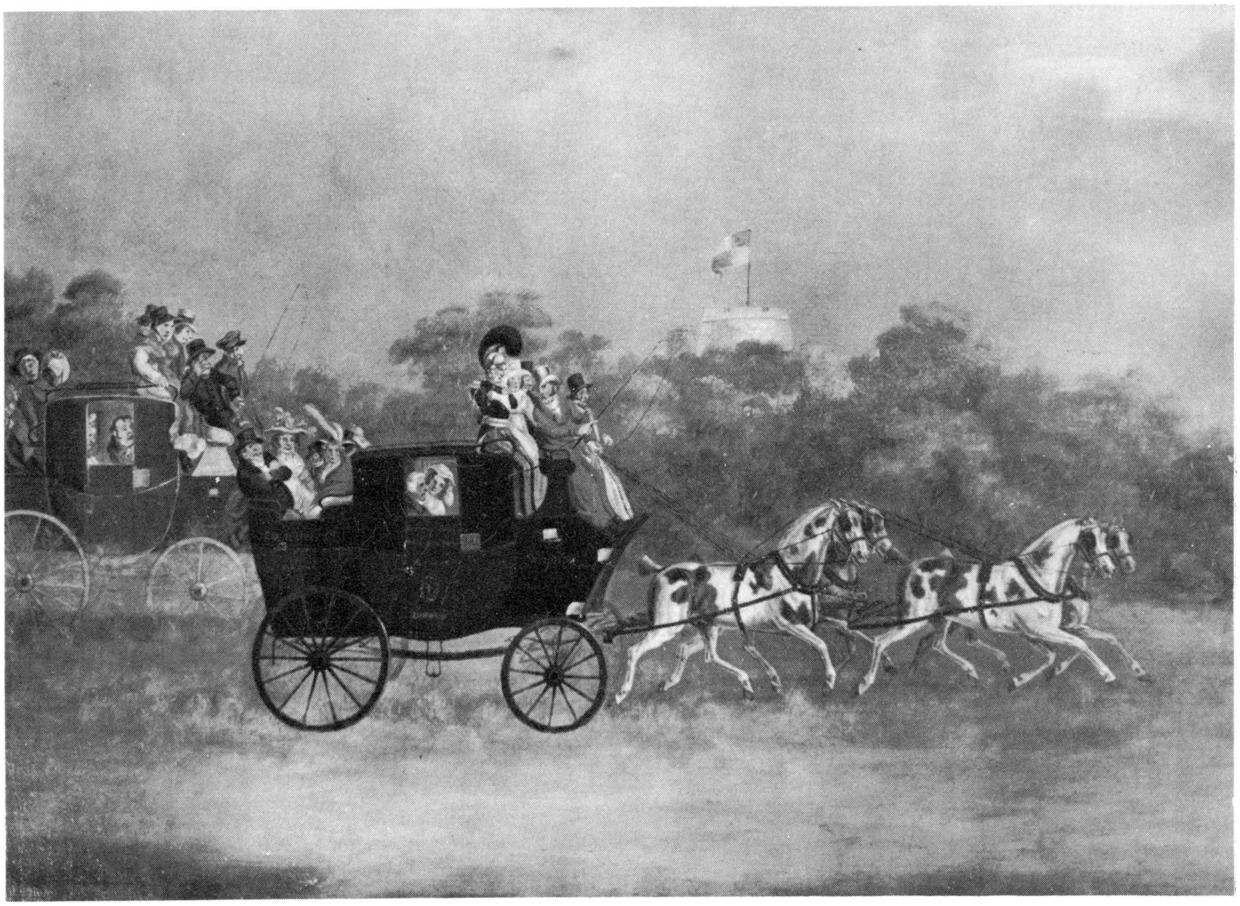

Canvas. $12\frac{1}{2} \times 18\frac{1}{2}$ in.

WILLIAM HEATH. 1785–1840
The London-Windsor Coach
Courtesy of The Lord Fairhaven

One of a pair

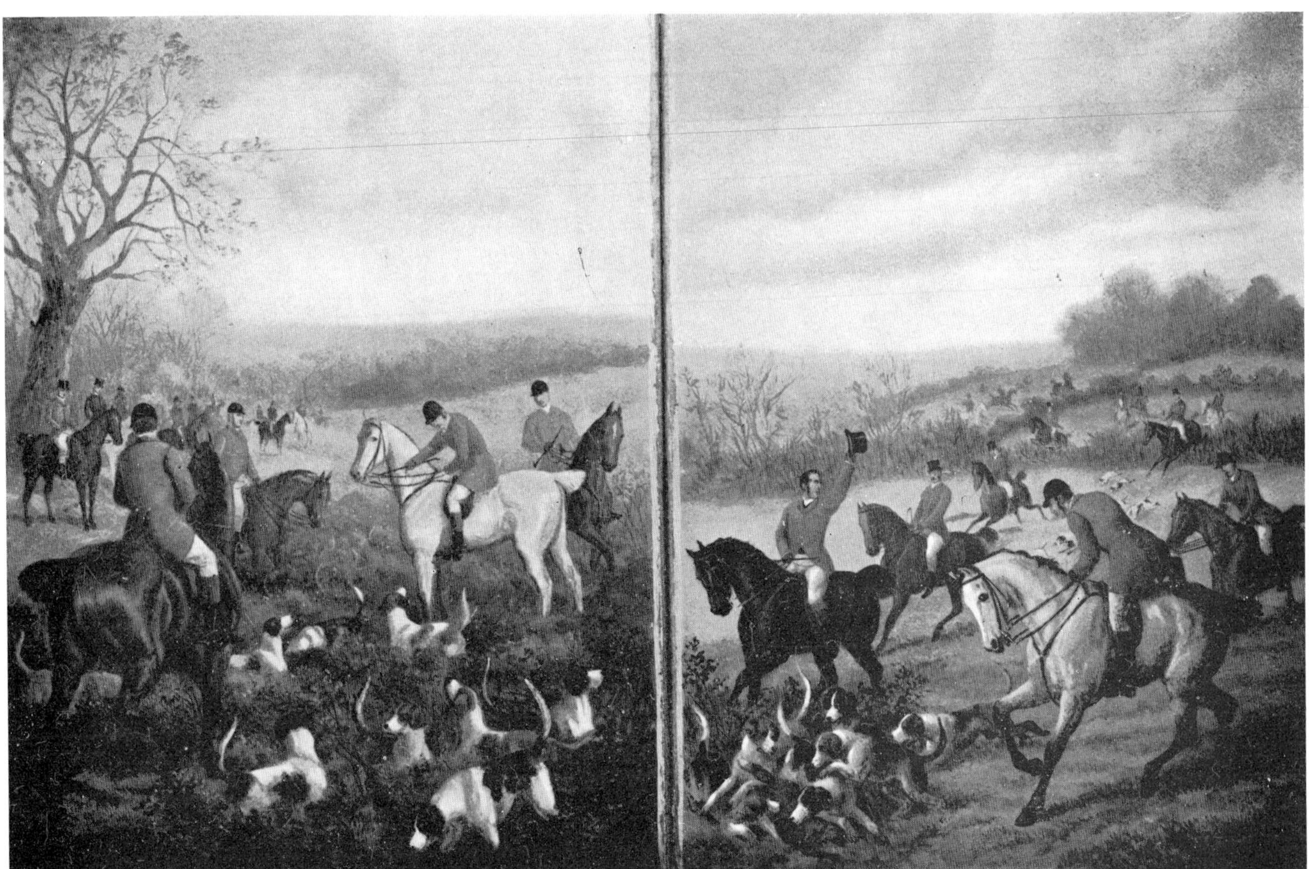

Oil. 17½ × 14 in. E. B. HERBERT (early 19th Century) From a set of 4

Foxhunting scenes

Courtesy of Messrs. Frost & Reed Ltd., Bristol & London

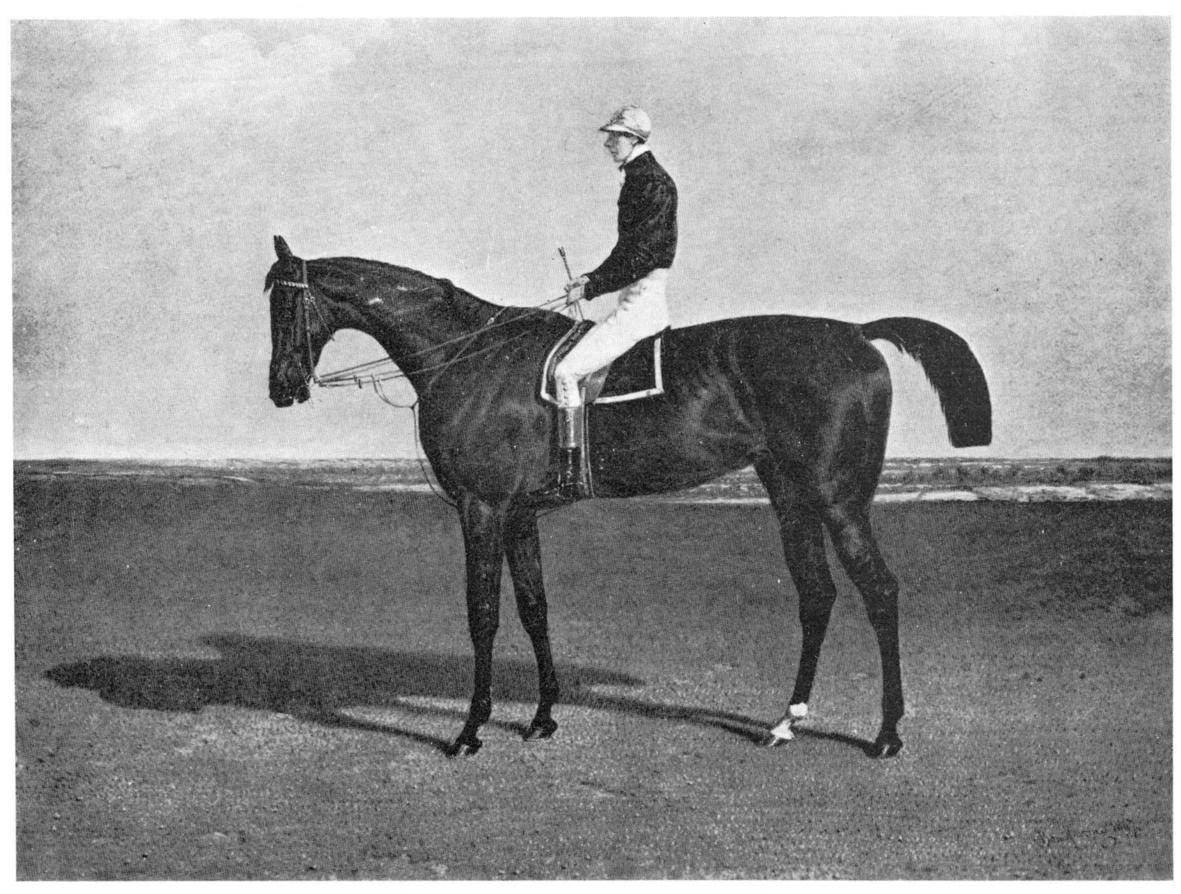

Oil. 13 × 18 in. BENJAMIN HERRING, **Junior. (b. 1830, d. 1871).** S & D. 1867

'Hippia' with Jockey up. Oaks winner 1867

Courtesy of Messrs. Frost & Reed Ltd., Bristol & London

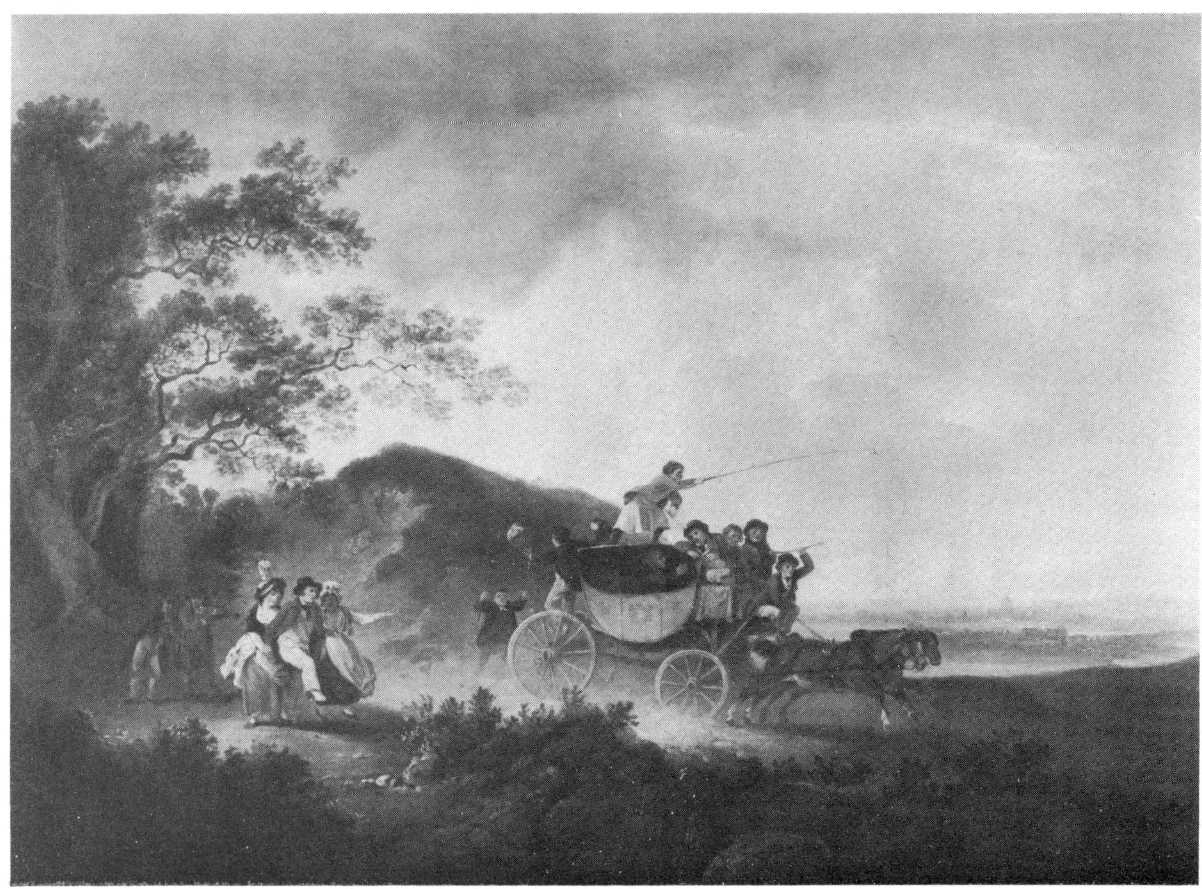

Canvas. 18 × 24 in.

JULIUS CAESAR IBBETSON. 1759–1817
Jack in all his Glory
Courtesy of Messrs. The Fine Art Society Ltd., London

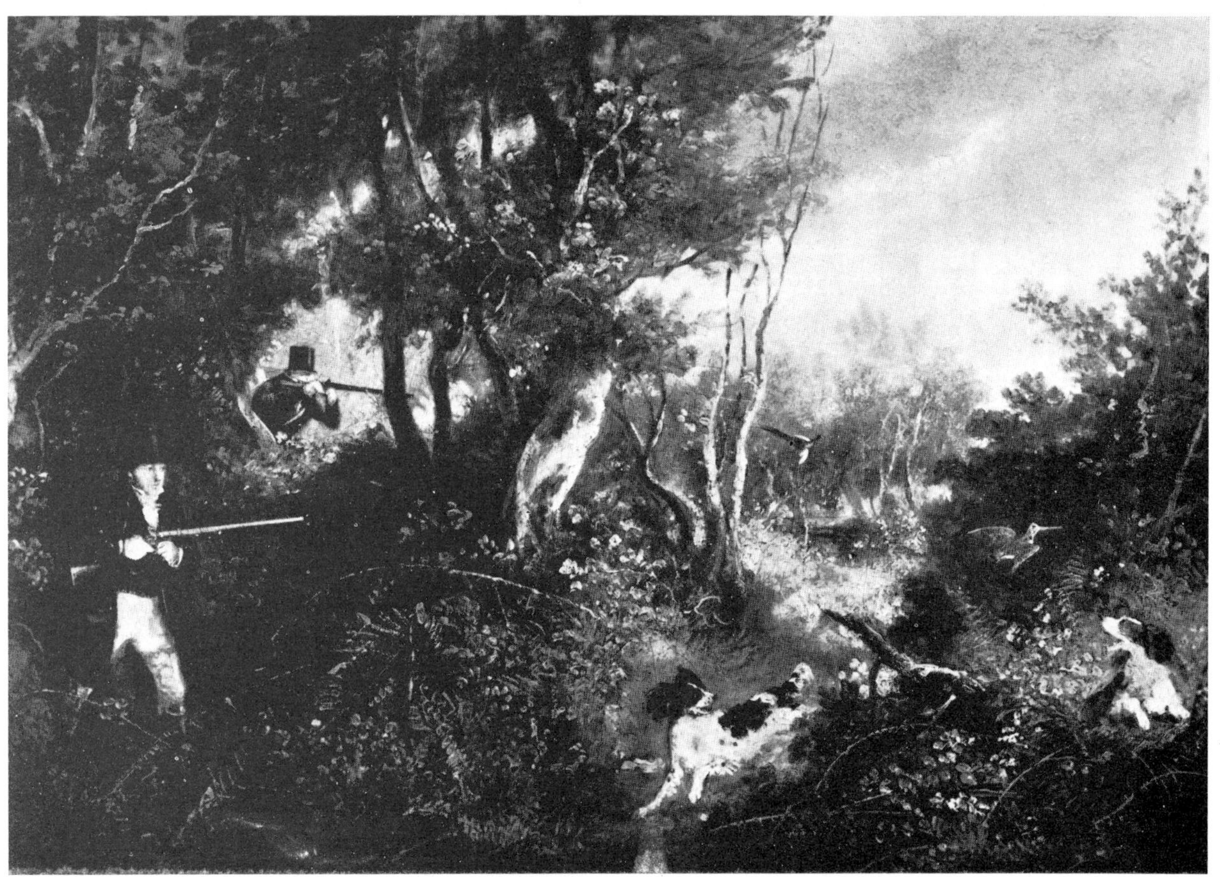

Oil. 11 × 15 in.

W. JONES. op. 1744–1745
Pheasant & Snipe Shooting
Courtesy of Messrs. Frost & Reed Ltd., Bristol & London

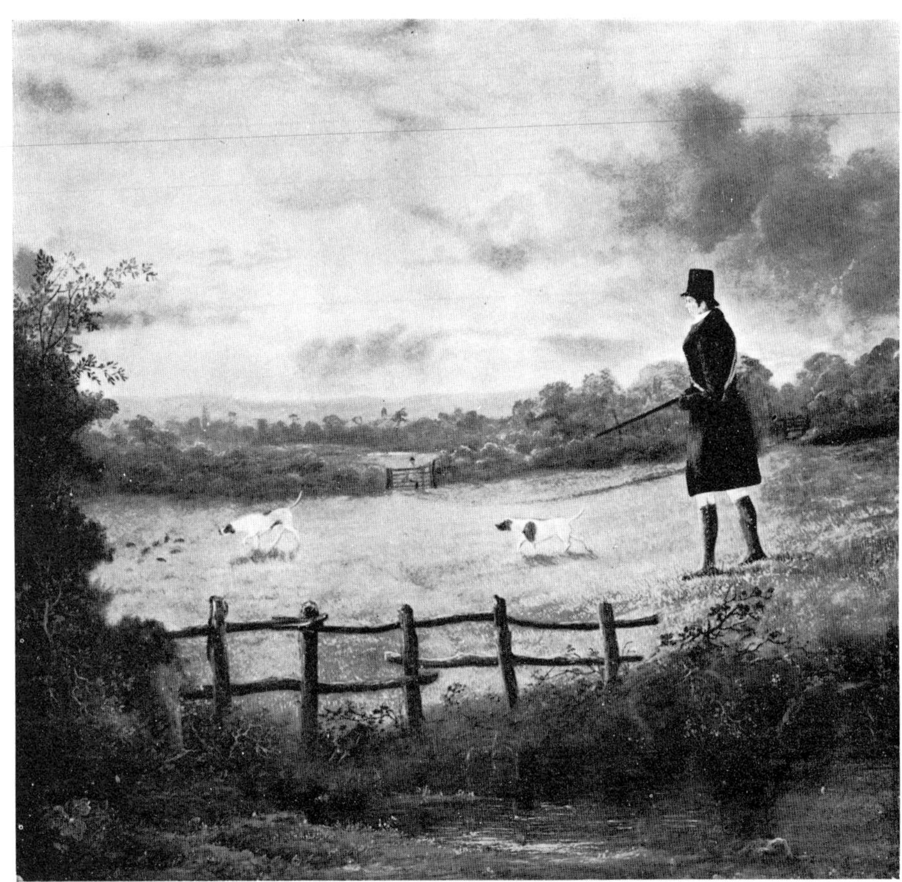

Oil. 31½ × 32¾ in. J. JOYNER. op. 1825–1833 S & D. 1832
Partridge Shooting
Courtesy of Messrs. Frost & Reed Ltd., Bristol & London

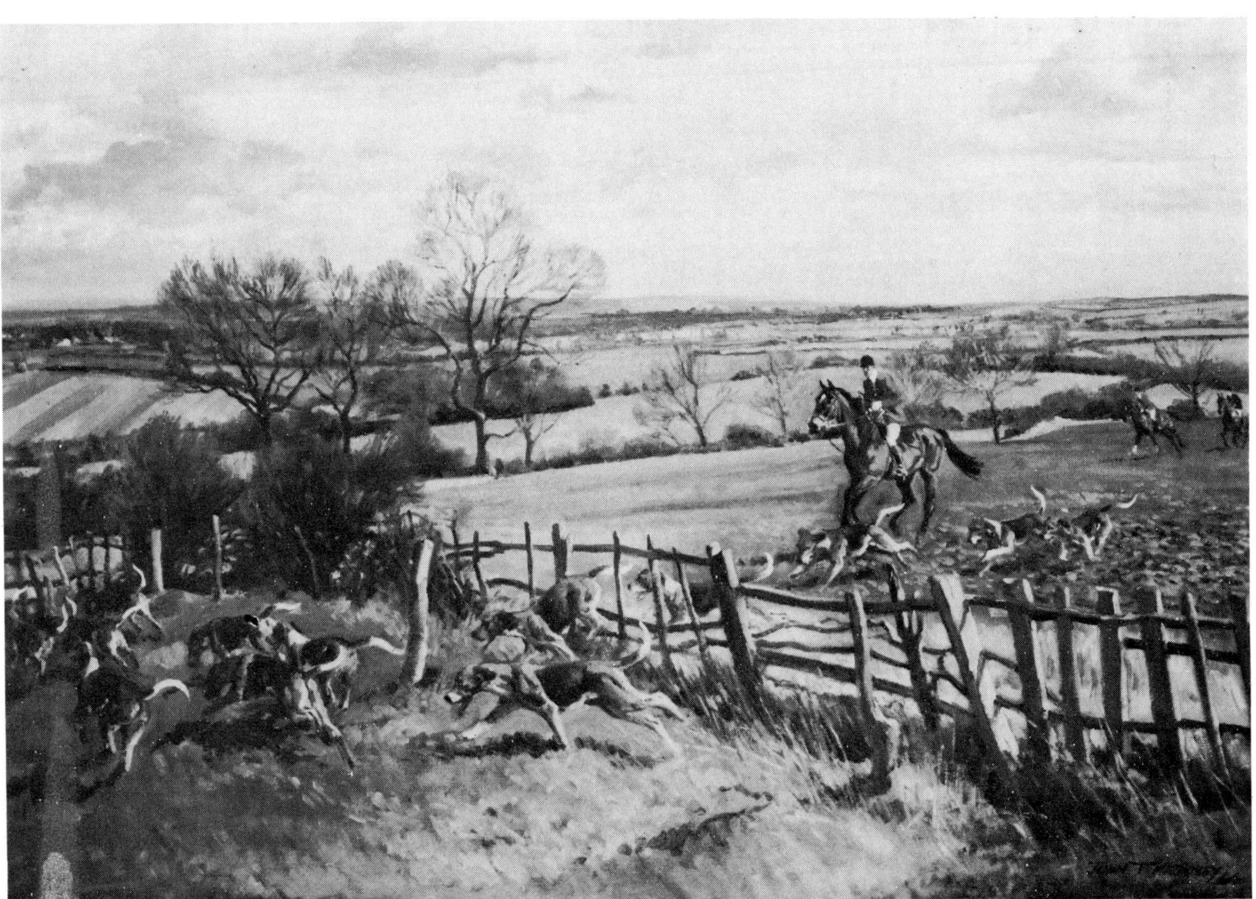

Oil. JOHN T. KENNEY. b. 1911 S & D. 1964
The Fernie at Saddington
Courtesy of the Artist

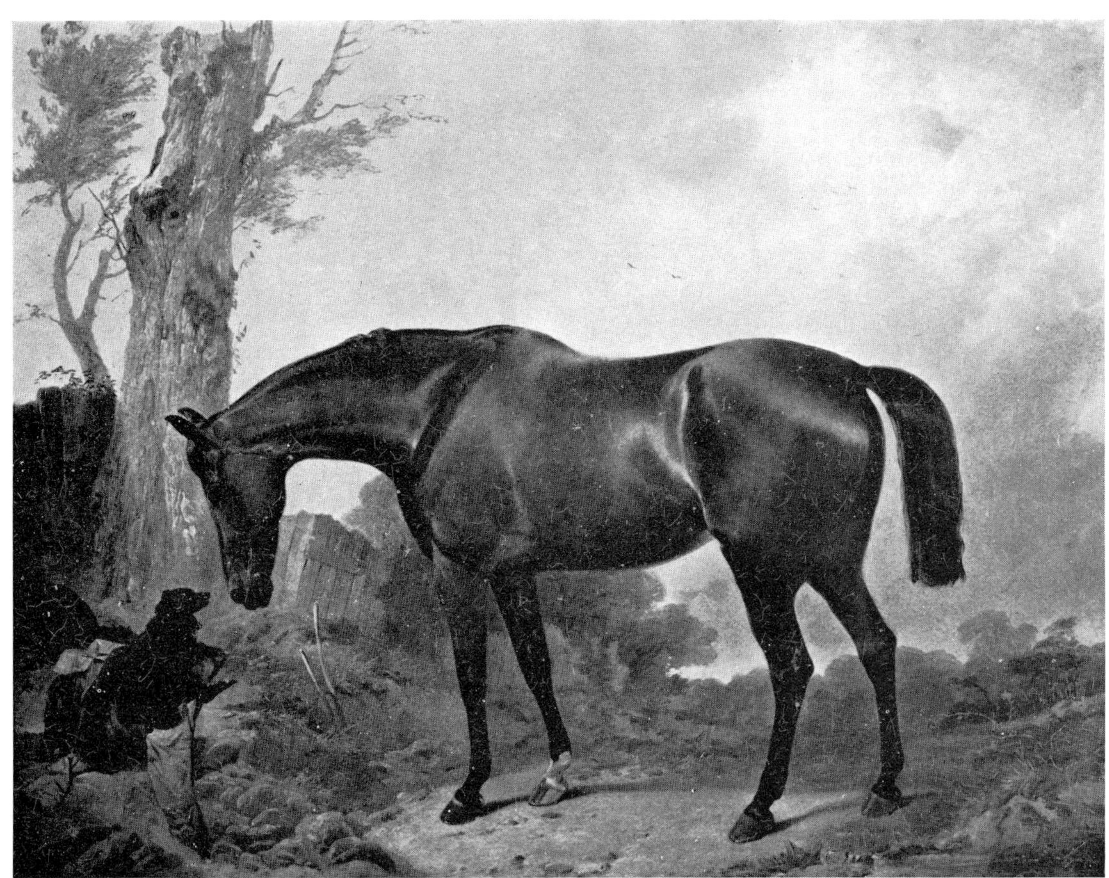

Canvas. 28 × 36 in. SIR EDWIN LANDSEER, R.A. 1802–1873
Good Friends
Courtesy of Messrs. Frost & Reed Ltd., Bristol & London

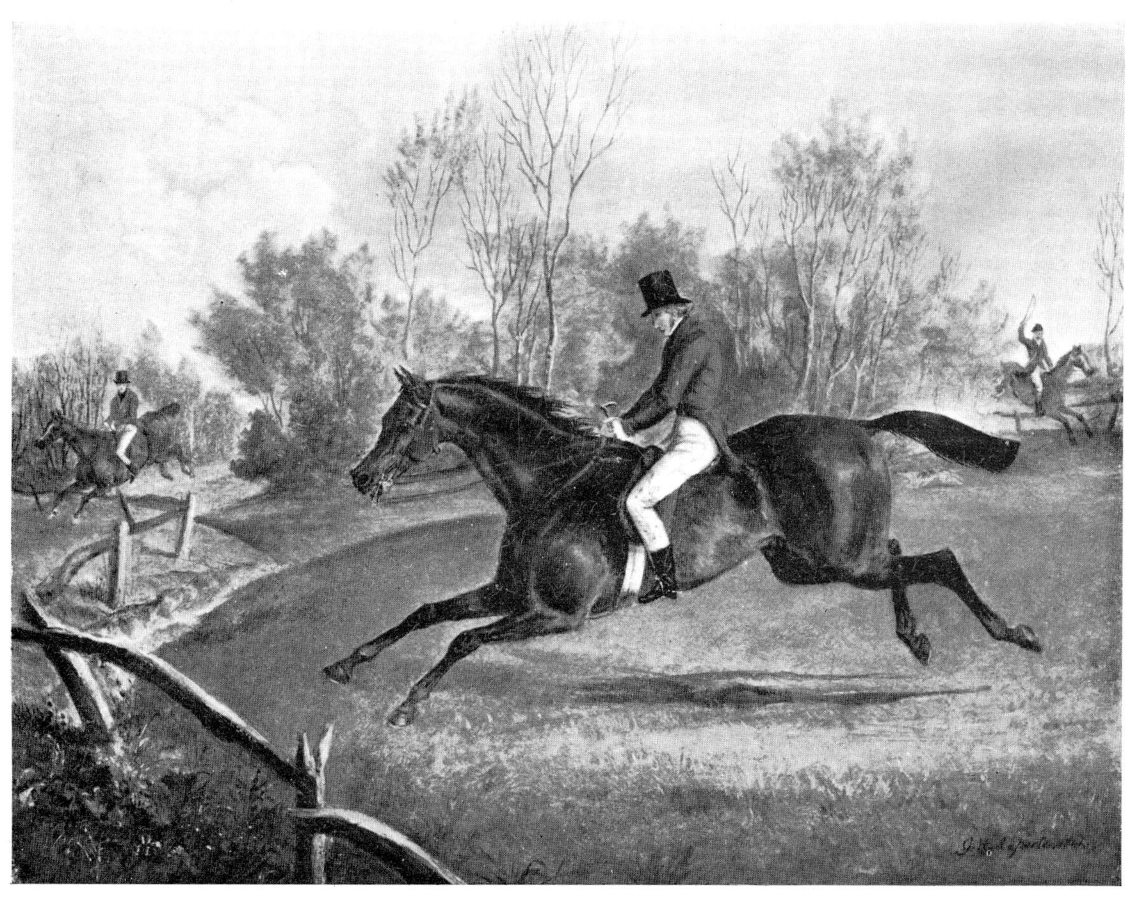

Oil. 12 × 16 (one of pair) GEORGE HENRY LAPORTE. 1799–1873 S & D. 1841
The Fence – A Doubtful Moment
Courtesy of Messrs. Frost & Reed Ltd., Bristol & London

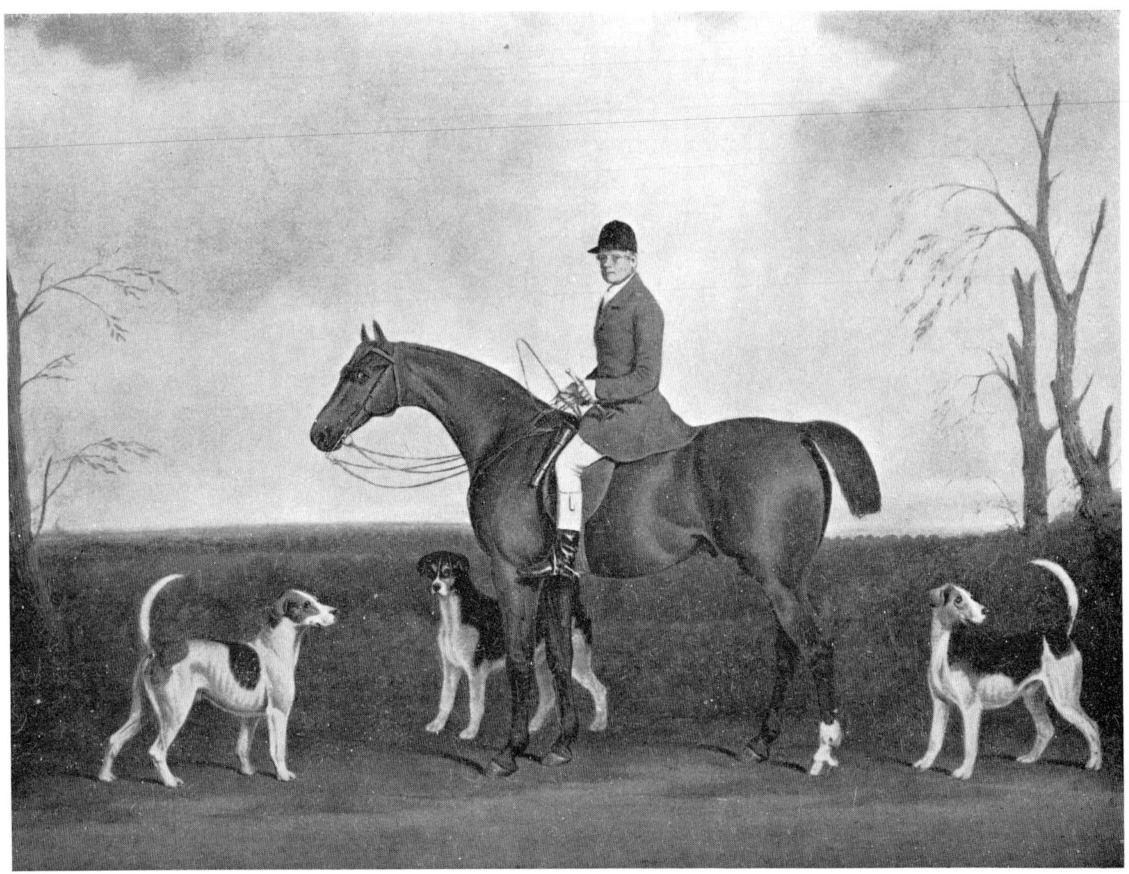

Oil. 28 × 36 in.

JAMES LODER of Bath. op. 1820–1857
Huntsman with Hounds
Courtesy of Messrs. Frost & Reed Ltd., Bristol & London

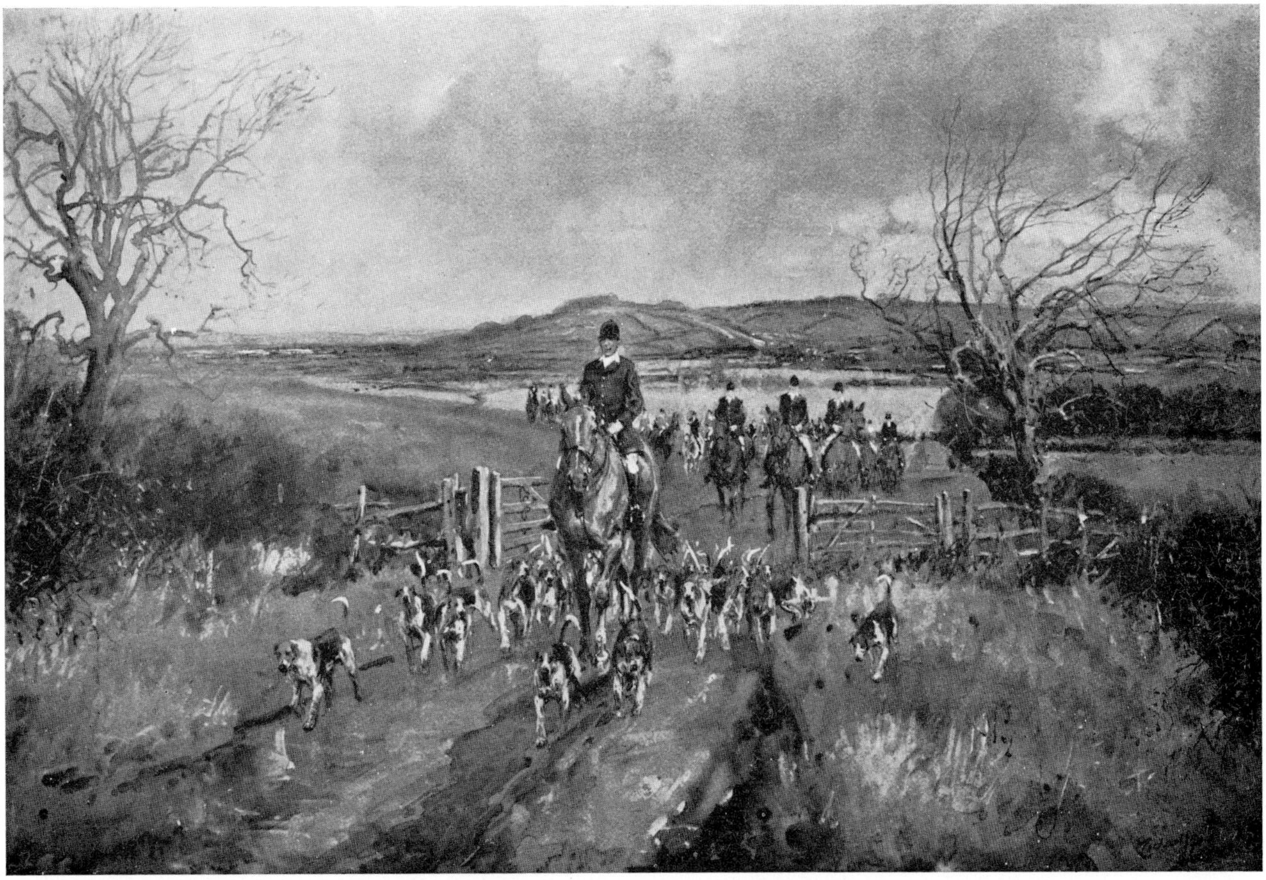

Water-colour $13\frac{1}{4}$ × 20 in.

MICHAEL LYNE. b. 1912
Pytchley – Returning to Hanging Houghton
Courtesy of Messrs. Frost & Reed Ltd., Bristol & London

Signed

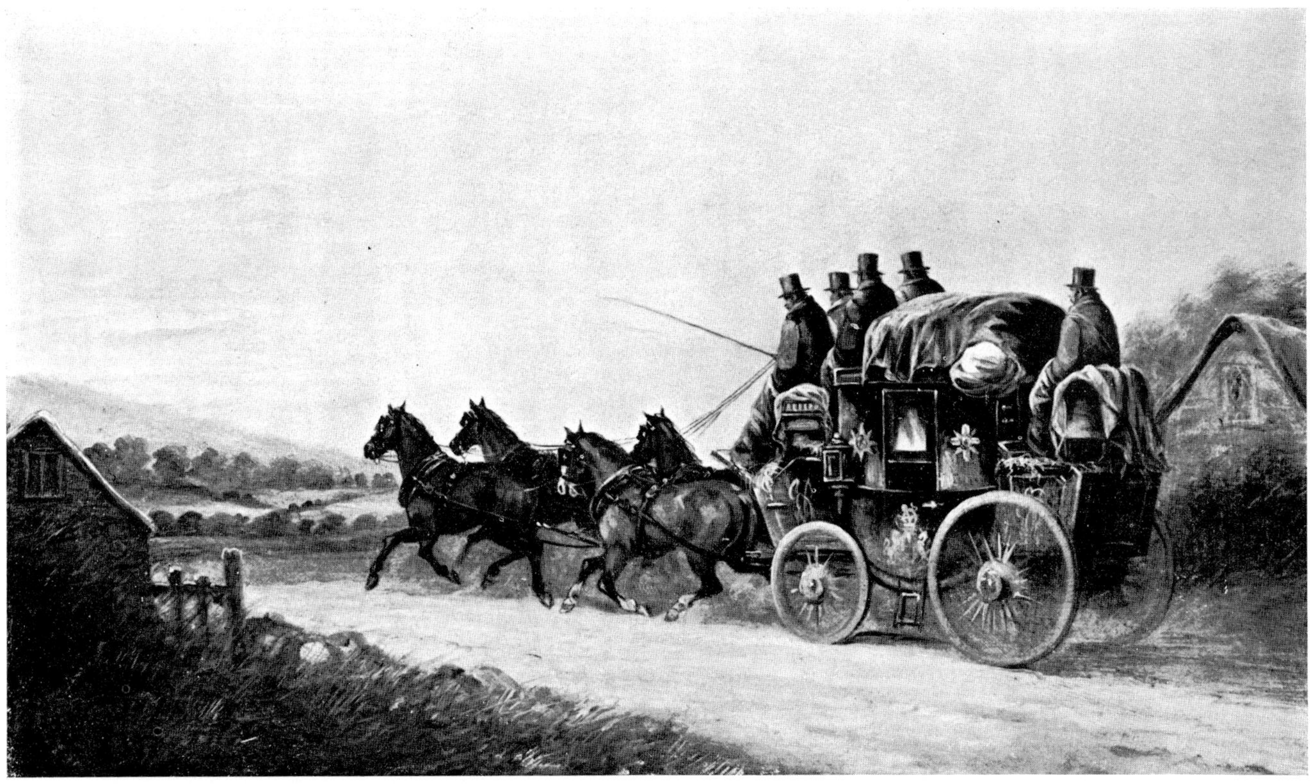

Canvas. 12 × 20¼ in. J. C. MAGGS. 1819–1896 Signed

Photograph by courtesy of Arthur Ackermann & Son

Now in the collection of Mr. R. D. Werner

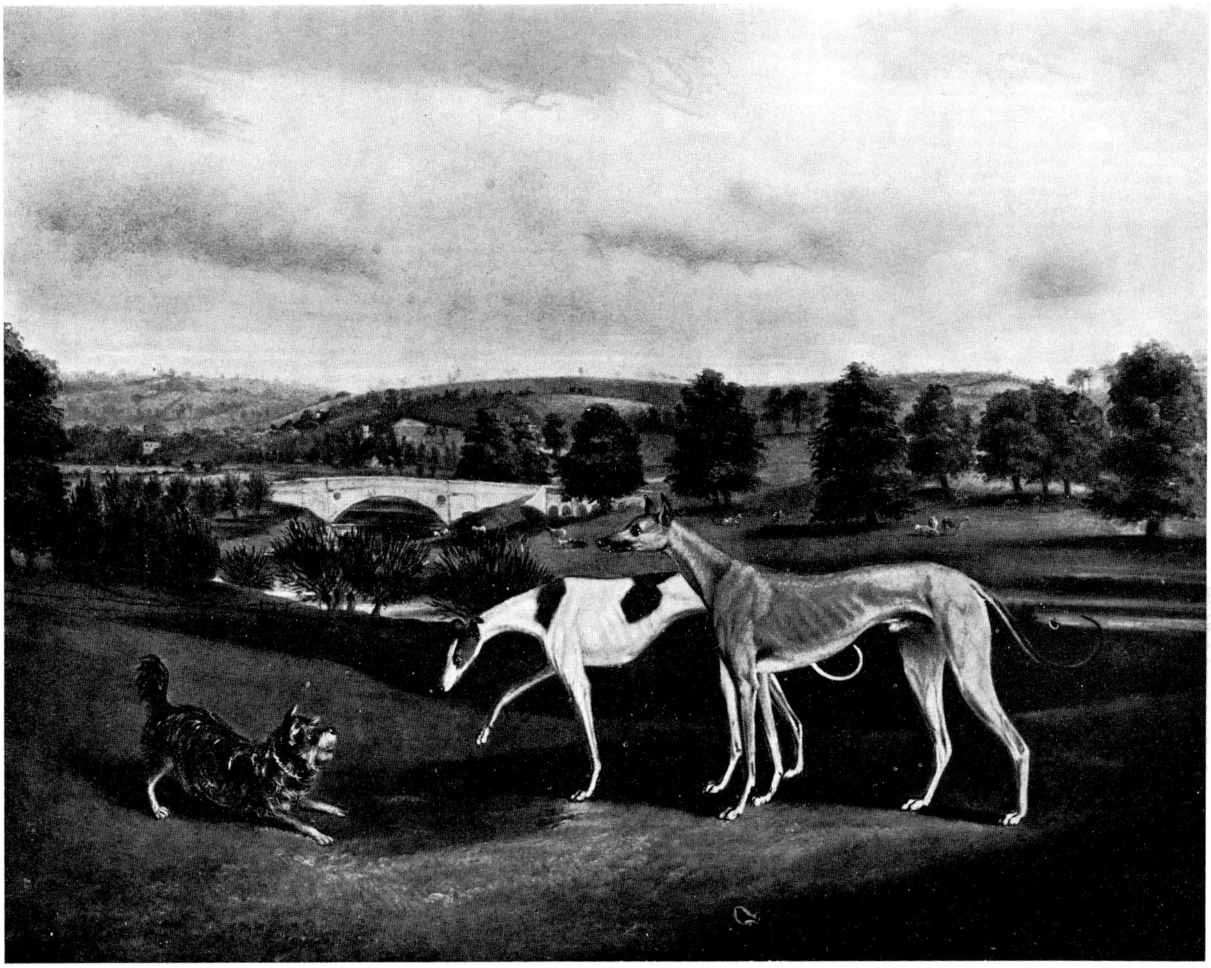

Canvas. 32 × 43 in. J. C. MAGGS. 1819–1896 S & D. 1850

Two Greyhounds and a Terrier in a Park

Courtesy of Messrs. Frost & Reed Ltd., Bristol & London

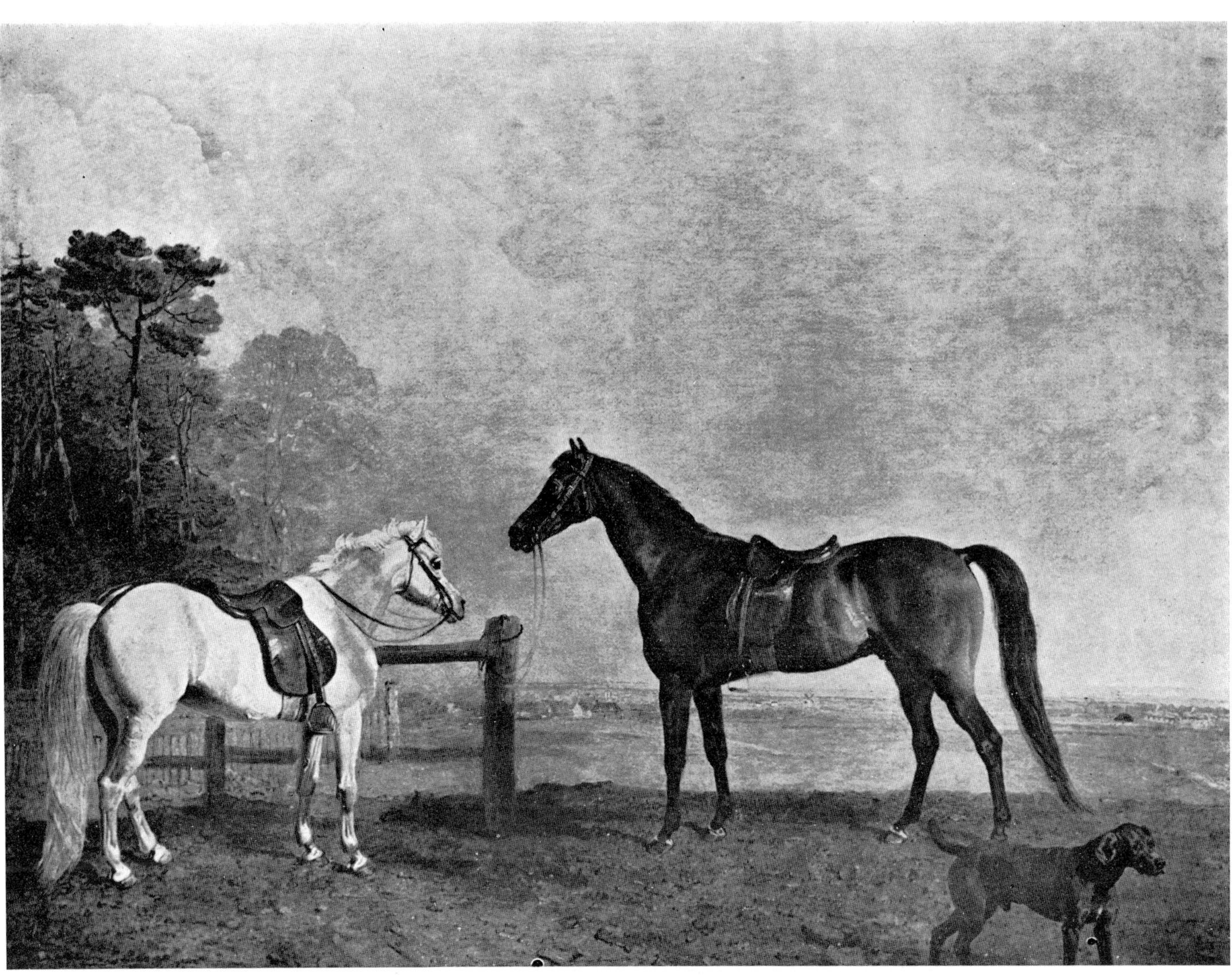

Canvas. 40 × 50 in. BENJAMIN MARSHALL 1767–1835 S & D. 1828

Two Horses & Dog on Newmarket Heath with distant view of Newmarket

Courtesy of Messrs. Leggatt Brothers, London

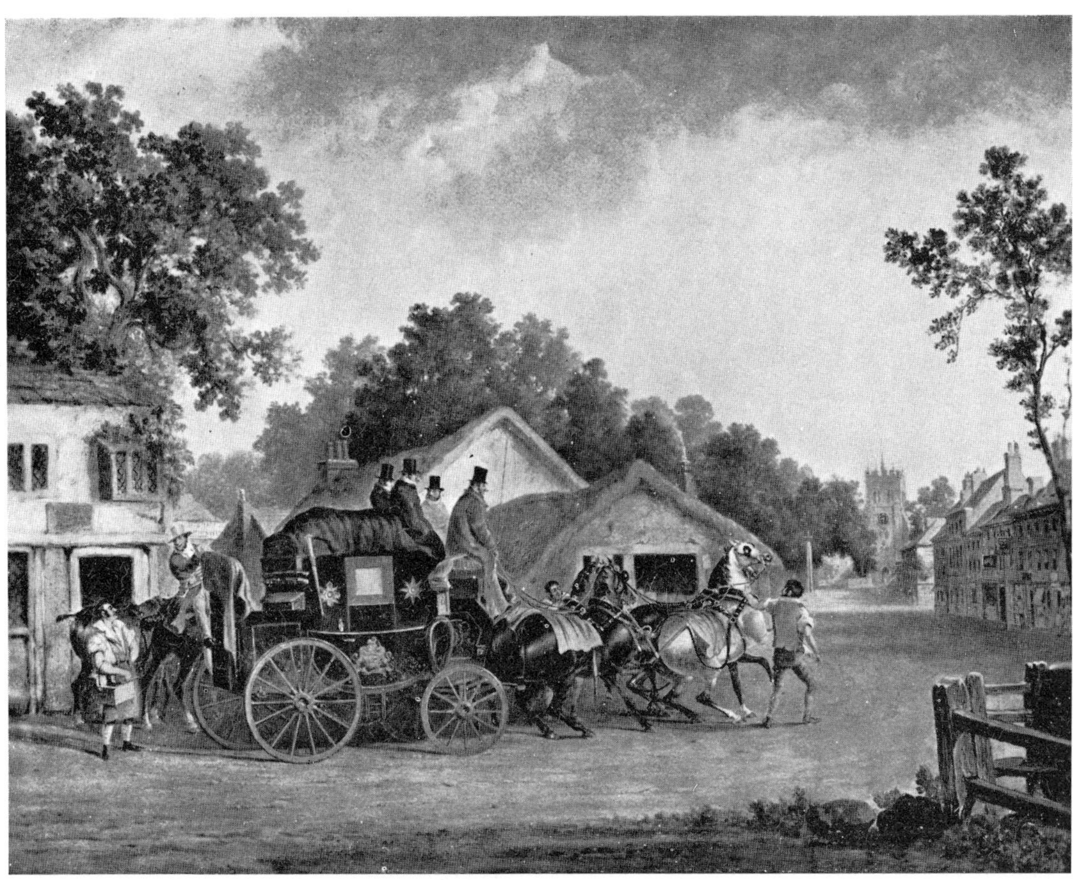

Oil. 26¼ × 36 in. A. ANSON MARTIN. op. 1840–1861 Signed

The York-London Mail Coach Leaving Bedale, Yorks

Courtesy of Messrs. Frost & Reed Ltd., Bristol & London

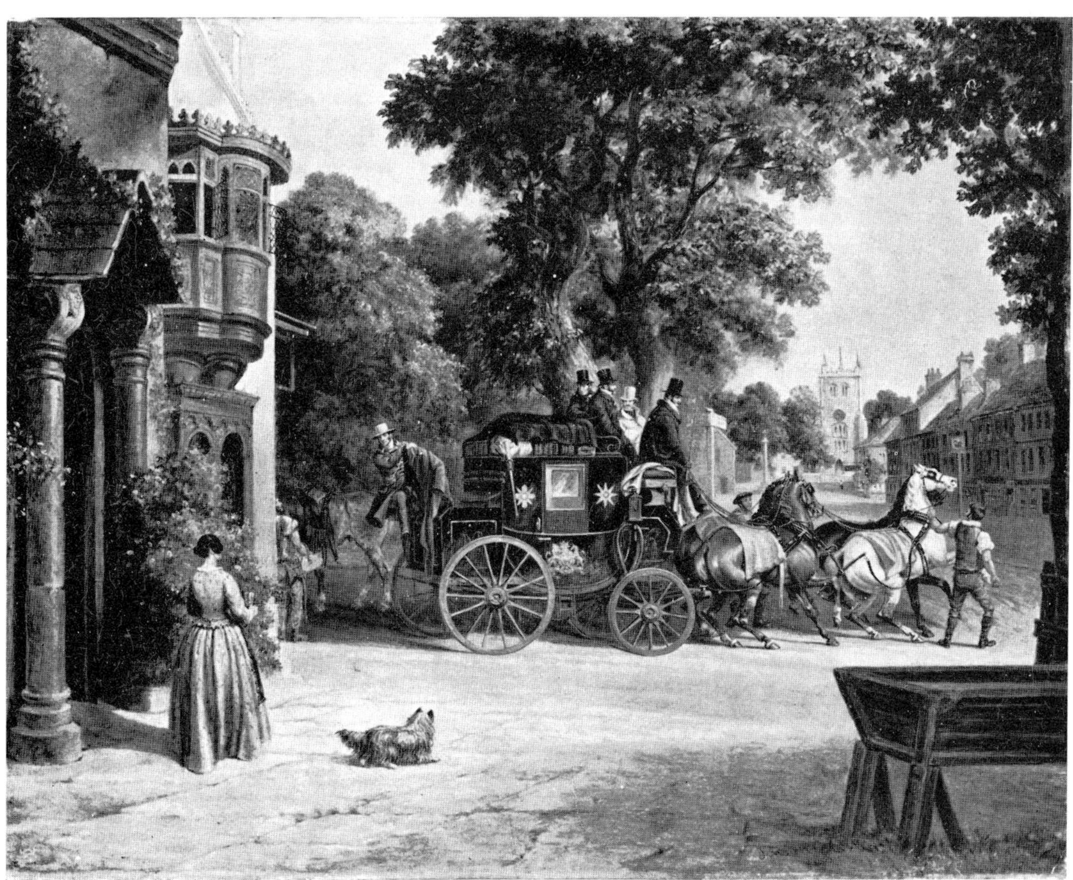

Oil. 28 × 36 in. ANSON MARTIN. op. 1840–61 & S & D. 1853

CHARLES COOPER HENDERSON 1803–77

The Exeter-London Mail Coach leaving Shaftesbury

Courtesy of Messrs. Needham's Antiques, New York

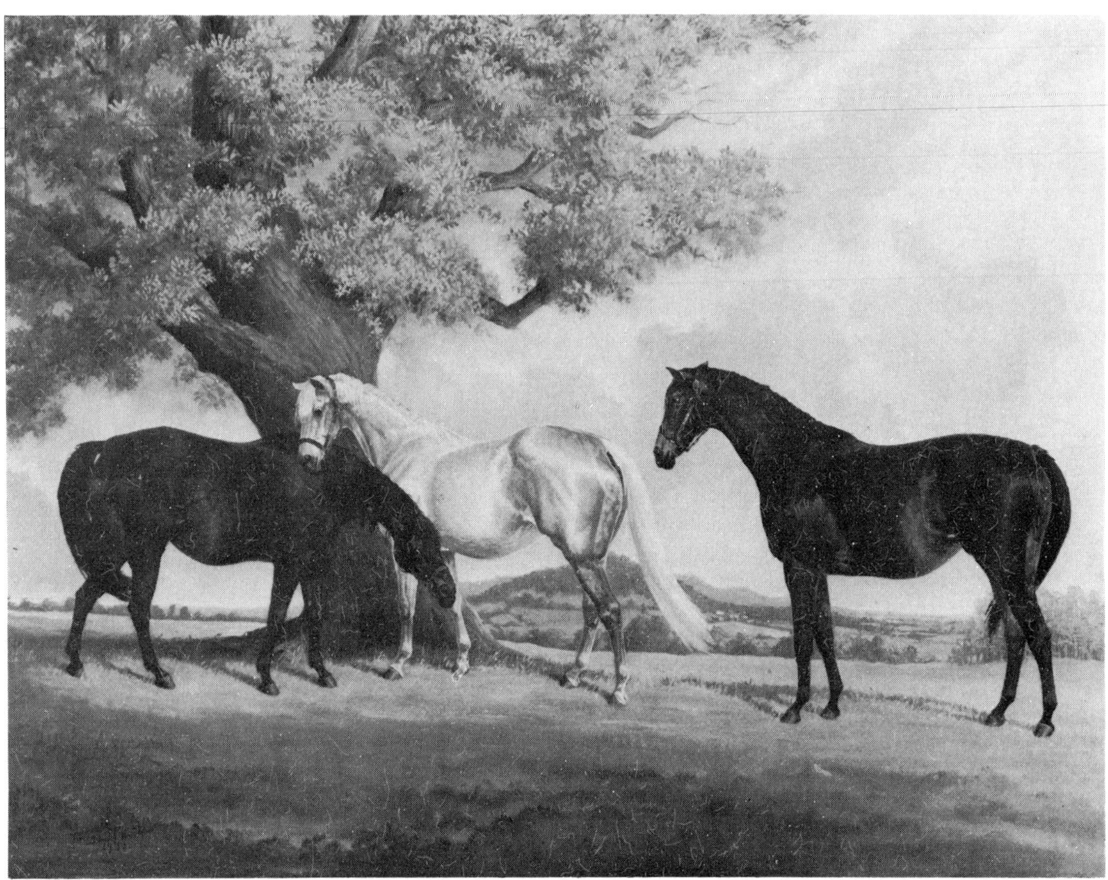

Canvas, 28 × 36 in. JULIET McLEOD. b. 1917 S & D. 1950
'Snowberry', 'Myrobella' and 'Sun Chariot'
Courtesy of Messrs. Arthur Ackermann & Son, Ltd., London

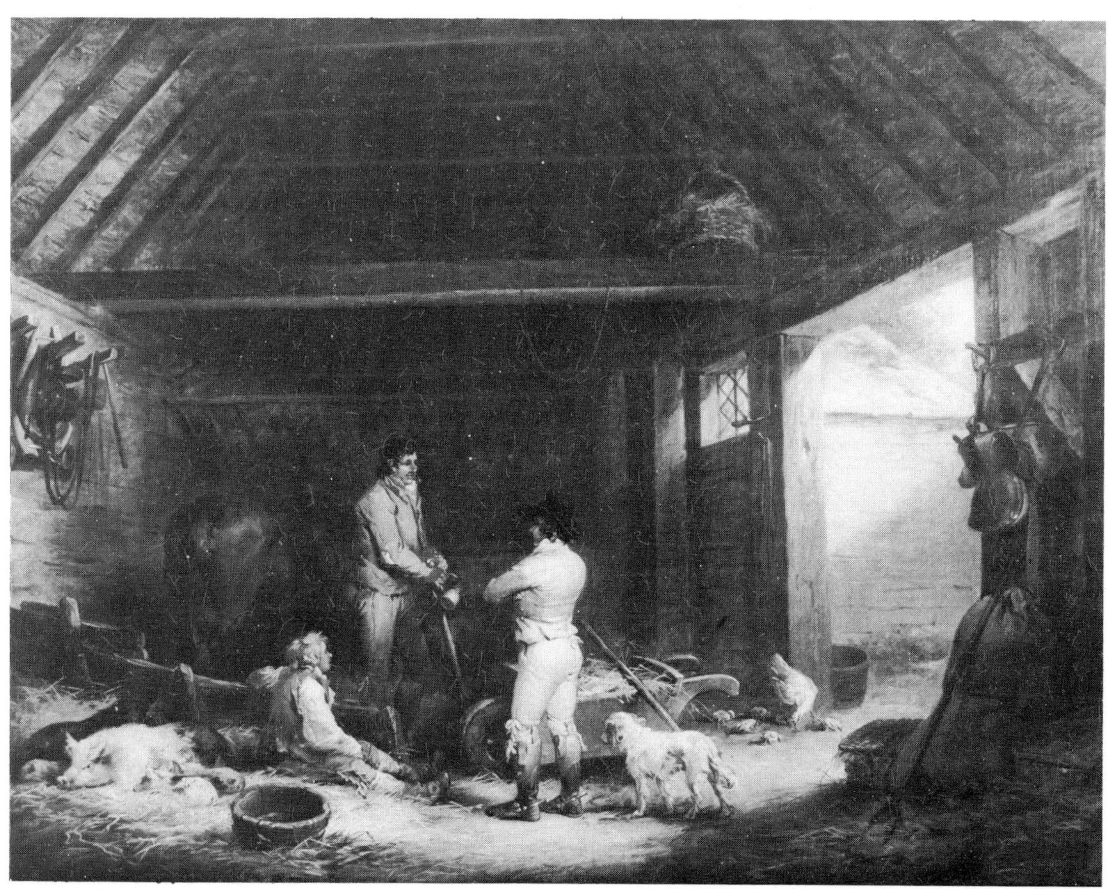

Canvas. 28 × 35 in. GEORGE MORLAND. 1763–1804
Evening, or the Post Boy's Return
Courtesy of Messrs. Leggatt Brothers, London

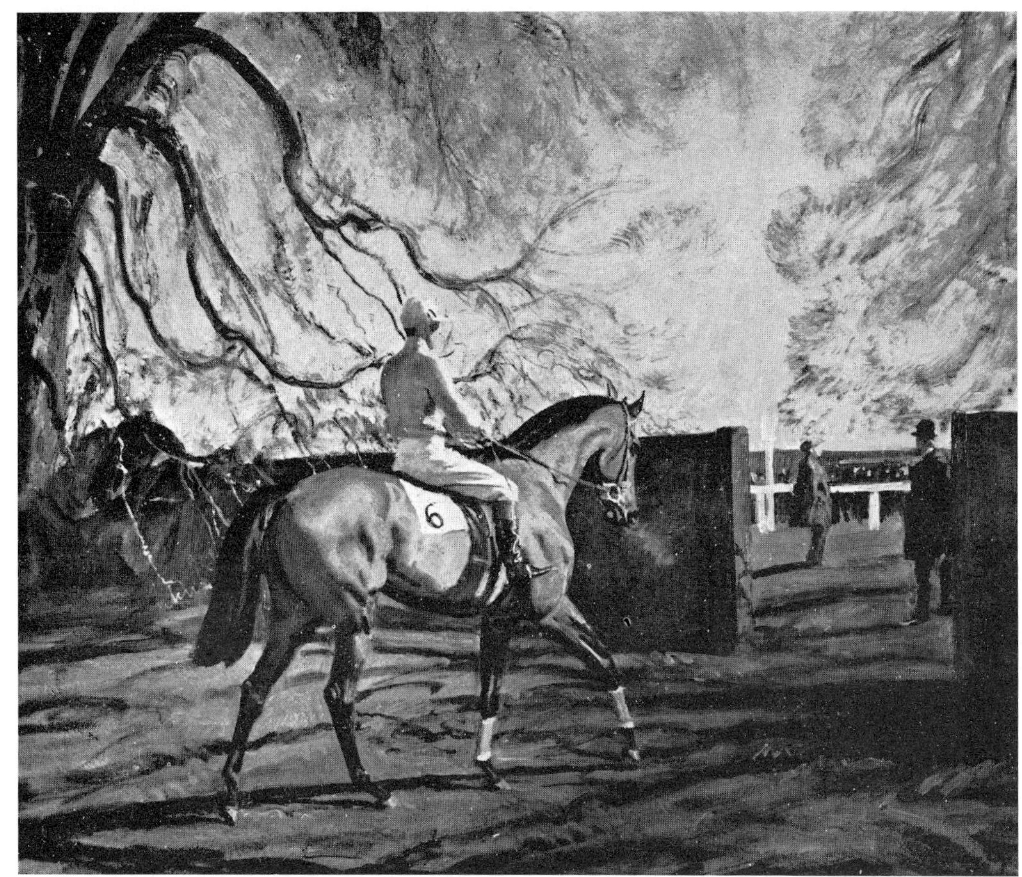

Oil. $24\frac{3}{4} \times 30$ in. SIR ALFRED J. MUNNINGS, PP.R.A. 1879–1959 Signed

Going Out at Kempton

Courtesy of Messrs. Frost & Reed Ltd., Bristol & London

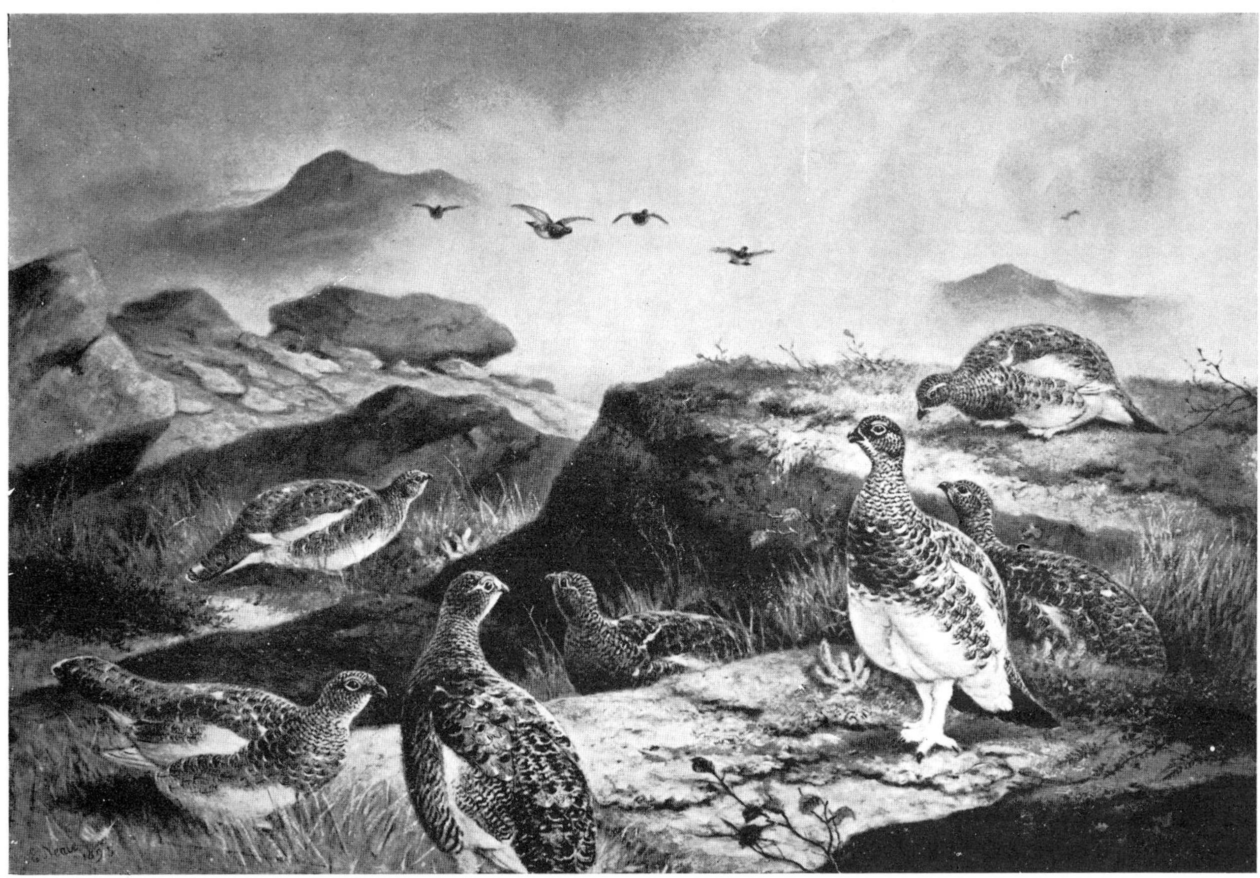

Oil. $26\frac{1}{2} \times 39$ in. E. NEALE. c. 1850–1910? S & D. 1895

Ptarmigan

Courtesy of Messrs. Frost & Reed Ltd., Bristol & London

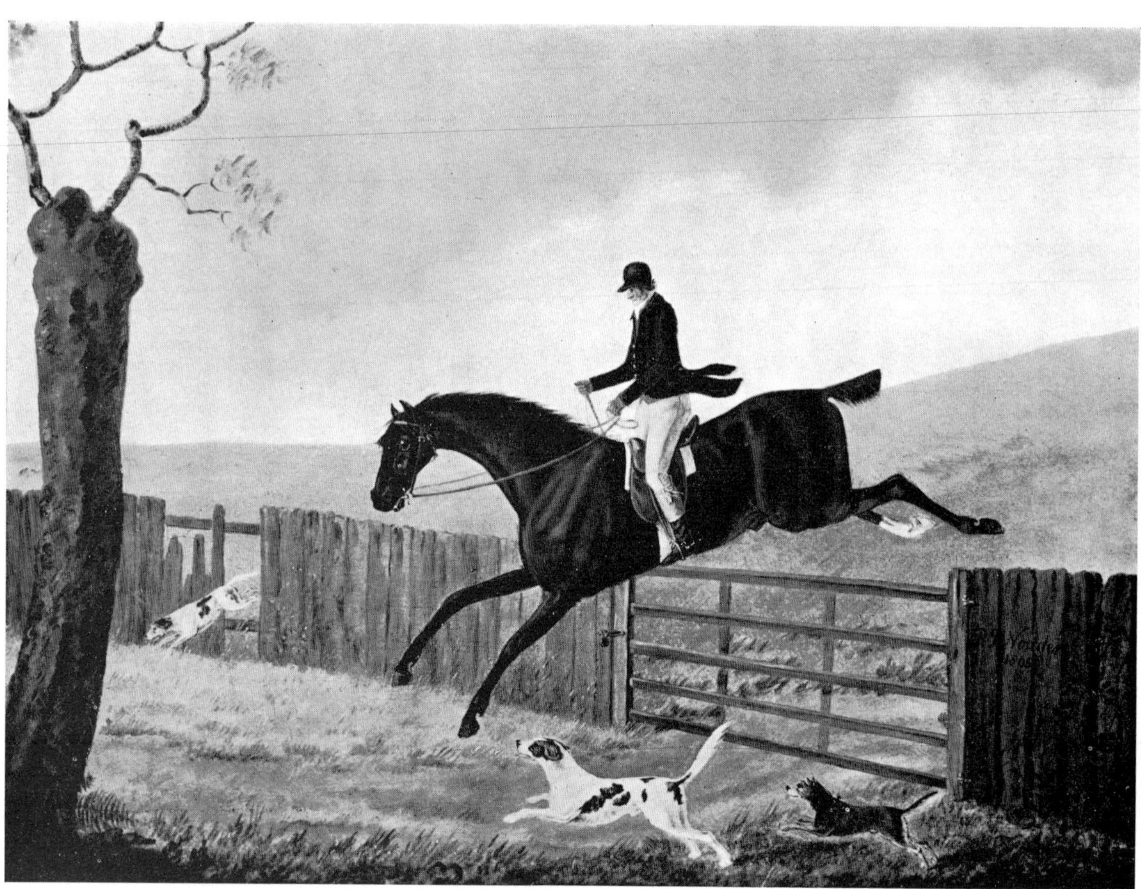

Oil. 14 × 17½ in. R. P. NODDER. op. 1793–1820 One of a set of 4

Courtesy of Messrs. Frost & Reed Ltd., Bristol & London

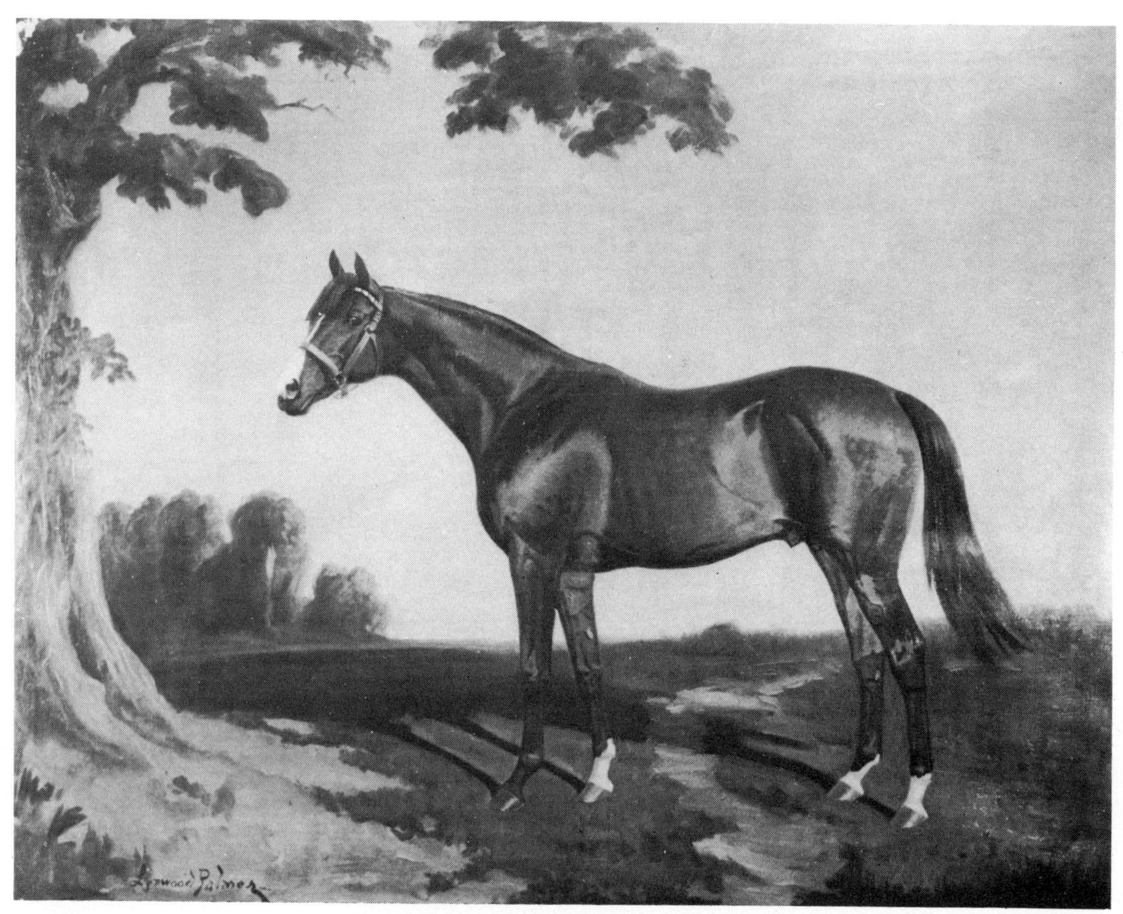

Canvas. 32½ × 41½ in. LYNWOOD PALMER. 1868–1939 Signed

'Royal Lancer' Winner of the St. Leger 1922

In the Museum & Art Gallery, Doncaster

PLATE 34

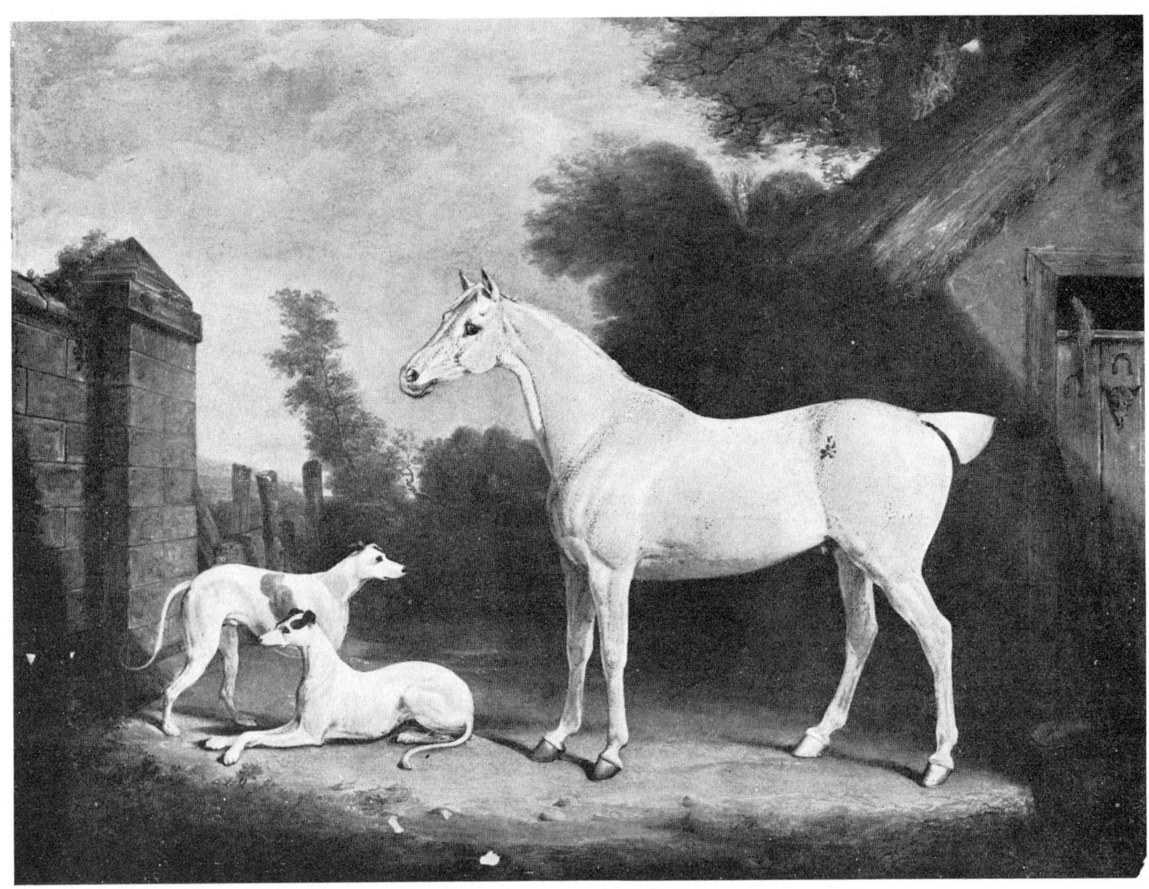

Oil 30 × 40 in.

STEPHEN PEARCE. 1819–1904
Portrait of a Greyhorse with two Greyhounds outside a Stable
Courtesy of Messrs. Frost & Reed Ltd., Bristol & London

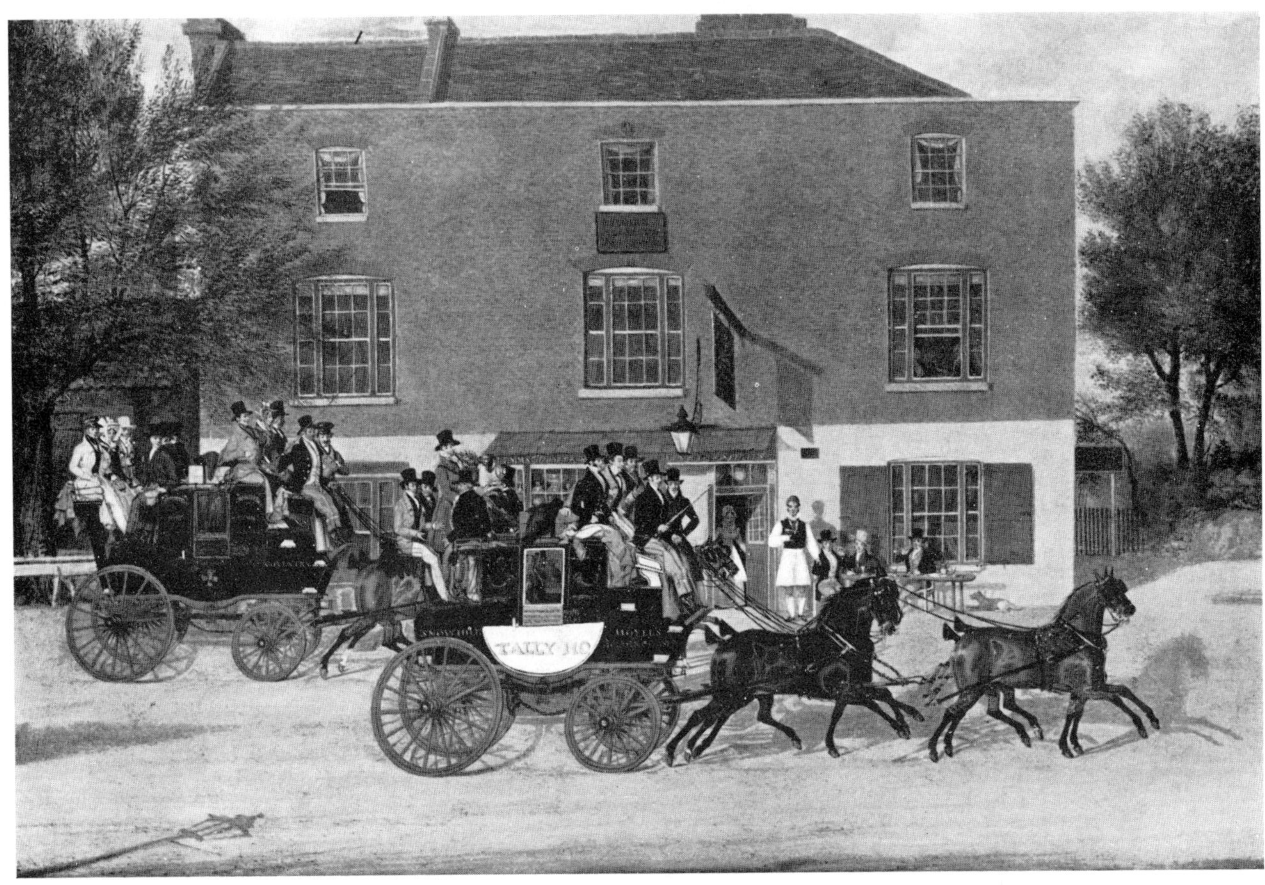

Canvas. 20 × 30 in.

JAMES POLLARD. 1792–1867
The Birmingham Tally-Ho Coaches passing The Crown at Holloway
Courtesy of Mr. N. C. Selway

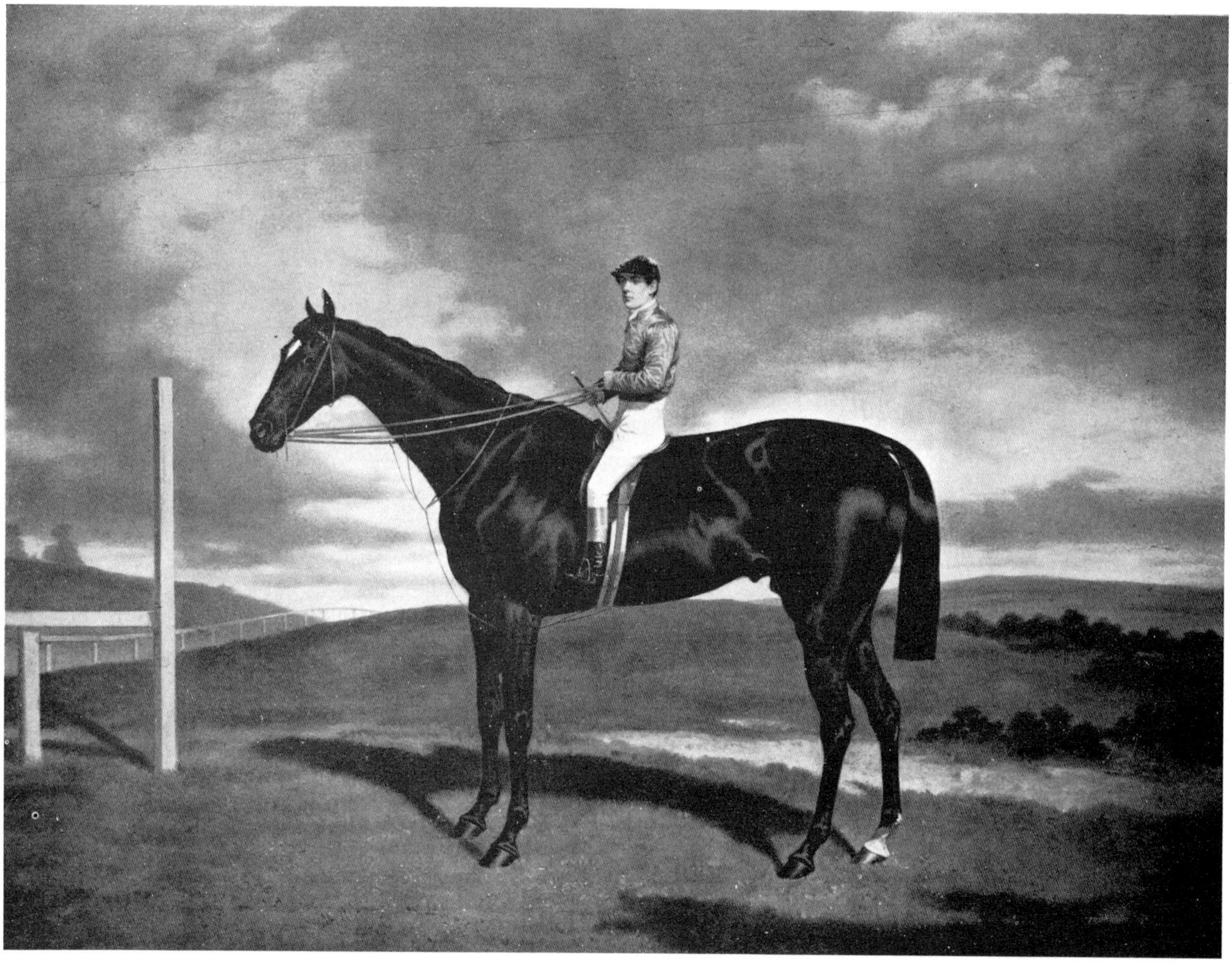

Oil. 28 × 36 in.

A. F. de PRAEDES. op. 1852–1879
The Racehorse 'Leamington' with Jockey
Courtesy of Messrs. Frost & Reed Ltd., Bristol & London

S & D. 1852

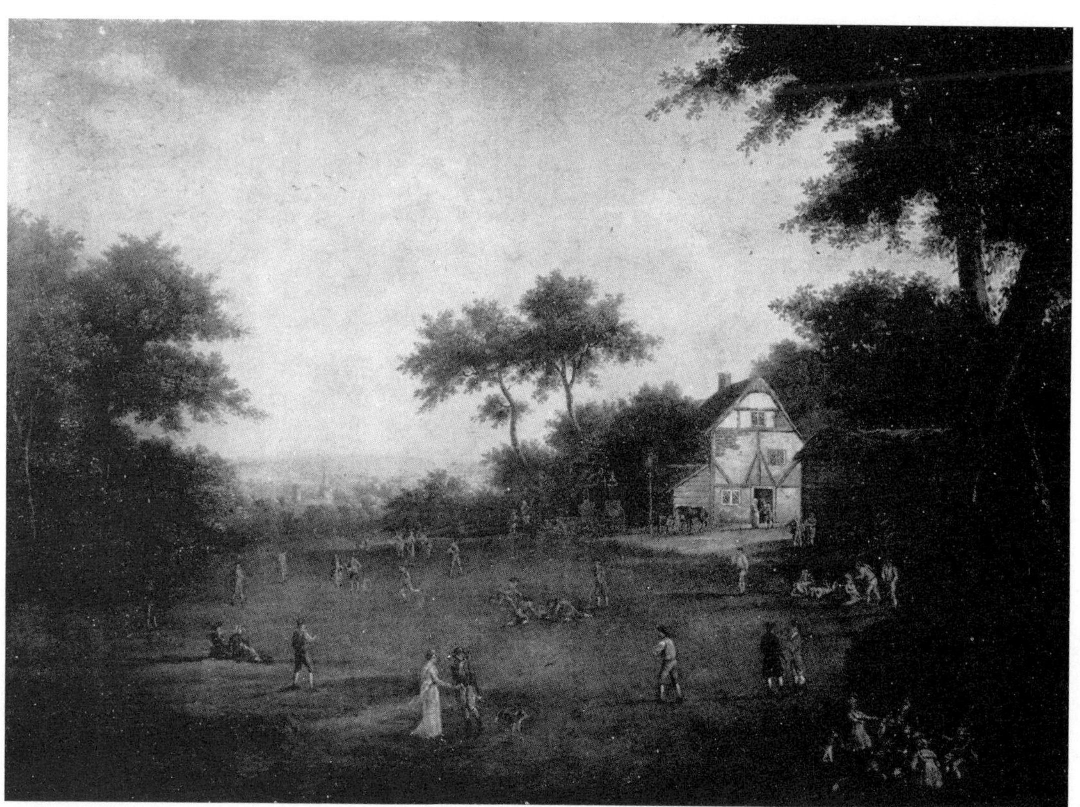

Canvas. $33\frac{1}{2}$ × 48 in.

JOHN R. READE of Bedford. op. 1773–1783
A Cricket Match
P.O.U.

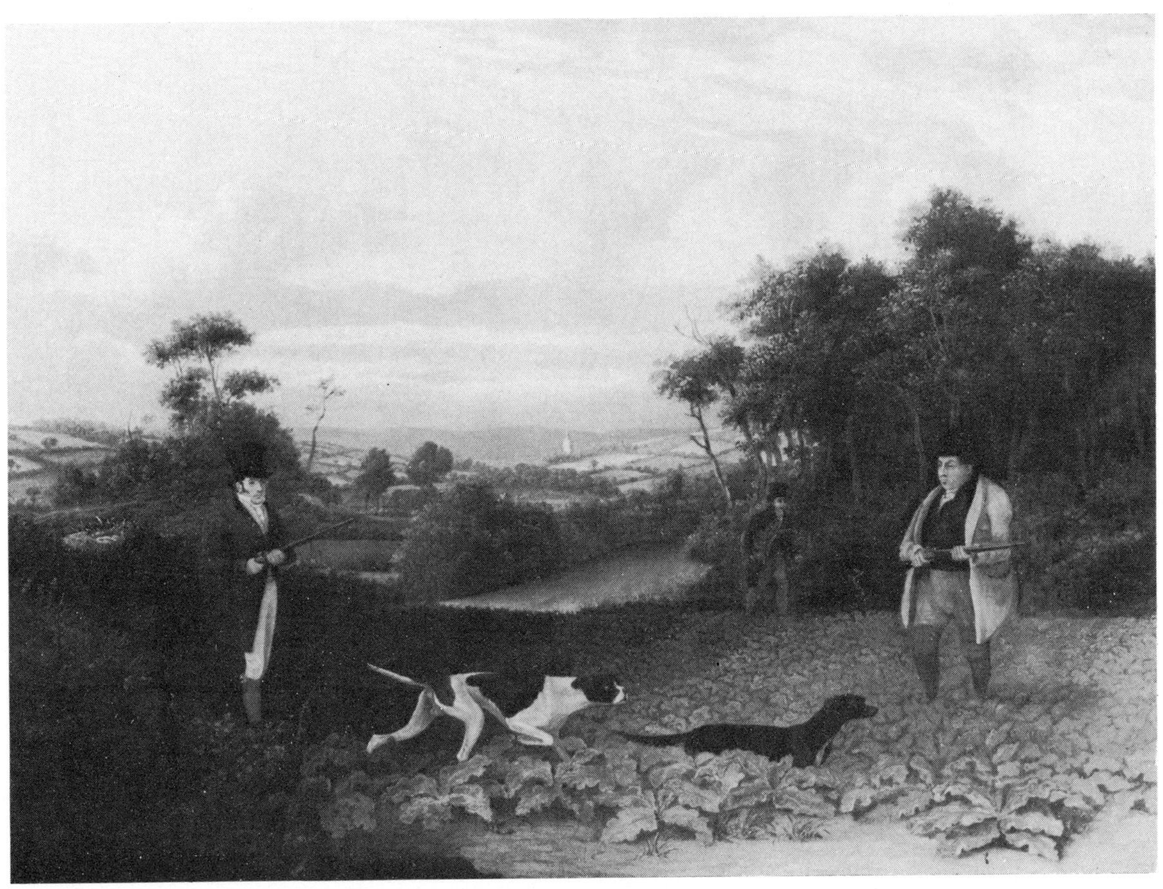

Canvas. 18 × 24 in. GEORGE REED S & D. 1823
Mr. T. Reed and Mr. T. Squires with Pointers on Cudham Hills, Kent
Courtesy of Messrs. Oscar & Peter Johnson Ltd., London

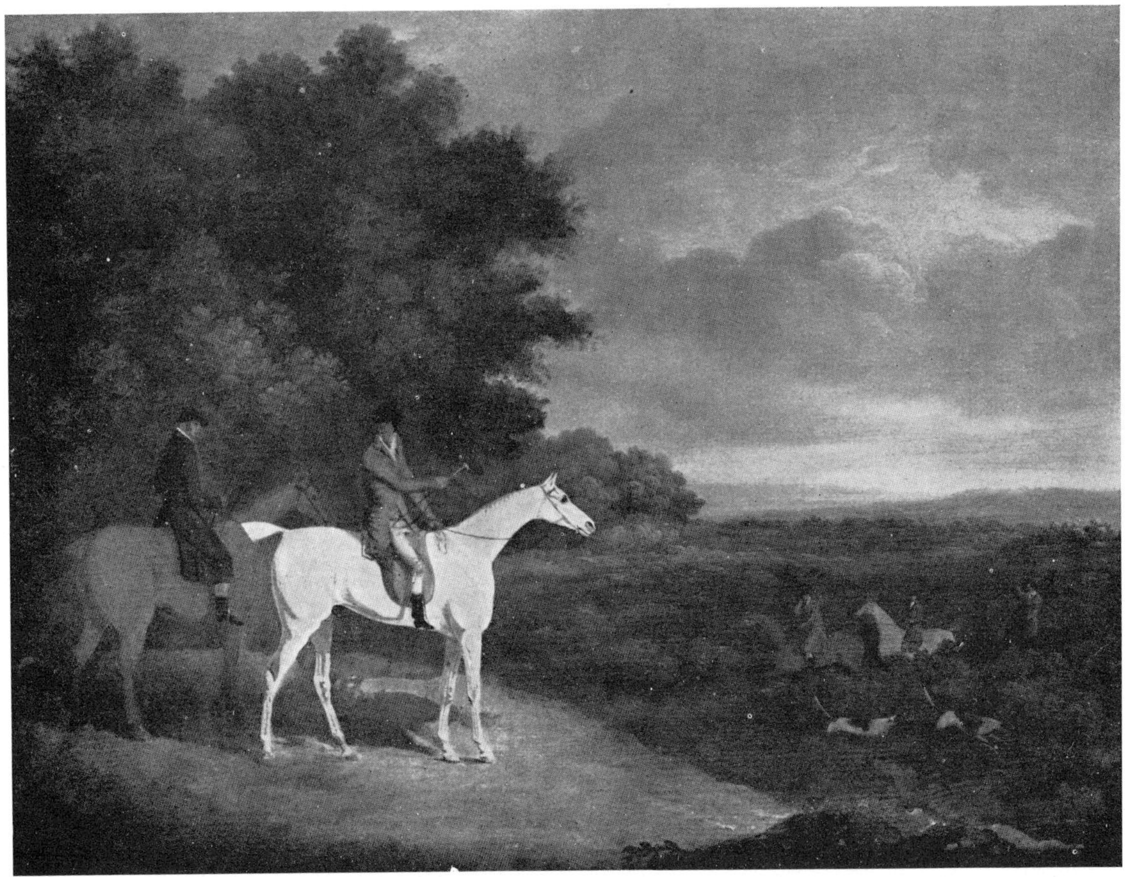

Oil. 27 × 35 in. PHILIP REINAGLE, R.A. 1748–1833
Gone to Cover
Courtesy of Messrs. Frost & Reed Ltd., Bristol & London

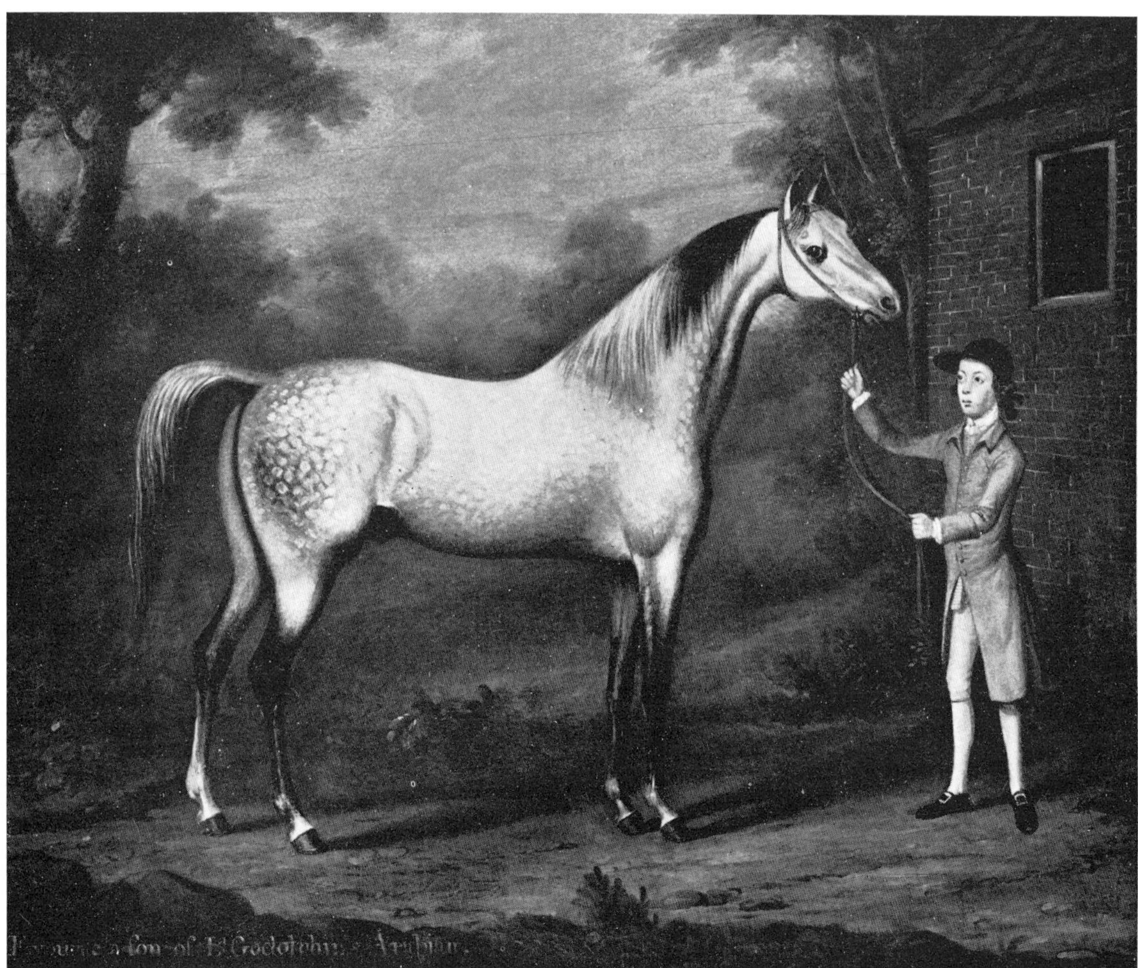

Oil. 40 × 50 in. RICHARD ROPER. op. 1749–1765 S & D. 1762
'Favourite' Son of Lord Godolphin's 'Arabian'
Courtesy of Messrs. Frost & Reed Ltd., Bristol & London

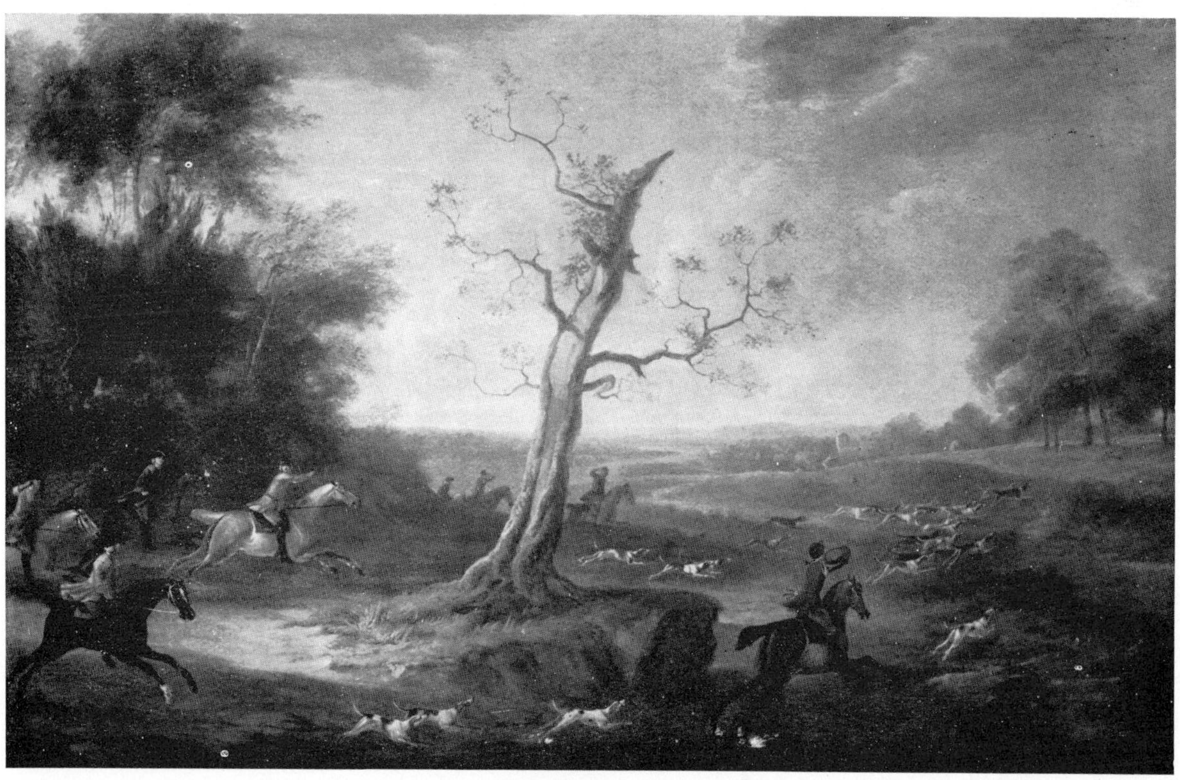

Canvas. JAMES ROSS. op. 1783 Dated 1783
A Hunt
P.O.U.

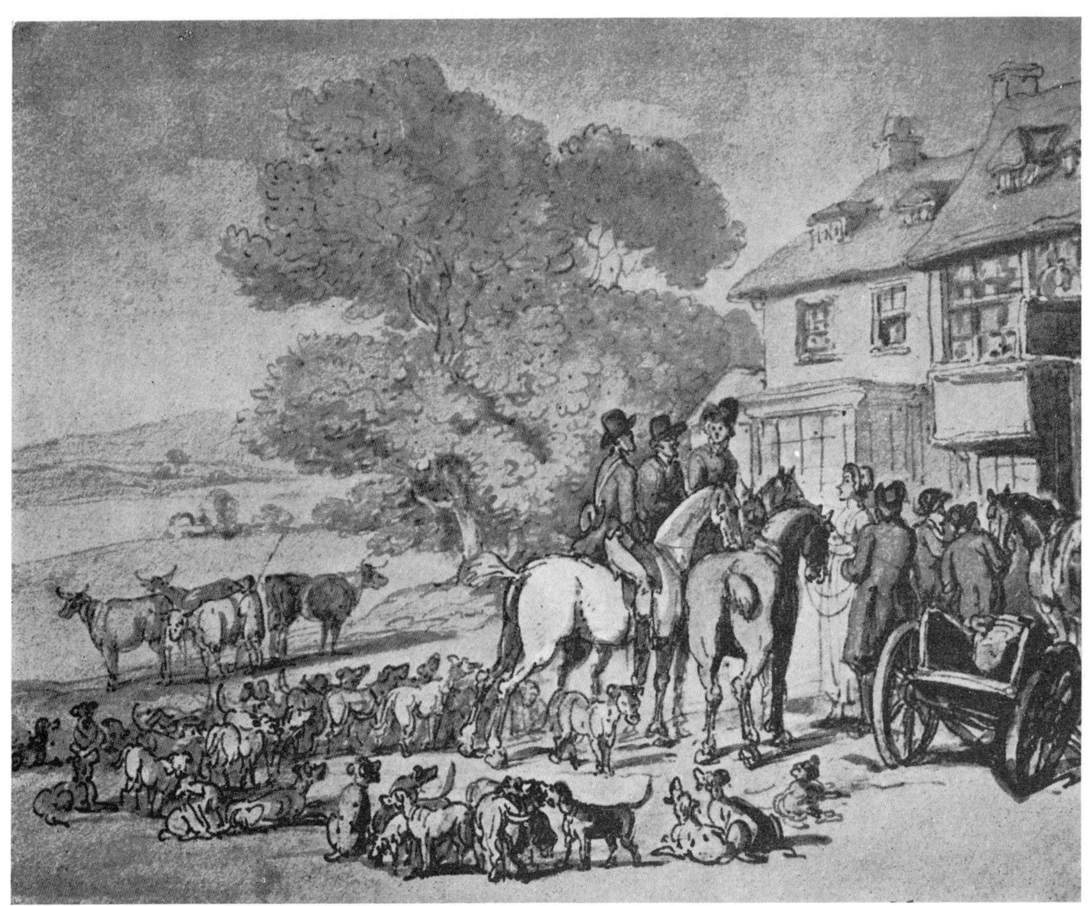

Water-colour 7 × $8\frac{3}{4}$ in. THOMAS ROWLANDSON. 1756–1827
Foxhounds Meeting outside an Inn
Courtesy of Messrs. Frost & Reed Ltd., Bristol & London

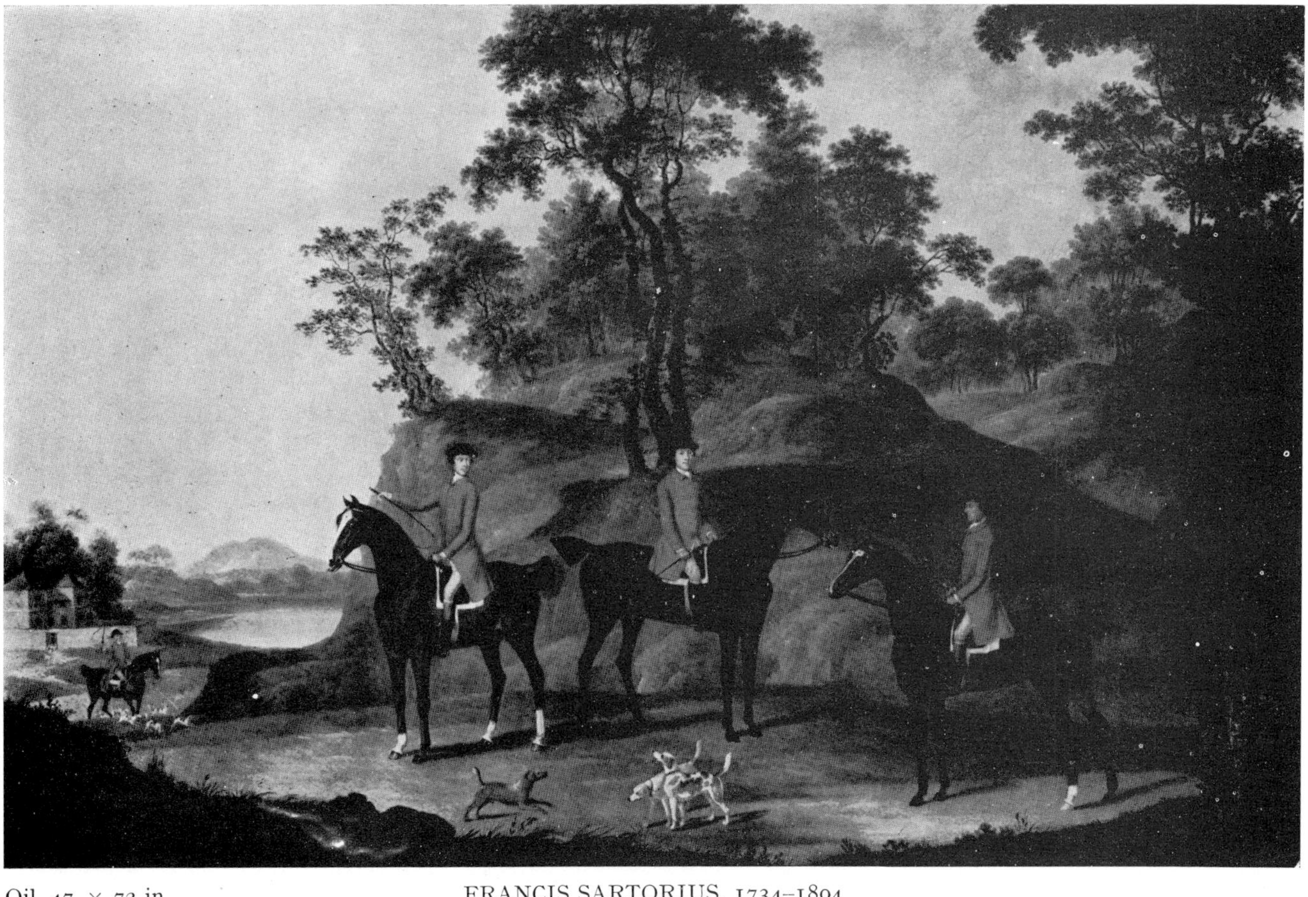

Oil. 47 × 72 in. FRANCIS SARTORIUS. 1734–1804
Foxhunting Scene
Courtesy of Messrs. Frost & Reed Ltd., Bristol & London

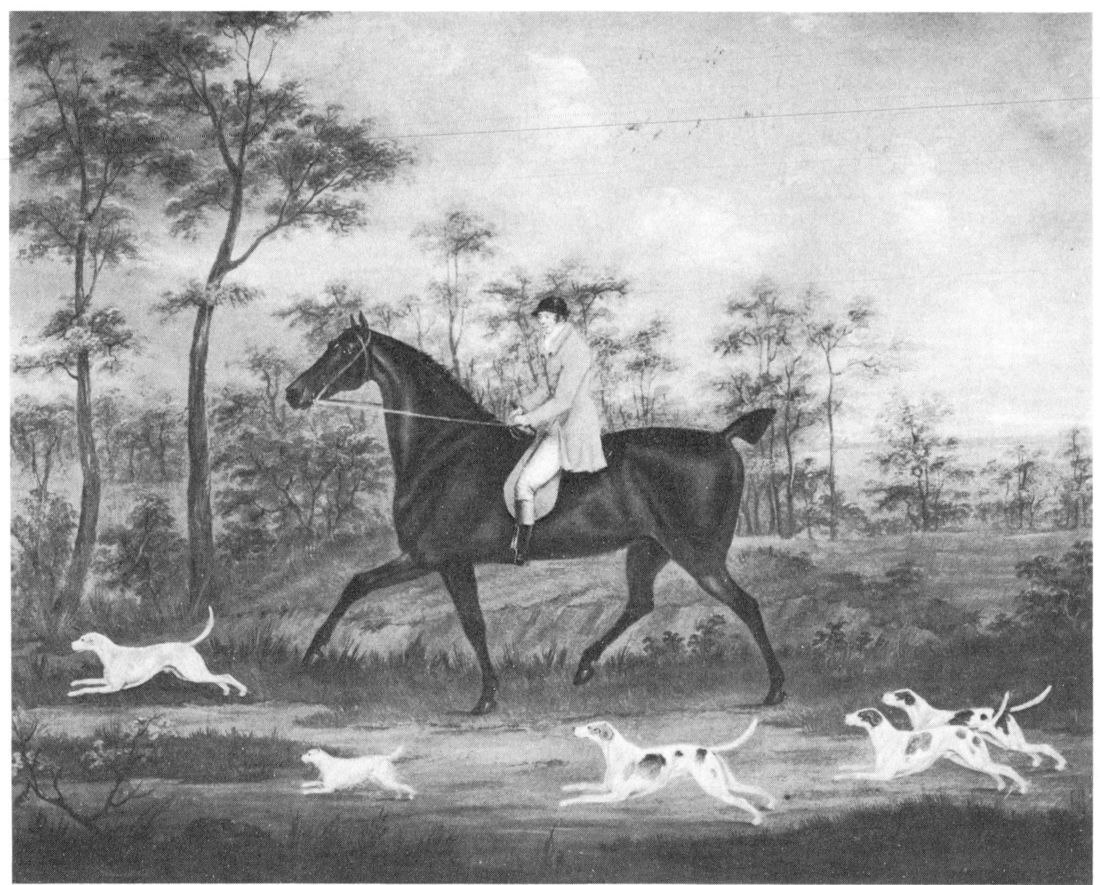

Canvas. 17 × 21 in. JOHN F. SARTORIUS. 1775–1830 S & D. 1832
Photo by courtesy of Arthur Ackermann & Son
In the collection of the late Lord Rootes

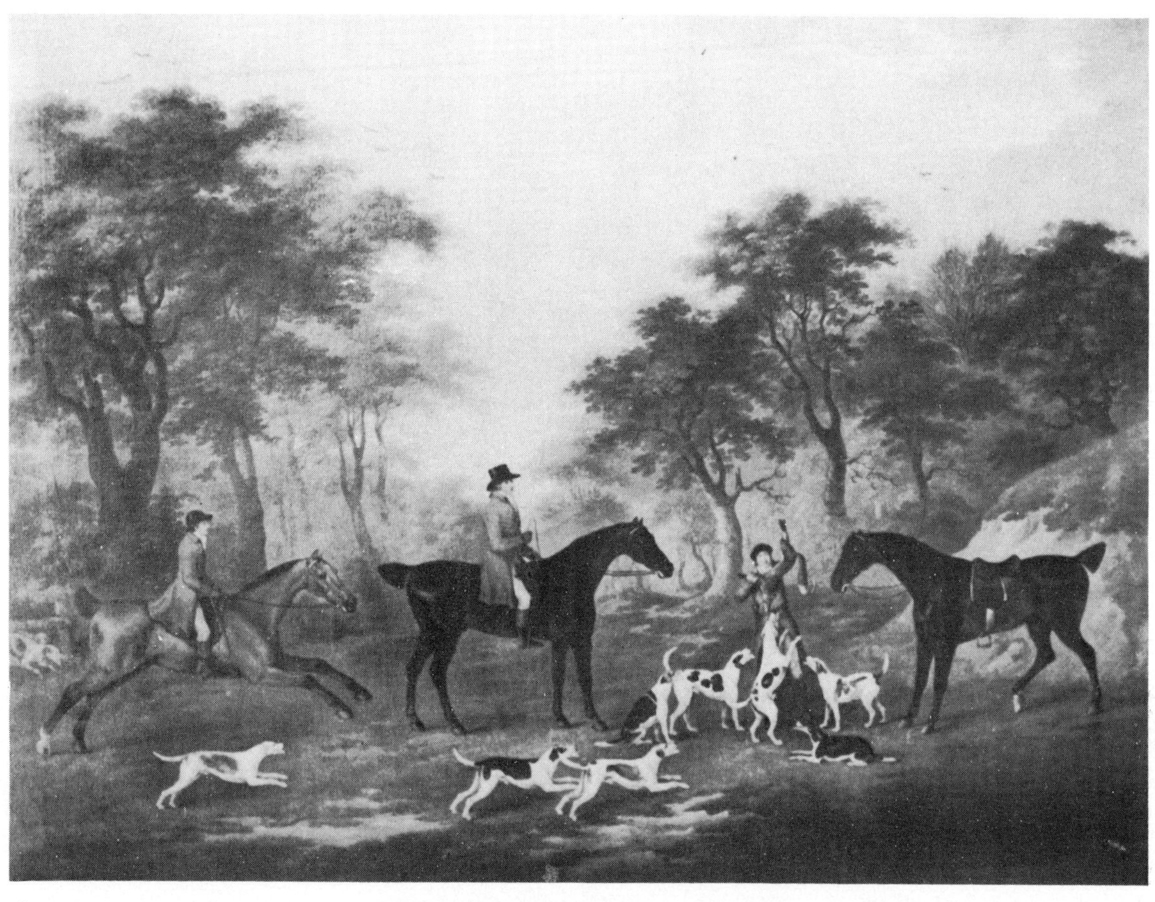

Canvas. 41 × 52½ in. JOHN NOST SARTORIUS. 1759–1828
Sir William Rowley, Bt. with the Essex & Suffolk Hunt near Stoke by Nayland
Courtesy of Sir Joshua Rowley, Bart

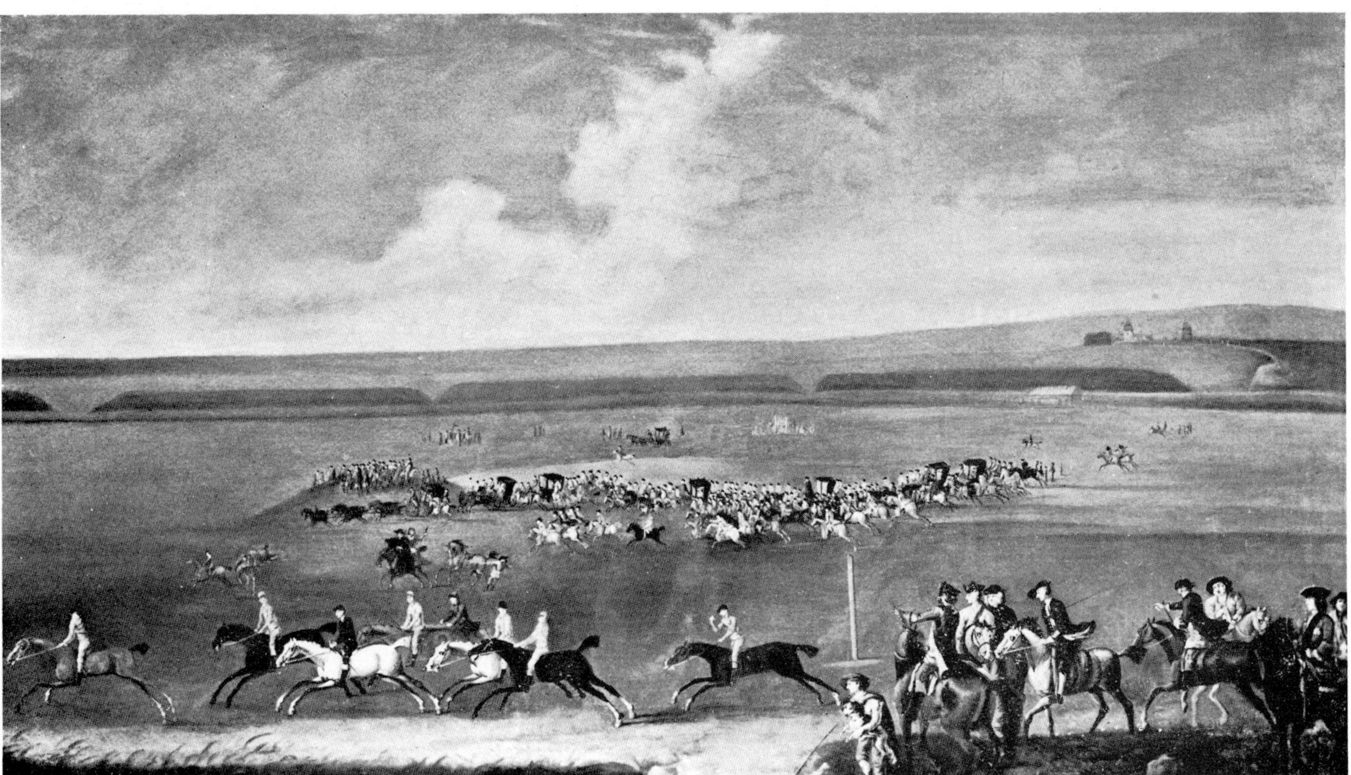

Oil. 33 × 57 in.

JAMES SEYMOUR. 1702–1752
A Race in Progress on Newmarket Heath 1750
Courtesy of Messrs. Frost & Reed Ltd., Bristol & London

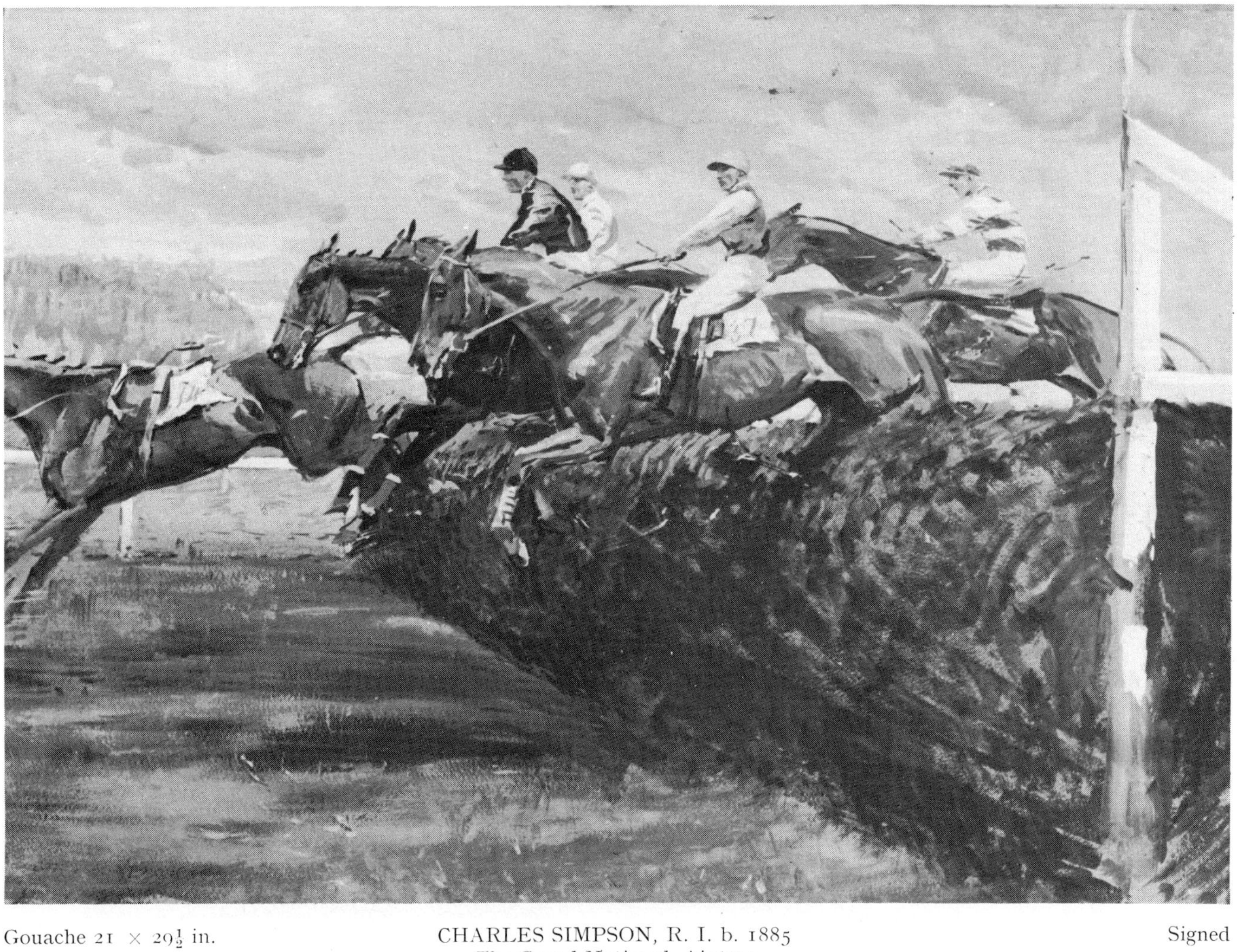

Gouache 21 × 29½ in.

CHARLES SIMPSON, R. I. b. 1885
The Grand National, Aintree
In the Dunedin Art Gallery, New Zealand

Signed

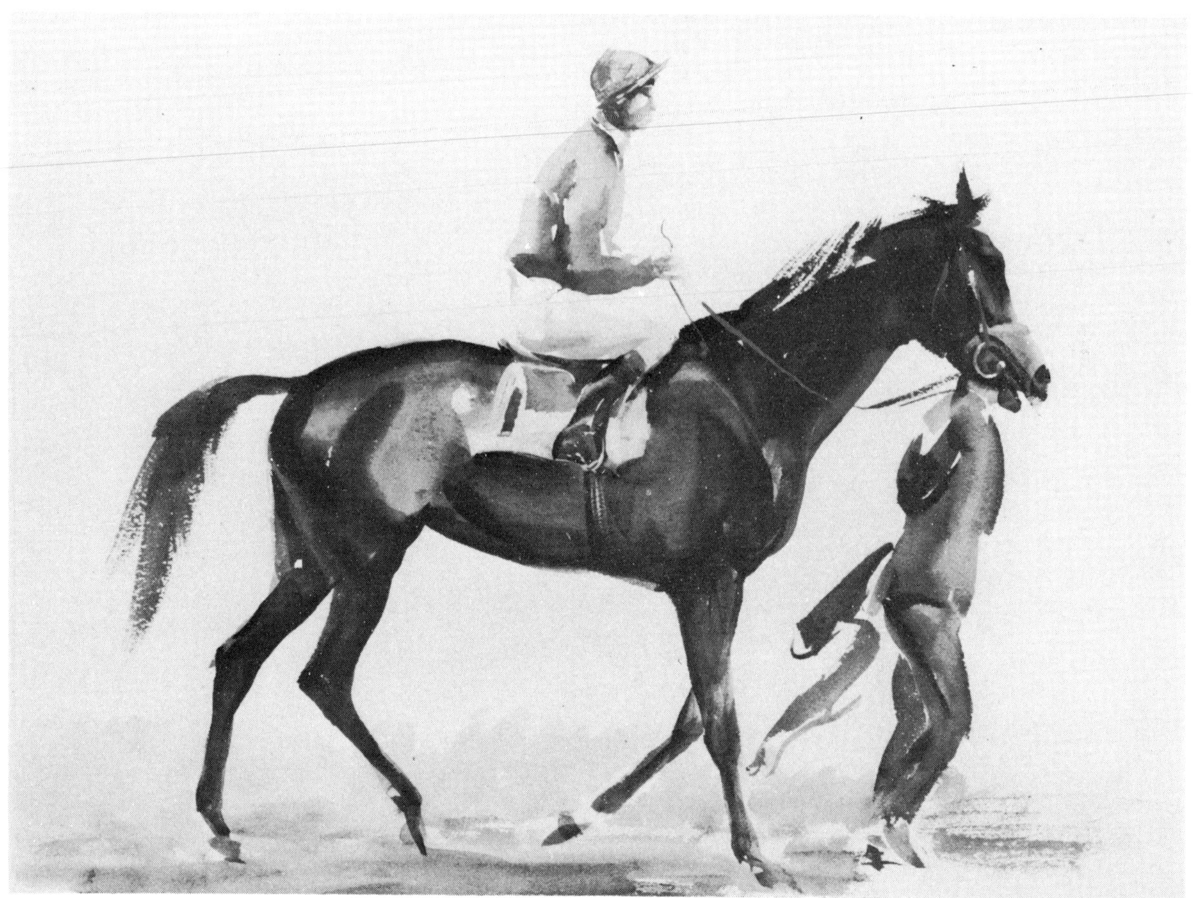

Gouache. 16 × 20 in. JOHN SKEAPING, R.A. b. 1901 S & D. 1963
Two Year Old Filly
Courtesy of Messrs. Arthur Ackermann & Son Ltd., London. Now in the collection of Mr. D. Taylor

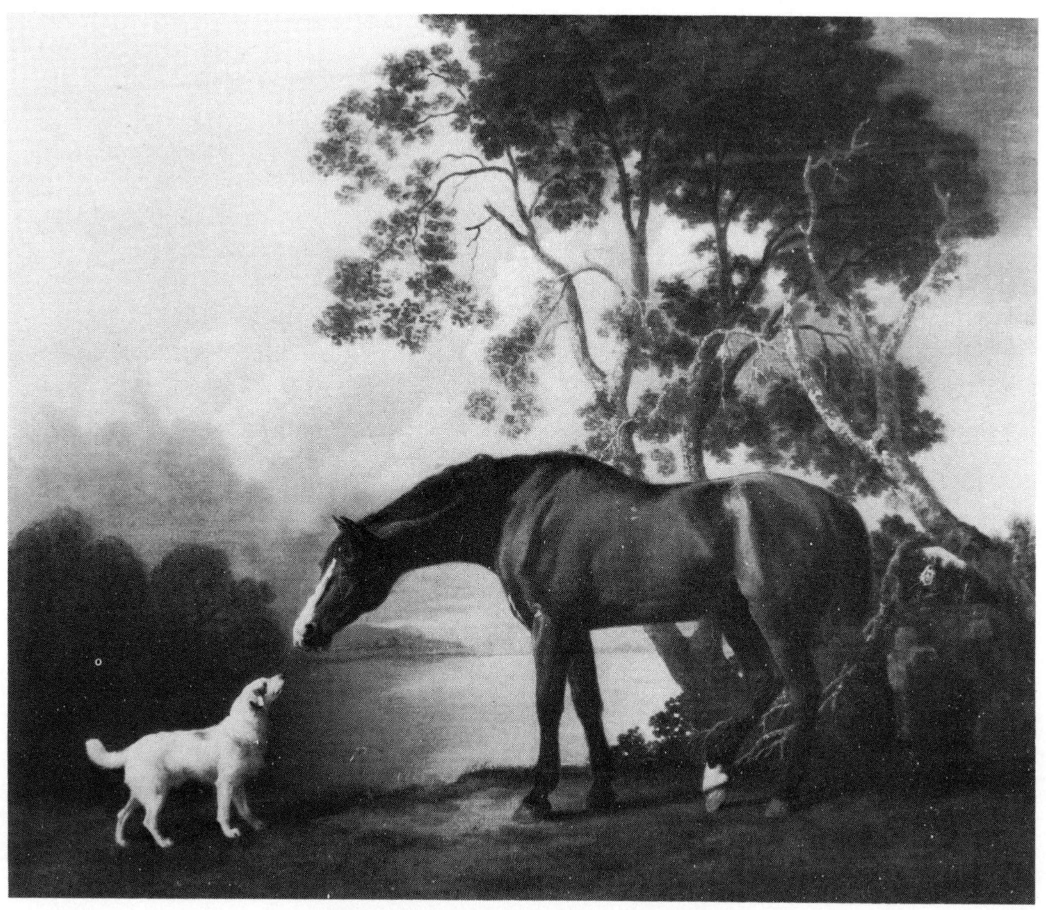

Canvas. 24 × 29 in. GEORGE STUBBS, A.R.A. 1724–1806 S & D. 1769
A Bay Horse and a White Dog, near a Lake
Courtesy of Messrs. Leggatt Brothers, London

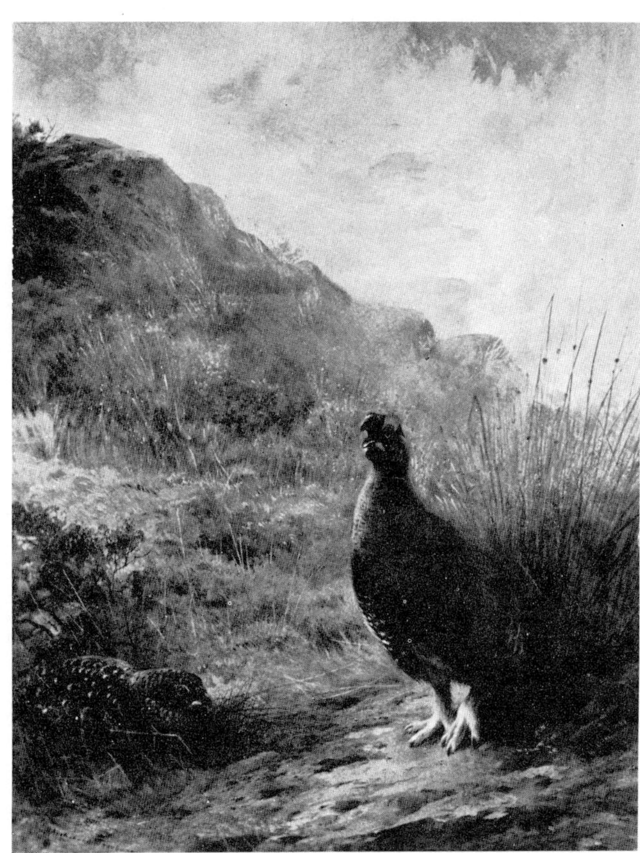

Water-colour $29\frac{3}{4} \times 21\frac{3}{4}$ in. ARCHIBALD THORBURN. 1860–1935 S & D. 1904

A pair of Grouse

Courtesy of Messrs. Frost & Reed Ltd., Bristol & London

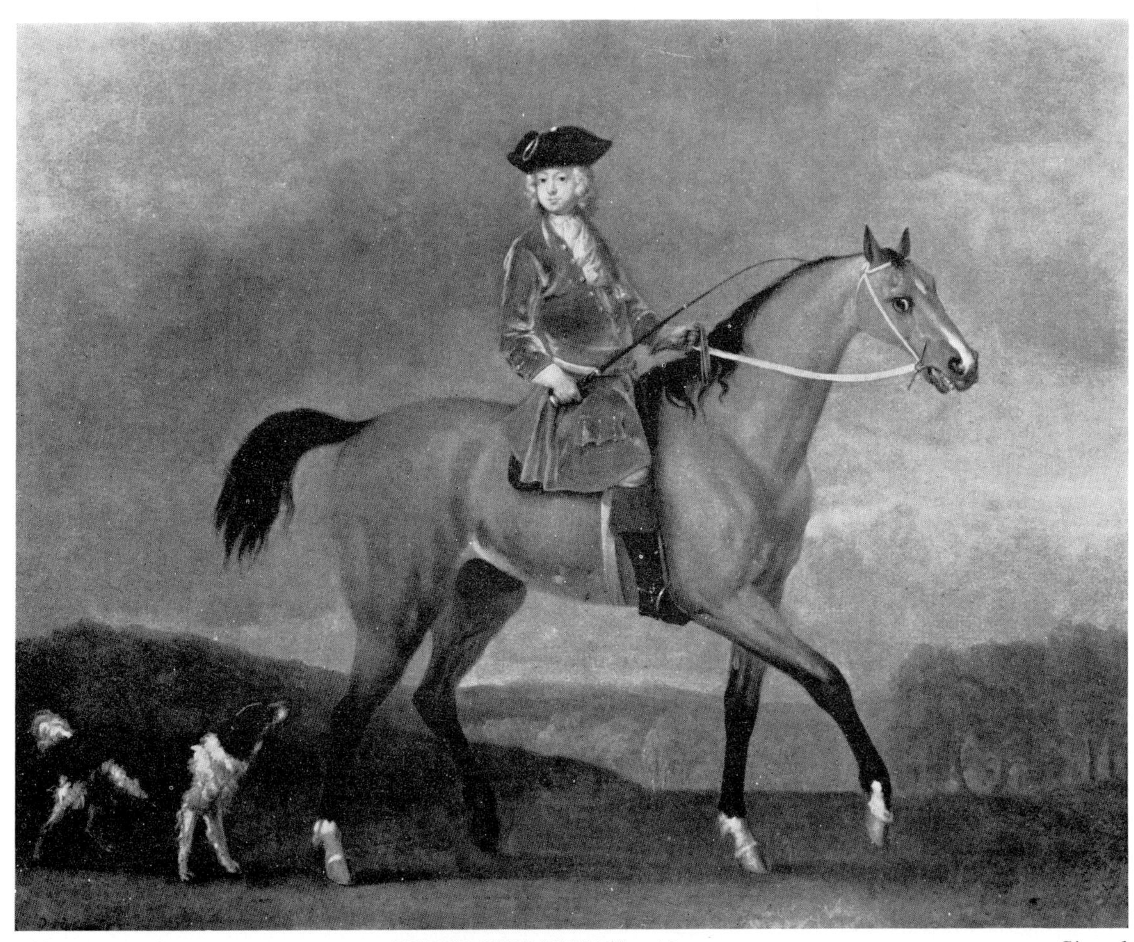

Oil. 39×49 in, PETER TILLEMANS. 1684–1734 Signed

Mounted Rider and Dog

Courtesy of Messrs. Frost & Reed Ltd., Bristol & London

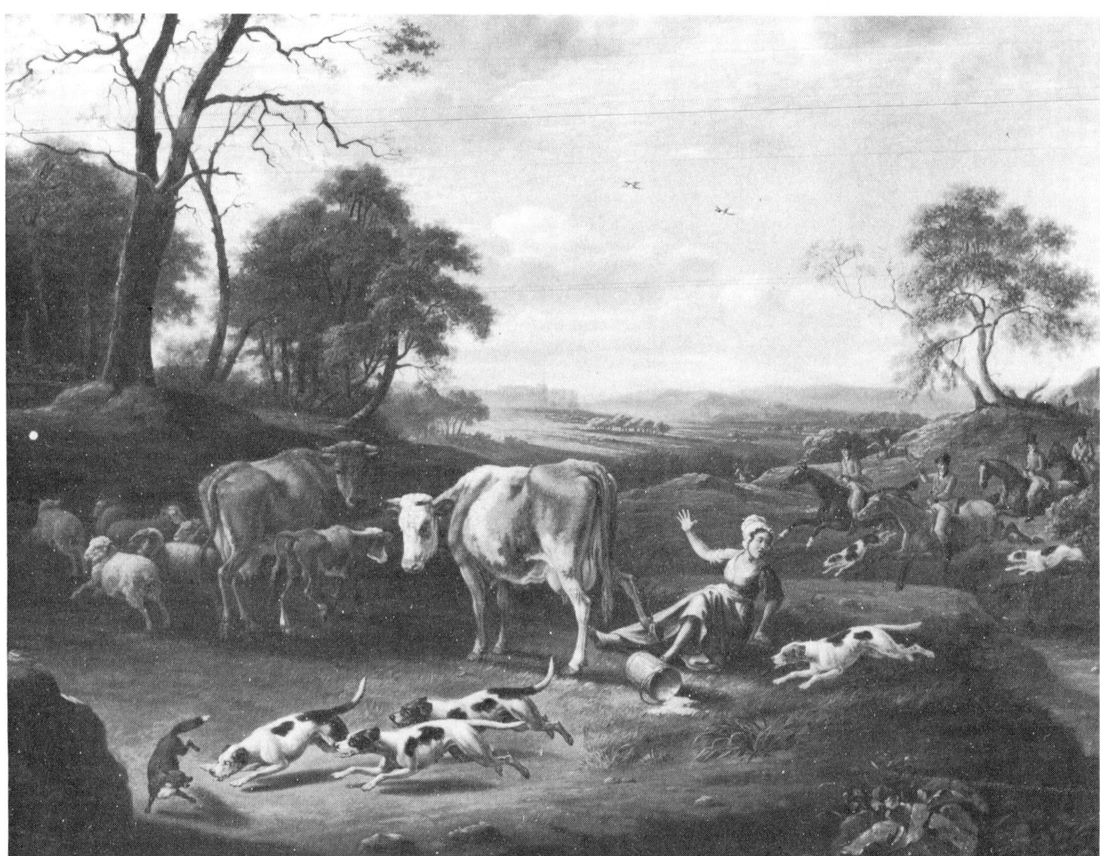

Canvas. $27\frac{1}{2} \times 35$ CHARLES TOWN of London. 1780–1850 S & D. 1827

The Royal Hunt at Windsor

Courtesy of The Lord Fairhaven

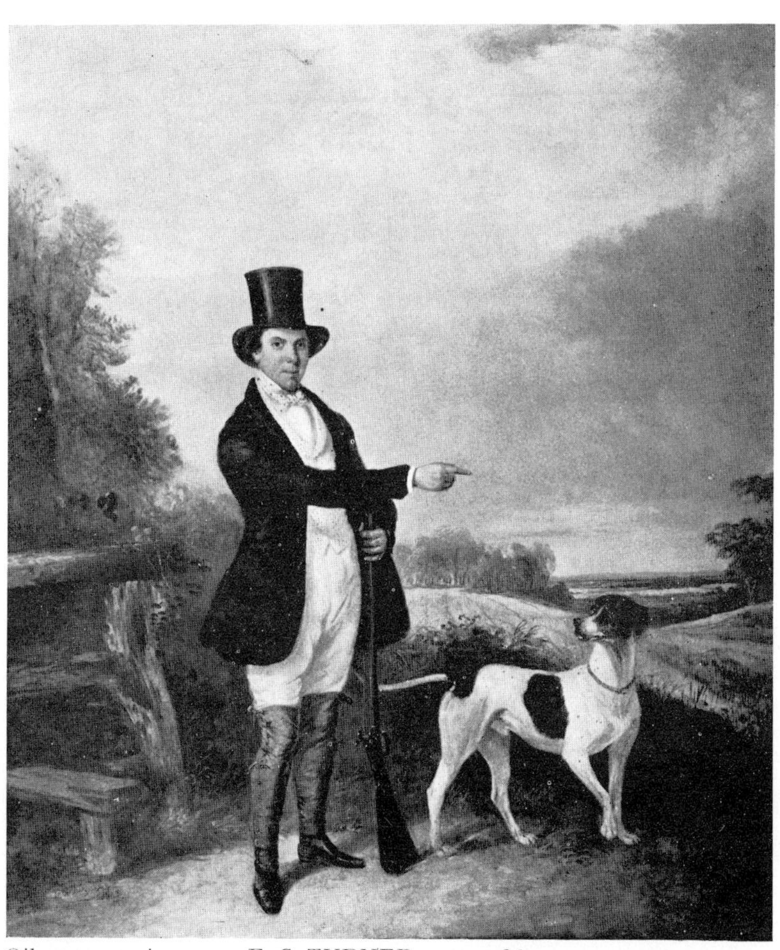

Oil. 30×25 in. F. C. TURNER. 1795–1865

Sportsman in a Landscape

Courtesy of Messrs. Frost & Reed Ltd., Bristol & London

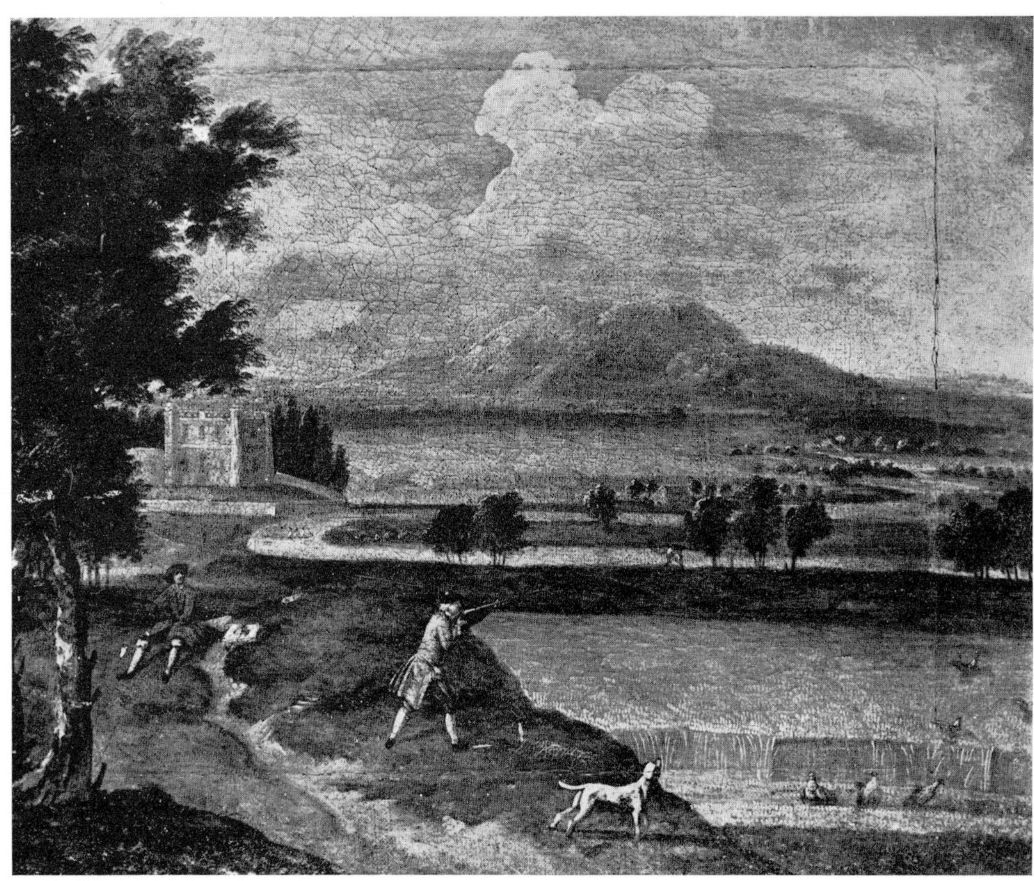

Canvas.

JAN VAN DER VINNE. 1663–1721
Gentleman out Shooting on his Estate with Dog & Loader
P.O.U.

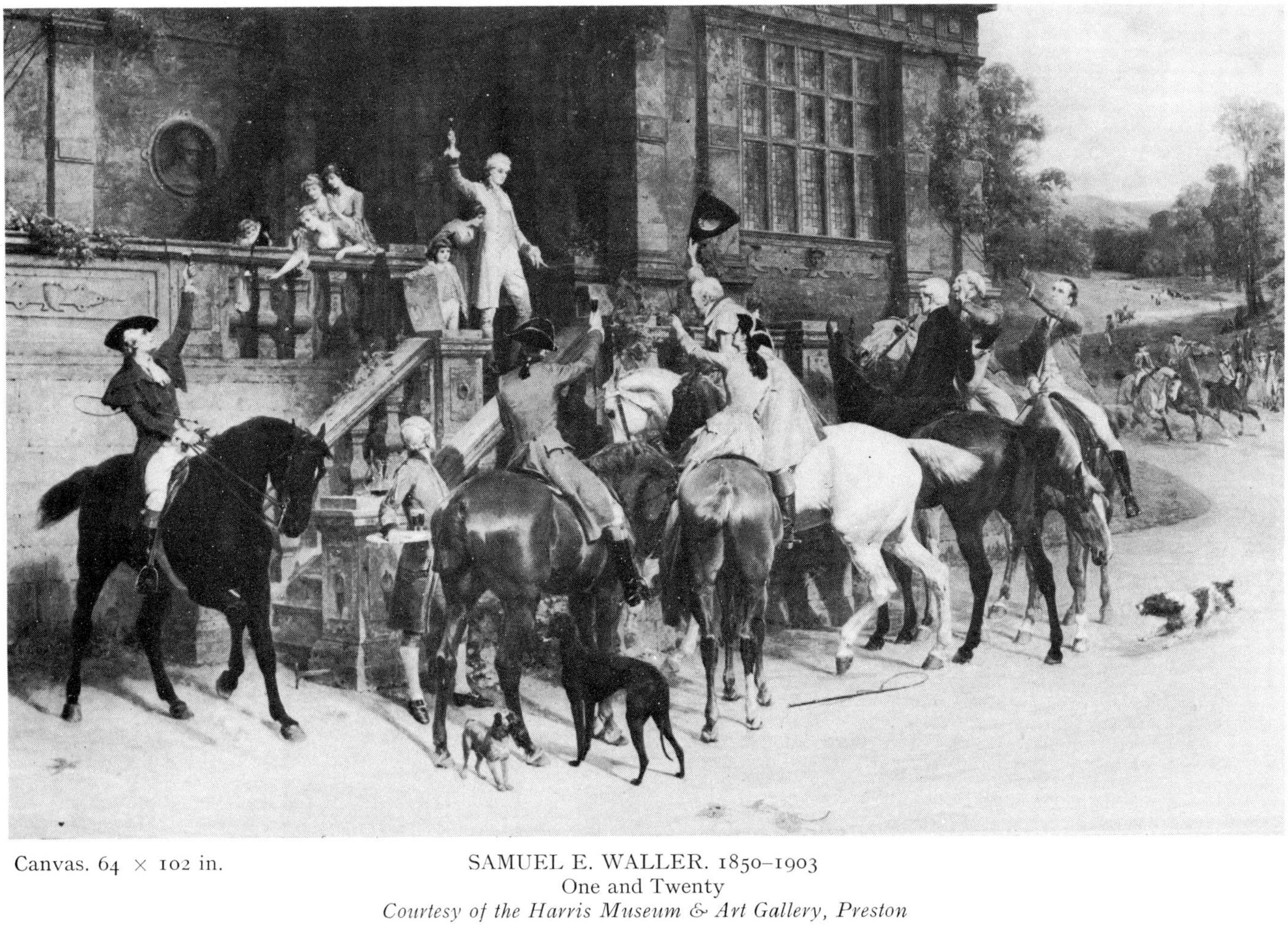

Canvas. 64 × 102 in.

SAMUEL E. WALLER. 1850–1903
One and Twenty
Courtesy of the Harris Museum & Art Gallery, Preston

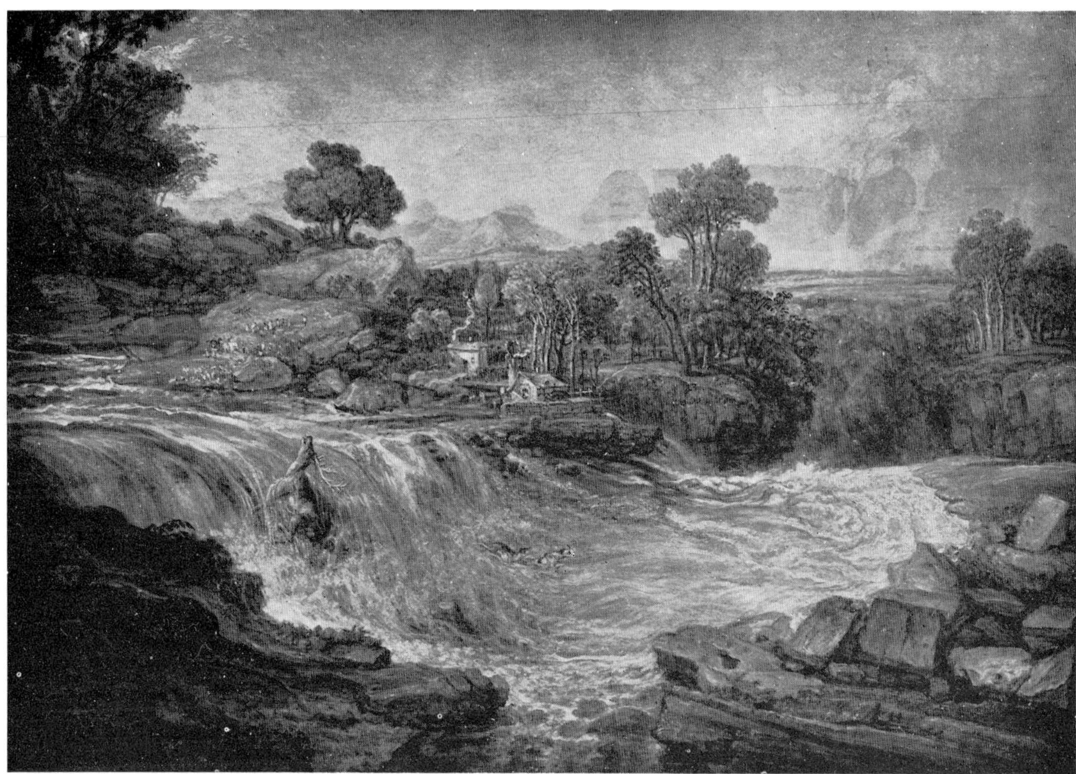

Oil. 28 × 40 in.

JAMES WARD, R.A. 1769–1859
Hunted Stag, The Clyde Falls
Courtesy of The Tate Gallery

S & D. 1852.

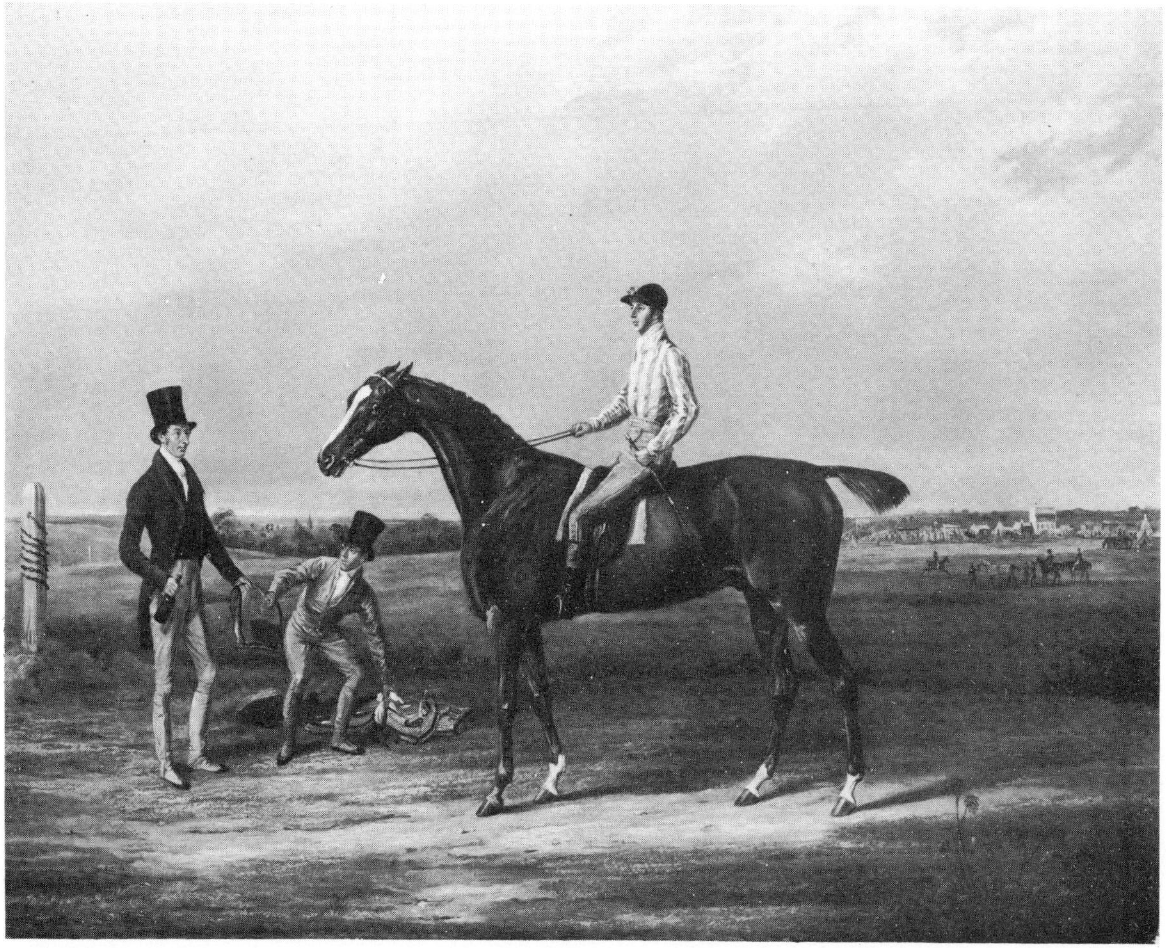

Canvas. $33\frac{1}{4}$ × 42 in.

WILLIAM WEBB. op. 1819–1828
'Euphrates'
Courtesy of Mr. & Mrs. Paul Mellon

S & D. 1825

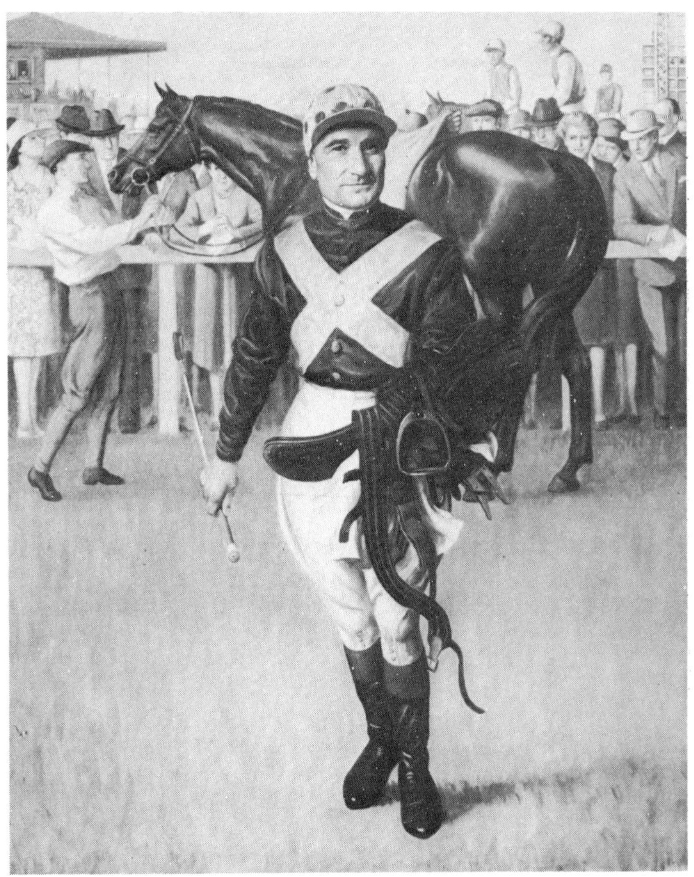

Canvas. 50 × 40 in. WALDRON WEST. b. 1904
D. L. Jones; Senior Jockey 1963
Courtesy of Mr. D. L. Jones

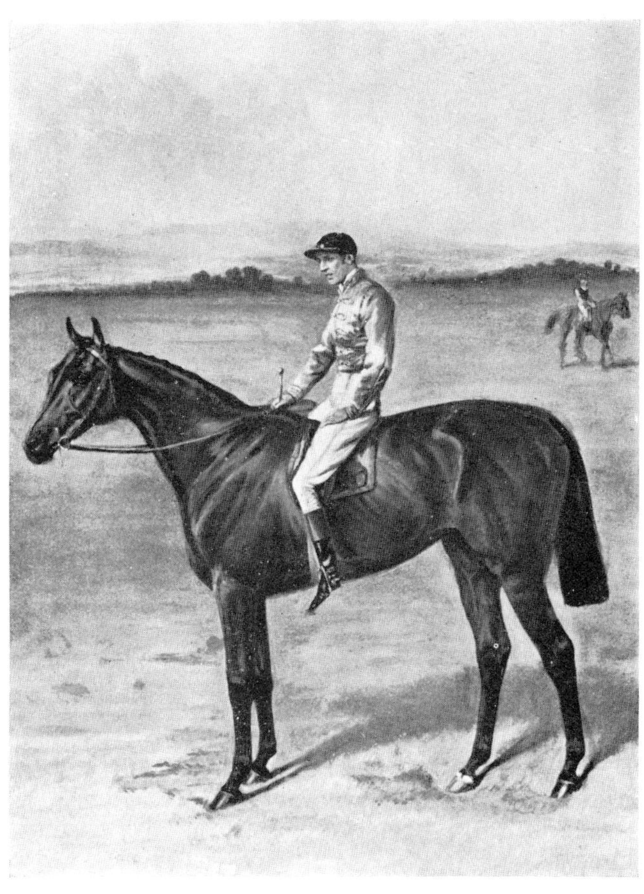

Oil. 24 × 18 in. J. A. WHEELER. op. 1821–1877
'Ormonde' winner of the Triple Crown 1886, with Fred Archer up
Courtesy of Messrs. Frost & Reed Ltd., Bristol & London

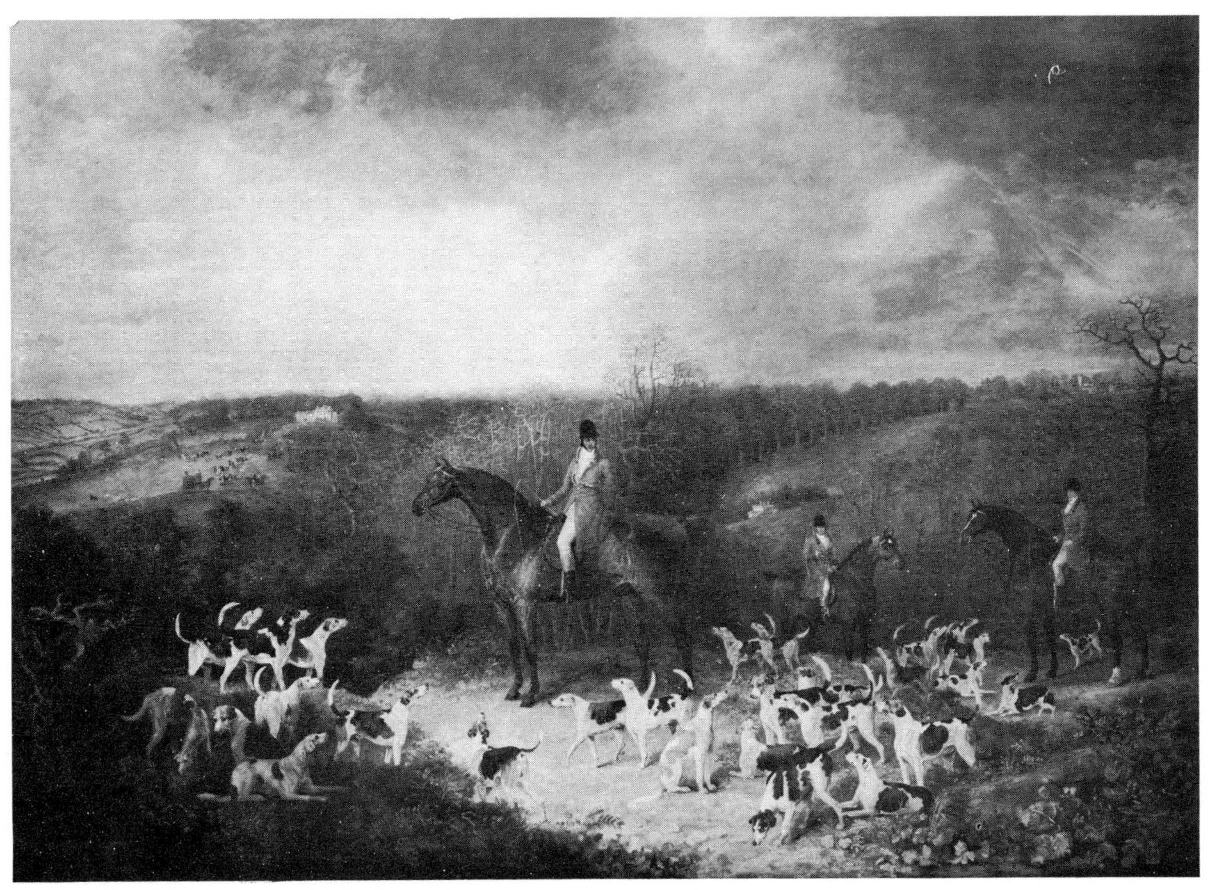

Canvas. 57 × 81 in, DEAN WOLSTENHOLME. 1757–1837
Lord Glamis and his Staghounds
Courtesy of Mr. & Mrs. Paul Mellon

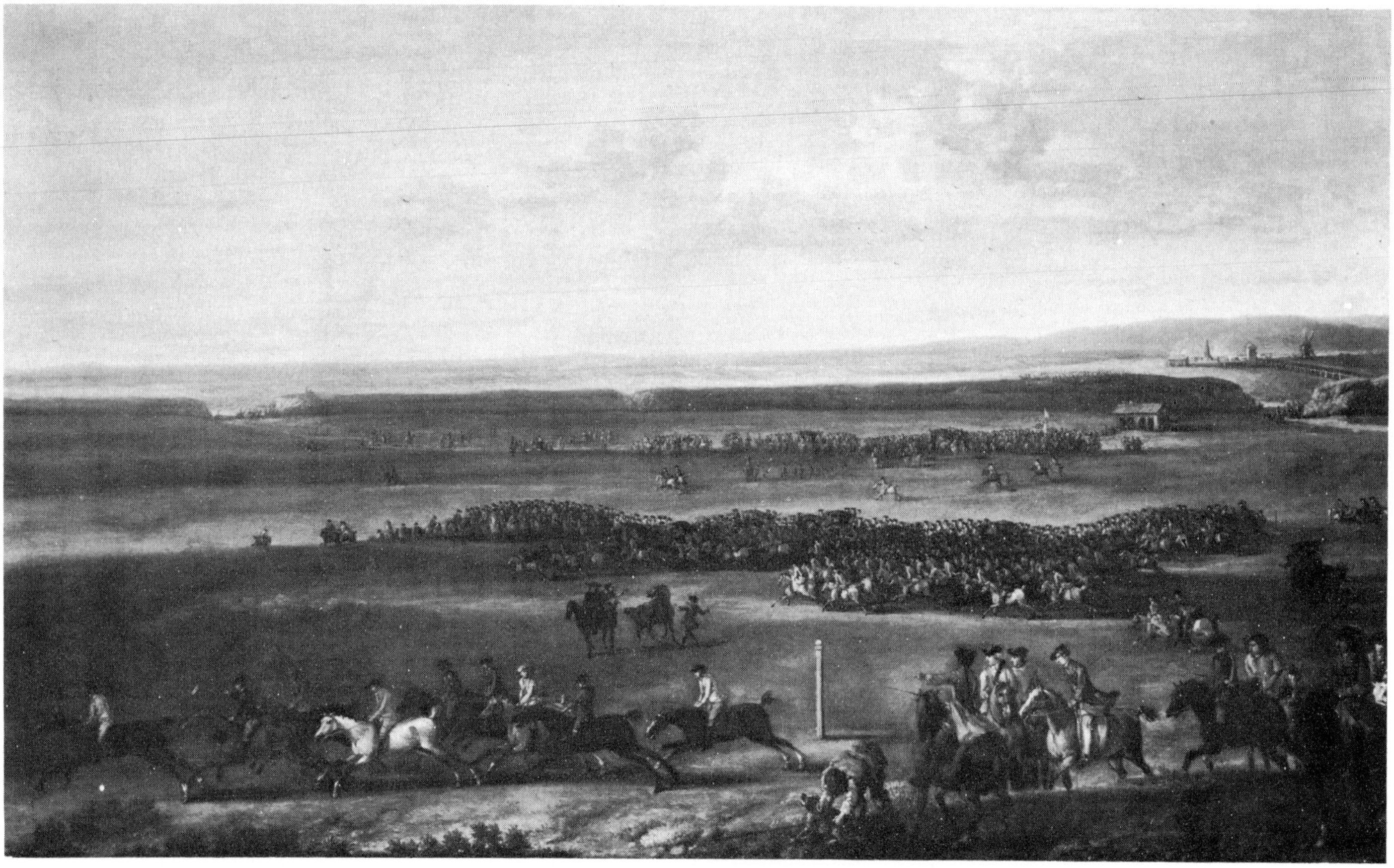

Canvas. 37 × 58 in. JOHN WOOTTON. 1678?–1765 Signed

The Prince of Wales at a race meeting on Newmarket Heath

Courtesy of Messrs. Oscar & Peter Johnson Ltd., London

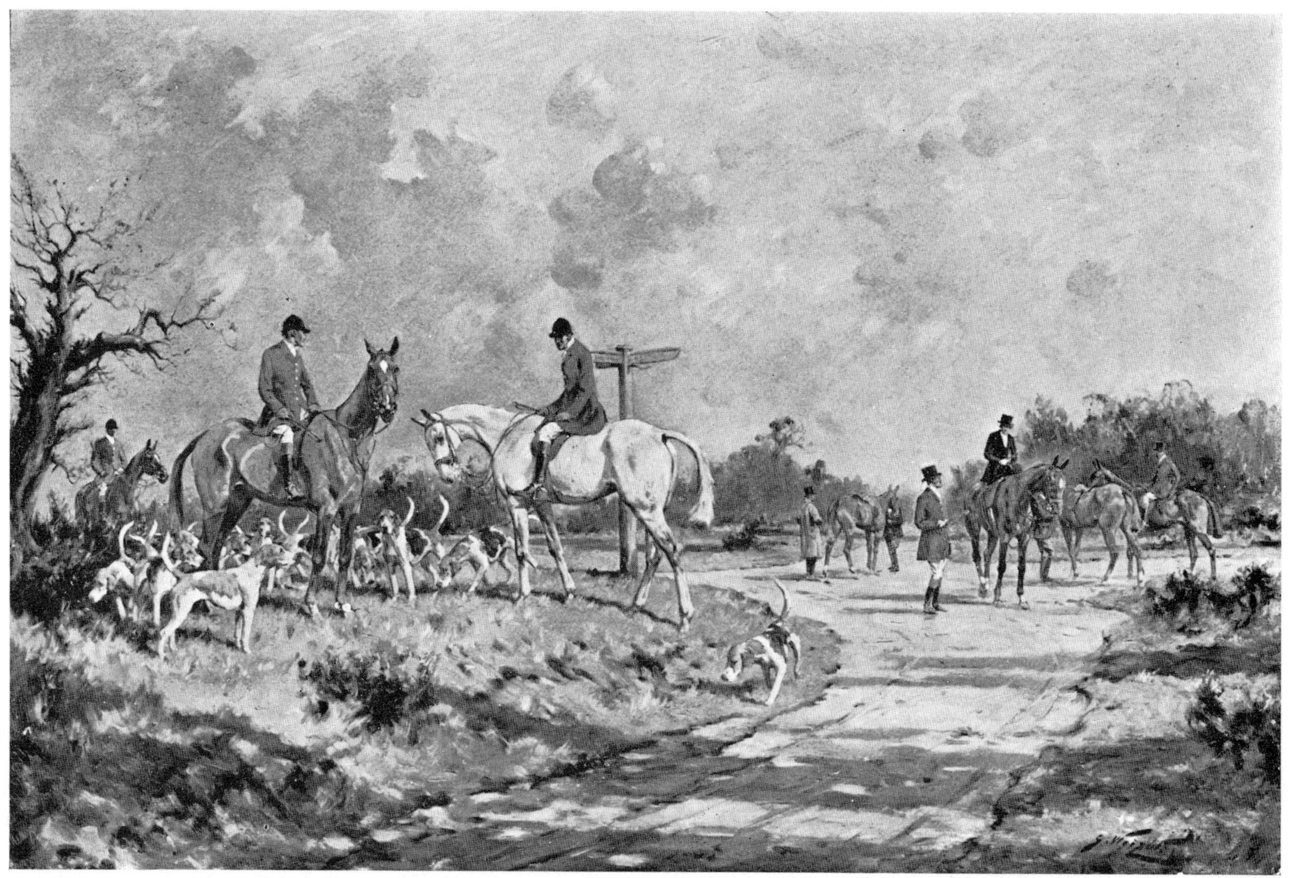

Oil. 24 × 36 in. GEORGE WRIGHT. 1860–1942 Signed

The Meet

Courtesy of Messrs. Frost & Reed Ltd., Bristol & London

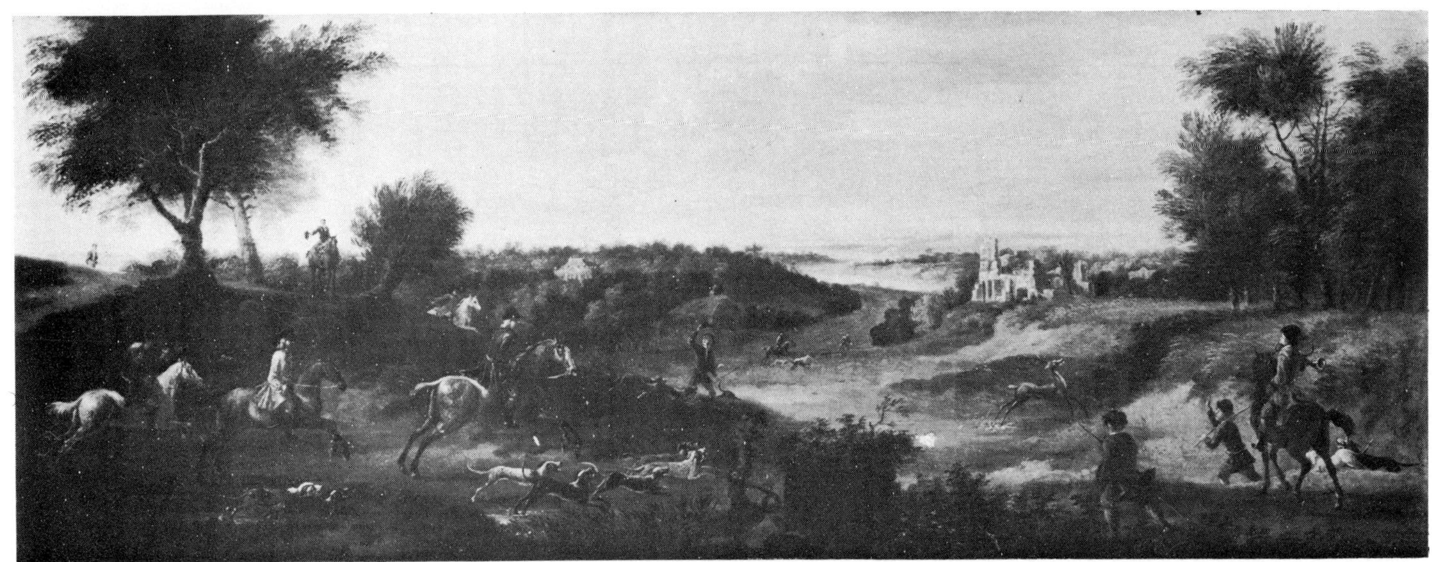

Canvas. 21½ × 56 in.

JAN WYCK. 1640–1702
A Stag Hunt

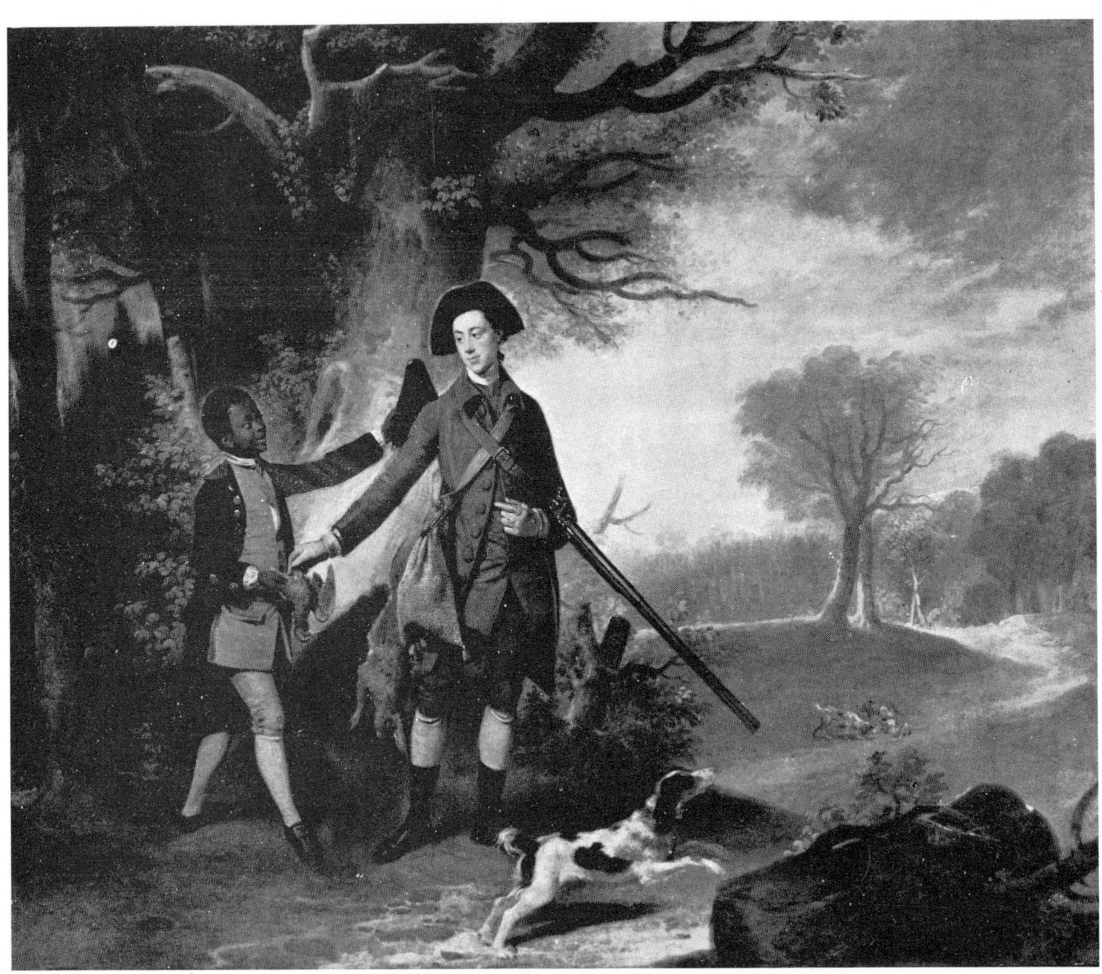

Canvas. 44½ × 53 in.

JOHN ZOFFANY, R.A. 1725–1810
The 3rd Duke of Richmond out shooting with his Servant
Courtesy of Messrs. Leggatt Brothers, London

c. 1765